Jessica Adams began her career at *Elle* magazine and is the astrologer for international editions of *Vogue* and *Cosmopolitan*. She is a team editor on the *Girls' Night In* and *Kids' Night In* series for War Child and No Strings which has raised over £1 million. She is the author of five novels including *The Summer Psychic*. Visit www.jessicaadams.com.

www.booksattransworld.co.uk

Also by Jessica Adams

SINGLE WHITE E-MAIL
TOM, DICK AND DEBBIE HARRY
I'M A BELIEVER
COOL FOR CATS
THE SUMMER PSYCHIC

and published by Black Swan

THE NEW ASTROLOGY FOR WOMEN
21ST CENTURY GODDESS
(with Jelena Glisic and Anthea Paul)

and published by Corgi Books

ASTROLOVE

Jessica Adams

ASTROLOVE
A CORGI BOOK: 9780552155342

First publication in Great Britain
Originally published by the Penguin Group (Australia), 2006

PRINTING HISTORY
Corgi edition published 2007

1 3 5 7 9 10 8 6 4 2

Set in 11/13pt Joanna MT by
Falcon Oast Graphic Art Ltd.

Corgi Books are published by Transworld Publishers,
61-63 Uxbridge Road, London W5 5SA,
a division of The Random House Group Ltd,
in Australia by Random House Australia (Pty) Ltd,
20 Alfred Street, Milsons Point, Sydney, NSW 2061, Australia,
in New Zealand by Random House New Zealand Ltd,
18 Poland Road, Glenfield, Auckland 10, New Zealand
in South Africa by Random House (Pty) Ltd,
Isle of Houghton, Corner of Boundary Road & Carse O'Gowrie,
Houghton 2198, South Africa,
and in India by Random House Publishers India Private Limited,
301 World Trade Tower, Hotel Intercontinental Grand Complex,
Barakhamba Lane, New Delhi 110 001,India.

Printed and bound in Great Britain by
Cox & Wyman Ltd, Reading, Berkshire.

Papers used by Transworld Publishers are natural, recyclable products made
from wood grown in sustainable forests. The manufacturing processes
conform to the environmental regulations of the country of origin.

CONTENTS

ASTROLOVE

WELCOME TO *ASTROLOVE*

How well are you coping in the love jungle? Maybe there is something to learn from Brad Pitt, Madonna, Ellen de Generes and Oscar Wilde, whose horoscopes were used in the research for this book. *Astrolove* is for singles and couples – of all sexual preferences. And although it's primarily about Sun Signs, it also covers the mysteries of Moon Signs, Mercury Signs, Venus Signs, Mars Signs and Rising Signs – all of which should help to unveil your partner's secret bits! In this book you'll also be able to use astrology to peer into the future. When are you most likely to date, relate, mate, procreate or separate? Astrology can help you time it right – and cope better, too, if the *merde* does hit the fan.

1 SPEED DATING AND ONLINE RELATING

If you only have five minutes to get to know somebody, their Sun Sign is an excellent guide. With just one piece of information – the sign the Sun was in on the day they were born – an astrologer can draw up what's known as a Solar Chart. Suddenly, it's possible to extract twelve important pieces of information about that Sun Sign, all drawn from the twelve houses of the horoscope wheel.

Gemini women are curious by nature. But why do they need to investigate life at such a deep level, and in such a penetrating way? Simple: Pluto, the planet of depth and intensity, rules Gemini's Sixth House of daily life.

Aries men are drawn to networks, clubs and teams because Uranus, the planet of groups, rules their Eleventh House of friendship. There is a belief that Aries men have problems co-operating and collaborating because they are too self-interested. Wrong. They do well in societies, associations and bands. They feel at home in a group.

Twenty-first century love is faster than ever. Jane Austen is probably revolving in her grave at the sheer speed of it. We begin relationships by staring at a photograph of someone on a website, or ticking boxes on a piece of paper, while potential dates are shunted on and off our table.

Astrology suits this first-look approach to the human race because it has two systems – Sun Signs and Solar Charts – that were created specifically for daily newspapers, which rely on quick-fixes of information to get their point across. As long as you remember that what you are about to read here are column inches about your partner rather than a full biography, you'll get the quick information sound bite you need. For the complete picture of the bride (or the bridegroom) stripped bare, you will need to read about their Moon Sign, Mercury Sign, Venus Sign, Mars Sign and Rising Sign as well. That comes later in the book!

For now, Sun Signs show you who people are before you get to the naked truth. Remember, though, Sun Sign dates are averaged so if you or your partner were born on the last or first day of a sign, check your time, place and date of birth at www.astro.com for pinpoint accuracy. So what are you waiting for? Love bunnies of the world, log on and start your search engines!

WOMEN

Aries Woman MARCH 20–APRIL 19

She carries a bee in her bonnet and an entire hive in her hairdo. Sometimes this works out well – her amazing enthusiasm and drive can create an incredible buzz. But sometimes it's a disaster. Nobody gets out of control like Aries gets out of control – and it can do damage.

Mars is her wildly energetic ruling planet. Fire is her ruling element. But there is more to Aries than this. Pluto, the planet of endings and new beginnings, makes important patterns in her horoscope. Pisces, the fishes – a water sign – rules her secret self. Aries women often unconsciously set up situations where they start fires and then have to put them out, or they attract crisis and then have to fix it.

However, Aries woman responds well to challenges. She finds them incredibly exhilarating. She also understands the natural cycle of crisis and change in life, which she has a deep respect for, no matter how much it pushes her to the wall. Consequently, Aries does well in jobs or families where she is in charge of damage control. Fighting situations or people that threaten to engulf everything and everybody in their path also gives her a chance to confront her own wild side.

It is no accident that so many of the dramatic endings or battles in Aries' life revolve around other people's money. Pluto rules her zone of joint finances. Where business, cash, possessions or property are concerned, the Aries woman tends to attract periodic crisis. Each crisis has a cleansing and purging effect, though. Pluto's job is to bring everything back down to ground zero so that new beginnings can be made. Aries woman intuitively understands this organic process in her life. She knows crisis clears a path for progress.

Mars rules the fight or flight response in people. With an Aries woman, it's usually about fighting rather than fleeing. Her nose twitches when she senses a threat. And it twitches even more if she senses a battle for control. It's her job to mark territory, defend what matters and protect what (or who) she cares about. This in turn teaches her about her own raging, uncontrollable, highly inflammable side. What she seems to attract from the universe is often a mirror reflection of her own nature – that part of her which is white-hot and unstoppable, and determined to take everything in its path. In facing this and fighting it, she also learns how to fight it in herself.

For Aries woman to understand this wildly uncontrollable aspect of her personality can make it easier for her to manage her life. The alternative? Too much crisis. Too much burnout. Too much destruction. And, it has to be said, sometimes awful damage.

The world needs Aries for her enormous energy and courage. She's the woman you want around you most in just about any overwhelming, critical or dangerous situation you can think of. At the same time, she has a wild energy and a ferocious passion which can in itself be damaging. Nobody moves faster than a woman born under the sign of the ram – give her ten minutes and she will cover ten kilometres! In turn, though, she needs to be more aware of the effect she has on her own life, as well as on other people. Helping her realise this just might be your job . . .

Taurus Woman APRIL 20–MAY 20

To understand Taurus, look to the Second House of her Solar Chart, which shows what she values most. It is ruled by Gemini, the sign associated with information and the written word. Gemini in turn is ruled by Mercury, the planet of quotable quotes, desk-diary wisdom, thoughts for the day, bright ideas and brainwaves. And the paper-jungle planet Mercury also rules the Fifth House of her chart, which rules how she expresses herself.

On top of all this reverence for books and bits of paper, you'll find pedantic, nitpicking Virgo in charge of her Fifth House too. Details *really* matter to Taurus. She's a reader, a researcher, a skimmer, a sifter and a sorter. Good grief, the woman actually uses bookmarks!

Taurus is a practical earth sign. This woman doesn't do waffle and she doesn't do padding. Taurus wants to know what matters, why it matters and where it is. End of story. Lots of them look as if they should have glasses on the end of their nose.

Taurean women work or live quite happily with computers. Aquarius (the laptop and PC sign) rules her Midheaven. For Taurus, Google is God, and God is often Google. The sheer volume of the Internet overwhelms her, though. What's important? What's not? Why can't somebody invent filters for the filters?

The Moon rules her Third House of information and communication – having the right facts makes her feel more secure. Pluto, the planet of depth, and Scorpio, the sign of obsession, rule her Seventh House. One of her lovers or professional partners in life has shown her how to focus. She has been known to forget to breathe when poring over one of her books.

Money, property and business – particularly when they involve family, colleagues or partners – bring out her inner lawyer or academic, or even trigger her spiritual beliefs. Jupiter rules the financial and lifestyle zone of her chart. Somehow, sooner or later, it all gets mixed up with the law, the library, or even her personal bible – whatever that is. All the more reason for her to develop a healthy respect for facts as well as figures! But there is more to the Taurus woman's craving for detail. Her natural rulership of the Second House in astrology ensures that she is born with a mental balance sheet.

The Second House is about keeping score, and Taurus is an expert at sorting out the debts and credits in her life – be they financial, emotional or even sexual. Be careful. Some of them keep ledgers in their heads. She always knows where the figures are in the columns of life. And don't *ever* give her a contract and expect her to sign it without trawling it first.

Sensible Saturn rules her zone of knowledge. She can be forgiven for doing everything by the book. Without Taureans, the world would be chaotic. She cuts through mental clutter, dumps the junk, keeps order, knows the rules – and knows what matters! Even if she never goes any further than high school, she is a natural student or guru with an astonishing nose for facts, figures or the deeper meaning in life. If you can't hire her, move in with her – and if you can't move in with her, at least ask her to be your personal research assistant.

Gemini Woman MAY 21–JUNE 20

She is curious by nature, and she feels it is her duty to look more deeply into things in order to correctly diagnose people, problems and life. Penetrating Pluto rules her approach to work, and plenty of Gemini women find careers where they are required to probe, scrutinise, research, scan and analyse for a living. If this isn't the nature of her profession, then her diagnostic skills will be used on her friends instead. When a Gemini woman puts your relationship under the microscope, you'll really know you've been dissected – but don't worry, it's just part of the service.

By her twenties, she learns that the right picture tells the correct story. She has a natural feeling for images, photographs or artwork that communicate a message. Neptune, the planet of vision, rules her Midheaven soul journey, which revolves around looking properly and truly *seeing*.

As a little girl, Gemini always asks 'Why?' and will not stop until she knows the cause behind the cause behind the cause. As an adult, she is the last person you should invite to dinner if you don't want someone probing your personality. It's not because you will necessarily be interrogated, but do be aware: your soul will be trawled later.

If she finds a job where detective work is part of her professional world – in the police force, in the paparazzi, or in the medical or caring professions – as her love partner you may find you are let off the hook, as all her energy is poured into the job. Otherwise, expect her X-ray eyes to be turned on you, your friends or your family. In Gemini's world, there is always a story behind the story, and her curiosity will not allow her to rest until she has discovered it.

She prefers sports like tennis, where opponents can be psyched out, or games like chess or poker, where second-guessing is part of the challenge. Gemini women are often unfairly painted as lightweights by some astrologers, but she is always looking for deeper clues, even when she's being entertained.

Gemini eyes typically look straight through you or gaze off into space. In both instances, she is looking for answers. This is the last person in the world you should try to fob off in a relationship, and if you even *think* about infidelity, you will be psychoanalysed within an inch of your life.

Are her conclusions about you, her job and the world always right? Not necessarily. But that won't stop her from continuing to look for answers. She can do this in the pages of her diary, or in long, intense conversations with colleagues, lovers or friends. In the land of Gemini, though, there is faith in knowledge. She just knows the truth is out there, somewhere, if only she can get her hands on the right clues.

Evaluation, examination and data are her things, even if she only applies them to her girlfriends' love-lives or her recipe collection. At the highest level, though, this woman can change lives and save lives with her unbelievable gift for investigation.

Cancer Woman 21 JUNE–JULY 22

Venus, the planet that rules beauty, colour and design, rules the Cancer woman's home zone – so even her student bedsit is run like a private estate. That word *private* is important too: Cancer needs closed doors so she can express herself – creatively, emotionally or sexually. Secretive Pluto rules her Fifth House, so her private life and her creativity need to be fenced in and walled off. Ask a Cancerian woman what her sign is, and she'll probably say 'Trespassers Will Be Prosecuted'. She knows who to let in and who to keep out. Don't even *think* about gatecrashing. Access to her life is by invitation only.

Aries is at the top of Cancer's horoscope. It's about boundaries and territorialism. She has a powerful sense of place. Leo rules her Second House: she values luxury, and she'll pay anything for the most dazzling clothes or the best plants for her garden. Alternatively, if she's really lucky, she'll end up with a partner who brings the entire package with him, or be born into a family that makes her dream home possible. If not, she'll organise the swimming pool herself. And the statues.

All this gorgeousness and brilliance can make her a target, though. There is something about her fearless Aries Midheaven and the influence of proud Leo on the Second House that makes Cancer push other people's buttons. Her love of home is well known. Less well known, perhaps, is her effect on those who see her in her natural habitat, and automatically find themselves reaching for a rotten tomato or a water pistol. Cancer's response? It is a dignified version of the well-known football chant 'Come and have a go if you think you're hard enough'. Her Aries Midheaven gives her an edge. Consciously or unconsciously, though, she does seem to provoke tomato attacks.

In all honesty, though, most Cancer women are far less interested in ducking and diving than just posing – with a good-looking lifestyle as an accessory. Her real estate matters, because she is ruled by the Moon, but it has to be a beautiful chunk of real estate too, because she was influenced by someone in the family tree who was attuned to art, fashion, beauty or design.

Capricorn, the sign of status, hierarchy and achievement, is on her descendant. One of her lovers has taught her all about finding a solid niche – preferably at the top end of town, rather than on the ground floor of the local sink estate. She needs to be *established*.

Here's something peculiar to this sign – a sensitivity to eclipses. Cancer is ruled by the Moon and she understands the battle between the Sun and her own planet when the sky goes dark overhead. It reminds her of how easy it is to disappear, unless you make a point of shining brightly. For this reason, Cancer women are like a Tracey Emin exhibition, a tour of Buckingham Palace, a Dior show and a picnic in the country – all on the same day.

You'll have to get in first, though. Remember the 'Keep Out' sign? Only visitors with a pass make it into Cancer World, and you'll have to make her feel completely safe with you before she'll even *think* about pulling up the drawbridge. That's her challenge to you!

Leo Woman JULY 23–AUGUST 22

There are no invisible Leo women. She assumes that people will always be looking, so she makes an effort. It is impossible to generalise about each Leo woman's taste, but she definitely doesn't do drab. When she goes to a ball, gets married or accepts an award, she wears the kind of outfit that shouts 'I am the Queen! Look at me! Shut up, everybody!' She always comes with 20 per cent extra free razzle-dazzle and ra ra ra.

Leo women do not get lost at shopping centres. They stand on the escalator, radiating Leo-ness and are immediately noticed. If they are forced to wear work uniforms or to live in dribble-covered jeans (the price of motherhood), then they just spend more time and money on their hair instead. The cut or the colour is always dramatic.

They all secretly want to be Tori Amos, Madonna or Kate Bush. It's a shame that so many of them are tone-deaf, because they are born to be in rock bands. Leo has rulership over the Fifth House in astrology, which is linked to self-expression. This sign is also ruled by the Sun, which rules showing-off. As little girls they yodel into a hairbrush in front of a mirror.

They understand display and presentation better than anybody else, and they know how to advertise and promote themselves – and they all have jobs or hobbies that allow them to impress and amaze everyone within a five-kilometre radius. If their careers don't give them space to be noticed and appreciated, then they will find a weekend passion that does.

Every Leo woman is a natural winner or a natural authority on *something*. She may be a cook, a fashionista, a swimmer or a surfer. Whatever she has mastered in her life, remember that challenging her authority is a bad idea. If you do, you will be frozen out with an icy stare or run over later with a Sherman tank. Remember too that she loves a celebration. And she has no problem with self-celebration either . . . when Leo gets engaged, wins an award or gets promoted, very few people will escape The Big Announcement.

Leo women use their names and initials in business, on their writing paper . . . or just about anywhere they can. As teenagers, they grab a Dymo machine and label everything. As mature women, they can be tempted to have monograms engraved on their dressing gowns and address books. Their businesses and companies are often eponymous, too – and really desperate Leo women will even refer to themselves in the third person in conversation!

Mercury rules her group zone. She likes joining teams, associations or networks where she can get together with other people to get a message across. Powerful Pluto rules her family zone. Someone in her family tree taught her about how power works and how to use the kind of ultra-confident tactics that help her to hang on firmly to the controls.

Never forget what she has done, who she is and where she belongs in the scheme of things! It's natural that Leo women should be counted among the movers and shakers in life – and the players, winners and performers. Do you disagree? Better buy some earplugs. But if you rain on her parade, be careful. Nobody is more loyal to Leo than the members of Team Leo. Are you on the team as well? You might as well join up. It's much more fun . . .

Virgo Woman AUGUST 23–SEPTEMBER 22

Someone in her family tree was always thinking about the future or dreaming about tomorrow. Jupiter rules the bottom of her chart, which is where her astrological DNA comes from. Life is often about the rest of her life for Virgo. It's speculative. Hopeful. A promise of bigger and better – or just more, more, more!

One of her lovers was, or is, a dreamer. Pisces, the sign of fantasy and wishful thinking, is on her descendant. One of her exes (or her current partner) has left a stamp on her personality. No matter how practical she tells herself she is, there is a part of her that is always wishing, hoping and pressing her nose up against the glass.

Libra, the sign of couples, rules her zone of property, possessions and money. All those bank brochures that show glossy photographs of young couples hugging each other as they flash their credit cards around are targeted at Virgo. She finds it hard to separate romance from white goods and white goods from romance. The longing for stuff is often mixed up with the longing for a partner.

There is a link between Jupiter, the planet that encourages her to live in the future, and the Ninth House of her chart, which is ruled by Taurus, the shopping (and window shopping) sign. Tomorrow is often in the front window of Bloomingdales, David Jones or Selfridges.

Fiery Mars rules her zone of joint finances. Before they even *think* about commitment, Virgo women need to sort out the fine print on the mortgage, the joint credit card, the hire-purchase agreement, or even the inheritance. The potential for arguments over cash or possessions is always there, because of the influence of Mars here. Virgo women need to understand what they are getting into when they enter a de facto partnership or a marriage. Romantic? Absolutely not. Vital? Absolutely *yes*!

Two simple rules for happiness for Virgo: live in the present (or, as Eckhart Tolle would have it, the power of now), and don't necessarily expect a split-cycle air conditioner to bring you happiness. Or a Lalique vase.

Virgo triggers all our romantic fantasies. She actually has the courage to live the Hollywood romantic dream – her love-life often resembles the best scenes from *Breakfast At Tiffany's* mixed up with *Pretty Woman* via *When Harry Met Sally*. She really understands 'Heroes', the David Bowie song, too. But, most of all, Virgo needs to get herself into a relationship where fantasy is enjoyed for its own sake, but firmly left behind when it's time to do the his-and-hers tax.

Lots of them develop a sense of humour about their insatiable longing for the good life, and it's one of the reasons why they make their partnerships work so well. What's wrong with gazing at seventeen-room mansions in a real estate window if you're still content to hold hands in a cheap café afterwards?

Libra Woman SEPTEMBER 23–OCTOBER 22

She plays student *and* teacher at various points in her life, and it's obvious in her personal relationships as well as her professional connections. Some Librans gravitate towards careers where life revolves around a long list of lessons, instructions or directions. Others just have friendships, partnerships or outside interests where they are required to play pupil or professor. She likes double acts. But they have to be educational too.

Libra acquires mentors throughout her life, but she also acts as a mentor for others. Jupiter, the planet of knowledge, rules Libra's zone of communication. Mercury, the planet of information, rules her zone of education. The getting of wisdom is an endless process.

Even if it's Libra who is guiding somebody else, she classically finds she learns as much from the experience as the person she is supposed to be helping. It's in her nature to want to absorb life lessons, even if she's supposed to be showing others the way at the same time.

Want a free piece of advice? Looking for a lecture? Want to know the ins and outs? Go to Libra. You may get it anyway, whether you ask for it or not. They all have their special subjects, hard-won experience, folk wisdom or inside knowledge to share – and it's hard for her not to pass on what she knows. It's her way of showing you that she cares, dammit. If you have a few special subjects of your own, you will also be flattered by Libra's genuine interest in what *you* know. Everyone has a Mastermind subject. What's yours? This woman always wants to know more. It's her way of connecting and relating.

Lots of them study forever, taking endless classes and courses, or they work their way up through the upper echelons of academia, acquiring an increasing string of letters after their names. They do well in careers where they are put in charge of interns or junior staff, and in any field where they are constantly forced to go on refresher courses, or do endless amounts of research and updating. She uses restaurant napkins as mini whiteboards to explain things. Or she gets into bed and says, 'Tell me about beekeeping'.

What is new to you may be old news to her – consequently, you couldn't ask for a better tour guide in your life. Similarly, if you find yourself in a relationship with her that is *Dead Poet's Society* meets *To Sir With Love*, you will know she has slotted you into the role of senior headmaster or headmistress. Here's another film that often resonates with Libran lives: *A Star Is Born*. She often ends up outstripping or out-earning the person who begins life as her teacher!

Sexually, she can be drawn to relationships straight out of *Lolita* or *The Graduate*. An age gap or an experience gap helps her fall into the student–teacher pattern in bed, just as she pursues it in other areas of her life.

Love translates as a little learning in a Libra relationship. To keep things interesting, make sure you swap the guru–disciple roles around. That way, you'll both benefit. Life is an escalator to her. Exchange your roles on the steps from time to time, and keep moving.

Scorpio Woman OCTOBER 23–NOVEMBER 21

She has exactly the same number of relationship breakdowns, financial losses, professional failures and illnesses as other women, but nobody handles it as well as the Scorpio woman, who is here to show the rest of us how to surrender, release and then start again. She is dignified when it all goes wrong for her, but it just adds to her legend.

There is something noble about her ability to crash, burn and keep going, thanks to classy Leo at the top of her Solar Chart. If she loses an election or a court case, she is remarkably graceful about it. If she loses her partner to another woman, she can hold her head high – even smile. She is an impressive class act, especially when deep in *merde*.

She is a powerhouse, and classically has a role in relationships, family or professional life that puts her in control. On the occasions when she loses that, her ruling planet Pluto takes over and the famous Scorpio process of death and rebirth begins. It's been compared to the phoenix rising from the flames, and all of them do it. She knows how to admit when the game is over, and she also knows when it's right to make a comeback too.

What Scorpio's fans all realise, of course, is that her losses actually empower her. And ironically, the more Scorpio bottoms out in life, the more admired she becomes – and the greater loyalty and awe from friends, family or colleagues she inspires. Most of the time she is one of life's winners. When it doesn't work for her, though, she performs the famous Scorpion withdrawal dance – pulling back and burrowing down.

From there, it's just a matter of regrouping, rethinking and re-energising. There is no question of crawling around looking for sympathy, or wailing that life is unfair and God is a bastard. Scorpio recognises that we all have to lose out in life sometimes, and it's the way you handle it that dictates your future success. On one buttock she has the word 'Start' tattooed, and on the other she has 'Again'. Mars, the fighter planet, rules her daily life.

Scorpio women intuitively understand Japanese history better than any other sign of the zodiac. What do you do when you've been brought to your knees? Answer? Come back fifty years later with Mitsubishi, Toyota, Sony and sushi franchises. Friends who are in trouble gravitate towards Scorpio, because she is a survivor who understands how to handle mushroom clouds.

Here's something else Scorpio knows how to do: she occasionally backs down with people, because she secretly has another agenda. This is also what helps to give her the upper hand, either in relationships or in her career. The woman who is born in October or November knows when it's worth conceding sometimes, in the interests of her own personal Plan B. And the nature of Plan B? You'll never know.

She attracts loyalty and admiration, even from her enemies, because of the way she handles herself when times are tough – and if you are divorcing her, she makes an honourable opponent. Be careful, though. Her tactics and strategies are never naïve. This one knows exactly what she's doing and why when she finally backs out of the game.

Sagittarius Woman NOVEMBER 22–DECEMBER 21

Live and let live is her attitude. Uranus, the planet of freedom and independence, rules her zone of ideas. Sagittarian women are self-starters, and believe other people should be too. Their personal and professional lives are full of forks in the road –

and although these are the same forks that occasionally separate them permanently from family, friends, lovers or colleagues, they also make it possible for Sagittarius to move forward.

Energetic Mars rules this woman's zone of self-expression. Life is a permanent green light to her – there are always new projects to pursue – but in order to move ahead, the Sagittarian woman typically has to work independently of other people.

She's always open to new places and new horizons. The journeys are sometimes geographical (which is why she has such a reputation as a traveller), or they can be creative or professional. The magic word in all this is new, though. That's what Mars on her Fifth House is all about: the starter's pistol, the new day, the new dawn.

Here's a phrase you'll hear a lot if you're living with this woman, or even just loving her: 'You do your thing, and I'll do mine'. Sometimes she doesn't even have to say it – it's just there in her body language or in the expression on her face.

Jupiter is her ruling planet. She runs on optimism, hope and big plans. Tomorrow is always another day, which is why Sagittarius handles divorce or separation so well. She is a free spirit who wants and needs to go her own way in life, and who has no problem allowing her ex-partners to do the same thing. This sign bounces back surprisingly well from a break-up, or even a professional separation. Change is good. Life goes on. It's in her nature to move on and move forward, and to give other people the space to do this too. As a result of this angle on life, her career or relationships are characterised by various declarations of independence. They give her the motivation she needs to pursue all the amazing possibilities that she knows are out there.

The past is a foreign country, as L.P. Hartley once wrote, and it's usually the future that intrigues this woman. With practical Virgo on her Midheaven, she is also far more work-focused than other signs. That's why every new path leads to a new plan and, eventually, a new project. Sagittarius always has something cooking.

Is she the least coupley of the signs? Not if you have a partnership that allows for genuine autonomy. She is talented at long-distance love or relationships with people who have dramatically different goals, ambitions or plans to her own. If the marriage or partnership has the kind of structure that allows her to keep breaking away periodically, it may develop a unique rhythm all of its own, like a bungee jumper on a very long rope.

She is relentlessly positive, with genuine faith in the future, enthusiasm for anything new, bags of independence – and incredible energy. And if her connections to people sometimes fall by the wayside? Don't hand her the Kleenex. She's already moved on, baby.

Capricorn Woman DECEMBER 22–JANUARY 19

Someone in her family tree was a fighter. She has inherited this fearless approach to life. It's in her astrological DNA. If she has any charts for family members, she should look at everyone from her father to her great-grandmother.

She's awfully strong. The unyielding, masculine planet Saturn is her ruler. She has uncompromising values. Aquarius is on her Second House. She can be staunchly idealistic about her ethics, morals and principles (what she won't sell-out for), or equally rebellious about money or business. Swing a punch at Capricorn at your peril!

Experiences with friends or groups teach her about secret winning strategies or subversive ways of defending or attacking. Powerful, hidden Pluto rules her zone of friendships and group involvements. She fights according to the rules, so remember that if you are divorcing her or challenging her in business. She expects other people to behave the same way. She lives by protocol and respects the regulations.

Balance, equality and fair play really matter to Capricorn. Libra is on her Midheaven. Time and again she is drawn to double acts, sparring partnerships or us-against-them situations. Libra is about balancing the scales. One of the reasons women incarnate as Capricorns is to invite one-on-one challenges where two people or two sides must work things out. Woman to woman or woman to man? It doesn't really matter, but her *raison d'être* is a fair fight.

The strange dichotomy of Saturn, the planet of clocks, and Mars, the planet of action, in her Solar Chart teach her a lot about timing. Hold off or move in? Hang back or go for the KO punch? Fast or slow? Stop or go? The more experience she gains in her personal or professional life the better she becomes at managing the games she plays.

There is no typical physical Capricorn type, but look at her eyes. They are watchful and careful. There can be a seriousness or intensity about Capricorn women as well. They're not here to muck around. They're here to win.

Saturn is a planet that teaches through pain. Rolling with the punches makes her even more determined to get it right next time. What doesn't kill her makes her stronger, but it also makes her triumphant, in the end.

One of her lovers is destined to teach Capricorn woman how to be self-protective – how to shield herself. That ultimately forms part of her strategy for coping with life. More than anything else, though, she is guided by Aries at the immum coeli of her chart, and Saturn, her ruling planet, on the ascendant. Capricorn women have a sexy, impressive mixture of absolute fearlessness and tough, worldly-wise experience that makes them the strongest, most astonishing lovers or wives to have on your side.

Aquarius Woman JANUARY 20–FEBRUARY 18

Someone in the family tree was a sensualist. A shopper, perhaps, or a devoted foodie. This has worked its way into the Aquarian woman's astrological DNA, and despite some of the clichés you might read about her (memo: she does not knit her own vegetables), she is strangely drawn to the good life.

Uranus is her planetary ruler, and it encourages her to find herself in groups. Follow an Aquarian woman for long enough and you will soon hit her tribe. It may be a tight circle of friends or a big global charity. In any case, she has a strange habit of gravitating towards people who will give her the space she needs to indulge her lust for life.

Jupiter, the planet of greed and overindulgence, rules her Eleventh House of groups. Her friends can lead her to successful excess – or she'll drift into networks of people who allow her to access her sensual, good-lifer side. Bring it on! 'Waiter, one more wafer-thin mint!'

Neptune, the fantasy planet, rules her zone of shopping and spending. A surprisingly high number of Aquarian women find that consumerism (or good restaurants) leads straight to bliss. It's not what you might read about her in standard astrological texts, but she can buy a magazine daydream just as successfully as any other sign.

This woman has a lot of needs to feed, on a daily basis. Cancer and the Moon rule her Sixth House. But less is never more in this case – if anything, Aquarius typically wants more . . . and more . . . and more. Are there food issues in her life? The Moon/Cancer rulership of her Sixth House may hold the key, along with the mother–daughter relationship. Sometimes, the influence of a grandmother or stepmother will also provide the key.

Jupiter is about luck as well as about excess. It brings abundance, and more than enough to go round. Its position in this woman's chart promises gain through group effort – or, at the very least, the kind of company that can always be counted on to produce a good wine list and plenty of life's second and third helpings. Her friends are invariably feelgood.

Aquarius can't forget her socially conscious ruling planet entirely, though. There is typically an uneasy awareness of political, economic, global or humanitarian issues with this sign. She knows all about the haves and the have-nots, even if she counts herself as the former.

She can question herself long and hard about ownership, consumerism and the exploitation of the world's resources, or she can head for hedonism with her tribe. It all depends on how balanced her life feels at the time. This sensual, intensely sociable woman is an enigma to herself as well as to her lovers. Is she a happy hogger of the gregarious good life, or a tortured First Worlder, stuck on a fat-cat planet? Only she can tell you.

Pisces Woman FEBRUARY 19–MARCH 19

She is funnier than most astrology books give her credit for – Sagittarius rules her solar Midheaven. Someone in the family tree was witty too; Gemini rules the bottom of her chart, which is where her parents, relatives and ancestors lie.

Neptune is her planetary ruler. It enables her to melt and morph into other people, whenever she wants to. Lots of Pisceans are brilliant mimics or natural actors for this reason. She's not only funny, she also knows how to fake being *anyone*. Even you!

Neptune is also about masks and smokescreens. Piscean women find it easy to hide their true personalities behind bits and pieces they pick up from here, there and everywhere. Some of them do it professionally. Others just do it in their relationships or among their friends. This is partly why Pisces is so famously hard to pin down. There are times when even she has forgotten who she really is.

She believes in hair and make-up, and in jokes, clowns, theatre, film, television, music, cartoons and comedy. How could she not, when Sagittarius, the sign of the comedienne, has such a hold over the top of her Solar Chart?

Her real thoughts and feelings are down there somewhere, but you may need to wait before she can settle down long enough to reveal what is there. And be prepared – some of them never do. Pisceans can spend a lifetime experimenting with a range of masks.

Why the cover-up job? It's partly to do with her need to

entertain and amuse, and partly to do with her famous imagination. Don't overlook her sensitivity and rawness, though. She can feel horribly exposed without her day-to-day act.

She is so skilled at grafting bits and pieces of other people onto herself that she also has an uncanny understanding of how it feels to inhabit someone else's skin. Taking on other people's beliefs, their words, their style – even their substance – for a while can allow Pisces to genuinely get inside the souls of her fellow human beings.

Theatrical Leo rules her zone of work and daily life. She needs to entertain, even if she's stuck on an assembly line putting biscuits together. Jupiter, the ruler of Sagittarius, sits at the top of her chart. It's all about exaggeration. She knows how to pull out what she wants from her repertoire, and push it as far as it will go. She doesn't do real. Or ordinary. Instead, the Pisces woman does art imitating life imitating art imitating life, and it can be highly entertaining, if you're in the right mood. And if you're not? She'll go away and come back with something else to amuse you. Or she may just give up. She needs an audience!

Pisces needs people who love, admire and appreciate her wit and her imagination, her sense of humour and her self-expression. She also needs a lover who understands and appreciates the woman hidden away beneath all the layers, though. With patience and compassion, even you might get there eventually – once she sees it's safe to come out!

MEN

Aries Man MARCH 20–APRIL 19

The myth is that he's a competitive, aggressive gorilla – like Mel Gibson in *Braveheart*, but with more testosterone. The reality is that he's a born leader with a canny appreciation of group dynamics and big creative cravings.

Cancer and the Moon rule his family zone. Someone in Aries' family background understood the importance of clan bonding, so when he leaves home he has useful tools with which to keep things cohesive. He believes in the idea that cooperation brings progress for everyone and he can be quite idealistic about it.

This is a man who has had so many educational experiences (on his travels, and at school or university) that he can communicate with a wide range of people – even those from radically different backgrounds or nationalities. This makes it easier to work or play with the group. The education or the travels, by the way, are encouraged by Jupiter, the explorer, and Sagittarius, the traveller, which rule his Ninth House of discovery.

This man is also someone whose lovers and partners in the past have taught him a lot about harmony (and brilliant people skills). Consequently, although there may be some tension about his undoubted place at the top of the tree (his Aries Sun cannot be ignored entirely) there is also a big emotional pull leading him towards an 'all for one, one for all' Three Musketeers approach.

Aries learns some fascinating lessons about ego and showing-off as he goes through his twenties and thirties. It's like a free course in What Not To Do. Self-expression matters to him, because Leo rules his Fifth House, so he always has something to show, give or display. Yet, the biggest conflict in his life isn't about the clash between stardom and being one of the gang, it's actually about his desire to freely please himself versus satisfying other people's expectations.

It is common to find Aries feeling stuck between delivering the kind of 'show' that he knows has worked before and genuinely trying to do something alternative – even something quite radical. You'll often see this dilemma being played out in his career or in his other pursuits. It reflects the dichotomy between Aquarius and Leo in his chart.

He is not quiet, nor is he Mr Invisible. He operates at a loud volume, with incredible power. After all, Mars is his planetary ruler. But everyone tends to accepts his place in the scheme of things too – it leads to a special kind of harmony.

Life will give him one or more leading roles. The mythological picture of a self-centred human Sherman tank is quite wrong – the Aries man has a huge charge in his chart, coming from the Eleventh House of friendship, mateship, cooperation and teamwork. Some of them find it in committees, others find it in political parties, charities, football teams or professional associations.

He's Captain Kirk and he's Captain Fantastic. Always get to know his gang, though. It's part of who he is, and the dynamic he shares with his circle will give you amazing insights.

Taurus Man APRIL 20–MAY 20

The myth is he's a money-grubbing sensualist with several investment portfolios and Rolexes. The reality is he's tempted by delicious sins, but held back by his own value systems. Sometimes the temptations are financial, sometimes they're sexual. And there are other dark vices to resist too – anything from booze to gambling to carb bingeing!

Taurus is always aware of temptation. It seems sinful or forbidden to him, and it goes against his other values. If he is left-wing, for example, it may come in the form of naughty taboos like selling out to the corporate fat cats. Or if he is right-wing it may be an attraction to a filthy femme fatale from the Labour Party.

Most of the time, though, the deeper, darker world he wrestles with is linked to sexual demons. These devilish activities (or people) vary, depending on his background and his value system. These life choices lure him and confront him, all at the same time. What pulls Taurus in the direction of sordid sinfulness? Most of the time it is the wonderfully forbidden nature of what is on offer. He longs for people and experiences that draw him into the shady depths.

Do you know a Taurean who is like a robot? Seemingly

asexual, or distant and cold? You may have found one who is pretending to be an Aquarian, so he can keep all that sinful lust at a safe distance. He can do that because cool Aquarius rules his Midheaven. In this case, when Taurus is not self-disciplined and strong enough to contain and restrain himself, he can cut out altogether and bypass the world of lust. The result? Dr Spock in the deep freeze.

What are his own, personal seven deadly sins? You will discover a lot about Taurus by asking him. Greed may be high on the list for only some of them as, contrary to myth, a significant number of Taureans have turned their back on cash to pursue values with a capital V. Taureans who stay true to their values (and their values are always defined by their seven-deadly-sins list) are impressive. Deeply masculine, extremely strong and somehow far more savvy about life than the other signs, they have amazing self-knowledge and self-respect because they have stared their demons down and decided their ethics, morals, principles and beliefs are more important to them. They have nerves of steel!

My filing cabinet reveals married Christian Taureans who have dallied with naughty single women and card-carrying members of AA who are always feuding with booze. Also on the list are eco-warriors who struggle with their conscience over money, and even former heroin addicts. All of which makes Taurus more sympathetic to others, somehow. His demons are *all* our demons, and you have to admire a man who can successfully fight them off. He'll never stop being fascinated by his own dark side. His lifelong struggle with it defines who he is, what he does and how he lives.

Gemini Man MAY 21–JUNE 20

Ah, yes, Gemini. The chatty, superficial jack-of-all-trades with the emotional depth of a budgie. Or is he? The fact is, this man is philosophical about life and death – and yet inspired by the small things too. There's a darkness behind the lightness.

A practical, utterly realistic attitude towards the inevitability of death is one of Gemini's trademarks. If you listen to the music of Geminis like Bob Dylan, Paul Weller, Paul McCartney or Morrissey you will hear far more about funerals and graves than you might expect. Gemini has no illusions about existence – he knows it's all about endings, and that gives him an unusual appreciation of how precious life actually is.

Gemini finds life weird (especially when he travels – mad Aquarius rules his zone of tourism) and wonderful (Pisces on his Midheaven means he is constantly working on professional projects or weekend interests that inspire him). On a creative level, he also finds life beautiful.

Oddly, this perspective on his existence sits side by side with a gritty acknowledgement that it could end tomorrow in a coffin, for himself or others. Better than any other sign, he understands impermanence. 'This too shall pass' is his motto. When the mourning is over, though, Gemini stops to smell the roses.

His own life is typically subject to the kinds of endings and sacrifices that would create neuroses or depression in other signs. He takes on a role or mission – a career or calling – and then he loses it or is forced to give it up. He settles into what he fondly imagines is a settled lifestyle, and it comes to a screeching halt. The legacy of this is rewarding, though. Gemini knows how to let go and move on. Quite literally, he believes that life is too short. That's what happens when Pluto rules your Sixth House.

Gemini retreats into his own space on a regular basis. From this he learns how to be more contemplative, more meditative – and far less tied to other people. He has the soul of a poet, the heart of a painter, the mind of a photographer and the spirit of a musician. However, the energy for all this can only be found after his periodic vanishing acts – encouraged by Pisces on his Midheaven.

At some point in his relationships, Gemini will end up with a partner who teaches him about the search for meaning; a person who looks for the patterns in life or the point of it all. This relationship will ring loud bells with Gemini, because his lover is putting him in touch with his own need for a bigger philosophical or spiritual picture.

And what does Gemini learn from all these various partners in his life? Basically, it is to find God in the details. This sign cannot escape loss, endings, death and partings, but he is blessed in being able to move on and see the big picture. Have you lost someone close to you? Look at the Gemini man's perspective on life and death – and living and dying. He has a unique angle on the human condition that you won't find anywhere else.

Cancer Man JUNE 21–JULY 22

More mad things have been written about Cancerians than any other sign. You know the story: he's a shy agoraphobic, neurotically dependent on family, home and cookbooks, who will kill anyone who stops him going home for Christmas. The reality? He is actually a ballsy explorer and a compulsive traveller – with a *big* mobile phone habit.

Cancer man is often painted as an appallingly domesticated creature who sits indoors with a tartan rug on his knee, rejecting any holiday destination that is more than 50 kilometres away from his bedroom slippers. The reality is astonishingly different. He is fascinated, hypnotised and even gobsmacked by new faces and places. Other people's beliefs, norms, sexual proclivities, local customs and social rituals enchant him – even if all he's doing is exploring a different social class or a small country town.

Clever Mercury rules his Twelfth House, his secret self, and also his Third House, his computer and telephone zone. The Cancer man is basically a closet journalist (no matter what he does for a living) and, more obviously, a methodical reporter of the facts (with all the detail you could desire).

He is precise with details and skilled at logical analysis, with Virgo and Mercury on his Third House. This special ability, combined with his permanent fascination with other places and faces, makes him a natural anthropologist – or, at the very least, a wannabe foreign correspondent.

What is 'foreign' to Cancer, of course, depends on how far he can actually travel. Cancerian George Orwell went to Wigan Pier and wrote a book about it. The Dalai Lama went from Tibet to India. Sir Edmund Hillary went from New Zealand to the top of Everest. Cancer never fully assimilates in any new place, though, no matter if he is moving there or travelling there. After all, home is beautiful, home is peaceful, home has romantic appeal . . . the Moon is his ruler, and the Moon describes what pulls people back to safety.

Cancer is very far from being the agoraphobic creature of astrological cliché, however. After all, exploring is routine to him, thanks to Jupiter's rulership of his Sixth House. He constantly finds himself involved in tasks or projects that require him to seek out the big picture.

Cancer is always on the attack or defence – in fact, he can be surprisingly combative and aggressive in his approach to new places and people. He typically has a highly provocative way of tackling the world – and a desperate need to tell the rest of us about whatever he finds. Ballsy Mars and Aries rule his Midheaven – his life direction.

It's a very long way from Mr Tartan Rug, but would you have it any other way? Bring a map on your first date and leave it on the table. That should start a conversation or four.

Leo Man JULY 23–AUGUST 22

He's a natural authority figure with a deep understanding of how power works – an all-powerful father, captain, team leader, teacher, expert, manager, boss, executive, commander, officer, director or lead singer. This authority role is hard for him, however, and he can spend a lifetime sweating over the pros and cons of being top dog.

His childhood and adolescence taught him a lot about how

power actually works. Observing the way one or more family members handled him (or other people) has given him an insight into the nature of control, and consequently he is sharply aware of how people-politics operates. Penetrating Pluto and Scorpio rule his family tree.

Lesson One for Leo is simple: how do you manage the rebels? This question is important for two reasons. First, he tends to fall in love with people who are highly independent, wonderfully individual and free-spirited. Second, some of his biggest problems in life have been with people who are mad mavericks. He loves outsiders. But he can't stand being disobeyed either. Both loving and hating these kinds of people teaches him that leadership is all about (a) respecting them and (b) setting up a power structure in which they won't cause problems. Crazy Aquarius and Uranus rule his Seventh House of enemies and opponents.

Leo has to learn (usually the hard way) about boundaries. Sometimes they need to be firmly maintained, or even set down with enormous force. At other times, the boundaries need to be moved or even thrown away. Leo struggles with this creatively.

And here's another thing: Leo's values dominate his life. This also makes his role as king rather difficult, because others are constantly imposing their values on him. Taurus, the sign of principles and ethics (usually connected with money!), rules his Midheaven. Financial issues follow him around. And, each time, he has to confront what he believes.

This eternal grappling with the perils of power and leadership often puts Leo in a position where he is forced to change a particular system, set-up or structure. Some rules stay, of course (Leo has a shrewd appreciation of when the rules are working for him), but he is also bold about calling a revolution if it seems necessary, thanks to the Aquarian influence on his descendant.

If his family is like an unholy cross between the Simpsons and the Osbournes, he will change the rules. If his workplace (or his weekend organisation) is run like *The Banana Splits*, he will blow it up and start again. It's what Leo was put here to do. When Leo finally has the power structure he needs, however, nobody makes a better king.

Hire Kenneth Branagh's version of *Henry V* on DVD if you really want to cheer him up. He'll identify with the troubled king so much, you'll have to drag him away. Nevertheless, his constant struggle with the rights and wrongs of power makes him eminently qualified to actually possess some.

Virgo Man AUGUST 23–SEPTEMBER 22

Lock up your daughters. Here comes the vitamin-guzzling, iron-pumping, dentist-worshipping, shirt-washing neurotic of many a dodgy astrology book. Did you know Nick Cave was a Virgo? I rest my case. This man is actually quite a different beastie altogether. Forget the vitamin myths. He's a controversial speaker, thinker and writer with some surprisingly unpopular opinions – that's what's *really* interesting about him.

It's all about the brain for Virgo – and possibly the voice box. He is a passionate speaker and a compulsive generator of ideas and opinions. He is also secretly braver than even he consciously understands, so in the face of opposition he continues to publish and be damned (or at least to stand up in front of an audience and have rotten tomatoes thrown at him).

He's clever but very few people appreciate his concepts or opinions. The non-conformist sign Aquarius and its rebellious ruler Uranus both control his Sixth House of daily life and work. Virgo is true to himself, and it can make people hopping mad.

His goals and aspirations typically revolve around education, the media, publishing, mass communication or the connections he can make between people, places and ideas. He also has an unusual capacity to make love to his computer – and his library – with the kind of intensity that other men reserve for their partners. Don't make the mistake of interrupting him when he is working on an idea. He's wedded to it, the way other men are wedded to lovers.

He is barely conscious that he is a closet egomaniac – but with a sneaky, secret Leo side to his personality, he is. He needs it in order to defend himself against the scepticism of the people who just don't get it.

Putting his ideas into words always seems to involve a power play between himself and his audience – even if it's just you and the other guests at a dinner party. Because Sagittarius and Jupiter rule the Fourth House, someone in his family tree was a true believer (politically, spiritually or philosophically). Consequently Virgo can also become quite evangelical about what he knows to be true. Changing the way people think can become a lifetime's occupation: it satisfies Virgo's inner preacher, but (if he succeeds) it also promises to vindicate his belief in himself.

Virgo also takes on jobs, hobbies, passions, tasks and projects (for professional or personal reasons) that require him to be on the outside in some way – or miles ahead. In order to get his message across, Virgo tends to look for a niche where he has permission to reach as many people as possible: teaching is one option, creating a website is another. Others become taxi-drivers, so they can lecture 200 new passengers on their views every day of the week. Better ask the driver his Sun Sign before you hop in.

Libra Man SEPTEMBER 23–OCTOBER 22

Now here's a sexual thrill-seeker who *genuinely* loves the buzzier aspects of the Zeitgeist. So much for the rather bland creature of legend, whose bottom is permanently scarred from so much fence-sitting. Libra habitually stirs things up! He is a dancer and a lover, not a fighter – but his response to the world at large is energetic, combative and dynamic. He also knows how to generate electricity. He expresses himself sexually (or creatively) in exciting, surprising ways, and he knows how to either create a buzz or detect one, and then fool around at the centre of it. Wild Aquarius and electrifying Uranus rule his Fifth House of self-expression.

The Libran man's planetary ruler is Venus, which astrologers have long connected with love and lust. Consequently, making conquests (even repeatedly, with the same partner, natch) is vital to his sense of self. Lust brings out the satyr in him. He finds freedom in sex, and sex in freedom. With Scorpio in his Second House, he also deeply values passion and erotica, and the world of sexual taboos. A routine marriage or relationship kills him – remember, he is perpetually seeking to be turned on, like any other piece of electrical equipment.

Tension, temper and heightened emotions are part of the territory. He either seems to attract them in the people around him or he generates his own lightning bolts and electrical storms – that's Aries on his descendant. Creatively, emotionally and sexually, Libra turns things upside down. He lives where the wild things are, and more predictable or conservative environments deny his personality. Some Librans actually froth at the mouth. Some just dance naked in a storm.

Libra also seeks fantasy in his reality, on a regular basis. This explains some of his professional choices, or even his daily routines – which make no sense to other people – but it can also explain another Libran trap: issues with drugs and alcohol. Pisces and Neptune rule his Sixth House of daily life. He's not averse to an escape hatch.

These men are in touch with the Zeitgeist on a daily basis. They use their sixth sense at work or in their normal lives, and consequently know how to read the general mood. They are particularly good at detecting where the next buzz is coming from, and as soon as it arrives, they obligingly hurl themselves in. It's not like Libra to be left out of the dance – particularly when it promises the kind of thrills and spills that give him permission to genuinely express his personality.

One or more partners/lovers in his life have been movers and shakers. Balls of fire. Ever-ready batteries of pure, unmitigated energy. Consequently, he's learnt to do a lot more than just go with the flow; he basically drives a Harley Davidson through it.

Previous dates or partners – or even the person he's with now – remind him that life should be a buzz, and if it isn't, he'd better start living or working somewhere else.

Scorpio Man OCTOBER 23–NOVEMBER 21

This man is shockingly candid when it suits him, and permanently haunted by his sins . . . when you eventually find out what they are, you will also understand why they had to be so deeply concealed. Sin attracts him. Sin *is* him. Nevertheless, when the time is right, Scorpio will usually tell all. The shell-shocked look on the faces of his partner, friends and colleagues is usually there because Scorpio has had one of his confessional moments. When Scorpio finally opens up, jaws clang on the floor.

One of his ancestors or relatives set up a family pattern showing him that honesty, even shockingly candid behaviour, was perfectly normal. Aquarius and Uranus, which rule truth at any price, rule his Fourth House of family background. Throughout his life, his need to be absolutely up-front with other people remains like an itch he has to scratch – and, sooner or later, Scorpio finds himself giving in. He's always got a jack-in-the-box confession.

Everyone sins, but Scorpio is more deeply aware of what shames or disgraces him than other men. He is also by nature a detoxer. Pluto is his ruler, and Pluto always brings the *merde* up from under the floorboards, sooner or later.

Scorpio believes that skeletons rattling around in closets or dark secrets can actually pollute the atmosphere. So it's almost impossible to begin a new relationship with a Scorpio man - without some confessional scene, one wild and stormy night. It may be what he did to his ex. It may be what he did to a small rabbit called Godfrey. It may be a Mafia hit he got mixed up in. But you'll hear all about it.

Scorpio sins and *then* covers it all up. The concealment has a purpose, though. More than any other sign, this one chooses a life path where he must take a leading role or even a place in the spotlight. For one reason or another, he ends up being hard to miss. (Leo and the Sun rule his Midheaven.) Consequently, discretion and concealment become necessary tactics. They are part of who he is. The pressure of covering up can only last so long, though, as Scorpio picks his moments, then confesses. But remember this – he'll only come clean when it suits him!

Scorpio's philosophical, political, spiritual or religious values are extremely dear to him, but so is his image. Consequently, it takes much soul-searching before he is prepared to come clean, both detoxing and transforming situations in a shocking way. Whatever his religion (or lack of it), Scorpio is essentially a Catholic at heart. He sins and then he seeks absolution – or at least understanding – from other people.

There is a raw power about this sign that affects all of us, because Scorpio is so unafraid to be human. The side of him that sins reflects us too. And the side of him that wants to get it all out in the open is also appealing. He's real. He's deep. As in *deeeeeep*. That's Scorpio for you. Made for Oprah Winfrey. It's what empowers him, you know.

Sagittarius Man NOVEMBER 22–DECEMBER 21

He's a big-picture thinker who uses his large perspective on life to focus on the tiny details. Telepathic Pisces and Neptune rule his Fourth House of family background. A relative in the family tree was highly intuitive or even genuinely psychic, so Sagittarius has grown up with the idea that relying on a sixth sense is okay.

Sagittarius is insatiably curious – even voyeuristic – in his need to know. Jupiter, the planet of knowledge, is his ruler. Be careful. Relentless Pluto rules his hidden side, and the reality is that there will be days when you may suspect that he is secretly unable to leave anyone or anything alone. It's the spy sign. And the no-stone-unturned sign too.

He typically gazes down on life from a lofty perspective.

Sagittarians enjoy jobs, hobbies or interests that give them the long view – flying, international aid work, astrology, philosophy, science, jobs that involve long-haul travel, riding, skiing, sailing and climbing are all typical. He lives with the big picture.

He classically enjoys exploring everything from a multiplicity of angles too, which once again accounts for his passion for the outdoors, travel (it broadens the mind, after all) and any job or hobby where information must be examined from a broad range of different perspectives.

All of this makes Sagittarius feel rather omniscient at times. If he is typical of his sign, he would rather have a cosmic or universal grasp of reality (God's view!) than anything as low-rent as an ordinary angle. And, above all, he would rather travel the world and see behaviour from a variety of perspectives than stay landlocked in a small town.

His intuition means Sagittarius often identifies things below the surface that other people miss. And it is astonishing how often Sagittarius finds himself being a witness to other people's secrets – even their sins. Because of this, Sagittarius also has to make moral and philosophical decisions along the way. He has the advantage of an elevated view of life – and second sight as well. When that involves him as a witness (or potential judge and jury) he has to ask himself if he really wants to play God after all. Should he accept the cosmos (and humanity) with all its flaws, or not?

His unconscious obsession with seeking out other people's dark sides or their crimes and misdemeanours is one aspect of his relentless curiosity and his insatiable interest in what is really going on in every hidden corner.

There is a huge irony in the fact that Sagittarius has such a broad and sweeping view of life, but still singles out the small stuff too. Virgo, the sign of minutiae and the trivia in life, sits firmly on the Sagittarian man's Midheaven. That's why the big picture always gives him the smaller story.

Capricorn Man DECEMBER 22–JANUARY 19

Capricorn is often, and mistakenly, described as a frightfully serious, social-climbing, professionally ambitious, pinstriped pessimist. But, hang on a minute. Elvis Presley was a Capricorn, so please, don't step on his blue suede shoes. The Capricorn man is dominated by romantic Venus and Libra, sitting on the Midheaven of his Solar Chart. And Venus rules his Fifth House of lust too. Forget the pinstripes!

When you're in a relationship with him, Capricorn is a sensitive and emotional talker, thinker, singer or emailer, and all his important goals are romantic ones. Throw away the idea that he is some uptight corporate climber; he is far more driven by his feelings and his passions than that.

His big challenge – which may not surprise you – is learning to love himself. This can take years. Until he manages to achieve this unconditional acceptance of himself, he can end up with unsuitable partners whose view of him is simply a mirror image of his own low self-opinion. Consequently, the relationship never lasts.

Capricorn knows all about feeling scared and defensive. Cold Saturn is his ruling planet. However, he also knows that unconditional love can work miracles. At least one of his partners in life will turn out to be precisely the kind of caring, protective type who can help melt the ice, thanks to Cancer on his descendant. And in many ways, it is only when he finally makes a commitment (and receives one in return) that Capricorn feels he has come home again. He truly believes in the mad miracle of love.

When Capricorn finally finds the real thing (you, perhaps?) he is entirely capable of dancing on the ceiling – permanently. In fact, when he is happily matched, Capricorn goes much further than the other eleven signs, and may even be found clambering up the ivy outside your apartment with a rose between his teeth.

Once his walls and barricades are being taken apart by the

power of the heart chakra, Capricorn is capable of being the kind of romantic action hero that Mattel probably had in mind when they created Ken for Barbie. He is impulsive – sexually or emotionally. He is fearless. He is prone to standing outside his lover's window at four o'clock in the morning, singing 'It Must Be Love'. That's what Capricorn is made of!

Someone in his family tree was an action man or action woman, because Aries rules his Fourth House. And Capricorn trusts impulse. He feels comfortable with it. In many ways, it is a release for him. No wonder his relationships are packed with so many wild romantic gestures.

There are good reasons why a partner is the key for Capricorn: it validates his sense of self-worth, and that by itself is enough reason for him to keep striving and serenading. No wonder he is the only sign to truly put himself on the line on St Valentine's Day, despite the risk of pain!

Aquarius Man JANUARY 20–FEBRUARY 18

This one is supposed to be as emotional as Frosty the Snowman and as mad as a March hare on E. True or false? Well, it's quite true that Uranus is his ruling planet, and so he does spend long periods of time losing himself in the joy of chaos – not to mention unparalleled anarchy.

Life never stands still for Aquarius – partly because his own unpredictable energy guarantees that nothing in his world will ever be normal or routine. Does this rattle his cage? Not at all. On the contrary, Aquarius only longs to join in with the loopiness. When an Aquarian forgets to watch out for potholes, though (or lightning bolts or stray cannonballs), all hell can break loose. Watch out for Uranian electrical shocks!

Why do so many Aquarian men seem to land in one disaster after another? Typically, it's because he equates 'new' with 'good'. Anyone or anything that has just entered the picture is accepted, no matter what awful results it might promise later. He thinks impulsively and he plays with life like an adolescent;

consequently, he hits SNAFU situations more than any other sign of the zodiac.

Life with Aquarius is rather like being with someone who is both the creator of the chaos and the observer of it too. Clever Gemini rules his zone of self-expression. Even when he's part of the mayhem, part of him is standing back and analysing it.

Aquarius is pulled between two opposite reactions. First, there is the side of him that everyone knows from ancient astrology books – Mr Cool, Calm and Collected. This part of his personality knows how to distance itself from whatever is taking place, and appreciates the perspective that comes from being disconnected and brilliantly analytical about life. But he alternates between two roles: he also throws himself into the deep end of dizzy disaster. That's Neptune's rulership of his Second House – he values chaos. And after that? He pulls himself out of the whirlpool and becomes the rather distant, intellectual, heavily analytical creature of legend – always looking for a pattern, be it scientific, philosophical, artistic, literary, astrological or psychological. Professor Aquarius is likely to be as much a part of your life as Kid Crazy. You have been warned!

Somewhere in between mad eternal youth and detached outsider, Aquarius eventually finds his middle ground. But not before he has pulled the rug, shaken up the snow dome, shocked the customers and scared the dog. No matter how much he might secretly long to play the intellectual, Aquarius is far too involved in life's madness at a grassroots level to ever entirely remove himself from the game.

If you are deeply organised by nature and need a system or a plan, you'll have trouble with this man. If you need to go white-water rafting in the madness of life, though, this is your tour guide. Just remember to come up for air periodically.

Pisces Man FEBRUARY 19–MARCH 19

Ah, yes. Apparently, this is the gentle, candle-burning poet who swoons if he hears an Enya tour rumour. Hopefully you've encountered the other Pisces, though. He's the real one. And he's also a man with a mission. The visionary crusader with a cause.

All Pisceans have an ideology, a conviction or a burning belief – and all are prepared to rally the troops if necessary. Jupiter, the faith planet, rules his Midheaven. More than any other sign of the zodiac, this one has the heart of a crusader.

Neptune rules him. It's the church planet. He can develop an almost religious fervour for the ideas, ideals or causes that speak to him. Pushy Aries and fiery Mars rule his Second House too, so he values action. It's not enough for him to just *feel* the faith. He has to act on it too. And he is often on the attack or defence; Pisces is not only far more aggressive than most astrology books let on, he also knows that a fighting spirit is worth a million bucks. That's fearless Mars on his Second House again.

Who is the enemy in Pisces World? Inevitably it is someone (or a whole bunch of someones) who are blind to the real truth. And the real truth, of course, is in Pisces' possession. Or at least he can't see any other possibility. Tunnel vision is his prerogative with Neptune, the planet of blind spots, as his planetary ruler.

Someone in the family tree was a thinker, talker, student, teacher, writer or reader, as Gemini and Mercury rule his Fourth House. Consequently, the world of ideas and opinions is second nature to Pisces.

And, there's more: he also falls in love with clever, methodical types, thanks to Mercury's rulership of his soulmate zone. All of this persuades him that he's going to need more than blind faith in his cause – he's going to need a manifesto too. Goodbye Mr Flippy Floppy Fins, hello Mr Brilliant Strategist. He's probably picked it up from you, you know . . .

Pisces is far more savvy with the facts than he is usually given credit for. And not only that, when he is armed with these facts ('The truth! And nothing but the truth!') he is ready to sail into battle. All he needs, apart from the spirit, is the logical argument.

The devil is alive and well in the Piscean psyche, and he lives somewhere 'over there', inhabited by people who might as well come from another planet, for all he understands them. Blame Pluto on his Ninth House, but Pisces always feels the gaps between himself and the distant non-believers.

A Sun Sign seldom describes what a man looks like, but where Pisces is concerned, there are certain trademark facial expressions. Begin with the eyes. They may be malfunctioning (lots of them are as blind as bats) or working well, but also noticeably glazed over – as if Pisces is seeing a misty and inspiring vision of the Truth. Then, in a flash, the eyes can be as piercing as a fox terrier's when you're on the wrong end of a sausage! It will be obvious on your first date with him, and still there when he's an old man.

2 PREDICT YOUR LOVE-LIFE FUTURE

WHAT'S IN STORE TO 2010?

Picture the scene: David Beckham, killing time in a hotel room, November 1996. Overhead, Venus, the planet of love, is passing through the Seventh House of marriage in his Solar Chart. Mars, the planet of action, is passing through his Fifth House of sex. In his room, a TV set is showing the new Spice Girls video.

According to Beckham's autobiography *My Side*, that was the moment Victoria 'Posh Spice' Adams made an unforgettable impact on him. 'I had to find a way to be with her,' he remembers. And after the magic month of November 1996? Well, the rest is history. Or, at least, a couple of purple thrones, three children and a lot of matching leather trousers – plus an alleged affair or two.

When Elton John announced his intention to marry David Furnish on April 25 2005, his Seventh House of marriage was also busy as the South Node and Jupiter passed through. The South Node is about past life connections. Jupiter is about big plans. And when Anne Heche met Ellen de Generes? Pluto was in her Seventh House. It's the planet of obsession, passion and intensity – and pushes new love affairs to the brink.

In astrology, any time planets and points pass through the Fifth House and/or the Seventh House, anything from a momentous first meeting to a life-changing commitment is possible. People fall in love, have one-night stands or give birth during these cycles. Don't get too excited, though. Planets and points in the Fifth House and/or Seventh House can also signal serious tests of commitment, and occasionally a separation or divorce too.

Remember Loosgate? It challenged the public face of David and Victoria Beckham's marriage. It took place in April and May 2004. David had an eclipse in his Seventh House. Victoria had a Full Moon in her Seventh House too. Planets in the Fifth House and Seventh House are destiny's milestone markers for lovers – for better or worse. It all depends on the energy of the planets and points that are travelling through those houses.

The ballad of Ted and Sylvia . . . and Bill and Monica

Ted Hughes met Sylvia Plath at a party on February 25 1956, a momentous first meeting, recorded in the Gwyneth Paltrow film *Sylvia*. Ted had Mercury in his Seventh House that night, and Mars, Saturn and the North Node in his Fifth House. Sylvia had the Sun in her Fifth House too. They married on 16 June 1956 when Ted had the North Node in his Fifth House and Chiron in his Seventh House. Sylvia had Mars in her Fifth House.

A similar pattern was repeated when Ted Hughes published his poems about his long-dead wife, *Birthday Letters*, on January 29 1998. He had the New Moon, Neptune, Uranus and Jupiter in his Seventh House and Pluto in his Fifth House. Even though she had long since passed over, Sylvia's Scorpio chart was also showing Mars and the South Node in the Fifth House on the same day.

The complicated Plath–Hughes relationship is a good example of how planets in the Seventh House and Fifth House of both partners can influence the timing of a fated marriage or affair. And also how planetary cycles affect us, even on the other side!

February 1997 was a big month for Leos Bill Clinton and Monica Lewinsky. Clinton received a Valentine's Day greeting from her in the *Washington Post* that month (it was a quote from *Romeo and Juliet* addressed to Handsome, from M). According to

BBC News, Clinton received something rather more interesting still on February 28 – a fortnight later – the day of the infamous navy-blue-dress date.

In February 1997, the Sun, New Moon, Mercury, Venus, Jupiter and Uranus were all in Bill's Seventh House while Pluto was in the Fifth House. As Monica is a Leo too, she was experiencing exactly the same cycles.

Now read on to find out more about the effects of planets in the Fifth House and Seventh House in *your* life. They rule your mating, dating and relating cycles, and it's your Solar Chart (your Sun Sign chart) that tells the story – but all the work's been done for you right here, so all you need to do is look at the following tables.

Do you have your Natal Chart too? Compare the two. You'll find that Fifth House and Seventh House cycles often echo each other.

All about the Fifth House

Below are some of the objects, experiences and issues that can turn up when planets travel through the Fifth House. Typically, sex or children dominate.

★ One-night stands
★ The pill
★ Children
★ Pregnancy
★ Viagra
★ STDs
★ Crushes
★ Fantasies
★ Sex therapists
★ First dates
★ Flirting
★ Pornography
★ Vibrators
★ Erotica
★ Tantric sex
★ Hookers
★ Orgasms
★ First kisses
★ Adoption
★ Infatuation
★ Cruising
★ Speed dating
★ Online dating
★ IVF

- ★ Nannies
- ★ Love rivals
- ★ Parenthood
- ★ Virginity
- ★ Condoms
- ★ IUDs
- ★ Affairs

All about the Seventh House

Below are some of the objects, experiences and issues that can turn up when planets travel through the Seventh House. Typically, serious partnership dominates.

- ★ White weddings
- ★ Civil partnerships
- ★ De facto commitments
- ★ Ex-partners
- ★ Separation
- ★ Divorce
- ★ Commitment
- ★ Marriage guidance counselling
- ★ Engagements
- ★ Vows
- ★ Pre-nuptial agreements
- ★ Elopements
- ★ In-laws
- ★ Love triangles
- ★ Honeymoons
- ★ Lawyers
- ★ Priests
- ★ Broken engagements
- ★ Remarriage
- ★ Impulse weddings
- ★ Second honeymoons
- ★ Infidelity
- ★ Love in sickness and in health
- ★ Soulmates

What you need to know!

Here is a list of key Fifth House and Seventh House Solar Chart cycles taking all the twelve signs up to 2010, so you know when the temperature is likely to rise. When the planets and points (Sun, Moon, Mercury, Venus, Mars, Jupiter, Saturn, Uranus, Neptune, Pluto, Chiron, North Node, South Node) are fated to travel through these hot zones of your horoscope, you'll reach turning points, traffic lights and crossroads – sexually or emotionally. Check your Sun Sign (normal star sign) below to find out when.

ARIES
When planets and points are in Leo, they are in your Fifth House.
When planets and points are in Libra, they are in your Seventh House.

TAURUS
When planets and points are in Virgo, they are in your Fifth House.
When planets and points are in Scorpio, they are in your Seventh House.

GEMINI
When planets and points are in Libra, they are in your Fifth House.
When planets and points are in Sagittarius, they are in your Seventh House.

CANCER
When planets and points are in Scorpio, they are in your Fifth House.
When planets and points are in Capricorn, they are in your Seventh House.

LEO
When planets and points are in Sagittarius, they are in your Fifth House.
When planets and points are in Aquarius, they are in your Seventh House.

VIRGO
When planets and points are in Capricorn, they are in your Fifth House.
When planets and points are in Pisces, they are in your Seventh House.

LIBRA
When planets and points are in Aquarius, they are in your Fifth House.

When planets and points are in Aries, they are in your Seventh House.

SCORPIO

When planets and points are in Pisces, they are in your Fifth House.
When planets and points are in Taurus, they are in your Seventh House.

SAGITTARIUS

When planets and points are in Aries, they are in your Fifth House.
When planets and points are in Gemini, they are in your Seventh House.

CAPRICORN

When planets and points are in Taurus, they are in your Fifth House.
When planets and points are in Cancer, they are in your Seventh House.

AQUARIUS

When planets and points are in Gemini, they are in your Fifth House.
When planets and points are in Leo, they are in your Seventh House.

PISCES

When planets and points are in Cancer, they are in your Fifth House.
When planets and points are in Virgo, they are in your Seventh House.

THE CYCLES OF THE PLANETS IN YOUR FIFTH AND SEVENTH HOUSES

The section after this will give you the *how* and *why* of your cycles, which you discover simply by finding out when the planets are passing through your trigger signs. All dates are averaged for world time zones, so there is a chance a planet might start its Fifth or Seventh House cycle the day before or the day after the one listed here – depending on where you are at the time! For total accuracy to the hour and day, check at www.astro.com.

SUN

2006–2010 Sun in Aries March 20–April 19
2006–2010 Sun in Taurus April 20–May 20
2006–2010 Sun in Gemini May 21–June 20
2006–2010 Sun in Cancer June 21–July 22
2006–2010 Sun in Leo July 23–August 22
2006–2010 Sun in Virgo August 23–September 22
2006–2010 Sun in Libra September 23–October 22
2006–2010 Sun in Scorpio October 23–November 21
2006–2010 Sun in Sagittarius November 22–December 21
2006–2010 Sun in Capricorn December 22–January 19
2006–2010 Sun in Aquarius January 20–February 18
2006–2010 Sun in Pisces February 19–March 19

NEW MOON

2006 New Moon in Virgo September 22
2006 New Moon in Libra October 22
2006 New Moon in Scorpio November 20
2006 New Moon in Sagittarius December 20
2007 New Moon in Capricorn January 19
2007 New Moon in Aquarius February 17
2007 New Moon in Pisces March 19 (An eclipse, so it's ultrapowerful.)
2007 New Moon in Aries April 17
2007 New Moon in Taurus May 16
2007 New Moon in Gemini June 15
2007 New Moon in Cancer July 14
2007 New Moon in Leo August 12

2007	New Moon in Virgo September 11 (An eclipse, so it's ultra-powerful.)
2007	New Moon in Libra October 11
2007	New Moon in Scorpio November 9
2007	New Moon in Sagittarius December 9
2008	New Moon in Capricorn January 8
2008	New Moon in Aquarius February 7 (An eclipse, so it's ultrapowerful.)
2008	New Moon in Pisces March 7
2008	New Moon in Aries April 6
2008	New Moon in Taurus May 5
2008	New Moon in Gemini June 3
2008	New Moon in Cancer July 3
2008	New Moon in Leo August 1 (An eclipse, so it's ultrapowerful.)
2008	New Moon in Virgo August 30
2008	New Moon in Libra September 29
2008	New Moon in Scorpio October 28
2008	New Moon in Sagittarius November 27
2008	New Moon in Capricorn December 27
2009	New Moon in Aquarius January 26 (An eclipse, so it's ultrapowerful.)
2009	New Moon in Pisces February 25
2009	New Moon in Aries March 26
2009	New Moon in Taurus April 25
2009	New Moon in Gemini May 24
2009	New Moon in Cancer June 22
2009	New Moon in Cancer July 22
2009	New Moon in Leo August 20
2009	New Moon in Virgo September 18
2009	New Moon in Libra October 18
2009	New Moon in Scorpio November 16
2009	New Moon in Sagittarius December 16
2010	New Moon in Capricorn January 15 (An eclipse, so it's ultra-powerful.)

2010 New Moon in Aquarius February 14
2010 New Moon in Pisces March 15
2010 New Moon in Aries April 14
2010 New Moon in Taurus May 14
2010 New Moon in Gemini June 12
2010 New Moon in Cancer July 11 (An eclipse, so it's ultrapowerful.)
2010 New Moon in Leo August 10
2010 New Moon in Virgo September 8
2010 New Moon in Libra October 7
2010 New Moon in Scorpio November 6
2010 New Moon in Sagittarius December 5

FULL MOON

2006 Full Moon in Aries October 7
2006 Full Moon in Taurus November 5
2006 Full Moon in Gemini December 5
2007 Full Moon in Cancer January 3
2007 Full Moon in Leo February 2
2007 Full Moon in Virgo March 3 (An eclipse, so it's ultrapowerful.)
2007 Full Moon in Libra April 2
2007 Full Moon in Scorpio May 2
2007 Full Moon in Sagittarius June 1
2007 Full Moon in Capricorn June 30
2007 Full Moon in Aquarius July 30
2007 Full Moon in Pisces August 28 (An eclipse, so it's ultrapowerful.)
2007 Full Moon in Aries September 26
2007 Full Moon in Taurus October 26
2007 Full Moon in Gemini November 24
2007 Full Moon in Cancer December 24
2008 Full Moon in Leo January 22
2008 Full Moon in Virgo February 21 (An eclipse, so it's ultrapowerful.)

2008 Full Moon in Libra March 21
2008 Full Moon in Scorpio April 20
2008 Full Moon in Scorpio May 20
2008 Full Moon in Sagittarius June 18
2008 Full Moon in Capricorn July 18
2008 Full Moon in Aquarius August 16 (An eclipse, so it's ultrapowerful.)
2008 Full Moon in Pisces September 15
2008 Full Moon in Aries October 14
2008 Full Moon in Taurus November 13
2008 Full Moon in Gemini December 12
2009 Full Moon in Cancer January 11
2009 Full Moon in Leo February 9 (An eclipse, so it's ultrapowerful.)
2009 Full Moon in Virgo March 11
2009 Full Moon in Libra April 9
2009 Full Moon in Scorpio May 9
2009 Full Moon in Sagittarius June 7
2009 Full Moon in Capricorn July 7 (An eclipse, so it's ultrapowerful.)
2009 Full Moon in Aquarius August 6 (An eclipse, so it's ultrapowerful.)
2009 Full Moon in Pisces September 4
2009 Full Moon in Aries October 4
2009 Full Moon in Taurus November 2
2009 Full Moon in Gemini December 2
2009 Full Moon in Cancer December 31 (An eclipse, so it's ultrapowerful.)
2010 Full Moon in Leo January 30
2010 Full Moon in Virgo February 28
2010 Full Moon in Libra March 30
2010 Full Moon in Scorpio April 28
2010 Full Moon in Sagittarius May 27
2010 Full Moon in Capricorn June 26 (An eclipse, so it's ultrapowerful.)

2010 Full Moon in Aquarius July 26
2010 Full Moon in Pisces August 24
2010 Full Moon in Aries September 23
2010 Full Moon in Taurus November 21
2010 Full Moon in Gemini December 21 (An eclipse, so it's ultrapowerful.)

MERCURY

2006 Mercury in Libra September 13–October 2
2006 Mercury in Scorpio October 3–December 8 (Mercury Retrograde Alert* October 28–Nov 18)
2006 Mercury in Sagittarius December 9–27
2006 Mercury in Capricorn December 28–31
2007 Mercury in Capricorn January 1–15
2007 Mercury in Aquarius January 16–February 2
2007 Mercury in Pisces February 2–27 (Mercury Retrograde Alert February 14–27)
2007 Mercury in Aquarius February 28–March 18 (Mercury Retrograde Alert February 28–March 8)
2007 Mercury in Pisces March 19–April 10
2007 Mercury in Aries April 11–27
2007 Mercury in Taurus April 28–May 11
2007 Mercury in Gemini May 12–29
2007 Mercury in Cancer May 30–August 4 (Mercury Retrograde Alert June 15–July 10)
2007 Mercury in Leo August 5–19
2007 Mercury in Virgo August 20–September 5
2007 Mercury in Libra September 6–27
2007 Mercury in Scorpio September 28–October 24 (Mercury Retrograde Alert October 12–October 24)

*A Mercury Retrograde Alert indicates you should avoid major discussions, signed documents or a heavy reliance on computers, post or telephones at this time.

2007	Mercury in Libra October 25–November 11 (Mercury Retrograde Alert October 25–November 1)
2007	Mercury in Scorpio November 12–December 1
2007	Mercury in Sagittarius December 2–20
2007	Mercury in Capricorn December 21–31
2008	Mercury in Capricorn January 1–January 8
2008	Mercury in Aquarius January 9–March 14 (Mercury Retrograde Alert January 28–February 19)
2008	Mercury in Pisces March 15–April 2
2008	Mercury in Aries April 3–17
2008	Mercury in Taurus April 18–May 2
2008	Mercury in Gemini May 3–July 10 (Mercury Retrograde Alert May 26–June 19)
2008	Mercury in Cancer July 11–26
2008	Mercury in Leo July 27–August 10
2008	Mercury in Virgo August 11–29
2008	Mercury in Libra August 30–November 4 (Mercury Retrograde Alert September 24–October 15)
2008	Mercury in Scorpio November 5–23
2008	Mercury in Sagittarius November 24–December 12
2008	Mercury in Capricorn December 13–31
2009	Mercury in Capricorn January 1
2009	Mercury in Aquarius January 2–21 (Mercury Retrograde Alert January 11–21)
2009	Mercury in Capricorn January 22–February 14 (Mercury Retrograde Alert January 22–February 1)
2009	Mercury in Aquarius February 15–March 8
2009	Mercury in Pisces March 9–25
2009	Mercury in Aries March 26–April 9
2009	Mercury in Taurus April 10–30
2009	Mercury in Gemini May 1–14 (Mercury Retrograde Alert May 7–14)
2009	Mercury in Taurus May 15–June 14 (Mercury Retrograde Alert May 14–31)
2009	Mercury in Gemini June 15–July 3

2009 Mercury in Cancer July 4–17
2009 Mercury in Leo July 18–August 2
2009 Mercury in Virgo August 3–25
2009 Mercury in Libra August 26–September 18 (Mercury Retrograde Alert September 7–18)
2009 Mercury in Virgo September 19–October 10 (Mercury Retrograde Alert September 19–28)
2009 Mercury in Libra October 11–28
2009 Mercury in Scorpio October 29–November 16
2009 Mercury in Sagittarius November 17–December 5
2009 Mercury in Capricorn December 6–31 (Mercury Retrograde Alert December 26–31)
2010 Mercury in Capricorn January 1–February 10 (Mercury Retrograde Alert January 1–14)
2010 Mercury in Aquarius February 11–March 1
2010 Mercury in Pisces March 2–17
2010 Mercury in Aries March 18–April 2
2010 Mercury in Taurus April 3–June 10 (Mercury Retrograde Alert April 18–May 11)
2010 Mercury in Gemini June 11–25
2010 Mercury in Cancer June 26–July 9
2010 Mercury in Leo July 10–27
2010 Mercury in Virgo July 28–October 3 (Mercury Retrograde Alert August 20–September 12)
2010 Mercury in Libra October 4–20
2010 Mercury in Scorpio October 21–November 8
2010 Mercury in Sagittarius November 9–December 1
2010 Mercury in Capricorn December 2–18 (Mercury Retrograde Alert December 11–18)
2010 Mercury in Sagittarius December 19–31 (Mercury Retrograde Alert December 19–30)

VENUS

2006 Venus in Libra October 1–24
2006 Venus in Scorpio October 25–November 17

2006 Venus in Sagittarius November 18–December 11
2006 Venus in Capricorn December 12–31
2007 Venus in Capricorn January 1–4
2007 Venus in Aquarius January 5–28
2007 Venus in Pisces January 29–February 21
2007 Venus in Aries February 22–March 17
2007 Venus in Taurus March 18–April 12
2007 Venus in Gemini April 13–May 8
2007 Venus in Cancer May 9–June 6
2007 Venus in Leo June 7–July 14
2007 Venus in Virgo July 15–August 9
2007 Venus in Leo August 10–October 8
2007 Venus in Virgo October 9–November 8
2007 Venus in Libra November 9–December 5
2007 Venus in Scorpio December 6–30
2007 Venus in Sagittarius December 31
2008 Venus in Sagittarius January 1–24
2008 Venus in Capricorn January 25–February 18
2008 Venus in Aquarius February 19–March 12
2008 Venus in Pisces March 13–April 6
2008 Venus in Aries April 7–30
2008 Venus in Taurus May 1–24
2008 Venus in Gemini May 25–June 18
2008 Venus in Cancer June 19–July 12
2008 Venus in Leo July 13–August 6
2008 Venus in Virgo August 7–30
2008 Venus in Libra August 31–September 24
2008 Venus in Scorpio September 25–October 18
2008 Venus in Sagittarius October 19–November 12
2008 Venus in Capricorn November 13–December 7
2008 Venus in Aquarius December 8–31
2009 Venus in Aquarius January 1–3
2009 Venus in Pisces January 4–February 3
2009 Venus in Aries February 4–April 11
2009 Venus in Pisces April 12–24

2009 Venus in Aries April 25–June 6
2009 Venus in Taurus June 7–July 5
2009 Venus in Gemini July 6–August 1
2009 Venus in Cancer August 2–26
2009 Venus in Leo August 27–September 20
2009 Venus in Virgo September 21–October 14
2009 Venus in Libra October 15–November 8
2009 Venus in Scorpio November 9–December 1
2009 Venus in Sagittarius December 2–25
2009 Venus in Capricorn December 26–31
2010 Venus in Capricorn January 1–18
2010 Venus in Aquarius January 19–February 11
2010 Venus in Pisces February 12–March 7
2010 Venus in Aries March 8–31
2010 Venus in Taurus April 1–25
2010 Venus in Gemini April 26–May 20
2010 Venus in Cancer May 21–June 14
2010 Venus in Leo June 15–July 10
2010 Venus in Virgo July 11–August 7
2010 Venus in Libra August 8–September 8
2010 Venus in Scorpio September 9–November 8
2010 Venus in Libra November 9–30
2010 Venus in Scorpio December 1–31

MARS

2006 Mars in Libra September 9–October 24
2006 Mars in Scorpio October 24–December 6
2006 Mars in Sagittarius December 6–31
2007 Mars in Sagittarius January 1–16
2007 Mars in Capricorn January 17–February 26
2007 Mars in Aquarius February 27–April 6
2007 Mars in Pisces April 7–May 15
2007 Mars in Aries May 16–June 24
2007 Mars in Taurus June 25–August 7
2007 Mars in Gemini August 8–September 28

2007 Mars in Cancer September 29–December 31
2008 Mars in Gemini January 1–March 4
2008 Mars in Cancer March 5–May 9
2008 Mars in Leo May 10–July 1
2008 Mars in Virgo July 2–August 19
2008 Mars in Libra August 20–October 4
2008 Mars in Scorpio October 5–November 16
2008 Mars in Sagittarius November 17–December 27
2008 Mars in Capricorn December 28–31
2009 Mars in Capricorn January 1–February 4
2009 Mars in Aquarius February 5–March 15
2009 Mars in Pisces March 16–April 22
2009 Mars in Aries April 23–May 31
2009 Mars in Taurus June 1–July 12
2009 Mars in Gemini July 13–August 25
2009 Mars in Cancer August 26–October 16
2009 Mars in Leo October 17–December 31
2010 Mars in Leo January 1–June 7
2010 Mars in Virgo June 8–July 29
2010 Mars in Libra July 30–September 14
2010 Mars in Scorpio September 15–October 28
2010 Mars in Sagittarius October 29–December 7
2010 Mars in Capricorn December 8–31

JUPITER

2006 Jupiter in Scorpio January 1–November 24
2006 Jupiter in Sagittarius November 25–December 31
2007 Jupiter in Sagittarius January 1–December 18
2007 Jupiter in Capricorn December 19–31
2008 Jupiter in Capricorn January 1–31
2009 Jupiter in Capricorn January 1–5
2009 Jupiter in Aquarius January 6–December 31
2010 Jupiter in Aquarius January 1–18
2010 Jupiter in Pisces January 19–June 6
2010 Jupiter in Aries June 7–September 9

2010 Jupiter in Pisces September 10–December 31

SATURN

2006 Saturn in Leo all year
2007 Saturn in Leo January 1–September 2
2007 Saturn in Virgo September 3–December 31
2008 Saturn in Virgo all year
2009 Saturn in Virgo January 1–October 29
2009 Saturn in Libra October 30–December 31
2010 Saturn in Libra January 1–April 7
2010 Saturn in Virgo April 8–July 21
2010 Saturn in Libra July 22–December 31

URANUS

2006–2009 Uranus in Pisces January 1–December 31
2010 Uranus in Pisces January 1–May 28
2010 Uranus in Aries May 29–August 14
2010 Uranus in Pisces August 15–December 31

NEPTUNE

2006–2010 Neptune in Aquarius January 1–December 31

PLUTO

2006–2007 Pluto in Sagittarius January 1–December 31
2008 Pluto in Sagittarius January 1–January 25
2008 Pluto in Capricorn January 26–June 14
2008 Pluto in Sagittarius June 15–November 26
2008 Pluto in Capricorn November 27–December 31
2009 Pluto in Capricorn January 1–December 31
2010 Pluto in Capricorn January 1–December 31

CHIRON

2006–2009 Chiron in Aquarius January 1–December 31
2010 Chiron in Aquarius January 1–April 19

2010 Chiron in Pisces April 20–July 18
2010 Chiron in Aquarius July 19–December 31

NORTH NODE

2006 North Node in Pisces June 20–December 31
2007 North Node in Pisces all year
2008 North Node in Pisces January 1–7
2008 North Node in Aquarius January 8–December 31
2009 North Node in Aquarius January 1–July 27
2009 North Node in Capricorn July 27–December 31
2010 North Node in Capricorn all year

SOUTH NODE

2006 South Node in Virgo June 20–December 31
2007 South Node in Virgo all year
2008 South Node in Virgo January 1–7
2008 South Node in Leo January 8–December 31
2009 South Node in Leo January 1–July 27
2009 South Node in Cancer July 27–December 31
2010 South Node in Cancer all year

THE TWENTY-EIGHT MAJOR LOVE AND SEX CYCLES

Sun in the Fifth House

The Sun sheds light on sex and children now, no matter what stage of your relationship you are up to – and no matter if you are single or attached. The cycle lasts around three weeks.

★ If you have a son or daughter, this cycle will turn a spotlight on their personalities and lives. If there are other planetary cycles at the same time as this one, the presence of the Sun will clarify exactly what is going on, and what you need to pay more attention to. Your kids may well be the centre of attention now – doing well, winning prizes or showing-off.

★ If you marry now, all eyes will be on your bump (if you are pregnant), on the kids (if there are stepchildren) or on the immediate prospects of you going into a hotel room and becoming impregnated. Attention will be paid to the children issue at this time. If you don't want them or can't have them that's going to be a focal point too, so be ready.

★ If you break up now, it may be a more public split than you would like. Be prepared to be singled out for attention (no matter if you are out together, or by yourself) and it's almost certain that other people will be talking about you. It's the kind of cycle when dignity rules, and good posture will win the day. If you're shy? Take heart. It's over in a few weeks!

★ Sexually, this phase in your relationship will test your confidence and help to build it too. You can shine more brightly in bed in this cycle, and even become a bit of an all-star, porn-star performer. As long as you don't sit up like a seal at the end and clap your flippers together, you should be okay. Any test to your sexual self-esteem will help you increase it.

★ Separation at this time may also lead you and/or your partner to focus on the children who are left behind, or the babies you never had. The spotlight may well turn on a previous termination or miscarriage. And if one partner didn't want children, that may be the temporary focus of all the thoughts and feelings too. One way or another, it's likely to be all about the kids.

★ If you fall in lust now, your partner may have one or more planets in Leo, or have some Solar qualities: that means they will be well known, and maybe even have their Warholian fifteen minutes of fame. Look for a distinct aura or glow, a reasonably healthy ego, a leading position in the world or in their career, and a vibe that says 'Look at me'.

★ Your identity will be tied up with your love-life in this cycle, so if you are single, you may find yourself defining yourself by your exes, or by the interest you're drawing from potential dates. If you're in a relationship or marriage, you'll also sort out who you are by working out where you stand in the partnership. Your ego is tangled up with your sex life.

★ If you are single and determined to avoid both children and sex in this cycle (and even Internet-only flirtation) then you will be astonished at how creative you become. The Sun's energy will be channelled into projects or passions that allow you to express yourself, and from dance to poetry, you should be able to find an outlet for your inner oomph now.

Sun in the Seventh House

For a few weeks, the state of your love-life will be the centre of your attention, as all other areas of your life take second place while you track past, present or future partners.

★ If you are single, you could be attracted to (or by) someone who has planets in Leo or a distinctly Solar personality. That means rather proud by nature, extremely well known in their world, impossible to miss in a crowded room, and with a house, car or wardrobe that says 'Oi, look at moi'. If you're really lucky, a genuine celebrity could be your shag.

★ If other cycles are affecting the Fifth House and Seventh House at the same time as this one, the presence of the Sun will help to clarify things and make the emotional or practical basics of the situation extremely obvious. When a New Moon takes place during this cycle too, it also gives you a chance to move forward and start making some big decisions.

★ Your ego, pride and self-esteem will be linked to your ex-partner in many cases during this cycle. The kind of relationship you once had with them, or the connection you have with them today, will enable you to define who you are and how you feel about yourself. You'll identify more with being their ex, and look at your self-esteem accordingly.

★ If you have an enemy or opponent (a love rival, for example, or a dastardly, divorcing wife or husband) then they will be hard to miss now. The Sun in the Seventh House will no doubt find your enemy looking for attention or demanding to be recognised. Sometimes it's just a simple case of old-fashioned showing-off. You'll gain clarity on their motives now.

★ In a marriage or existing relationship, the Sun will show you all the good stuff – and the not-so-good stuff. It illuminates almost everything about the way you are together, from sex to the kids to the finances. You may find yourself paying more attention to the vows you have made, or the promises that have been exchanged. What's 'we' all about?

★ It's possible that you could start to draw quite a lot of attention as a couple. You'll be in the spotlight as a unit of two much more than if you were both flying solo. This can turn you into a double-act to be reckoned with, as long as you are both comfortable about the fact that so many people are staring or talking. In some cases, cameras will be involved.

★ Needless to say, if you marry during this cycle, you can't really hope to get away with a discreet ceremony in a cave, tucked away in the Outer Hebrides with only a sheep as a witness. The Sun in the Seventh House is about lights, cameras and red carpets. In fact, it will be frankly astonishing if one of you isn't wearing white, silver, gold or diamonds now.

★ If you're splitting up now, it will also be hard to hide yourself away. There may be a very public separation, for whatever reason. Perhaps it's you who's making things abundantly clear to the world. Perhaps it's your former partner. In any case, it's fairly likely that a lot of pride will also be on display. And perhaps the odd ego. Either way, people are looking!

New Moon in the Fifth House

When the Sun and Moon join forces, you arrive at a green light – the start of a brand new lunar cycle, in fact. Allow a couple of weeks either side of the actual day.

★ Your unconscious and your conscious mind will work together now. Your dreams may back up what you are organising in your life sexually, emotionally or in terms of children. There is no question of separating your moods, memories and emotions from your goals now; they are interwoven. You'll make up your mind now, via the help of your heart.

★ Your self-esteem and identity will be tied up with your role as a parent (if you are pregnant or have kids) or with your ability to nurture, protect and care for your lover. If you're single and have no ties, the week of the New Moon may present you with a new dating prospect; if so, expect to find a parent–child dynamic in the relationship.

★ If you give birth at this time, your baby will be astonishingly typical of his or her Sun Sign, because the child's Moon Sign is in exactly the same place! The birth may draw a lot of attention for some reason, or you may feel as if everyone's watching, talking or standing by with a camera. New Moon children have a strong sense that Mum and Dad are as one.

★ Here's another interesting possibility – if you are single at this time, you may attract (or be attracted to) potential lovers who have one or more planets in the sign of the New Moon. So if you're an Aries, you may find people with a Leo signature in their chart start hovering. Or if you're a Taurus, it may be a noticeably Virgoan type who finally lands you in the sack.

★ If the New Moon falls in the same sign as your own Moon Sign (for example, you're a Scorpio with the Moon in Pisces, and you're hitting a New Moon in Pisces in your Fifth House) then expect to feel unbelievably focused, but also extremely emotional – in the manner of your Moon Sign! Back to the Scorpio example: you'll act and feel like a Pisces.

★ The New Moon can often be a trigger for other cycles – particularly the outer planets and points like Jupiter, Saturn, Uranus, Neptune, Pluto, the Nodes and Chiron. The seventy-two-hour period around the New Moon may bring in all kinds of now-or-never decisions, or stop–go, yes–no turning points that reflect the larger themes that are going on in your life.

★ If the New Moon falls in a sign that is opposite to one of the signs which is big in your chart, then you'll feel weirdly ready to go on all matters romantic, sexual, emotional or parental – but also rather confronted and divided. For example, if you're an Aries but you also have planets in Aquarius, the Leo New Moon might leave you feeling a bit unbalanced.

★ The same applies to Taureans with planets in Pisces; Geminis with planets in Aries; Cancerians with planets in Taurus; Leos with planets in Gemini; Virgos with planets in Cancer; Librans with planets in Leo; Scorpios with planets in Virgo; Sagittarians with planets in Libra; Capricorns with planets in Scorpio; Aquarians with planets in Sagittarius; and Pisceans with planets in Capricorn.

New Moon in the Seventh House

The New Moon in the Seventh House can bring in new relationships, engagements, weddings, separations and divorces! Allow a couple of weeks either side of the actual day.

★ This cycle can function as the green light that begins all the other Fifth House and/or Seventh House cycles taking place now. By itself, it can signify the start of a new relationship, or just a one-night encounter. However, if the New Moon runs alongside other cycles (particularly involving slow-moving planets) this may be the love of your life calling.

★ Equally, if you have been wondering when to move on a separation or divorce, you may just find the New Moon does it for you. The circumstances around you finally fall into place, or your (about to become ex) partner takes the initiative, or the third person in a love triangle starts up the kind of pressure that gives the break-up more momentum.

★ If you are single and sizing up a new date, the chances are he or she will have one or more planets and points in the sign of the New Moon. So if you're a Sagittarian, you may be looking at someone who has a strong Gemini signature in their chart. Or if you're a Capricorn, it may be a person who has (say) Venus in Cancer, or the Midheaven in Cancer.

★ Here's the rest of the list: Ariens may find Libran types feature;

Taureans will notice Scorpio types around; Geminis will find people with Sagittarius planets hover; Cancerians will find Capricorn types; Leos will find Aquarian types; Virgos will find Piscean types; Librans will find Aries types; Scorpios will find Taurus types; Aquarians will find Leo types; and Pisceans will find Virgo types. You'll also typically get an 'opposites attract' feeling.

★ The issues in your love-life now will also be typical of the sign of the New Moon. For a Taurean, it's all about secrets, power and control. For a Capricorn, it's all about domestic life, family ties or parenthood. For a Sagittarian, it's all about communication. To get a better idea of the issues, focus on the sign chapters in the 'More About' sections.

★ If you're battling your ex-partner or a love rival when the New Moon is in the Seventh House, their tactics and approach are likely to characterise the qualities of the New Moon sign. So if you're a Leo dealing with an Aquarian New Moon, your enemy may be crazy and unpredictable – rather like a jack-in-the-box. In other words, for the duration of the New Moon, your sparring partner or feuding rival will take the approach of the sign of the New Moon. Sometimes they'll actually have a planet or point in that sign as well.

★ Aries finds the opponent uses charm; Taurus finds the opponent uses sex or power; Gemini finds the opponent uses the moral high ground; Cancer finds the opponent uses his or her position; Virgo finds the opponent uses deceit; Libra finds the opponent uses aggression; Scorpio finds the opponent uses money; Sagittarius finds the opponent uses his or her way with words; Capricorn finds the opponent uses the family, or Mum, or the kids; Aquarius finds the opponent uses drama and theatrics. This in turn will help you fathom a strategy!

Full Moon in the Fifth House

When the Moon and Sun are opposite in the sky, there is a tug of war going on that affects everyone down below. Allow a couple of weeks either side of the actual day.

★ If things have gone beyond the point of no return in your marriage or relationship, the Full Moon is going to make everything glaringly obvious. It's very likely that your partner's friends or your friends – or that other group or team that someone belongs to – will be an issue too. Sorting all that out will take time, energy and long baths.

★ When the Moon is full in your Fifth House, it's pushing the following buttons: neediness, cravings and sexual or emotional appetites. You may try to satisfy what is lacking through food. It's a classic comfort-eating opportunity! The Sun opposite the Moon now will shed light, in the most scorching and obvious way, on what you're not getting – or who.

★ The Fifth House rules pregnancy, parenthood, the behaviour of your children and the world of other people's children. With a Full Moon you can expect to face an unbalanced or lopsided situation, which is all about somebody's needs not being met. This may be yours or those of your tantrum-throwing two-year-old. Tune in, but strategise later.

★ Tuning in and acting later in the week (or in the month) is a good idea when the Moon is fighting the Sun, because you, the child or the adult concerned is likely to be acting irrationally or emotionally, and may be motivated by passing moods or memories that have no practical purpose in the present. It's a wobbly time – wait until life feels more stable!

★ It's not just you, either – remember, Full-Moon energy affects everyone. The ripple effect that spills out at this time can also make waves in your emotional life, your sex life or your relationship with the children. You may do or say nothing that rocks the boat, but on a global level you're likely to be affected by ripple after ripple from much bigger stones.

★ At this time, the Sun will be emphasising your friendships and your group involvements, and those people are likely to be the big focus in your life. Don't be surprised if these also make waves or push emotional buttons, though. The Moon is pulling on the Sun at this time, just as much as the Sun is pulling on the Moon. So once again, proceed with caution.

★ If you have planets or points in one or even both of the signs of the Sun and Moon at this time, then you're likely to feel the effects more strongly. For example, if you are an Aries with a Libra rising sign, then a Full Moon in Libra is going to highlight all the things inside yourself you can't reconcile – or it will play out typical Aries–Libra issues in a relationship.

★ If you give birth at this time, your baby will see both parents as dramatically different people. They will typically turn into a good, creative problem-solver, because the child in question is being born with a huge Sun–Moon conflict, which will need constant reconciling. One or both parents may have planets or points in either the sign of the Sun or the Moon. If so, the child will bounce off that parent as a role model for years to come.

Full Moon in the Seventh House

This is a classic indicator of a new romance or even a wedding where one or both partners are privately saying 'Ummm . . .' Allow a couple of weeks either side of the actual day.

★ Even if what is now taking place in your life is cause for celebration (a honeymoon, a new business venture with your partner, a liberating divorce) you can still expect mixed feelings. The Moon is in the Seventh House now, opposite the Sun in your First House. So there's a conflict between 'Me, me, me' and 'Us, us, us', even if you're drinking Bollie!

★ If you are single you may attract people with one or more planets in Cancer at this time (the influence of the Moon). There is an even stronger possibility that you'll draw in people who have planets or points in the sign of the Full Moon. So if you're a Libra, you may find yourself on the dance floor with a woman whose Mercury sign is Aries. (Don't tread on her.)

★ Here's the rest of the list: Ariens attract Libran types; Taureans attract Scorpio types; Geminis attract Sagittarian types; Cancerians attract Capricorn types; Leos attract Aquarian types; Virgos attract Piscean types; Scorpios attract Taurean types; Sagittarians attract Gemini types; Capricorns attract Cancerian types; Aquarians attract Leo types . . . and, bizarrely, Pisceans attract Virgo types. You pull in your opposite sign . . .

★ Despite all this magnetic attraction, though (and remember, it may be them salivating over you, as well as the reverse), there are likely to be a few inner or outer conflicts. Someone may be attached. Or you may have doubts. Maybe they're shilly-shallying. To understand why, read up again on the Planet/Sign descriptions in the 'More About' section.

★ If you have an enemy or opponent in the game of love, play it cool at this time. The Full Moon is likely to make you or the other person rather irrational and emotional. Don't let a passing mood dictate your strategy. It's likely that your or their inner child will be running the show. And this is no time to let a six-year-old dictate the terms of your life.

★ I have no idea why some astrologers and so many witchypoo

types insist that a Full Moon is a great time to press ahead with decisions or to cast mad rituals involving bat crap. Two of the biggest forces in astrology are opposite now. They are like boxers in a ring, facing off. Now, why would that be a good time to launch anything? And if you don't believe me . . . The Asian tsunami happened around a Full Moon. So did D-Day. Lots of battles in the course of history have also been launched around the time of a Full Moon – obviously because of the advantageous light, but cosmically, all the tensions of war do sum up a Sun–Moon opposition. We're talking mixed feelings now! Even if you're tying the knot in a frock.

★ It's just a few days, though – so no sweat. Though you should pay attention if the Full Moon is obviously picking up the Seventh House cycle of a major outer planet, like Saturn, Uranus, Neptune or Pluto. I don't know if Jennifer Aniston has an astrologer, by the way, but she is an Aquarian and her divorce became official a week or so after a Full Moon.

Mercury in the Fifth House

Communication is the key to everything in this cycle. Even X-rated subjects are up for discussion when Mercury the messenger passes by.

★ If you are separating now, you can expect several discussions about the children, or one extremely long fax! If there are other cycles taking place affecting the Fifth House at the same time as this one, then Mercury will help you put feelings into words. It will assist you in communicating clearly. Emotions can be filtered through the brain, which is useful . . .

★ If you are marrying now, and there are children from another relationship, expect plenty of discussions about their welfare – and the role that you want your offspring to play. If there are other cycles taking place in the Fifth House during this one, Mercury will help you to keep discussions about the children logical and connected.

★ If you are marrying now and there are no children, you'll still have the discussions anyway. Alternatively, expect much discussion from other people about your prospects of parenthood, and perhaps an annoying interrogation session or three from your relatives. If you haven't yet talked about the 'P word', then you will. Even on your wedding night!

★ Don't be surprised if a Tracey Cox book falls off the shelf in front of you now, or if you find yourself randomly tuning into a radio station and picking up a program about the G-spot or the history of sex on Sparta. Mercury rules the written and spoken word, and this planet has a funny way of getting you to think about/talk about/read about shagging!

★ You will see this warning posted in the Mercury tables: Mercury Retrograde Alert! It means you should avoid major discussions, signed documents or a heavy reliance on computers, post or telephones at this time. So although it seems to be time to talk turkey, hold off. Otherwise Mercury Retrograde will leave you feeling like Foghorn Leghorn.

★ Mercury Retrograde means the planet appears to be going backwards. Consequently, love letters go missing, new lovers never call, and you sign your children up for an expensive school and have to tear up the contract later. The written or spoken word is dodgy now. It's not to be trusted.

★ Reassuringly, once Mercury is out of the dodgy zone, you'll find that everything returns to normal. That's your cue to book the dirty weekend in Dusseldorf or to take your lover out to dinner so you can have The Talk. This cycle is excellent if you are dealing with heavy emotional issues or delicate subjects. It enables you to be articulate – and to listen too.

★ If you have a child in this cycle, they will be fairly typical of the sign that Mercury is in now. So if you're an Aries and you have a Mercury in Leo baby, you'll find they are a bit of a performer.

Mercury in the Seventh House

You're going to find out loads of information about your ex in this cycle – or about that potential date in your life. Already hitched? It's time for some coupley-type discussions.

★ If you are single now, someone who has a lot of Mercurial qualities may be hovering. They could have planets and points in Gemini or Virgo, which are the two signs ruled by Mercury. In any case, this is someone who talks cleverly or talks a lot. They seem witty, switched on, and read the newspaper in bed or turn on the radio post-sex.

★ This is a classic cycle for fact-finding, information processing and question-and-answer sessions. You'll be more curious about your ex-partner, your current partner or a future date now. Mercury may give you an amazing opportunity to sit down with them and talk, or you may be given the information from a third party, thanks to the glories of email.

★ Watch out if Mercury is retrograde – it's clearly marked in the Mercury tables. I doubt if you will find a single astrologer on the planet who will sign a wedding contract when Mercury is retrograde. Even if the marriage works out, you'll find the groom has spelt his surname wrong, or someone gets drunk and leaves the precious scroll in the back of a cab.

★ When Mercury is retrograde, never take anything that people say to you or put in writing too seriously. Allow a large margin for error, or for people to change their minds. Once again, very few astrologers I know would try to sort out their marital or relationship plans when this planet is going backwards. What seems to be written in stone will be pure jelly!

★ If you are fighting someone or they are being mean to you, then also bear in mind that for the duration that Mercury is retrograde, the words will go backwards and forwards – or the communication may break down altogether. Never underestimate the part that a computer virus or a dodgy telephone can play at this time. Leave the peace conference until later!

★ If Mercury is behaving, though, then it's definitely time to allow communication in the door – especially if the issues between you and your feuding ex-partner or your love rival have become heavily emotional and utterly irrational. Even if you have to clap your flippers together like a dolphin and make 'Aaargh' noises, you'll still get your message across.

★ And you'll hear them better too . . . Mercury rules your ability to tune in, comprehend and understand. This is a very good period to have things spelt out to you and to articulate what you normally only feel in a physical or emotional way. Of course, it's about putting things into words, but it's also about nodding your head a lot and, above all, tuning in.

★ If you are moving in together, having a first date (also known as an initial interrogation) or tying the knot, you can expect the discussions to have the same dynamic as a UN summit. The exact wording of the vows, for example, will keep you going for months. And more than anything else, it's the communication you have with a date that will count.

Venus in the Fifth House

Ah, Venus. If this cycle takes place when there are encouraging planets also active in your Fifth House and/or Seventh House, we could be looking at *major* love action in your life.

★ This is a great cycle for patching up arguments over sex or children, or just helping you to make the peace if one of you has been an utter bastard/a conniving cow/a shameless fornicator. Venus is about scales, harmony and balance. This planet's influence will enable you to shake hands or kiss and make up, or your erring partner will take the lead.

★ Having a baby now? They will be typical of the sign that Venus is in during this cycle. So if you're a Capricorn having a son, he'll have a strong streak of Taurus in his chart. If you're an Aquarian having a daughter, she'll have a huge dose of Gemini in her chart. For more information on how your offspring will develop, read the 'More About' section.

★ Oh God, he's so good-looking. Oh God, she's so gorgeous . . . Venus in your Fifth House brings in the hunks and the babes. The object of your lust may have planets in Taurus or Libra (the signs that Venus rules) too. He or she will certainly approximate your idea of sex on a stick. Let's hope other planets are involved, though, or it will *only* be about the looks.

★ If you marry in this cycle, don't be surprised if everyone immediately starts thinking in terms of your future babies – along with you. Venus has a way of romanticising parenthood in this cycle. The wedding itself is likely to be storybook, and the bride deeply and unapologetically feminine. Expect Romance with a capital R and a B for Barbara Cartland.

★ The mood now can be so romantic that you need to be hip to the other cycles that may be taking place. For example, if you're convinced that you've just met the love of your life but you also have Saturn in the Seventh House in this cycle, then you need to get slightly more real. Venus is wonderful. It's like eating chocolate-dipped roses. But buyer beware.

★ Sex becomes more seductive now. It's all about the music, the sheets, the candles, the G-strings, the lingerie, the accessories, the lighting. One of you will be noticeably more yin than the other partner now, whose yang bits will be more obvious! That means strong role-playing now, be you straight, gay or lesbian. One partner's softer and more receptive now!

★ Needless to say, this is a brilliant cycle for soothing any troubled sexual waters. You can coax a condom onto your lover and he won't fling the Vaseline at you. You can casually mention a Viagra prescription at the same time that you are offering a full-body massage. You can gently raise the topic of fluffy pink handcuffs over breakfast in bed . . .

★ If you have children, then you'll either enjoy them hugely in this cycle (making you want to go back to bed and make more of them) or you will be given a much-needed break in your relationship with them (especially if you are having a tough cycle alongside this one). Venus is about the art of relating at the highest levels – even with demented toddlers!

Venus in the Seventh House

Astrologers in magazine columns around the world will promise you all sorts of things when this cycle hits. It can produce love miracles, sure. But look at the bigger chart picture too!

★ This cycle will make a wedding particularly romantic, no matter what other cycles may be taking place. It can sweeten and lighten the atmosphere, and make grown men weep. If the other cycles you have at this time are generally supportive of commitment, you could be onto something. And if they're not? At least you'll (temporarily) have hearts and flowers.

★ What if your marriage is like the Wars of the Roses? What if you and your boyfriend are acting out the worst scenes from Armistead Maupin novels? Venus can help you to realign the relationship. One of you will be in the right time, place and mood to try to calm things down, and even attempt a genuine peace settlement. The cosmos is on side now.

★ If you meet someone new now, they will be mind-blowingly attractive to you. You'll be passionate about the package, so hopefully the contents will be worth your energy as well. Venus describes people who seduce you. You may only need one photograph or one glance across a crowded room – but it's all about the face. And the body. And the clothes.

★ This cycle classically produces a honeymoon period in a new relationship, or a second honeymoon feeling in an existing relationship or marriage. Not surprisingly, it can coincide with real honeymoons too. If other cycles are operating alongside this one, Venus will fill in part of the canvas with beautiful, rose-tinted paint. Even if it's a weird abstract artwork!

★ People who have planets in Libra or Taurus (the two Venus-ruled signs), or planets in the sign that Venus is actually in, may be in focus now. So if you're a lesbian Libran, you may find the dyke who just arrived on her motorbike has Mercury in Aries – because Venus is in Aries for you right now. A full list of all the possibilities for dating and mating follows . . .

★ If you're an Aries, Libran types may hover. Taurus? Scorpio types. Gemini? Sagittarius types. Cancerians can pull in Capricorn types now, and Leos can pull in people with one or more planets in Aquarius. Virgos? Pisces types. Scorpios? Taurus types. Sagittarians? Gemini types. Capricorns lure Cancerian types, Aquarians pull Leo types, and Pisceans pull Virgo types.

★ The above rules aren't inevitable, but they happen often enough to be worth mentioning. You may find your existing partner or date's approach to seduction becomes strangely typical of the sign that Venus is passing through.

★ This applies no matter what signs your partner actually has in their horoscope package: the sign opposite to you on the zodiac rule, which towers over the Seventh House, uncannily describes the way other people act with you in relationships – particularly when Venus, the seduction planet, is passing through. And of course, if your partner really does have planets in the sign that Venus is in now, the overall effect will be magnified.

Mars in the Fifth House

★ Mars is the planet of action, impulse and initiative; also the planet of flying saucepans and sex in the lift, between floors. It doesn't waste time and it doesn't muck around. Ooh-er.

★ You'll want sex *right now* when this cycle hits. Or your partner – or potential new date – won't want to wait. The shagging may be particularly athletic and sweaty. Sometimes competition spurs you on too. So if the one that you want is also wanted by somebody else, you may be determined to get in first. Impulsive first dates often happen now.

★ If you have a baby in this cycle, they will be strangely typical of the sign that Mars is in when it happens. So if you are a Pisces and you give birth to twins now, both of them will have Cancerian qualities – no matter what their actual sign is. Want to know what the terrible twos will be like? Look at the sign Mars is in now: that's how the kid will lose it!

★ To continue: if you're an Aries, your child will throw theatrical Leo-like tantrums around age two. Taurus? The toddler will be hung up on detail. You're a Gemini? The child may pair off with someone, so it's two against one. Cancer? Your child has Mars in Scorpio – there will be poo issues. Leo? Your child has Mars in Sagittarius. They'll try to toddle to freedom.

★ If you're a Virgo, your child's terrible-two period (actually their Mars Return) will see them losing it like a Capricorn – cautiously. Libran parents have kids who get angry like Aquarians (suddenly, unpredictably). Scorpios have Pisces-style tantrums (tears!). Sagittarians have fist-whirling Aries-style kids, Capricorns have children with a Taurean approach to anger (it may involve toys or the piggy bank), Aquarians have kids who lose it like Geminis (noisily, or ranting into the Fisher-Price phone) and Pisceans' kids will just chant 'Mummmyyy!'

★ Remember, the above rule only applies if you actually become a parent when Mars is in the Fifth House. And here's something else about the birth – it's likely to be faster than you thought, or there will be a real action-stations feeling in the hospital or birth centre. Don't necessarily expect the soothing ambient-music-choreographed-birth of your fantasies!

★ Back to sex. Particularly sex between men! You'll really become aware of role-playing and stereotyping now, no matter whether you're a bear or a drag queen. Mars is all about traditional, unreconstructed, yang–yang male qualities. So one of you is really going to pick up on that and get a Martian on your ass. Possibly literally. The sex roles will be unusually distinct.

★ Lesbian couples will also find a weird, role-playing dynamic enters into the bedroom. One of you is just going to be aware of her masculine side much more sharply – that's all. It may not necessarily be the partner who always takes the lead, either. There's room for experimentation in this cycle. But it will bring out the tough grrrrl in one of you!

★ Fights, arguments, rants and raves are common now, because one of you is being far too pushy or impatient (or just intolerant). Sex or love rivals are usually the topic *de jour*. Happily, once the boundaries are drawn or redrawn, you may find that Mars drives you back to bed. It's an energy that you can play with safely, if you know how to handle fire.

Mars in the Seventh House

★ If your marriage or relationship is on shaky ground, this cycle will flush out the hidden tension. Single? You or someone else can't be bothered waiting.

★ Love can begin with a crash, bang and wallop in this cycle. It may actually start with real physical action, which is typical of Mars – one of you arm-wrestles the other in a pub, or one of you manages to crash straight into the other person's car. If you normally move slowly in love, you may wake up blinking and amazed at the sheer speed of it all.

★ Anger or irritation will be much more obvious, even in a happy relationship or marriage. One of you feels as if the other person is pushing the boundaries, or taking more than their share. The other feels defensive, because he or she is under attack. Mars is here to get both of you to set reasonable limits, and to honour the fact that you're as mad as hell.

- ★ Some couples are so Zen-like (damn those meditation classes!) that they pull off the astonishing feat of channelling the Mars energy into goals that they achieve together, with remarkable speed. Mars can definitely work for you, if you're prepared to consciously harness it this way. You'll do more together, faster, than you could ever do alone.

- ★ Be very conscious of the fact that if you have an enemy, opponent or love rival (the curse of the annoying ex, perhaps?) then he or she is likely to be a lot more active now. Your attack and defence mechanisms will be primed too. The rule with Mars is to get angry constructively, without hurting yourself and others. And on no account drunk-dial.

- ★ You can definitely take strong, firm steps to try and tackle the person who is against you, though – and this is a key time if you are separating or divorcing. Just be conscious of Mars's worst excesses and try to avoid them, or to avoid triggering them in the other person. That means lose the anger, the impulse, the speed and the desire to hurl vacuum cleaners around.

- ★ Bring on the manageable side of Mars, though! That means taking the initiative and organising counselling or legal advice, writing firm, stern but fair letters (ask a sensible friend to check before you send), and making it really clear that there are certain boundaries in your emotional, sexual or domestic space that the other party can't cross.

- ★ Phew! But guess what? If other cycles are supportive of new love or big leaps forward in an existing relationship, Mars can be a blessing. It can speed things up, stop the boring procrastination and bring a huge blast of energy – and a real lust for life and each other – into the picture. Love at first sight can happen now, and so can impulsive proposals.

Jupiter in the Fifth House

Jupiter makes everything bigger and better, and it has a remarkable way of producing the 24-carat gold lining in any cloud. Some over-the-top sexual experiences are on offer now!

★ You may give birth to a child who has one or more planets in Sagittarius in this cycle, or who is Jupiterian: that means, bigger or taller than everyone else, noticeably upbeat and positive (one of life's smilers), a born student or teacher, a keen traveller, and funny as well – maybe even a natural comedian. Are they a big baby? Ouch. Blame Jupiter.

★ Jupiter is a safety net planet. Even if there are issues with your pregnancy, child, adoption or stepchild, you will find that Jupiter protects you from the worst. In fact, you could easily find that clouds turn into instant silver linings, thanks to Jupiter's famous reputation for saving the day and turning problems into pluses. What appears to be bad news may, in the fullness of time, end up adding more magic, more meaning and more of everything to your family life.

★ Luck may play a part in your pregnancy now. If you want a boy, you'll get a boy – if you want a girl, you'll get a girl. Alternatively, the child itself may be blessed, fortunate or lucky in some way. There may be lavish christening presents, an inheritance in the works or plenty of good omens around. Expect lots of toys, or doting relatives or godparents.

★ If you begin a new relationship now, you may be called The Lucky Couple. Alternatively, one look at your partner and you will feel blessed. They are likely to have one or more planets in Sagittarius, or to be Jupiterian. That means funny, well-travelled (or from another country), a student or teacher of life, and philosophical and positive by nature.

★ If you've split up with your partner and there are child custody, maintenance or access issues, this cycle can help enormously. Jupiter's presence in your Fifth House can help you develop meaningful relationships within the family, even if you're living apart. It can assist you in taking the raw materials of a break-up and actually, weirdly, gaining from them.

★ Opportunities to adopt, opportunities to become pregnant, opportunities to become a godparent, aunt, uncle, grandparent . . . this is what Jupiter is famous for. Annoyingly, you won't be able to pinpoint any of the exact outcomes ahead of time. But rest assured, this planet will do what it can for you, according to your allotted karma in the cosmic wheel.

★ If you're a sexual opportunist, you'll probably go to excess now. And even if you're not, you'll be astonished at what can happen if you let yourself follow Jupiter's clues. Whatever you privately consider to be over the top will probably be on offer. For conservative types, that means spa baths with strangers. For erotic adventurers? Orgies are entirely possible.

★ Needless to say, this is a fantastic cycle for resolving sexual or fertility problems. If you have a history of abuse and need to heal, or if you are grappling with IVF or one partner's perpetual Brewer's Droop, then Jupiter can help. People who are generous with their time and energy (very typical of Jupiter) may well turn up, or a real stroke of luck may assist.

★ Single women who have been chanting 'No men, no men' for several decades will be pleased to see how many doors open to potential relationships now. But unless you have planets in the Seventh House at the same time (or the Nodes, or Chiron), don't make the mistake of thinking that this is big commitment time. It may just be a happy interlude. Jupiter expands whatever it touches. So expect more partners, more frequent sex with the same partner, or sex that shakes you all night long. Just like the AC/DC song!

Jupiter in the Seventh House

This cycle lasts around a year. If you are miserable and want to get out of a relationship, it can help make the process easier. Single and looking for love? Your chances are higher now.

★ If you are happily settled with a partner during this cycle, then you'll want more. The chances to expand as a couple will be there too. Financially, a door may open that allows you to buy a property you both love, or take an extensive and expensive trip overseas. If you've been de facto forever, you may finally get hitched. Or add kids . . . or a new business.

★ If you are fed up with your partnership in this cycle, Jupiter will bring you an opportunity for a meaningful relationship – preferably one that you can believe in, as opposed to one that seems lacking. You'll get this in one of three ways. Through successful counselling; through the arrival of a new love; or through an amicable split – and a good ex-relationship.

★ If you are single you may be attracted to someone who has one or more planets in Sagittarius now, or a person whose personality or job is Jupiterian. This means a traveller, a teacher, a perpetual student, a comedian, a religious type, a spiritual type, a publisher, a foreigner or (yes, it does happen) someone who is much bigger or taller than you are.

★ Weirdly, even your opponents and enemies can bring benefits at this time. They won't know it, of course, but their presence in your life during a Jupiter transit guarantees that even when they're trying to be vile, they're actually doing you some good. You'll be amazed at how easy it is to end feuds in this cycle too. Just be Jupiterian – optimistic and funny.

★ That word *optimism* is crucial to understanding this cycle. Jupiter makes you believe that good things are possible. This may be behind one of the most famous outcomes of this transit – the arrival of Ms or Mr Right, after a dry spell of 19500 years. Single people in this cycle seem to open up, expect more, want more and believe more; miracles often follow.

★ If you marry in this cycle, the wedding or honeymoon is likely to be over-the-top in some way. Or, to put it another way, divinely excessive. Alternatively, you might keep the ceremony simple, but the emotions will be profoundly larger-than-life. It's the kind of optimism that can carry almost any union forward, so let's hope it's sound underneath.

★ Watch out for Jupiter's famous reputation for turning the *merde* in your love-life into solid gold. So you're breaking up with someone? Weirdly, he'll turn out to be your business partner a few years from now, and he'll make you rich. So you're with a woman who triggers your fear of commitment? Great. She'll teach you life-happiness skills for later on.

★ The key to everything now is Jupiter's insistence that you hope for more, you believe in more and you want more. This applies to the connection you have with your ex too. A former partner can become a new friend now, even if you were hurling domestic appliances at each other years ago, or an ex can introduce you to your next lover!

Saturn in the Fifth House

You won't have this cycle again for around twenty-nine years. Use it to educate yourself about the realities of sex and kids. It's a chance to acquire L-plates and then graduate up to Ps.

★ The process of pregnancy or adoption is likely to be hard work in this cycle and may involve a waiting game, or a long learning curve. Things will feel completely different once this cycle is over. The timing involved, the people or the situation are going to set up obstacles in your pathway. These slow you down and allow you to learn more . . . and more.

★ If you are single you may wonder if you are ever going to have sex again at various points in this cycle. Fear not! And the phrase is used advisedly. Fear is one of Saturn's main trademarks. If you find yourself dealing with performance anxiety, insecurity about your libido or your orgasms or *anything* – hit the books. Saturn rules patient self-education.

★ It's possible that a child (your own, or someone else's) may become a burden in this cycle. Once again, you will feel very differently about things once Saturn has left your Fifth House. Along the way, you will learn to accept that Saturn's toolbox is the only one to have: inside the box you will find wisdom, patience, maturity and a get-real approach.

★ This is not the kind of cycle when you can get away with wild one-night-stands, mindless orgies or great big dumb relationships. Weirdly, each of them will have to teach you something, and often the lesson can be impossibly hard. Above all else, do not practise irresponsible sex in this cycle. Saturn has a way of forcing you to become responsible.

★ Don't be surprised if sex in an existing relationship or marriage becomes a duty. Maybe that's okay – for a lot of couples, it is. If you resent feeling as if every time you climb into bed you're going to work, though, listen up! Saturn rules authority. Convert this planet's energy by becoming an authority on shagging (start Googling now) and then practise.

★ If you are single you may fall in love with someone who has one or more planets in Capricorn now, or a Saturnine type. That means your love object is an authority figure – probably with a senior role, or a respected position in the world. They might be older, or just seem that way, because they're awfully mature, serious and sensible.

★ Be careful! You may be putting obstacles in your own path in this cycle. If you are in a relationship, you may be unconsciously starting arguments so that barriers go up and real sexual intimacy is impossible. Or you may be freezing your partner out in other ways. If you are single, you may also be self-sabotaging on dates. So . . . what scares you about closeness?

★ If you work at it for long enough, you can end up with a virtual PhD in parenting, sexual technique, emotional common sense, intimacy, adoption, fertility and all the other areas associated with the Fifth House. You'll be slowed down by life again and again while Saturn gives you a chance to learn, absorb and practise. Bless the mistakes now. They help.

Saturn in the Seventh House

This cycle lasts for around two years, and if you're married or in a relationship, it will test you. If you're single or dating, you'll learn a huge amount about love.

★ If you're roaming solo in the jungle of love in this cycle, you may be attracted by one of the older gorillas. Lovers who look as if they could teach you something about the real world may turn up now. So will people who are a lot more mature, sensible and practical than you. Will it work out with them? It depends how much you value their rock-like love.

★ People who have one or more planets in Capricorn or have jobs or personalities that are Saturnine may become involved with you now. That means men with hot-shot jobs, women with positions of authority, people who went grey young, people who are vulnerable to Eeyore-like gloom and ambitious types who are practical enough to wait for success.

★ Fear can keep you away from people now! It may come disguised as shyness, anxiety or ultra-caution. You'll make your own obstacles now, if you're scared of rejection, or even just scared of being in a new relationship. Ask wise, impartial, objective friends what they think about the situation . . . they'll tell you how you're building brick walls around yourself.

★ What brought you and your partner together? It needs to be something more than alarmingly attractive buttocks or sexy credit cards in this cycle. Saturn will test you and test you and test you – until you find out if the marriage or relationship is really built on solid foundations. Is what you have together enough to last another twenty-eight years?

★ Saturn likes traditional values and old-fashioned merits. It's not particularly interested in superficial qualities, which is why it famously busts up so many Hollywood marriages based on looks/career/status when it arrives to do its stuff. What Saturn wants from you is simple: maturity, common sense, patience, wisdom, hard work and a solid structure.

★ If you marry in this cycle, then you're unlikely to rush into anything, and may have to deal with obstacles on the path from proposal to engagement to wedding to honeymoon and beyond. The obstacles slow you down and make you think even more seriously and fully about your commitment. The wedding itself is likely to be *frightfully* straight, by the way.

★ If your ex-partner or your love rival is playing the role of the enemy now, it will undoubtedly feel like a burden. Cultivate Saturn's qualities to cope, and remember the way you currently feel won't last beyond this cycle. Saturn's best coping mechanism: handling the opposition like the wise old man or wise old woman you know you are. Or want to be.

★ No matter if you are single and waiting (and waiting and waiting) or settled (and working and working) or recently separated (and learning and learning) there is much to gain from Saturn. It has a reputation for being the complete bastard of the zodiac, but in fact, what you learn about life and love now is a reality check that will make the future *better*.

Uranus in the Fifth House

This is a long-running cycle, so the effects you read about below won't happen to you every day of the week – but over the next few years, quite a few of them will probably crop up.

★ This is the classic cycle for surprise pregnancy, so if you don't want to be surprised, chain yourself or your partner to the contraceptive pill. If you do become pregnant now, you may produce a boy (when you were promised a girl) and may be the astonished parent of twins (when it was the last thing you wanted). All things are possible. Stay cool and be flexible.

★ If you are single, and even if you're not, you may be suddenly and wildly attracted to someone who has planets in

Aquarius, or whose life and personality is Uranian. That means they're into alternatives – in food, music, film, clothes and lifestyle. Computers, science, and all aspects of the New Age (especially astrology!) also fall into this category.

★ If sex is boring and predictable then you need to actively change that, or Uranus will have a funny way of turning your personal snow dome upside down and shaking it extremely hard. Whatever or whoever it takes to get rid of the boredom will suddenly appear, rather like a Monty Python foot. A change of status now (for example, single to married) may rev things up.

★ Sexual preferences, partners, positions and turn-ons that you once thought were weird may now seem positively normal. It's very likely you'll be up to stuff that you know would give your friends, family or colleagues a major cardiac arrest if they knew! If you marry or pair up in this cycle, it may be an act of rebellion too. Who cares what the world thinks?

★ Freedom will also be a big theme in your relationship with children – either your own, or other people's. You may want to break free of any routines, expectations or family set-ups that tie you down, or make you feel restricted on any level. Equally, if a child or teenager in your world is feeling stifled by school (or by you, alas) expect mad, wild rebellion.

★ Uranus rules new inventions, so you'll be up for anything that the Japanese can throw at you in the sex toy department. The same applies to interactive DVD pornography, and particularly the fusion between sex and the Internet. You're in an experimental mood in this cycle, so what used to turn you on will now look very seventeenth century. *Vive la revolution!*

★ You'll want to try out domestic arrangements that give you more space, freedom and independence if you are living with someone now. Any situation that confines you or makes you feel like a hamster going round on a treadmill will probably kill your libido. Sex will become an effective barometer of how free you actually feel: pay attention to it.

★ Suddenly bolting out of a marriage to enjoy the thrills of a one-night-stand, or even walking out of a marriage in search of a totally unlikely, unthinkable lover is another classic effect of this cycle. Uranus is neither ethical nor unethical. It just appears whenever you need real freedom and excitement – but yes, there will be consequences . . . so do as you would be done by, as the English say. Or . . . do what ye will, but harm none. A 'wrong' relationship often feels right now.

Uranus in the Seventh House

This cycle takes a few years to complete, so you won't feel its effects every day. The following effects are typical, though, and you may experience some or all of them.

★ If you are single you may fall in love with someone who has one or more planets in Aquarius in this cycle, or someone who is a recognisably Uranian type. They may be involved with computers, astrology, alternative entertainment/art, groups dedicated to social change, science or – Uranus is always unpredictable – nude wrestling or another eccentricity.

★ Lightning-bolt attractions are typical of this cycle. It's great if you're single, although if you're a Bridezilla waiting to happen, watch out – there are absolutely no guarantees about a long-term commitment here! If you are married or in a steady relationship, the lightning-bolt attraction can seriously threaten what you have. But take a closer look at your crush . . .

★ It's just as likely that the person who excites you so much is a mere catalyst for change. You may not want to hear that, but wait until the electrifying, lightning-bolt attraction has hung around for a while. It's entirely possible that this isn't the real thing after all. Instead, it's just a wake-up call to get you to make changes in your existing relationship.

★ Freedom is the thing with Uranus in the Seventh House. You have to have your own space, time and emotional oxygen when this planet is around. You need wildness and the unexpected in your love-life, and domestic routine will begin to seem just awful. Rather than ignoring Uranus and hoping it will go away, try to consciously change your life now.

★ At this time you will be organising your love-life in new, different and unconventional ways which large numbers of people will not really understand and some may even be visibly threatened by. That's fine. You're actually on the cutting edge of social change in your world now, which is why, single or attached, you feel like you're always experimenting.

★ If you're single now, your priority is being true to yourself. Love or lust has to be completely authentic now, or it won't work. There have been other times in your life when you've compromised, faked it, or gone along with certain partners or dates for the sake of being with someone. Uranus won't let you stand for this any more. You've got to be you!

★ The last thing you expected to happen to your partner, to you or to the relationship is probably going to be the first thing that comes up. You are now in the surprise zone, and occasionally you will be in the 1000-watt shock zone too. Stay flexible in this cycle. Keep moving. Use anything that happens as an excuse to make changes. Don't get weirded out.

★ Forget fixed patterns in your relationship or marriage. The way it used to work for you, before this cycle began, is something you'll probably have to leave behind. The reasons for the radical change in your partnership could be anything from one partner's weird new hobby (they're never there on Tuesday and Thursday nights) to . . . *almost anything at all*.

Neptune in the Fifth House

This cycle runs for years, and you shouldn't expect to see these effects every day of the week! Nevertheless, what follows are some common outcomes of Neptune's influence.

★ Total, brain-numbing confusion is not unusual when Neptune passes through the Fifth House. Should I stay or should I go? Should I be with Rob, or should I be with Renee? Do I really know what I want, or am I really a banana in human form? Needless to say, when the fog descends, leave the alcohol or drugs alone. They'll just distort the picture further.

★ Sex can become more sensitive now, fuelled by soulful feelings like compassion, kindness, empathy and unconditional love. You may be drawn to Sacred Sex, or the *Kama Sutra*, or one of you may be having problems so the other devotedly becomes celibate for a while. This cycle is about less grunt and more soul. It elevates everything to a higher level.

★ Deception, trickery, evasion and lies are some of Neptune's less appealing aspects in this cycle. If you're playing the part of El Dodgy, be aware that life is unlikely to become much clearer for you as a result of your behaviour – if anything, it's likely to bamboozle you! What if it's the other person? Trust your sixth sense and put your mind at rest – sensibly.

★ If you're single in this cycle you may be fascinated by lovers who have one or more planets in Pisces – and particularly those who have Neptune patterns in their charts. You may end up with poets, surfers, musicians, potheads, photographers, psychics, drinkers, film-makers, artists, healers – and anyone who is (a) special and (b) not from this planet.

★ Don't be surprised if you attract a partner who needs to be rescued by you in this cycle. As long as you are making meaningful sacrifices (as opposed to confused acts of martyrdom) you may find you approach a new, spiritual level of loving. It may suit your beliefs, for example, to put yourself last in the story, and give unconditionally to your lover now.

★ Sexually you'll be looking for total escape and possibly nirvana as well in this cycle. The combination of sex and drugs or sex and alcohol may give it to you. Your fantasies may revolve around spas, waterfalls and oceans. Soft-focus pornography and erotic prose may also provide the escape route you want. You'll want candles and incense with *everything*.

★ If you are married or in a steady relationship and find your partner mysteriously disappears in this cycle, then you can expect clarity to arrive once this Neptune cycle is over. In the meantime, the exact circumstances of your partner's whereabouts may be lost in a classic Neptunian 'fog' and it may be more useful to investigate once the cycle is over.

★ Confusion may reign where fertility, pregnancy, adoption, stepchildren, sons or daughters are concerned. You will also find that parenthood, or the chance of parenthood, involves significant sacrifices. If you suspect you are receiving muddled information about fertility or kids in general, do not hesitate to get a clear second and third opinion.

Neptune in the Seventh House

This cycle is with you for some years, and you won't wake up to dramatic events every single day. Nevertheless, these are some common (and classic) outcomes of this period.

★ If you are single, beware of total, brain-numbing confusion with potential dates. Misunderstanding signals, misreading people's intentions, getting the wrong idea and sending out mixed messages are all lovely examples of Neptune at work. Awful though it may seem, you may be better off spelling things out nice and c-l-e-a-r-l-y at this time.

★ The material and physical side of love will matter less in your partnerships in this period. You may not be all that interested in status, sex, security or money. You will be fascinated by the dream of a blissful, telepathic, highly spiritual union of souls, however. As long as your feet are on terra firma while you go looking for this, you may just find it!

★ Your partner may become more Neptunian at this time – don't be surprised if you encounter vagueness, confusion or a more spiritual approach to life in their personality. Drugs (prescribed or otherwise) and booze will probably have a much bigger impact on them than usual. If you're with Mr or Ms Dodgy, then sadly put your lie detector on standby.

★ If you're single you may be hypnotised by people who have one or more planets in Pisces, or a Neptunian profession or personality. That means artists, photographers, poets, film-makers, musicians, psychics, healers, religious types, surfers, drug fiends, drinkers, and pretty much anyone who is looking for an alternative to the dullness of cold reality.

★ If you end up in a feud with your partner, your ex-partner or a love rival, then be extremely careful. Your enemies may tell lies, tall stories or just deliberately distort the truth in this period. They may be sneaky and subtle – like a gas leak getting underneath the door. Surround yourself with practical, sensible friends and advisors to deal with the issue.

★ Your wedding is most unlikely to be conventional or (even) remotely practical now. You want fantasy, daydreams, bliss, nirvana and the blessing of a higher power. You want turquoise crystals in your socks and pink doves flying out of gilded cages! The vows will be much more crucial to you than others may expect. You want a mystical meeting of souls.

★ If you are in a partnership in this cycle and feel like a bit on the side, don't expect life to become any clearer once you've cheated. If anything, Neptune tends to build up the layers of mental fog and emotional confusion until you feel utterly bamboozled. Fantasies about sleeping with other people are also common now. Know where to draw the line, though!

★ At its highest vibration, Neptune in the Seventh House is all about gently discovering the pure soul qualities you love in each other – quite unconditionally, and without expectation. It's about making sacrifices for your partner, for all the right reasons. It's really a Buddhist approach to marriage and commitment; compassion and kindness are your guiding lights.

Pluto in the Fifth House

Pluto takes years to trawl through the Fifth House, so don't expect destiny to bang on the door every day. What follows are classic manifestations of its influence, however.

★ Sex is always taboo when Pluto is in the Fifth House. Of course, what's taboo to you may be tame to other people. It depends on what you consider to be forbidden. Group sex? Bondage? Spanking? Your first vibrator? Sometimes one phase of your sex life will end in this cycle to be replaced by a new way of shagging. It will be deeper too – and more intense.

★ If you are trying to become pregnant or to adopt in this cycle, then don't expect a smooth path from A to Z. You'll hit a series of critical stages throughout the whole process – some of which will dramatically end a few of your ideas, and others which will launch new attitudes or set-ups. Each critical stage will transform your attitude towards children and parenting.

★ If you're single you may be involved with people with one or more planets in Scorpio, or people whose jobs or personalities are Plutonian: police, criminals, people in life-or-death professions, hookers, underworld figures, sex therapists, plumbers (a very Plutonian profession), occultists, and almost anyone who deals with stuff that is buried or intense.

★ Don't be surprised if you find yourself in a relationship or marriage that goes through a number of endings and new beginnings in this period. That's just Pluto's way of getting you to change everything. The death and rebirth of the partnership will profoundly alter the balance of power, though. Expect a whole new order after each passing mushroom cloud.

★ Obsession with your partner or a potential date is also part of this cycle. Be prepared! It is likely to be all-consuming, verging on raging – this is what Pluto is famous for! If it's clear that the obsession is causing you pain, try this: transfer your fixation to a creative project or a sport that involves deep self-expression. It's a tried and tested cure that works.

★ If this cycle does remove a relationship or marriage from your life permanently, be aware of hidden power and control issues between you and your partner. Heighten your awareness of the part that children may be playing too, and be particularly aware of how easy it is for sons or daughters to be used in manipulative game-playing. Why go there?

★ On the last day of this cycle, look back at how much you've changed, sexually and emotionally, since it began. Typically, Pluto will have killed off some parts of your love-life (and yourself) and allowed something new in the door. Pluto always promises new beginnings, no matter how thoroughly and completely it finishes off what went before.

★ Some or all of your sexual preferences and fantasies are going to have to become secrets in this cycle. *Because* they are secret, they will feel particularly intense. Pluto is not an up-front planet and very little about your private life will be obvious to other people now. If 'they' think they know what you're up to or what you desire, 'they're' probably wrong!

Pluto in the Seventh House

This planet moves so slowly that it will be several years before it leaves your Seventh House. What you see below are common Pluto effects – but they won't appear every day!

★ There may be something taboo about your partner now – or a forbidden topic for discussion within your relationship. Talking about it will be hard, but this off-limits issue will come up repeatedly until you deal with it. In one case I know, a Gemini man had to face his dying wife's request for euthanasia. Pluto requires you to face 'uh-oh' subjects.

★ If you are single you may be obsessed by someone who has one or more planets in Scorpio, or a lover who has a Plutonian profession or personality. Typical examples include occultists, criminals, police, psychologists (anyone who deals with the dark side of existence!) and also plumbers, septic tank cleaners and any person who delves around in the muck of life.

★ It is possible that life-and-death issues will come up in your marriage or relationship now. One partner may be facing a dangerous illness, for example, or be working (or just living) in life-threatening situations. On a less confronting level, there may simply be questions about your will or inheritance, and what should happen to your property if one of you dies.

★ If your marriage or relationship survives in this cycle, it is going to have to transform. That is the most basic rule of Pluto's transit through the Seventh House! You can't stand still, or hope to remain unchanged by its influence. This planet insists that you detox yourselves and the partnership, and that you alter the structure so it lasts forever.

★ If your ex-partner becomes your enemy now, or if a love rival decides to conduct a feud with you, be extremely careful. If you enter into the game they are playing, it's possible that obsessive feelings could dominate you or your opponent. That can be dangerous. Keep sensible, down-to-earth supporters and friends close; listen to their views.

★ The whole point of this cycle is to allow you to have a genuine rebirth experience as the relationship you are in becomes profoundly changed – and resurrected – or it finally dies, eventually replaced by a completely new kind of partnership that makes your old attitudes and expectations seem obsolete. Either way, you're going to feel born again!

★ Everyone gathers dead wood over the course of a long-term relationship or marriage. This cycle is about recognising dead wood when you see it – and releasing it to the elements, rather than stubbornly trying to cling on, as if it was still part of the tree. Bits and pieces of your domestic life, love life and sex life that aren't meant to be there long term will go.

★ The potential is there for you to be one half of a power couple in this cycle. You may both find yourselves with the kind of financial, social or professional status that makes you the Bill and Melinda Gates of your social circle. If you've earned it, you'll get it. But part of the journey of arriving as a couple is going to involve the kinds of changes described above!

Chiron in the Fifth House

Some astrologers associate Chiron with healing, but I've found it's an indicator of outrageous attempts, sheer audacity and astonishing nerve. Here's how it works long term.

★ You may become pregnant against the odds in this cycle, either because you are over the usual age limit assigned to expectant mothers, or have been told that it's not possible for you to have children. Note the emphasis on the word 'may'! This is only one example of how Chiron works when it's passing through the Fifth House and there are many others.

★ Sexually, you'll be more inclined to believe ninety impossible things before breakfast (with apologies to Lewis Carroll). Your style now will be confident, daring and possibly predatory. Your greatest interest will be in scoring a bullseye. Chiron was a centaur, seldom seen without his bow and arrow. What (or who) hits the spot for you now?

★ If you have a son or daughter, or are an active aunt/uncle/godparent/step-parent, then you'll probably find you want more for the kids than other people think is normal, or possible, or even acceptable! Chiron is not an astrological force normally associated with discretion or caution. You're unlikely to want to toe the line where kids are involved.

★ Your choice of partner in this cycle may be daring too – or your partner's choice of you as their partner might provoke responses that range from eyebrow-raising to open-mouthed in other people. Sometimes just the fact that the two of you are together can push the boundaries of what's acceptable – at least in the eyes of conservative types.

★ Contraception may be just one area of your private life where you feel more inclined to take risks, or attempt the impossible. The withdrawal method might attract you for obvious reasons. So might chocolate-flavoured condoms, or calculating your fertility by the Moon. When Chiron is around, you're much more likely to consider the O for Outrageous option.

★ You may want to push the envelope where pregnancy, adoption and even christenings are concerned. It's unlikely you'll be particularly interested in what family, society or friends' opinions are; this is the kind of cycle when you'll be pulled towards what 'they' say you can't or shouldn't do. Paying a sperm donor? Natural birth? Calling the kid Zippo? Why not?

★ Trying something (or someone) impossible and getting away with it is what this cycle is all about. The astrological charts of several audacious acts and outrageous events in history show Chiron in a prominent position. It's not a negative or positive force in astrology – it's like Popeye – it just is what it is. You get to decide if you're being ethical or just baaaad.

★ Be aware that there are two risks with Chiron affecting the world of sex and children in your life. The first is that you might just miss the target you are aiming for – and have to deal with the ramifications. The second is that you will get what you want, but have to deal with other people's reactions. Only you can judge whether your attempt is worth it now.

Chiron in the Seventh House

Your inner Sex Pistol will emerge in relation to marriage, commitment and your ex-partners in this cycle. You'll discover *chutzpah* you didn't know you had. Never mind the bollocks!

★ You are now in the mood to marry someone who raises eyebrows all round, or sends plates and cutlery clattering to the floor. You're not supposed to be with them. Perhaps you shouldn't be with them. And, in some ways, it's absolutely impossible that you're with them! But guess what? You don't care. You'll be the biggest punk at your own wedding.

★ If you are in a steady relationship, don't be surprised if it operates in a way that confronts other people's expectations – and perhaps a few of your own as well. The domestic routine, the shared lifestyle or the financial arrangements in your partnership may seem unthinkable or (frankly) quite unachievable to more conservative people.

★ If you are single, the most outrageous act of all is probably remaining staunchly solo in this cycle. After all, it's not supposed to make you happy . . . is it? Another obvious option is the decision to be as promiscuous as your time allows. Once again, you're not supposed to do it, and you shouldn't be able to get away with it . . . but somehow, that's the whole point.

★ When it comes to your ex-partners, you'll be more inclined to push the envelope with them now. You are quite capable of making outrageous requests or demands of them. You are also capable of behaviour that makes their current partner want to ask for an oxygen mask. Is any of this wrong? Only your conscience can judge. Chiron certainly won't.

★ If you have made an enemy out of an ex-partner or even your current partner (or a love rival) then be careful. They are likely to be quite audacious in this cycle, and show astonishing nerve. Don't dismiss certain behaviour or tactics as impossible, unthinkable or off limits – because your enemy won't. And neither will you, natch, when you fight back.

★ Chiron is all about getting away with it (hopefully) and showing the world that you can do anything if you're determined enough. Funnily enough, this also applies to the sanctity of legal marriage, as recognised by the church. Don't be surprised if you want to bend the rules, twist the regulations, skew the vows and warp the whole goddamn institution!

★ Not surprisingly, some people privately organise open marriages when Chiron passes through their Seventh House. Others keep up the pretence of a straight family life and operate as 'tourists' in gay clubs on the weekends. Other variations on this theme include women who leave their husbands and kids to start lesbian relationships – or even Green Card marriages.

★ Chiron isn't particularly ethical or moral – but neither is it recognisably bad or evil. It's a neutral force in astrology, which involves a certain kind of *chutzpah* and audacity. It really depends what you use it for, but be careful. If you're going to get away with something now (and the odds are usually good), then be aware of all the repercussions.

North Node in the Fifth House

You'll feel calmer about your future karma if you work on the issues concerning pregnancy, children and sex that the North Node brings up now. Practise, practise, practise!

- ★ If you are splitting up now and children are involved, the karmic repercussions of this time will be considerable. Weigh things up as much as you can and try to work towards the kind of balance that secures things for the long term – and maybe into your next incarnation! If friends or the group become an issue, there may be past-life connections involved.

- ★ If you are marrying and one partner is inheriting children from the previous relationship, then it's possible that there is a karmic promise changing hands too, for the future. Ask yourself what is being gained or given up in this cycle. That probably holds the clues you're looking for. You're being asked to stretch yourself and learn re your own or other people's offspring.

- ★ If you break up now and a friend or the group in your life is a key issue, there is a very good case for past-life connections between all of you. What you do now – what you say, and how you behave – will either keep the spiral going into another life, or help to set you free. Are kids (or the lack of them) also connected? Work on this. It's your future karma.

- ★ Sexually and emotionally, the North Node describes what you are fated to learn, and even who you incarnated to be with at this time. No matter how many times you've done it, you may feel slightly clueless about sex in this cycle. And no matter how often you've been in relationships, it may feel as if you're learning to crawl. Keep going. It's in your destiny!

- ★ Don't be surprised if you become a parent now and it feels as if you've never done it before – even if you have triplets and eight adopted Vietnamese orphans. The North Node has a habit of turning up when you need to learn some aspect of parenthood that is missing from your repertoire. Getting it right means you've mastered a pre-ordained karmic task.

★ It's okay to feel like an absolute beginner in any new relationship you begin now. The person you have chosen (or the person who has chosen you) has been sent to help you develop. If other cycles in the Fifth House and Seventh House coincide with this one, you'll get a stronger idea about the abilities you need to work on most and what to develop.

★ It's possible that there will be a very clear-cut conflict between a group commitment and your love life at this time. You may shag a friend you've met through your local football team – and find you have to hush it up, because he's the captain and you're the referee. How about this common scenario? Your friends don't approve of your new lover. Aaargh!

★ The North Node is a wonderful, free, astrological educational tool. You won't have a chance to equip yourself with this kind of hard-won experience and learned knowledge in any other cycle. Watch out for the reverse of the friend/lover problem above, though. Are you denying yourself an affair because he's your friend's ex? Or because of peer disapproval? You may need to find the centre-point of the seesaw now to try and find a compromise.

North Node in the Seventh House

The North Node in the Seventh House is going to teach you a lot about 'We' versus 'Me' and particularly 'Me, Me, Me' versus 'Us'. It's your chance to earn good future karma.

★ Sometimes money and property is the future karmic connection between you now. If you get together with someone in this cycle and it immediately becomes obvious that one of you is doing an awful lot of giving while the other is simply receiving, take note. Even though you'll feel clueless, you need to get the balance absolutely right – it's your karma.

★ If there are other cycles taking place at the same time as this one, your relationship or marriage will have an incredibly fated, meant-to-be feeling. What you do with your partner this time round – how you treat each other – has karmic implications in future lives too, according to the North Node position. This is one bond that could go on . . . and on.

★ The karma aspect may explain the peculiar things that happen when you try to run away, avoid the person or cut ties with them completely. Bizarrely, they keep boomeranging back. You bump into them in the street. Or they find you in other ways. Sometimes there are contracts on paper that make a clean break impossible, so . . . you're forced to learn.

★ If you've been a sworn single before this cycle, you'll be strongly aware of the need to honour your solo time, your self-development and your self while dealing with the demands of a relationship. The South Node, which is always opposite the North Node, is in your First House of 'Me, Myself and I' at this time. You may really notice the tug of war!

★ If you stay single in this cycle, it may well be because you want to skip the problem outlined above. But the Nodes have a funny way of getting you to work on partnership issues anyway – so you may have to manage the situation with your ex. Or you may be involved in a business partnership that feels like a marriage and makes similar demands.

★ Get all the advice you can while the North Node is passing through the Seventh House. Nobody expects you to be an instant expert on relationships or marriage now, and karmically it may well be the case that you've never done this before in your life! (Or, at least, in other lifetimes.) If it feels new or strange, then keep going. You'll learn a lot.

South Node in the Fifth House

★ The South Node is the clearest indicator you'll have that your lover or child in this cycle is a familiar face from a past-life relationship. Old patterns from past lives re-emerge now.

★ If you give birth or adopt in this cycle, you may have the distinct impression that the small person now staring at you is a rather old soul. Plenty of astrologers would agree with you. The children who come into your life in this cycle have been through all sorts of situations and connections with you before. Does your toddler act like your mum? Now you know why.

★ Don't be too amazed if sex with a new lover feels completely instinctive now. It may well be that you've been lovers before, which is why you don't need to have a discussion about what they want or what you'd prefer. Alternatively, the problems you have with each other in bed may also feel completely familiar. And, ta-da, they're oddly easy to resolve.

★ If you get a same-old, same-old feeling with your partner now – especially sexually – then you may well be falling into a rut. It's just that it's a rut dating from 1647, which you may not have expected. The South Node is all about what you fall into, what you rely on and what you return to, because it's all so easy. Don't become too lazy, though!

★ Why are certain aspects of your sex life or your parenting so easy, though? Astrological tradition states it's because you've done them before – perhaps several times across lifetimes. It doesn't necessarily mean those patterns are good for you or even particularly enjoyable, though – so be careful! You may be leaning on learnt responses too much.

★ Not all those learnt responses are necessarily taking you anywhere. In fact, the more you ignore the obvious need to work a bit harder on your social life, your friendships and your group commitments, the more likely it is that you are retreating to what (or who) you know in your private life, or within the family. To regain balance, start stretching yourself.

★ This means not allowing yourself to do what comes naturally or easily, either in bed or as a parent. If it feels like you've done it a million times before you probably have, so why follow the same old knitting pattern again? Equally, it's clear that you have to put more effort into your social connections now. That's really what you're here to develop this time!

South Node in the Seventh House

You'd be amazed at how many partnerships at this time are made on the back of ancient, karmically binding agreements about loyalty, money, property, fidelity or family!

★ If you have a baby in this cycle, it may well be that you are returning an ancient promise to your partner, made several lifetimes ago. In that life, he may well have been a woman, and playing the mother role! Alternatively, you could have made pacts and vows in your last relationship that promised you would bear a child. And now look – you are.

★ If you marry or pair off in this cycle, there is typically an old, old feeling of familiarity about the person you are making a commitment to. Did you know each other in a past life? The South Node says you did. It's not just the fact that you've been staring across the breakfast table at each other for all this time – you may go back as far as ancient Rome.

★ Enemies are likely to be known to you from another lifetime too. This includes love rivals, or your ex (if the break-up was acrimonious). Believe it or not, you may have agreed to reincarnate to continue a battle in this life and to try and resolve it, once and for all. This might explain why trivial irritations feel like major problems – it's past-life emotion.

★ When you consider how bloody and inhumane most of our collective history has been over the centuries, you can understand why a battle over the phone bill can seem so wounding. The real issue is probably deeper and much nastier (a decapitation may have been involved, or a live chicken). Consequently, an argument about a bill can push old buttons!

★ A new relationship or marriage in this cycle may feel astonishingly easy. You slide into your respective roles and ease into domestic, sexual, emotional and romantic patterns which seem somehow . . . familiar. If you find yourself role-playing too often, though, you may need to change the patterns. The South Node can stall you, and hold you back.

★ The North Node is always in the First House when the South Node is in the Seventh House. So what you're really here to work on is yourself. Your personality, your self-image, your appearance, your sense of identity . . . all the 'Me, Me, Me' issues! Astrological tradition says this is actually what will be hardest now. It's going to stretch you and test you.

★ When this happens, it may be astonishingly easy to retreat back into the partnership. If you do so, though, you'll be ignoring one of the reasons you reincarnated at this time –

which is to work on the stuff about yourself while also juggling a relationship that, essentially, you've had a million times before. It's about 'Me' versus 'We' right now!

★ If money or property come up repeatedly, you can almost bet that you had a past-life agreement – possibly a contract or vow – that put cash, possessions or a home on the line. There may be a very strong sense that one of you is giving and one of you is receiving, or one of you is indebted, while the other one is in a position to pay. The wheel spins around!

LOVE-STYLES OF THE RICH AND FAMOUS

On June 3 1954, the novelist Iris Murdoch, immortalised by Kate Winslet in the film *Iris*, met John Bayley, an Oxford don, five years her junior. The North Node was in her Solar Seventh House, along with Mars – and Saturn was in her Fifth House.

In April 1936, the painter Augustus John introduced Dylan Thomas to Caitlin Macnamara. 'It was said that within minutes of being introduced, Dylan and Caitlin were in bed together, and didn't emerge for several days,' notes writer Virginia Nicholson in her book *Among the Bohemians*. At the time, Dylan had the Sun in the Solar Seventh House, a New Moon in the Seventh House, Mercury in the Seventh House, Mars in the Seventh House, Saturn in the Fifth House and Uranus in the Seventh House. Caitlin didn't stand a chance.

What happened when Elvis Costello saw his future soulmate Cait O'Riordan for the first time, playing bass with The Pogues? Saturn and Neptune were in his Solar Fifth House. And when Elvis went on to marry another soulmate, Diana Krall, a few years later? Chiron was in his Fifth House. And what about his original partner, Mary Burgoyne? Jupiter was in the Seventh

House on the day they were married. (All dates are from the biography *Complicated Shadows: The Life and Music of Elvis Costello*, by Graeme Thomson.)

Here are some more famous dates with fate that show how planets and points in the Fifth House and Seventh House shape destiny. In all these examples, the person named first is the partner whose horoscope patterns are being listed. Typically, though, the charts of couples tend to show that both partners are experiencing the effects of planets and points in the Fifth House and Seventh House at the same time – though in different ways. Remember, too, these are all Solar Chart (Sun Sign chart) examples.

Camilla Parker-Bowles and Andrew Parker-Bowles divorce
January 21 1995
North Node in Fifth House, Uranus in Seventh House,
Neptune in Seventh House

Brooke Shields marries Andre Agassi
April 19 1997
Pluto in Seventh House

Brooke Shields and Andre Agassi divorce
April 9 1999
Pluto in Seventh House, Chiron in Seventh House

Brooke Shields marries Chris Henchy
March 4 2001
Mars in Seventh House, Pluto in Seventh House, Chiron in Seventh House

Vita Sackville-West marries Harold Nicolson
October 1 1913
South Node in Seventh House, Venus in Seventh House, Mars in Fifth House, Neptune in Fifth House, Pluto in Fifth House

Madonna and Sean Penn divorce
December 4 1997
Sun in Fifth House, Jupiter in Seventh House, Uranus in Seventh House, Pluto in Fifth House

John Cleese marries Barbara Trentham
February 15 1981
Mercury in Fifth House, Mars in Fifth House, Chiron in Seventh House

Mia Farrow marries Frank Sinatra
July 19 1966
Mercury in Seventh House, Venus in Fifth House

Julia Roberts marries Lyle Lovett
June 25 1993
Venus in Seventh House, Saturn in Fifth House

Princess Anne marries Captain Mark Phillips
November 14 1973
Jupiter in Seventh House, Neptune in Fifth House

Princess Anne marries Commander Tim Laurence
December 12 1992
Sun in Fifth House, Mercury in Fifth House, Venus in Seventh House, Saturn in Seventh House, North Node in Fifth House

Princess Diana marries Prince Charles
July 29 1981
Uranus in Fifth House

Princess Diana gives birth to Prince William
June 21 1982
Jupiter in Fifth House, South Node in Seventh House

Princess Diana gives birth to Prince Harry
September 15 1984
Jupiter in Seventh House, Saturn in Fifth House, Pluto in Fifth House

Princess Diana and Prince Charles separate
December 9 1992
Mercury in Fifth House, Uranus in Seventh House, Neptune in Seventh House, Pluto in Fifth House

Prince Charles and Camilla Parker-Bowles marry
April 9 2005
Uranus in Fifth House

Princess Grace marries Prince Rainier
April 18 1956
Mercury in Seventh House

Sophia Loren marries Carlo Ponti
January 9 1966
Sun in Fifth House, Mercury in Fifth House, Saturn in Seventh House, Chiron in Seventh House

Lauren Bacall marries Humphrey Bogart
May 21 1945
South Node in Fifth House

Drew Barrymore marries Jeremy Thomas
March 20 1994
Chiron in Seventh House

Lisa Bonet marries Lenny Kravitz
November 16 1998
North Node in Fifth House

Eva Braun marries Adolf Hitler
April 29 1945
Uranus in Fifth House, Pluto in Seventh House

Barbara Bush marries George Bush Snr
January 6 1945
Mercury in Seventh House, Neptune in Fifth House, Chiron in Fifth House

Queen Elizabeth II marries Prince Philip
November 20 1947
Sun in Seventh House, Mercury in Seventh House, South Node in Seventh House, Chiron in Seventh House

Lenny Henry marries Dawn French
October 20 1984
Mars in Fifth House, Jupiter in Fifth House

Brad Pitt and Jennifer Aniston become engaged
January 1 2000
Jupiter in Fifth House

Brad Pitt and Jennifer Aniston marry
July 29 2000
Jupiter in Fifth House

Brad Pitt and Jennifer Aniston separate
January 8 2005
North Node in Fifth House

Sarah Ferguson marries Prince Andrew
July 23 1986
North Node in Seventh House

Mary Donaldson marries Crown Prince Frederik
May 14 2005
Venus in Fifth House

Madonna marries Guy Ritchie
December 22 2000
Mercury in Fifth House, Venus in Seventh House, Uranus in Seventh House, Neptune in Seventh House, Pluto in Fifth House, Chiron in Fifth House

Courtney Love marries Kurt Cobain
February 24 1992
North Node in Seventh House, Uranus in Seventh House, Neptune in Seventh House, Pluto in Fifth House

Kate Winslet and Jim Threapleton announce their separation
September 4 2001
Uranus in Fifth House, Neptune in Fifth House

Nicole Kidman and Tom Cruise announce their separation
February 6 2001
Pluto in Seventh House, Chiron in Seventh House

Prince Edward marries Sophie Rhys-Jones
June 19 1999
Mercury in Fifth House

DATES WITH FATE

Alongside the major cycles you've just read about, there are also specific dates in astrology when important, unusual and rare planetary patterns light up the heavens. These periods, listed below from 2007 to 2010, can change all our lives. Directly and indirectly, they can affect your private life and partnerships as well . . .

December 11 2007

Jupiter in Sagittarius conjuncts Pluto in Sagittarius

The effects of this powerful, fortunate meeting between the 'think big' planet and the 'power up' planet will register throughout December. Scorpios will find that their plans to increase their wealth or completely detox and change their financial affairs are given a cosmic push now. Scorpio is the sign most skilled at transformation, and once the facts and figures have been satisfactorily discussed, you should end 2007 with a long-overdue sorting-out period for business, property and finance – or with an entirely new lifestyle or income arrangement that gives you the control you want. Inevitably, Scorpio's finances are always bound up with their partner's, so this period of cash detoxing for you will also affect the chemistry in your marriage or relationship.

Aries should pick up the clues about a course, a foreign connection, a change of work or home location, or an ambitious overseas trip. If you're part of a couple then, you may need to make some of those famously tricky decisions about moving or travelling together versus having a long-distance relationship for a while. If you're single, though, you may well treat this change of location or course as a chance for new hunting possibilities in the love jungle. A note of obsession may be obvious, but it's a small price to pay for passion. Every bone in your body will tell you to travel, explore or learn more in December 2007, so follow the trail.

Virgos will find their house, flat, family or flatmate situation is strongly affected by the conjunction, and it may be time for a long-overdue ending – one that is empowering – or for a fortunate new beginning. As the conjunction is directly opposite your Midheaven, which is where you pursue your ambitions and create success, it's possible that changes on the home front will tally with professional shifts as well. That's obviously going to have a huge effect on your marriage or relationship at this time.

Pisceans will find December is a landmark in terms of their status, career potential, achievements or mission statement. You have been knocking down and rebuilding for years by the time this conjunction comes around. At this stage you may be ready to bring something to a fortunate conclusion once and for all, or be prepared to take the ashes of whatever is smouldering in your career and rocket up from the embers like a phoenix in an ejector seat. Whatever transforms now in terms of your ambitions, achievements or work situation will benefit you. Your partner is going to have to be completely clued in to what you are going through at this time, or there may be tension.

A NOTE ON TIMING FOR ASTROSURFERS

The dates when the planetary patterns become exact may represent the centre point of the whole process or the time when things suddenly start to roll without warning. Most of the major developments in our lives, from real estate sales to professional success, take weeks and months to come together. So what you experience during the dates in this section may be the grand finale, the halfway mark, or the beginning. The main thing is that – just like surfing – you need to spot the wave as it starts to swell, and be ready to jump on and stay on.

January 21 2008
Jupiter in Capricorn trines Saturn in Virgo

This combination of planets lends itself to empire-building, wealth accumulation and concrete opportunities. Capricorns will respond strongly to this onward-and-upward period, registering important contacts or choices at any time from late

December 2007, but it's the third week of January that will make it obvious to Capricorn that life is firming up and turning the corner. Long-distance people and places may be part of what takes place – or a course of study could be key.

Sagittarians are in a stronger position professionally and financially than they have been for some time in January 2008. In fact, what develops in their lives will include everything they believe in – a vindication of their optimism, a reward for their positive thinking, a slice of big, fat, dumb luck – but more importantly, there is a cosmic message that this opportunity has long-term potential. If you are with the right person at this time then he or she will completely understand that it's not the actual rewards that matter to you now – it's the fact that you believed, and it worked out!

Geminis should focus hard on concrete ways to add more to their lifestyle, jobs and sense of wellbeing – and look for ways to get a mortgage, lease, family situation, property investment or tenancy agreement on a firmer footing. Because Saturn is involved in the configuration in the heavens in late January 2008, there is a big emphasis on the passage of time. This is not a wham-bam launch pad for luck. It has staying power, so look ahead. If you both own property as a couple, or want to own more, then this time in your life will be decisive.

Cancerians will find this historic phase in their lives allows them to sort out their feelings about a marriage, a close relationship, separation, divorce, or a burning love-life question. When Jupiter trines Saturn a great deal will be clearer, and this is when Cancer can finally surf through a useful period of decision-making and emotional commitment to the future – whatever their personal choice ends up being!

Libra should consider all real estate and family options at New Moon time too (the Moon rules domestic issues), and be prepared to go with a rather benevolent flow in the third week.

If your birthday falls around April 28, August 31 or December 30 itself, then the first month of 2008 will set you up in at least one department of your life. Does your decision-making process then seem awfully mature, terrifyingly sensible, awesomely wise? Then fear not. You are tapping into the energy of Saturn, Jupiter and your natal Sun in a smart way. Above all else, your sense of self should be strengthened at this time if you catch the wave as it rolls towards you.

May and June 2009
Jupiter in Aquarius, Neptune in Aquarius, the North Node in Aquarius and Chiron in Aquarius

This is a remarkable period of our lives, when Jupiter and Neptune join forces in Aquarius with Chiron, and the Moon's North Node passes through the same sign as well. This moment in our lives is all about radical progress and moving into the future; as long as your extraordinary faith, hope and optimism does not lead you into la-la land now, the more grounded visions you have in this period will take off. Are you excited by what you imagine is possible? Does it seem to spell a brave new world for everybody else too? Then be prepared for even more remarkable developments. In fact, you could change the planet now. It's going to have an explosive effect on the relationship you are in at this stage of your life, and if you are single, it could attract some remarkably new and different people to your side.

A word of warning, though – this historic and unusual pattern in May and June may bring the loonies out as well, so be aware that the world's most radical fringe-dwellers are now going to be ultra-active. It's going to be a thought-provoking period for everybody, even if it's not particularly calm and reasonable.

Some astrologers associate Chiron with healing, but my own research shows that it's actually about daring, temerity, nerve, audacity and . . . balls. It seems to turn up whenever people think they can push the envelope, or do what 'they' say can't be done. And this period will have a big effect on your love-life, particularly if your Sun Sign is Leo or Libra.

Aquarians who were born around February 15 have a special

part to play in all our lives in May–June 2009, as they may be catalysts for progress in some way, or become living symbols for all our dreams and aspirations, particularly those which are about human progress. If you're in bed with one at the time, it will be almost impossible to shut them up, so be warned!

More practically, if you're a Scorpio, check out real estate now. Does it have a water feature or is it next to a river or a beach? Fantastic. This could be the great escape you have been fantasising about, as long as you read the fine print and get an inspection for termites. Family issues run deeper than that, of course, but what develops between May and June for Scorpio should elevate one situation involving parents, children or close relatives onto a spiritual level. Something remarkable could emerge from the decisions that are taken in mid-2009.

For Pisceans, May and June could coincide with a psychic awakening, a spiritual beginning or an extraordinarily creative phase with lasting effects. Your partner will need to be understanding and supportive or you may feel rather misunderstood. For Taurus, the middle of 2009 is a fantastic opportunity to test your career dreams against reality. If your ideals and aspirations are in line with what is actually possible, then some amazing things could happen. A special role is possible. So is a very special project. Never say never. But your partner is going to have to understand that it's all about You, You, You at this time, because your ambitions have seldom been so important to you.

Leos need to focus on their marriage, former partner, close relationship or love-life potential at this time. The focus is on big dreams. Weddings emerging from this period will be worth filming. Divorces that come out of this period will make sound spiritual sense for both your souls, in a bizarre, New Age, Byron Bay kind of way.

More vitally, with this amazing line-up of points and planets in Aquarius, 2009 is crucial for the planet. Sure, it will bring out the loonies – and some of them may be dangerous, unfortunately – but it's also true that extraordinary humanitarian movements that capture the imagination of people all over the world are finally possible now. Watch the signs in the media and follow your nose in your own community. Listen to the universe, because it will be practically yelling at you this year. What needs to change? Where are people or animals being denied freedom? What old, tired rules need to be jettisoned so the planet can move forward? That's what the highest potential of 2009 is all about.

With so much emphasis on Aquarius, the sign of humanitarian change, we are likely to see major alterations in the status of gay and lesbian people around the world. In fact, you may even see what amounts to a great leap forward.

June 2010
Jupiter in Aries and Uranus in Aries

Aries, revamp your image now, or aim to increase your reputation in some way. By 2011 you could be taking up more space on the stage of life or just physically looking better. If you have never really understood what a difference your packaging can make to the way you feel, consider how liberating it would be to look a certain way or present a certain image. Looking in the mirror in June 2010 is an excellent idea because it will get you thinking and show you what is possible. If you're single at this time you will attract a completely different kind of lover. He or she is responding to the new image you're presenting.

Cancerians can take the contacts, clues, emotions or possibilities that were in the ether on April 14 and move them forward. It is not enough to have a job now; you need a mission statement that will move you forward and make you feel as if you are accelerating with the human race, rather than sitting there watching the engine turn over in the name of a regular salary. A complete change of career direction is possible. So is a surprise promotion. New people or projects in your usual line of work could revolutionise what you are doing. June 2010 is a platform for 2011, though, so don't necessarily expect everything to fall into place now. It's crucial that your partner 'gets it' at this time, or you may find that your new direction in life is contradicting what they want for the relationship.

Capricorn, the planets are encouraging you to run your home life along new lines. Certain individuals and situations will practically fall into your lap, willing you to do so. A family arrangement or domestic set-up that is a departure for you could turn out to be beneficial on every level. Even sudden rips in the fabric of your life will turn out to be benevolent twists of fate, so knock nothing and be ready for everything.

Sagittarius, there is an enormous energy focus on children and babies – your own or other people's. A surprise pregnancy is not out of the question. However, the conjunction of Jupiter and Uranus is also about big ideas, and a brainchild you have about children in general or one child in particular could also come to term this year.

Space, freedom, room to breathe and to be true to yourself are huge themes in June 2010. Aquarians will respond strongly to the Zeitgeist now – the music, films, books and political changes – because freedom is their reason for living. Aquarians will find the words to express what the rest of us need to know, and any Aquarians who are big in corporate life, government, science, religion or entertainment in 2010 will turn out to be key figures in the shifting mood that precedes 2011. (All this also applies to people who simply have a planet in Aquarius too.)

The messages of Aquarian-influenced people in our media will move a lot of things forward at this time – and it's likely that this part of 2010 will have huge ramifications for gay and lesbian rights worldwide. Aquarius is about freedom and honesty – daring to be different – and demanding independence, non-conformity and truth, in a fake, fake, fake world! It has long been associated with alternative sexualities, which is why this period is likely to see some important global milestones for gay and lesbian communities.

3 MORE ABOUT HIM

If you haven't already looked up your partner's planet signs, turn to page 272 now. You probably already know his Sun Sign – it's his regular sign, the one you've read about in magazines or newspapers. To find out the inner workings of his soul, though (not to mention the contents of his boxer shorts), you also need his Moon Sign, Mercury Sign, Venus Sign, Mars Sign and Rising Sign.

HIS ARIES SIDE

If his Sun, Moon, Mercury, Venus, Mars and/or Rising Sign is in Aries then this sign will be a big part of his personality. Want to know if the Midheaven is there too? Check www.astro.com.

Is Mars in Aries? It's possible he can have a divorce, separation or parting of the ways that ends in all concerned air-kissing and handing over large bunches of roses, but it's unlikely. When things go bust for this man, they go bust with a foot through the door or a war of words in the street. He has the soul of a boxer, and it lies at the heart of his manhood.

Wherever his Aries planets or points are, this is probably the man most likely to smash a guitar, so bear that in mind the next time you start an argument in a music store. Yoga is a fantastic channel for an Aries-influenced man. It's a container for all his testosterone. Throwing things at politicians on the TV screen is a good way for him to maintain the rage and contain the rage too.

Sport is another fantastic outlet – there is no better natural contender for a spot with the New York Giants, even if he's the same shape as a Malteser.

Does he have Mercury in Aries? He's a tough talker and if you take him to see *Reservoir Dogs*, he'll probably come out talking like Mr Blue. He can try to croon like Pat Boone too, but he'll always sound like The Damned circa 1976, or an extra in a gangster movie talking out of the side of his mouth. Should your relationship ever hit the 'We've got to have a talk' stage, prepare for something that approaches the level of an Oxford–Cambridge debate, or a particularly gruelling current affairs interview.

He can be a damner and blaster, a four-letter-word hurler and a world-class screamer. His personal mantra is 'I'm as mad as hell and I'm just not going to take it any more.' But nobody is a better person to have on your side if you are fighting for truth and justice, and nobody is a more terrifying enemy either. You'll be astonished at how much damage one man can do with a computer, a letter to the editor, or as a guest on a radio talkback show.

Remember, if he has planets or points in Aries, that constitutes a substantial chunk of his personality. If it's the driving force in his character, he may even have a great dictator complex. Attack and defence will be big with him, and a great deal of his mental energy will go into strategising.

If he has several planets in Aries, or the planet Mars dominates his chart, then he's a born tactical thinker, and instinctively understands the inner workings of football coaches, military strategists or political spin doctors. He may not always be convinced that pacifism is the answer either. He thinks sometimes you've just got to punch people in the nose – or, ahem, blow them to smithereens. Even the *pacifists* punch the air at demonstrations.

He typically has a touch of Tarzan about him too . . . 'He made his kills and ate and slept, and swung on tirelessly through forests or across plains.' (Edgar Rice Burroughs, *Tarzan the*

Magnificent.) Tarzan was created when the Moon was in Aries. Tarzan's Midheaven is there too, and Mars is sextile the Ascendant and opposite the Sun. Clint Eastwood and Marlon Brando are Mars/Aries types too.

Mars/Aries types can be New Men or Unreconstituted Old Men, but they all like a bit of action. They do well in jousting contests, and daring and foolish polar exploration – or the more foolhardy kinds of backpacking. Sir Raymond Priestley, a member of the 1907 Antarctic expedition, is rumoured to have recommended Scott for leadership and Amundsen for efficient travel, but Shackleton (a true Mars/Aries type) for those hopeless situations when you are forced to get on your knees and pray!

The film director Peter Weir wisely cast Russell Crowe in the naval epic *Master and Commander*. With both the Sun and Mars in Aries, and Mars (the ruler of Aries) aspecting Venus, Crowe is perfect for playing the master/commander type. Actors with strong Mars and Aries signatures fit easily into the role of cowboy, gladiator or war hero because the archetype makes sense; there is a little of each inside them.

Sport is an obvious outlet for all this rampant testosterone, and Mars/Aries types are well known for playing it or being dedicated supporters of it. Football is a good outlet for their energy. They need a pitched contest, a feud, a stoush, a barney or a blue in their lives. At its least evolved, though, far away from the fabulous world of football, planets in Aries and strong Mars aspects can produce a man who is all too keen on guns or bombs, or hurling small animals.

At the very least, men with Aries planets or points find it extremely difficult to walk away from an argument – or even a potential argument – and turning the other cheek does not come easily to them. They're far more likely to wage an all-out war.

If the man in your life has aspects (patterns) involving the planet Mars as well as one or more planets in Aries, then he may need anger management courses. Mars is the ruler of Aries, so it's like having a double dose of the sign.

The other effect of a strong Mars/Aries dose in a chart is a complicated bloke who won't or can't express his feelings, because he's worried that if he does, all the anger will pour out and he'll chainsaw somebody's head off. To check for Mars aspects, have a look at his chart at www.astro.com and see if there are lots of lines stretching out from the Mars symbol: ♂ These show aspects – the conjunction, sextile, square, trine and opposition.

Extreme examples of Mars/Aries energy gone wild are a reminder that these men (particularly when young) need an outlet for their angry feelings. Come on down, Timothy McVeigh (the Oklahoma bomber) and Mark David Chapman (RIP John Lennon). This sign and planet combination is also common in the charts of world leaders who make pro-war decisions – or just start them.

Adolf Hitler, Tony Blair and George W. Bush all have big Aries and Mars themes in their horoscopes. This sign and its planet are *huge* on attack and defence.

Everyone knows that Albert Einstein, born with the Sun in Pisces, founded the theory of relativity. But he also contributed to the creation of the atomic bomb. Einstein was born with Mercury and Venus in Aries.

The intelligent Mars/Aries types get therapy or channel their emotions into sport or lobbying for a worthwhile cause. A passion for politics is extremely common too! It's a fine line, though. How does the Mars/Aries bloke in your life handle anger, or even the legacy of thousands of years of socially sanctioned male violence and aggression?

To really understand the highs and lows of living with Mars/Aries, read the classic work on football *Fever Pitch* by Nick Hornby. According to birth data from him in *Elle* magazine, Hornby was born with the Sun and Venus in Aries, and Mars sextile the Sun and Venus. His book is about football as a metaphor for life, and it's about a new kind of masculinity too.

Any man with a lot of Mars and Aries in his chart (whatever his Sun Sign actually happens to be) needs to look at anger – and, if possible, laugh at it. Or, better still, channel his psychological need for a great big male-on-male war into an Arsenal–Manchester United game. Football (American, Australian or British) is probably the ultimate safe Aries channel.

There is something very physical about the Mars/Aries combination too. It's about adrenaline addiction, fight-or-flight response and all our attack and defence systems. Feeling your heart pump in the back of the stadium when your team scores or your horse wins is one way of experiencing it. Hunting is another outlet: Henry VIII was born with the Moon in Aries, and Mars trine his Midheaven and Venus.

Mars/Aries types get angry, and if they don't do that, they just get . . . irritable. It's natural for them to feel the heat, though, and if they channel it properly, they can be brilliant fighters for a good cause.

Most of all, they need to manage their own masculinity and their notion of manhood as it stands in relation to those archetypal Mars symbols of the warrior, the soldier and the Testosterone Tyrant. And they probably also need to watch a lot of Michael Moore documentaries . . . Does your man have Aries Rising? Meet Mr Tough! He seems to be wearing a leather jacket all the time, even if he's not.

HIS TAURUS SIDE

If his Sun, Moon, Mercury, Venus, Mars and/or Rising Sign is in Taurus then this sign will be a big part of his personality. Want to know if the Midheaven is there too? Check www.astro.com.

Ah, yes, the human calculator! With a Taurus theme in his chart, this man will either put his values first ('Stuff the system and the salary, there's more to life than money!') or end up seriously rich. Either way, the Taurus type is hung up on money or values. He knows the price of everything and the value of everything too. He is a human calculator. He keeps his receipts with a vengeance. He also has strong views on art, and how much you should pay for it.

If Mars is in Taurus, then his energy goes into business, finance, investment or charity. It all depends on his values, which may be deeply capitalist or purely philanthropist. Sometimes he mixes the two, and ends up sitting on a fortune and giving half of it away.

Whatever planets or points are in Taurus, you'll soon see that some bull-influenced men are natural socialists and can see the point of Karl Marx, but others are guilty of excessive Donald Trumpery. In all cases, though, this man defines his manhood and masculinity by his attitude towards money and his economic politics. Comic Relief or tax relief? It really depends on the rest of his chart.

He is a natural businessman, or leans hard on values that have nothing to do with money and everything to do with his political or religious leanings. He makes a fantastic philanthropist. However, if he's not left wing or philanthropic by nature he can be an excessive shopaholic and a prime capitalist, and one Hilton Hotel on a trip is never enough.

Does he have the Moon in Taurus? It's the mark of trade unionists and big spenders alike. Being rich or poor affects his entire way of life. Being broke (or making it) shapes his personality. Is he a have or a have not? Are you? It matters more than you think, if you're going to live together.

I've met plenty of these types who 'don't care' about money, to the point where they give up high-earning jobs and pursue low-paying vocations instead. But guess what? A fixation with cash still underlines almost everything they do and everything they say. 'Capitalism was and is a paper Utopia, the most unreal product of wishful thinking of all the Utopias,' said George Bernard Shaw, born with a Taurus Moon and quoted in *Picture Post*

1938–1950 by Tom Hopkinson. Plenty of big earners and super spenders have Taurus themes in their charts, though.

Richard Branson has Taurus on the Midheaven. By the age of thirty-two his companies had an annual turnover of £50 million. Andrew Lloyd Webber has Taurus on the Midheaven. In February 2003 he was valued at £310 million. Donald Trump has it too. The Midheaven shows your direction in life: in Taurus, it describes the pursuit of what you value – be it truckloads of cash or something priceless, like the ability to donate large amounts of money to aid agencies, political parties or charitable foundations and change the world. (If you're curious, remember you can check the Midheaven, with a birth time, at www.astro.com.)

Men with planets and points in Taurus are funny about money. Earning it and spending it is their *raison d'être* or, alternatively, like Karl Marx, they see straight through capitalism and pursue other values instead. Either way they spend large chunks of their life being obsessed by the stuff. Look your man up!

For serious riches (I knew you'd ask) a man generally needs more than just a Taurean theme in his chart. Alongside the sign of the bull, you might also look for Scorpio influences and planets in the Second House and/or Eighth House. Men with points and planets in Taurus and Scorpio tend to be fixated with lucre, which is why they make so much of it. Alternatively, they are Robin Hoods. They either make it to give away, or they lobby the rich to give to the poor. Either way they are a tad obsessed.

Bill Gates, Ralph Nader (the consumer activist), Pope John Paul II (until recently head of one of the richest religions), Tiger Woods, Ted Turner and Donald Trump all have horoscopes showing major emphasis on these all-important Second and Eighth houses.

Here's the rich list (and the charity list too). The bull and the scorpion in combination can be formidable: **J. Paul Getty** – Moon, Midheaven and Venus in Scorpio; **Conrad Hilton** – Moon in Taurus, Venus in Scorpio; **William Randolph Hearst** – Sun, Mercury and Ascendant in Taurus; **Guy de Rothschild** –

Sun and Mercury in Taurus, Moon in Scorpio; **Bill Gates** – Sun in Scorpio, Moon in Taurus; **Elton John** – Moon in Taurus, Chiron in Scorpio; **David Beckham** – Sun and Mercury in Taurus; **Bono** – Sun, Mercury and Venus in Taurus, Moon in Scorpio; **Ted Turner** – Sun and Venus in Scorpio.

Big earners, big givers and bankrupts alike have Taurus themes in their chart. Men with Taurus planets can either indulge themselves or use money as a humanitarian power tool (and sometimes do both). When super-Taurus type Elton John married, his gift to new wife Renate was a heart-shaped gold pendant set with sixty-three diamonds. Afterwards they allegedly had a £50,000 reception where guests ate lobster, king prawns, oysters, scallops, smoked salmon, mud crabs, trout, lamb, venison, loin of beef, stuffed quail glazed with honey, pork, turkey and lemon chicken washed down with champagne, vintage wine and schnapps. Meanwhile, Elton's AIDS foundation has generated millions and changed the world.

With an emphasis on this sign and this house, your life becomes a mission statement of your values. If you value Louis Vuitton luggage (I saw Elton's old trunk on sale in a second-hand shop once and it was *huuuge*) then that is what you will pursue. If you value social justice more, you may join the Communist Party, but the whole thing will still essentially be about money. It's common for Taurus types to compromise and fall between the two, by the way: this produces the classic portrait of a luxury-loving big charity giver.

Sometimes, it has to be said, Taurus types accumulate security because they have been plunged into financial crisis by overspending – and the Monopoly consciousness begins. They crash and burn as often as they rise effortlessly to the top of the cash pile. But in either case, they always learn about what (and who) is truly valuable to them. When the boom collapsed on Wall Street in October 1929, the North Node was in Taurus. The North Node is about karma. In this case, though, it was kerching karma.

Unevolved Taurus types can reach a point where they know the price of everything and the value of nothing. Dating them can feel as if you are having dinner with a cash register or a catalogue. When they come to visit you at home, they'll be more interested in your interest rate than your way with curtains, and unless you are similarly inclined it can all become a bit . . . boring.

Men born with this chart signature are actually here to show us what is truly valuable, so if you do strike an empty-headed materialist, he is rather missing the point. Telling you about his new Armani suit is all very well, but what the rest of the planet is looking for is a truly accurate summary of what things are worth. We need to be updated!

Does he have Taurus Rising? There are two kinds of Taurus Rising men. The first group is radical. Their values are so important to them that they are prepared to put up with anything (being broke, being unpopular) to pursue their goals. The second type will remind you of Richie Rich. He's Designer-label Man, and he has a Designer-label car.

HIS GEMINI SIDE

If his Sun, Moon, Mercury, Venus, Mars and/or Rising Sign is in Gemini then this sign will be a big part of his personality. Is the Midheaven there too? Check at www.astro.com.

Men born with planets and/or points in Gemini have a way with words which is striking. They have a way of putting things. They often have catchphrases, or do that Laurie Anderson 'language is a virus' thing and infect every single one of their friends with a stupid new word. Frequently, the funniness of this new word/phrase/acronym/nickname is very hard to explain to other people. You have to be there. And you have to hear the way they say it.

Nobody takes more delight in naming things than the Venus in Gemini man. When he buys a company off the shelf, he spends weeks scribbling down ideas on the back of an envelope, and when he buys a car, it gets a nickname before it gets petrol. He likes songs where you can hear the lyrics properly and then read them, appreciatively, on the liner notes. He knows what Queen meant when they sang about Radio Ga-Ga, and his taste in art, music and books ranges from street smart and sharp to intellectually highbrow, depending on his education. As a child or teenager he learns code, and sends messages through Coke cans on strings.

This is diary-and-postcard man, and also message-T-shirt man – but only if it's cleverly ironic. I have known several to wear ties that are conversation pieces – either way, they think more about their wardrobes than most men.

Unless he has planets in Sagittarius, he will bore easily on a long overseas trek – but he loves short-haul flights, mid-range balloon exploration and bobbing around the waterways on a barge. The whiff of a freshly packed overnight bag is deeply arousing to him, as is the sight of a sleigh, a dog and a large furry hat with earflaps.

If you really want to upset him, take away his television set or his radio. 'No more podcasts for you, mister!' The man cannot bear camping trips unless he can find a newsagent too.

If you know someone who has a mixture of Gemini and Sagittarius influences in his chart, he will find it easy to be funny. In the privacy of your bedroom, he may turn out to be the best stand-up comedian you've ever heard. In fact, it may be impossible for him to ever be fully serious. Even if Gemini is the only factor in his chart, he'll still express himself with wit. Gemini rules not only the dictionary and the thesaurus, but also the tonsils and the larynx. Men with Gemini bits are funny not only because they know how to turn a phrase, but also because they know how to say it. There is nothing essentially amusing about the phrase 'I'm free', but when John Inman (three planets and points in Gemini) said it on *Are You Being Served?*, it suddenly became funny.

Ronnie Barker, best known for *Open All Hours*, *Porridge* and *The Two Ronnies*, wrote several scripts for *The Two Ronnies* as well, under a pseudonym. Some of his most famous sketches and jokes have involved that very Gemini area of word play, tricks of the tongue and tricks of speech.

Ben Elton, heavily influenced by the sign of Gemini, famously played with similes – another Gemini passion – in his scripts for *Blackadder*. In fact, together with co-writer Richard Curtis, he may have reinvented them as an art form. A turnip shaped like a thingy? Well, of course. And Baldrick always has 'a cunning plan' – another typical Gemini catchphrase.

Remember the catchphrases in Seinfeld like 'These pretzels are making me thirsty', 'Cable boy' and 'Get out!'? The two creators of the show, Jerry Seinfeld and Larry David, both have planets in Gemini. So does catchphrase king Matt Lucas (Little Britain).

If you take Scrabble seriously, don't play it with a Gemini-influenced man. He will make up stupid words, read out words backwards or refuse to play by the rules. If you live with a Gemini-influenced man for any length of time, prepare to enter his peculiar world and find various household objects/pets/domestic rituals renamed.

Why are they so witty? A lot of it comes down to the twin symbolism of Gemini. It deals in doubles, so if they can find another way of saying or putting something, then they will. They quite like tacky old double entendres – but they use them ironically, not as Benny Hill might have used them. If you want to entertain Gemini if he is stuck in hospital, bring him a thesaurus. I'm not joking. They love reading out loud from them too.

Men (or comedy shows) with planets in Gemini include **Ben Elton** – Venus in Gemini; **Billy Connolly** – Moon in Gemini; **Harry Enfield** – Sun in Gemini; **Michael Palin** – Moon, Mercury and Venus in Gemini; **Monty Python** – Venus in Gemini; **Larry David** – Venus and Mars in Gemini; **Spike Milligan** –

Moon in Gemini; **Oscar Wilde** – Midheaven in Gemini; **John Inman** – Moon and Mercury in Gemini; **Julian Clary** – Sun in Gemini; **Walt Disney** – Midheaven in Gemini; **Noel Coward** – Moon in Gemini; **Ronnie Barker** – Moon in Gemini; **Victor Borge** – Moon in Gemini; **Bob Hope** – Sun and Mercury in Gemini; **Eddie Izzard** – Midheaven in Gemini; **Jerry Seinfeld** – Venus in Gemini; **George Cole** – Mars in Gemini; **Peter Sellers** – Midheaven in Gemini; **Dudley Moore** – Venus in Gemini; **John Cleese** – Midheaven in Gemini; **Chevy Chase** – Mars in Gemini; **Eric Morecambe** – Moon in Gemini.

Does he have Mars in Gemini? Then his sharp retorts are extremely sharp (listening to him can feel like being lanced repeatedly with a javelin), so never push him too far or he might just tell you to f-f-f-fade away.

The Gemini-influenced man is a natural poet, postcard writer, blogger, short-story king, scriptwriter, copywriter and advertising genius. It all depends on education, time, money and ambition. At the very least you will keep his love letters for the rest of your life – long after you've broken up.

If he was born with the Sun, Moon, Mercury, Venus, Mars, Ascendant and/or Midheaven in Gemini, with tight aspects to Mercury from one or more other planets, then bear in mind that his brother or sister will also have a massive effect on his life and personality, for better or worse.

According to Mrs Gallagher, mother of the Oasis lads, Noel was born on May 29 1967. That day, the Sun and Mercury were in Gemini and Uranus and Pluto were both square Mercury. Five years later, on September 21 1972, his younger brother Liam arrived. A third brother, Paul, has written a book about the family: *Brothers: From Childhood to Oasis*. It's a wickedly funny account of what it's like to grow up being related to a Gemini type. As Paul recounts, Noel's sibling rivalry with Liam even extended to multi-million pound house purchases.

Does he have sibling closeness or sibling coolness, or has a brother or sister had a pivotal effect on his life and character? Go to www.astro.com and calculate his chart. If he has lots of lines stretching out from the Mercury symbol in the horoscope ☿, then you'll know!

Ray Davies of The Kinks has Mercury in Gemini and Mercury also sextile Jupiter and Mars. His relationship with brother Dave has never been easy. Kinks insider Hal Carter has seen a lot of Kinks break-ups in his time. 'Of course they keep breaking up,' he says in *The Kinks* by Neville Marten and Jeffrey Hudson. 'Ray will go off on his own and do a tour and Dave will go off to the States or something. Then Ray will write something new or set up a load of dates and they'll say, "Oh, we've got to have Dave; it's not The Kinks without Dave." So they hook up with Dave again and go out on tour, but within a couple of weeks they hate each other again.'

Paul McCartney was born with the Sun, Mercury and Midheaven in Gemini, in a rare triple conjunction. Mercury is also square the Ascendant and sextile the Moon. But Paul isn't the only musician in the family; his brother Mike is well known for his time with the band Scaffold and their 1967 (and only) hit 'Thank U Very Much'.

'Michael McCartney, Paul's brother, took longer to get used to the changes he's had imposed on his life,' Hunter Davies wrote in his 1968 book *The Beatles*. 'Paul has always been very close to his brother, in age and taste, more than George has been with his brothers, which made it worse for Michael.'

Some Gemini/Mercury types discover a brother or sister changing their lives. In the case of Christy Brown, author of *My Left Foot*, it was his brother Eammon who took dictation during his first attempt at an autobiography. Born on June 5 1932, Brown is a typical Gemini/Mercury type.

Does the man in question have Gemini Rising? Quick, clever and curious on the surface, he has a lighter-than-light quality that lets him slip in and out of dating situations more easily than most. Typically, he'll be full of questions too – he is a clearing-house for information.

HIS CANCER SIDE

If his Sun, Moon, Mercury, Venus, Mars and/or Rising Sign is in Cancer, then this sign will be a big part of his personality. Is the Midheaven there too? Check at www.astro.com.

Park him in front of a real estate agent, and even if he's renting a shoebox, he'll start thinking like a landowner, a gentleman farmer – or a property developer. He may have a gift for buying the worst house in the street and turning it into a goldmine. Renting is okay, but it's the moment he first turns the key in the lock of his own home that he approaches his personal epiphany. He needs his home – it is his fortress, his castle and his sanctuary. He understands why other people need their homes too, and is usually the man you most want feeding your plants or painting your bathroom when you're away. If he has planets in Taurus as well, he may have an instinct for gardening – particularly as he knows how much a decent rose garden can jack up a house price at auction time.

Whatever the rest of his chart looks like, a large chunk of him is Cancerian – so the care and protection of children, animals or vulnerable people in society will push his emotional buttons. Lots of Venus in Cancer men do amazing work for charities. Still more become the cornerstone of their families.

History does something to him – preferably his own, because unless he has planets in Sagittarius, he's not really interested in other people's. The English Venus in Cancer men cross their fingers and hope that King Arthur really is buried in Glastonbury, and spend their weekends traipsing around the Tor, just in case. Take him to a museum and he'll start channelling A.J.P. Taylor.

His nationality really matters, which is why the Scotsmen look like wannabe Bay City Rollers and the Americans have their baseball team on their baseball cap. The English are all terribly English (unless they are Northerners or Cockneys, in which case they sound like film extras from an Ealing comedy) and the Irish all go mad on St Patrick's Day, even if they happen to be in Kenya at the time.

They like songs that namecheck the streets or towns they know best, or music that promotes a local sense of familiarity. The Americans like to hear 53rd Street dropped into a song; the English like to hear about roast beef on Sundays.

He needs to belong, and if he doesn't have a close connection to his own flesh and blood, he will accumulate a 'family' another way. Family matters – oh, how it matters, for better or for worse. He's more aware of all the branches on the tree than most people, and he can become quite emotional about it. His relationship with his mother is either all love, all hate, or all love–hate. It's constitutionally impossible for him to feel detached about her. He needs a close relationship with his mother and/or grandmother in order to have a good lifelong relationship with women. If he does, his female side will be well developed and chicks will love him – platonically or sexually.

Aspects between the Moon and the personal planets and points – as well as a dose of Cancerian influence – typically put a man's mother at centre stage, for better or worse. Look at his chart on www.astro.com. Are there lots of lines stretching out from this symbol? ☽ Then Mummy really matters!

Emergencies and crises underline this emphasis on the family. A man with a strong Cancer/Moon emphasis in his chart will run straight to a parent if the going gets tough, even if he's past middle age at the time. If the family ties have been cut, then a substitute clan will be found as a sounding board. Sometimes this is a tight circle of friends, sometimes it's his own new family, which lots of them start just as soon as they possibly can.

If his relationship with his mother and his family generally was on solid ground, then you won't need any Dr Benjamin Spock books when you have a baby. He'll have an incredible natural instinct for parenting.

If the mother–son relationship was strong, you had better respect it. Nelson Mandela was born with the Sun in Cancer. His dream upon leaving prison was to visit his birthplace, the hills and streams where he had played as a boy, and the burial ground of his mother, which he had never seen.

'A mother's death causes a man to look back on and evaluate his own life. Her difficulties, her poverty, made me question once again whether I had taken the right path. That was always the conundrum: Had I made the right choice in putting the people's welfare even before that of my own family?' (Nelson Mandela in *Long Walk To Freedom*.)

If a man with the Sun, Moon, Mercury, Venus, Mars or other points in Cancer cannot find anything happy about his family or his mother, he will channel the feelings into his homeland. But those who had delightful childhoods and retain warm memories of home can become passionate about both in a way that those without Cancer planets find impossible to understand. Often, the best part of going away on holiday for them is coming home again and calling Mum.

'Homeland, sweet homeland' should be tattooed on his left buttock. The academic Cancer/Moon types gravitate towards history for this reason – either reading it, writing it or making it. They need to understand their roots, and they need to fully comprehend the country they were born in – the mother country, of course.

George Orwell, born with the Sun and Moon in Cancer, wrote *1984* as a future history and penned it out of his deep concern for England. *Animal Farm* was the alternative history of the Bolshevik Revolution. Like Nelson Mandela, Orwell channelled a lot of his passion back into his homeland and was fiercely patriotic on his own terms.

For a Cancer/Moon type, his home town or his country has exactly the same deep, emotional pull as a family tie; it's never just a chunk of land, it genuinely speaks to his soul – so you'd better be careful what you say about it! Sir Edmund Hillary, another Sun Cancerian, is reported to have said that while he has visited many countries and admired some of the most beautiful places in the world, he still feels fortunate to have been born in New Zealand. This, from the man who was the first human being to reach the top of the world!

Rupert Brooke, born with Mars in Cancer and the Moon opposite the Sun, wrote in his poem 'The Soldier': 'If I should die, think only this of me/That there is some far corner of a foreign field which is forever England.' It virtually became a mantra for World War I.

The real function of the sign, and its ruler the Moon, is to remind the rest of us where we came from, though – and where we belong. In a big city full of urban refugees from other places, it is the Cancerian and lunar types who will wheel out the barbecue for Australia Day, or start booking Irish pubs for St Patrick's Day. Patriotism can turn to jingoism – a criticism frequently levelled at George W. Bush – but nobody would doubt that the feelings are real. (He's a classic Cancer type, by the way.)

Cancer man needs his food. If he's Jewish he may have a thing about chopped liver. If he's Scots, haggis may bring tears to his eyes. You can give him nouvelle cuisine if you wish, but there is a part of him that just wishes the spirit of his great-grandmother would turn up with the family recipe book and throw lots of mashed potato at him.

Cancer rules food too, because it rules mothers: the Cancer man can be emotional about what he eats and doesn't eat, and he may either develop cooking skills himself or become a devotee of restaurants. A. A. Gill, the well-known English food critic, has the Sun and Mercury in Cancer, along with two outer planets and the North Node!

If you like hovering around health-food shops, then you will know that Terence Stamp, the toast of *Priscilla, Queen of the Desert*, also has his own product line now. Stamp has the Sun, Mars and Midheaven in Cancer. Boy George wrote a great macrobiotic cookbook with Dragana Brown, after she changed his life by changing what he ate. He was born with the Moon and Mercury in Cancer, both in conjunction! He famously said that he'd prefer a cup of tea to sex – very Cancerian. He does a mean hangover cure, though, if you happen to have a jar of umeboshi plums hanging around the fridge.

Does he have Cancer Rising? If his family made him miserable, you'll soon hear about it. And if they are his best friends and he rings them every day? You'll hear about that too. Where Cancer Rising goes, his family or background follows. He seems caring, and genuinely concerned about people – even a bit of a Gooey Louis. Aaah . . .

HIS LEO SIDE

If his Sun, Moon, Mercury, Venus, Mars and/or Rising Sign is in Leo, then this sign will be a big part of his personality. Is the Midheaven there too? Check at www.astro.com.

Take him to any Shakespearean drama and he will immediately identify with the king. If he has more than one planet in Leo, he will spend his childhood playing actor or director, or alternatively forcing the hamster to pretend it is in an Andrew Lloyd Webber production.

Remember, whatever his chart looks like, a substantial chunk of his personality is pure Leo, so he needs a career or part-time passion that allows him to show the world his star quality. An invisible life doesn't suit him, which is something his music and drama teachers usually discover to their cost the moment they start casting the school nativity play.

He carries himself like a knight of the realm, even if he is the same shape and height as a potato. He does Dignified, Distinguished and Distinctive better than any other Moon sign – and also Pretentious, Pompous and Ponderous, if you ask nicely.

None of this is fake. If he has the Moon in Leo, for example, then the Lion King is 20 per cent of his personality, and he is born to lead. People trust him in this role and he may rise to the top because of it, if the rest of his chart agrees. This is the Rolex Moon sign. It's also the Pol Roger champagne Moon sign.

Self-expression is his thing. Even if he has just one planet or point in Leo, there is a part of him which is good on a dance floor, happy on a stage, fine behind a microphone or quite comfortable to be shoved under a spotlight for any reason at all. He gravitates towards careers or weekend passions where there is a sense of occasion, and usually a chance for a dose of comfortable extroversion.

In astrology, Leo is the sign associated with the Fifth House, which rules entertainment, leisure and lust for life. Leo is about the dance, not the washing-up. It's about self-expression channelled through anything – after hours, or on the weekend – that gives him a chance to shine. Some of them are fortunate enough to end up in jobs where play also becomes work. But all of them know how to play . . .

Leo is ruled by the Sun. Men with this sign in their charts feed off warmth and radiate it as well. They like the body heat at stadium rock concerts, football finals, film premieres and beach parties. They respond well to central heating, perspiration and a sense of occasion.

This is the royal sign. Leo types do Events with a capital E. They celebrate birthdays, promotions, sporting victories, legal victories, film premieres, hit singles, christenings, weddings, bar mitzvahs – and anything else that gives them an excuse to dress up and experience a different kind of lighting.

Is he proud to be seen with you? Does he take quiet pride in the way you are seen as a couple? Does he have a wardrobe to be proud of? Then you'll know he's functioning properly, with all his Leo points and planets in place. This is someone who needs to hold his own out there, even if he can't always be the best. If life is one big waltz, then the Leo type needs to know that he's in command of all the moves – and preferably with a partner who can make both of them look good.

Try as he might, he doesn't understand wallflowers, introverts, dropouts or people who sit at home with the lights off in the middle of winter listening to The Smiths when they could be out there . . . showing-off. Some of them show-off all by themselves, and some of them only feel comfortable when they are doing it in groups of people who are being extroverts *en masse* – but all Leo types need the attention.

The Fifth House of astrology, which Leo rules, is the romance and sex house. If he has planets or points in this sign, he finds it hard to go it alone for very long. Part of him is permanently tuned in to old Fred Astaire and Ginger Rogers films, so be aware. He'll never admit it, but often the whole point of coupledom for him is that you get to go out together and be seen. Don't ever imagine you're going to be in a pizza-delivery-and-TV relationship if you get together with this man. Too much cocooning kills his life force.

He's fertile. He wants either kids or projects and plans that he can conceive, nurture and deliver. He longs for the christening, the champagne against the side of the ship or the balloons on opening night. If he has points or planets in Leo, then he is born to give birth – to sons and daughters, or to a creative brainchild.

He carries the life force in an obvious way, and he knows he is on the planet to go forth and multiply – or to be permanently fruitful in other ways. When Leo types become fathers for the first time, there is a tremendous sense of Mission Accomplished.

If he's not interested in having children or unable to have them, then he will pour himself into an area of life where he can have the satisfaction of starting something from a small seed and watching it grow.

If his Leo side is well developed, then this man will seem more alive, more positive and more vital than other men. The Sun, which rules this sign, is more closely associated with the life force than any other planet. Life is always full of promise for the Leo type. It is sometimes literally pregnant with possibility (if he's the paternal type) or symbolically full of amazing, unborn potential.

Do you know a man who has one child, another on the way and a big plan up his sleeve? Or do you know a guy who has just finished Plan A, is celebrating the conclusion of Plan B and is already bursting with Plan C? That's a Leo type, even if he only has one planet or point in this sign.

They are drawn to careers or interests that allow them to produce end results that carry their signature style or large chunks of their personality. This is not a man who does particularly well with paint-by-numbers instructions or prescribed forms of creativity. If he is forced to join a covers band, he will interpret his ABBA songs or his Led Zeppelin guitar riffs with the kind of time signature or chord changes that make the music unrecognisable . . . and yet uniquely his.

Pride has something to do with his need to put his stamp on his children or on the occasional creative brainchild. But it's also part of the Leo type's contribution to the world. You may love what he offers up, or have serious doubts about it, but without his dedication to his kids or the products of his talent or energy, the world would look rather samey. The whole point of doing his thing is that it's *his* thing.

Does he have one of the outer planets – like Uranus, Neptune or Pluto – transiting the Fifth House of his Solar Chart now? If he was born with the Sun in Scorpio, the Sun in Libra or the Sun in Leo, then the beginning of the twenty-first century will be an incredibly fertile time for him. Producing a son or daughter in these years will be an epic voyage of discovery for him. But in many cases, the Scorpio, Libra or Leo person – with planets or points in Leo – will also be on a major creative journey, and what he delivers in these years will have a major effect on his personality and his destiny.

Leo is ruled by the Sun. Even if this man only has around 20 per cent of his horoscope influenced by this sign, you'll find that New Moons and Full Moons have a strong effect on him. At New Moon, the Sun is in the same position as the New Moon. At Full Moon, the Sun and Moon stand opposite each other. These periods tend to shed light on his creative process, his fertility, parenthood or self-expression. Is he starting the process, halfway through it or finishing up? New Moons and Full Moons illuminate the famous fertility, creativity and productivity of the Leo type and give him a chance to turn the spotlight on this side of his life and personality.

If he has planets or points in this sign, style matters. Don't mistake it for fashion, either. Instead, look for the way he presents himself, the way he approaches life, the way he launches himself into anything where he's on display. Other people prefer substance over style. The Leo type knows that style can be the substance too. Why do anything unless you're going to do it in a way that increases his/your/our lust for life, all round? The Leo type believes that a sense of occasion is what separates us from the aardvarks, and he's probably right.

He has a romantic soul. The Fifth House, the natural home of Leo, is about flirtation, courtship and all the rituals involved in dating and relating. It's the fun part of commitment; the Jane Austen part. Whatever ultimately comes of your time together, you'll never forget the dance if someone with Leo planets or points is your partner.

Does he have Leo Rising? A lot of them look like Shakespearean kings or princes. Is it the hair, the jawline or the beard? No matter if they have masses of curls – or even a shiny bald head – they still manage to look impressive. All of them have secret hair issues. All of them are good at organising and directing too. Leo Rising can take any loose gathering of people, no matter how random and chaotic, and pull it into shape.

HIS VIRGO SIDE

If his Sun, Moon, Mercury, Venus, Mars and/or Rising Sign is in Virgo, then this sign will be a big part of his personality. Is the Midheaven there too? Check at www.astro.com.

Now, here's a man who never diverts from the script. His best man speeches get run through spellcheck and rehearsed with every comma and full stop in place. If he has more than one planet in Virgo, then his penchant for details may find its way into his career as well, and checking facts or figures may become a way of life.

Does he have an overload of Virgo planets and points? Then his bookcase will be filed alphabetically, by subject matter or possibly with the Dewey Decimal System. His CD collection will similarly look like a BBC Radio archivist has just moved in and taken over. Does he have planets in Cancer as well? Then the contents of his fridge has a profound influence on his emotional state, and he will never respond sexually unless the restaurant is right.

Even if only 20 per cent of him is Virgo, you'll notice an incredible sense of duty and service to other people. If he ends up as the boss, he'll still always be driven to do the right thing by others – as perfectly as possible too.

The Virgo type knows that details matter in a modern man's wardrobe. It's the little horseshoes on the ties, the width of the pinstripe or the invisible stitching on a hem that concerns him most. He judges furniture and art on the same basis. It's the small things that matter – like the precise amount of sheen on a Le Corbusier chair, or the fine lines on a limited-edition print.

He loves service – both receiving it (take him to Claridge's and he'll think he's in an episode of *Jeeves and Wooster*) and giving it (he can be unbelievably attentive in bed). He understands the concept of service better than anyone else too – even if he has just one planet or point in Virgo.

This man also makes a natural wordsmith, if the rest of his

horoscope agrees, and what he says or writes will be famously pointed and precise. Also picky, pedantic and perfectly polished. All Virgo types have opinions about music, books, films or art. They care about a weak chorus, an unconvincing ending, a boom in shot, or a stain on a Monet.

They are all natural critics, and if you ask them what they think of your favourite band, they will tell you. In great detail. Pedantically and mercilessly, to the point where you have to beat them around the head with a rolling pin.

He's funny about cigarettes and smoking – either clinging to his bad nicotine habit with the same tenacity that other people have for brushing their teeth, or waging a one-man campaign against dirty ashtrays and passive smoking. Men with Virgo planets can never take or leave smoking – they're practically political about their right to do it, or their right to get up and walk out if *you* do it.

He takes comfort in his routines too, be it an hour on the treadmill before work, a morning meditation session or a daily love affair with a sausage roll and a jam doughnut. It's all part of the daily ritual, and the daily ritual *matters*. Nobody else is quite as disgruntled if his Salute to the Sun is interrupted in the mornings. Nobody else fusses quite as much if his breakfast bong is taken away. None of them can ever forget they have bodies, and they either worship them like sacred temples or trash them like garbage dumps and then become overemotional when they read family medical encyclopaedias.

He needs his rituals, and by his twenties will decide if they're going to involve class A drugs and a reliable dealer, a chakra-balancing session in the morning and an Ayurvedic massage in the evening or a bottle of Evian a day and a pump session at the gym. Everything for a Virgo type comes back to how he *feels* – and he usually means physically.

It's the details that make him feel at home. When he looks around his flat or house, he can understand why William Morris needed to create such convoluted curtains, and why Frank Lloyd

Wright's woodwork looks like it was designed with a tape measure. He responds well to the subtle clinking of temple bells or a bird on the window. It's the little things that work best for him.

He shudders when television quizmasters let their guests get away with sloppy answers, and reaches for the encyclopaedia to check the spelling of Mississippi, or the sports reference books for the exact date of Donald Bradman's last appearance at the crease. Anally retentive? Absolutely. They put Post-it notes on their Post-it notes, and they run a highlighter pen through the TV guide.

He may well believe that the grass is always greener on the other side of the septic tank if he has planets or points in this sign. Mercury, his ruling planet, gives him an analytical and critical streak that can make it hard for him to ever feel completely content. Wanting what (or who) isn't available can be a classic Virgo dilemma.

What he needs to understand is this: the reason another house/job/lover/whatever looks so desirable – particularly in comparison with his own picked-over existence – is because it hasn't been picked over. Nor has it been scrutinised, pulled apart, dissected and then shoved under a microscope! Virgo types who believe happiness is always somewhere else need to bust their own perfectionist myths – particularly if the vision of loveliness or happiness they see elsewhere is far off, out of focus or lit by Hollywood. Does he have major Contentment Issues? Then he needs to understand exactly why it's the *unexamined* jobs, lifestyles or relationships that are so appealing. Could it (possibly, do you think) have something to do with the fact that they're, um, unexamined? Or even . . . fictional?

He is hardworking and excels in any area of life where progress is guaranteed if you just keep at it. He does well in a role where everything depends on practice. Virgo types are put on the planet to show the rest of us how beautiful a well-oiled machine can actually be. This is why so many of them instinctively feel at home in a gym, playing sport or committing themselves to music, chess or Latin – just about anywhere, basically, where manhood is defined by the ability to put in the hours. Hours turn into days, days turn into weeks and weeks turn into his entire life – but the Virgo type seldom feels fulfilled unless he finds a job or passion that requires endless amounts of time.

He has a strong sense of duty, and understands what his role is in the scheme of things. Virgo is associated with the Sixth House in astrology, which symbolises work, effort and service. For this reason, he has a different definition of success to most people. It's genuinely not about coming first or being at the top for this man. It's actually about the process of *working at it*.

Even if his Virgo side only constitutes 20 per cent of his personality, you'll notice the way he can slot neatly into a system. He may be the boss or he may be the reserve player, but he respects the fact that everyone has to have their place, their function and their role. Even the captain serves his team. Even the person on the bench, left behind to cut up oranges, has a duty to perform.

He understands that only individual commitment makes anything work – no matter whether it's a large corporation or an entire civilisation. For this reason, the Virgo type tends to function well as part of a team or a group. Other parts of his horoscope may pull him in the other direction, but if he has planets or points in Virgo, there is definitely something about him which is pure cog-in-the-wheel – even if he's actually driving the machine at the same time.

Virgo types are typically extremely sensitive to the idea that they may be letting themselves or someone else down. If this man feels that he hasn't put the work in, or that he's not dedicating himself, part of him dies a little. He needs to do his bit!

Does he have Virgo Rising? If his health is an embarrassment to him, he'll skip any mention of his body/lifestyle/gym/eating preferences/drinking habits altogether. Lots of them find their illness, allergies, delicate constitution or medical condition is the first thing others notice about them – and the first thing they see when they look in the mirror. The other kind of Virgo Rising bloke is far more common. This one goes on (and on) about his dislike of smoking, his preference for non-GM foods, his loyalty to organic farmers, his food-intolerance recipe books, his passion for the gym (or yoga, or running, or daily swims) and . . . you get the picture. His body is his calling card.

HIS LIBRA SIDE

If his Sun, Moon, Mercury, Venus, Mars and/or Rising Sign is in Libra then this sign will be a big part of his personality. Is the Midheaven there too? Check at www.astro.com.

Does he have Venus in Libra? Line up the hair products on the bathroom shelves and build an extra wardrobe. Equality really matters to him too – no matter if it's based on race, class, sexuality, gender or age. Whatever his horoscope looks like, if he has one or more planets or points in Libra, then you can expect his side of the wardrobe to matter as much as yours, and possibly more.

Does he have Mars in Libra? Then he takes his revenge by looking better than you – it's good grooming used as a weapon. He is also capable of charming his enemies to death, so beware the meaningful, broad smile. To understand what it's like to be attacked by a Mars in Libra man, imagine that Roger Moore is facing you in a tuxedo in a scene from a James Bond film. You'll soon appreciate how easy it is to be killed by lethal charm – and a well-cut white jacket.

With this Mars sign, energy is well suited to partnerships – personal or professional. If you're really lucky, you'll get to play Jimmy Page to his Robert Plant, or Mel Smith to his Griff Rhys-Jones.

Art is a very good outlet for a man with Libra planets. Painting – or even just wandering around the nearest art gallery – can help him to take the strain. He needs the kind of art, photography, design, fashion, art direction or architecture that he can develop a lifelong relationship with. If the rest of his chart agrees, he may even develop his love for aesthetics into a career or calling. Don't give him a website out of a box; he always wants to customise it. He gets make-up, too, when you're out shopping together, and he really does make a superb drag queen at fancy-dress parties.

Straight men with several planets in Libra spend an awful lot of time trying to convince other people that they're not gay. The gay men have a fantastic time, releasing their inner Sebastian Flyte. Bring me my teddy bear! Bring me my white flannels!

A Libra type needs a permanent relationship in his life to feel truly secure, but if he doesn't have someone to eat toast with in the mornings, he'll create a professional or business niche that involves a partner – a genuine double act. He functions better at karaoke if you invite him to sing a duet with you, and he likes it when you play Nancy to his Sid, or Bosie to his Oscar. The single men wander around with ex-girlfriends in tow, just so they still have the illusion of a double act. Or they team up with best mates and get a blokey duet going in the pub. Even if Libra is only 20 per cent of him, he still needs two-by-two action.

He never really feels at home on the planet unless he is doing something to even things up – equality, gender, third-world or class issues may push his emotional buttons, or he may be powerfully affected by environmental campaigns. Some Libran types act on it, some don't, but they all end up in 2 a.m. arguments about *what's fair*. Typically, he's sensitive to 'isms' of all kinds, from racism to sexism.

Does your man have a touch of velvet trouser about him? Just look at this list of men with a little bit of lovely Libra: **John Lennon** – Sun and Mars in Libra; **Marc Bolan** (T-Rex) – Sun and Venus in Libra; **Melvyn Bragg** – Sun, Mercury and Venus in Libra; **Brian Connolly** (Sweet) – Sun and Mercury in Libra; **Julian Cope** – Sun, Moon and Mercury in Libra; **Bryan Ferry** –

Sun in Libra; Sting – Sun and Moon in Libra; **D.H. Lawrence** – Venus and Moon in Libra; **Bob Geldof** – Sun and Mercury in Libra; **Bruce Springsteen** – Sun, Moon and Mercury in Libra; **Ian Thorpe** – Sun, Mercury, Venus and Midheaven in Libra; **Tim Robbins** – Sun and Venus in Libra; **Alex James** (Blur) – Mars in Libra.

Who's the only Olympic champion to wear pearls? Super-Libran type Ian Thorpe. In the days when I was a music journalist, I interviewed Bob Geldof about all sorts of things: his friendship with Prince Charles, his relationship with the Boomtown Rats, his life since Live Aid. Only one thing actually ate up twenty passionate minutes on the tape recorder, though, and that was our conversation about his priceless collection of punk clothing, donated to the Victoria and Albert Museum in London.

This is Julian Cope, another super-Libran, speaking to *The Face* in November 1981: 'My main plan is to get my hair cut really short, and just let my beard grow a bit. And get away from the pretty-pretty image.' And here's Alex James, from Blur, also talking to *The Face*: 'I always wanted to spend my twenties drunk and ridiculous, being an alcoholic idiot–genius who lived in Soho. But it's just not so elegant when you get older and start looking like a potato. Vanity's my saving grace, definitely.' Hair matters. Shoes matter. And yes, *carpets* matter as well. When they turn up to weddings, they look as if they've researched their look for weeks. And – oh my God! – they probably have.

Libran types tend to be female friendly. 'What I think I've learned about maturity for a man,' Sting told Q magazine halfway through his career, 'is that one route is to become Rambo or Chuck Norris, and the other is to become more feminine, to accept that part of your psychological make-up is from your mother.'

There is also a strange kink in the destiny of Venus/Libra that means they will spend large amounts of time in the company of females. They may exclusively have daughters, teach at a girls' school or work in the fashion business, for example. Or they may end up with social lives or careers where large gatherings of females dominate.

Christopher Reeve was a super-Libran/Venusian. And he was also Superman, of course, but not as boys in the 1950s knew him. 'By the late 1970s the masculine image had changed,' he wrote in his autobiography *Still Me*. 'People expected marriage to be a genuine partnership. Now it was acceptable for a man to show gentleness and vulnerability. It was even admirable for him to cook dinner, change diapers, and stay home with the kids. I felt that the new Superman ought to reflect that contemporary male image.'

Venus and Libra are often associated with peace, as opposed to war, but this isn't necessarily true. History shows that several prominent Venus/Libra types have been prepared to fight if they feel a situation is unfair enough. They're into equality, not necessarily peace at any price.

Fairness motivates them more than anything else. The Libran scales are a brilliant, timeless symbol of this need for perfect balance. Libran-influenced men commonly become involved in political or humanitarian causes because they feel the scales in some situation have become desperately lopsided. Some of them are into gender equality, others are dedicated to the environment, anti-racism, the anti-war movement or animal rights; all of them start twitching when they see injustice. Sting, Tim Robbins and Bob Geldof are well known for their commitment to the developing world and global harmony, as was John Lennon. But don't forget that Oliver North is a Libran too. It isn't always peace that's the issue, but primarily a vision of justice.

Bob Geldof became famous for Live Aid, Band Aid and Live 8. In Great Britain, he has recently made the headlines again for his stand against the iniquities of family law. He told *Word* magazine in 2003, 'The very language of family law is against men . . . It's not a gender-neutral law, even though it pretends to be.' This inequality is his new big issue.

The famous vacillation of Libra – an unwillingness to speak out and offend anyone, lest the scales be unbalanced – can sometimes work against these men. Their instinct for fairness becomes suppressed just in case it results in dinner-party detonating arguments. A man born with a strong Libra/Venus theme in his chart who hasn't found a cause or a mission is missing the point, though. Ultimately, he wasn't put here to become popular; he was put here to correct imbalances and injustices, and the popularity part of the deal is just a tool to get things done.

Does he have Libra Rising? You'll be charmed. Whatever he's like on the inside (and remember, this may be the only Libra thing about him) there is a bit of kissy-kissy about this man. He knows how to do mwah-mwah, and he also knows how to behave at afternoon tea.

He may be wearing a suit when you first meet. If so, it will be beautifully cut. Only when you get inside his bathroom will you really discover the lengths to which he goes to to put his look together, though . . . Libra Rising organises his hair, his facial hair, and his ties in his own way.

It's not surprising, perhaps, to find out that he regards physical appearance as a kind of personality trait. He's got big opinions about blondes v redheads v brunettes too.

HIS SCORPIO SIDE

If his Sun, Moon, Mercury, Venus, Mars and/or Rising Sign is in Scorpio, then this sign will be a big part of his personality. Is the Midheaven there too? Check at www.astro.com.

His personality suits heavy metal, black comedy and Wagnerian opera – and it suits secrets, too, lots and lots of secrets. He doesn't have hobbies and interests, he has mad passions and consuming obsessions. If he has other planets in Scorpio as well, then his sexual tastes, fascinations and preferences will define his personality – even though you may be the only person who ever really gets to understand it.

He understands why John Cleese in *Fawlty Towers* yelling 'Don't mention the war!' to German tourists is funny. He is drawn to anything and anybody that goes where you're not supposed to. At various times in his life he'll be drawn to the occult or towards the off-limits aspects of sex, drugs and rock 'n' roll. He needs to duck in and out of the shadows occasionally – it restores his lust for life.

If he has more than one planet in Scorpio he may be a natural psychologist, and be compelled to examine aspects of human behaviour that make other people say 'Eurgh'. Alternatively, he may work in areas of the caring or medical professions where other people's dark bits – or even their private hell – is his nine-to-five domain.

He needs his music raw and emotional, and any song that begins 'La, la, la' makes him feel physically ill. He deals with relationship break-ups by reading poetry or listening to Jeff Buckley. By the way, it's not unusual for Venus in Scorpio men to find special resonance with artists, musicians and writers who died young or took their own lives. They don't find it creepy. These people just speak to them, that's all . . .

He craves emotional depth. Other people may snigger when The Bee Gees croon the question, 'How Deep is Your Love?' but a Scorpio type really, really *does* need to know. He likes a little mystery too. He always knows where the nearest haunted house is.

He is comfortable about dealing with the realities of death and dying, and doesn't turn away if people want to discuss the afterlife with him, or any of those other Scorpionic subjects that polite society usually ignores.

Take him to a fancy dress costumier and he'll always pick the devil outfit for a joke, but part of him also knows those horns are real. Some Scorpio types fight it, some give in – but all of them are well aware of their power-packed potential for sin.

Who flicks through Aubrey Beardsley catalogues until he

finds the bare-breasted bits? Who listens to Derek and Clive on his iPod on the train? El Scorpion.

He intuitively understands the machinations of power too. Take him to *Evita* and he'll probably find the plot awfully familiar. In fact, there may be moments when you suspect he could run his life like Argentina under the Perons, or the Mafia under the Godfather.

He is a survivor and may consciously – or unconsciously – be drawn to situations that push him almost beyond the point of no return, just so he can come back again. His phoenix-from-the-flames act may be a characteristic part of his personal and professional life. He can deal with AIDS, he can deal with suicide, he can deal with child sexual abuse – in short, he can deal with most of the stuff that makes other men turn pale.

If he has more than one planet in Scorpio, you'll swear that he has special powers. Look for an intense stare and a phenomenal amount of psychological – or even psychic – control. He is instinctively intrigued by spies, secrets, Roman scandals, ghosts and phantoms of all kinds, Ronnie and Reggie Kray – and, quite naturally, sex. He does not censor or edit his ideas, and they frequently concern subjects that other people find off-limits or appallingly taboo. Who ends up talking about Nazis, transvestites or the Crucifixion at a dinner party? The (drunk) Mercury in Scorpio male. Along with sex, the other two great Mars in Scorpio subjects are death and the occult. Who sits at the back of a spiritualist church with his jaw on the floor? A Mars in Scorpio man who has encountered mediumship for the first time.

If he has other planets in Scorpio, you may be dealing with a real player whose brain functions somewhere between Freud, Jung and Machiavelli. He'd sell his soul for total control, basically. He probably knows that absolute power corrupts absolutely, but that still won't stop him from trying to dominate his chosen industry or profession. He can be a regular Chairman Mao if you let him.

Is his Mars sign Scorpio? When he's on the attack or defence, he is nastier than Nick Cotton on *Eastenders*, or deadlier than an American werewolf in London.

I don't know if this is true, but I have been told that there is a relationship between the Mars in Scorpio man's need for power and his virility. When his professional control or his status plummets, so does his libido. Answers on the back of an envelope, please.

When I first became interested in astrology, the birth chart for Prince Charles made no sense at all. Prince Charles has the Sun and Mercury in Scorpio, and Pluto – the ruler of Scorpio – square the Sun. All this darkness in a chart suggests a weekend job with the Mafia or, at the very least, a life spent as Ozzy Osbourne's roadie. Scorpio and Pluto are about secrets, sex, death, taboo subjects and everything in life that is dark, intense, extreme – and usually hidden. Even if you wear a kilt and play the cello, though, if you have planets in this sign, you'll have to take a walk on the wild side eventually – and Prince Charles did.

If Pluto, the ruler of Scorpio, is making aspects (patterns) with other planets and points in your man's horoscope, he'll be even darker. Look at his horoscope at www.astro.com and if you see lots of lines stretching out from the Pluto symbol ♇ you'll know he's Scorpio in extremis . . . The aspects, by the way, are conjunctions, sextiles, squares, trines and oppositions.

The boys from the black stuff include: **Ozzy Osbourne** – Venus in Scorpio, Pluto trine Sun, square Venus; **Bon Scott** (AC/DC) – Moon in Scorpio, Pluto conjunct Mercury; **Lemmy** (Motörhead) – Midheaven in Scorpio, Pluto square Midheaven, trine Mercury; **Irvine Welsh** – Moon and Venus in Scorpio, Pluto trine Ascendant, square Moon; **Alastair Crowley** – Sun, Mercury and Ascendant in Scorpio, Pluto trine Mars; **Larry Flynt** – Sun, Venus and Mars in Scorpio, Pluto square Sun, Venus and Mars; **Prince Charles** – Sun and Mercury in Scorpio, Pluto square Sun, trine Mars; **Andy Partridge** (XTC) –

Sun and Mercury in Scorpio, Pluto square Sun and Mercury; **Marilyn Manson** – Mars in Scorpio, Pluto trine Mercury; **Bela Lugosi** – Mercury in Scorpio, Pluto trine Moon; **Henry Miller** – Moon and Mars in Scorpio, Pluto trine Venus; **Nostradamus** – Moon in Scorpio, Pluto sextile Venus; **Robert Louis Stevenson** – Sun, Mercury and Mars in Scorpio, Pluto trine Venus.

Andy Partridge is the heavily Pluto/Scorpio-influenced singer and songwriter for cult band XTC. According to *Mojo* magazine, his first idea for the cover of the XTC album *Skylarking* was a close-up of male and female pubic hair intertwined with flowers. The retailers didn't like it.

Sometimes it's sex, sometimes it's the occult, sometimes it's other off-limits stuff that does it for them. In his autobiography *White Line Fever*, Scorpio type Lemmy recounts how in 1975, Motörhead used a recording from Germany of marching feet and people yelling '*Sieg Heil!*' as their concert intro tape.

Near-death experiences and huge life crises (almost like little deaths) are common in the lives of strongly Scorpio types. They 'die' and are reborn – often after a professional, personal or health crisis. Linda Goodman, writing in *Sun Signs* in 1968, noted that Sun Sign Scorpios are associated with resurrection from the grave. 'One of the strangest patterns in astrology is the death of a relative in the family within the year before or the year after the birth of a Scorpio,' she writes. 'And when a Scorpio dies, there will be a birth in the family within the year before or the year after.' 'Pluto burns through the garbage. What you have left to work with is what you are,' says astrologer Debbi Kempton-Smith in *Secrets from a Stargazer's Notebook*.

Scorpio/Pluto types can be obsessive too. They can be self-obsessed (don't go there!) or manic about lovers, hobbies or jobs. Some astrologers associate this sign with a hypnotic stare. I haven't found that to be the case, but they do have a particular kind of energy that you will be very familiar with if you have ever haltingly taken a cup of tea to the door of the garden shed or their study while they are absorbed.

Does he have Scorpio Rising? The vibe is secretive, intense, powerful and controlled. The body language and the eyes say 'Impenetrable'. He's a little bit Mr Darcy, he's a little bit Heathcliff, he's a lot Iago. The rest of the chart will reveal if it's really *him*, though.

HIS SAGITTARIUS SIDE

If his Sun, Moon, Mercury, Venus, Mars and/or Rising Sign is in Sagittarius, then this sign will be a big part of his personality. Is the Midheaven there too? Check at www.astro.com.

What's out there in Wonderland, or beyond the looking glass? The man with planets or points in Sagittarius really needs to know. He's a daytripper, even if it all takes place in his imagination. He needs travel – or astral travel – and the more planets he has in Sagittarius, the more obvious it will be.

At least 20 per cent of his personality is Sagittarian if he has Mars placed here. He may be a lifelong student of life or informal teacher of life lessons to others – or spend half his time exploring libraries or the Internet for big ideas.

If he can't find the time and money to engage in global roaming, he'll opt for weekend adventures closer to home. A lot of them are hikers, mountaineers, kayakers and bushwalkers. They're all closet Jack Kerouacs. His soul is global. He thinks in world terms, not the end of the street.

Men with planets and/or points in Sagittarius are funny when they try, but often funnier when they don't. Peter Cook had a Sagittarian signature in his chart. 'Peter was the funniest man in the world,' said Eric Idle, after Peter Cook's death, 'and all funny people know that. When he died he was universally mourned by all generations of comedians.' (Quoted in *Something Like Fire* by Lin Cook.)

Men born with personal planets and points in Sagittarius

know how to exaggerate. Peter Cook created characters who were hilariously over-the-top, from the grotty E. L. Wisty in his raincoat to Arthur Streeb-Greebling, a whisky-soaked colonel. Sagittarius is ruled by Jupiter, the planet ruling expansion and size. A lot of comedy is based on inflating human foibles and failings, so that they become larger than life and thus funnier; Barry Humphries, born with Sagittarius on the Midheaven, has it too. Dame Edna Everage is over-the-top in every way.

The Sagittarian side of a man's personality can express itself through arm-waving, dramatic gestures, brilliant comic writing, the exaggeration of amusing character traits, face-pulling, voice-manipulating or expert cartooning. Not all of them use it, but all of them have it, nonetheless. Think of Sagittarius-influenced Oscar Wilde's Lady Bracknell – she's every Victorian grand dame he'd ever met, inflated to ridiculous proportions. 'A hand-baaaaag?' When Sag types tell stories, they tend to do voices.

Monty Python's Flying Circus, which Michael Palin's diary records was named on a day when Mars was in Sagittarius (it has Gemini influences too), includes demented British housewives (pepper-pot women), ridiculously pompous heroic knights and giant feet – just for starters.

Clowns are very Sagittarian. They have exaggerated smiling or sad mouths, enormous hair, huge feet and over-the-top clothes. Here's an interesting point about professionally funny Sagittarian types: they know that anything larger than life is amusing, so they often pair themselves with people who are much taller/bigger or shorter/smaller. It plays up the difference and it makes the whole act work.

Men with planets and points in Sagittarius include: **Graham Chapman** (*Monty Python*) – Venus and Mars in Sagittarius; **Woody Allen** – Sun and Mercury in Sagittarius; **Oscar Wilde** – Mars in Sagittarius; **Lenny Bruce** – Ascendant in Sagittarius, Venus in Sagittarius; **Ronnie Corbett** – Sun and Mercury in Sagittarius; **Kenny Everett** – Sun and Mercury in Sagittarius; **Benny Hill** – Mars and Midheaven in Sagittarius; **David Jason**

– Sagittarius Rising Sign, Sagittarius Moon; **Brian Rix** – Mars and Midheaven in Sagittarius; **Ernie Wise** – Sun and Mercury in Sagittarius; **Evelyn Waugh** – Mars in Sagittarius; **Barry Humphries** – Midheaven in Sagittarius; **Terry Gilliam** – Sun in Sagittarius; **Peter Cook** – Mercury in Sagittarius; **Alan Alda** – Venus in Sagittarius; **Richard Wilson** (*One Foot in the Grave*) – Midheaven in Sagittarius; and **Harry Secombe** – Moon in Sagittarius.

Does he have planets in Gemini too? That's the other funny-man sign. Prepare to be permanently amused, if this is the case (and look at the Gemini section too, if you haven't already done so). Gemini types with a Sagittarius signature include **Ben Elton** – Sagittarius Rising Sign; **Billy Connolly** – Sun and Venus in Sagittarius; **Harry Enfield** – Moon in Sagittarius; **Larry David** – Moon in Sagittarius; **Spike Milligan** – Midheaven in Sagittarius; **Julian Clary** – Sagittarius Rising Sign; **Walt Disney** – Sun in Sagittarius; **Noel Coward** – Sun and Mercury in Sagittarius; **Ronnie Barker** – Sagittarius Rising Sign; and **Victor Borge** – Venus in Sagittarius.

Jupiter is the planet of growth and development, and it rules Sagittarius. It is natural for this man to constantly want to stretch himself and test the limits of everything that is familiar. Jupiter is also the planet of luck. People who know Sagittarian types well will typically tell you that they seem to be divinely protected. No matter how far they wander off the beaten track – and how many risks are involved – people with planets in Sagittarius always seem to have something, or someone, looking after them.

He typically has issues around freedom and restriction, independence and control, space and limits. This can be obvious from childhood (the day he escapes from his playpen is the day his mother knows she has given birth to a Sagittarian type) or even in middlescence, when the man with planets or points in Sagittarius suddenly decides he wants to spend his weekends wandering or pushing the envelope of what's acceptable or 'possible'.

Is the wanderlust sexual? Sometimes. But this man is just as capable of fidelity and long-term commitment if he has a partner who will let him explore – and escape – in other ways. He does need a lot of room to move, though. So it stands to reason that if your life together consists of you saying 'No', 'That's off limits' and 'For God's sake, come back here!' he will eventually snap under the strain and is likely to make a break for freedom.

Men with Sagittarian planets want to explore their options and push the boundaries so they can see first-hand what is out there. Their lives are typically spent experimenting with the fences that are around them – socially, geographically, professionally, sexually or personally. Can you stop him from wandering off? Not really. It's in his astrological DNA to want to roam. Does he push his luck? Yes, that is part of his psychological make-up as well. He can also push other people too far – particularly if these are the same people who are trying to keep him where they want him.

Even those Sagittarian types who live within the limits set up by other people – a certain kind of job, lifestyle, relationship or set of rules – are always gazing off into middle distance at life's other limitless possibilities.

He typically prefers to make up his own mind about where he should and shouldn't push the boundaries. At heart, he understands that life is a gamble, and unless you take your chances with it, you'll never know. In the process, Sagittarian types often change the rules of the game for the rest of us. Their desire for what is unexplored, new, uncovered, foreign, unfamiliar or apparently off limits teaches others where the boundaries really are.

The more they can take in – or the more they can have access to – the more a Sagittarian type feels at home in the world. He always sees the big picture, which is why he is so reluctant to stay hemmed in by other people's rules, regulations and expectations. He has an interesting relationship with authority figures for this reason, and it usually begins with his parents. Are they right or wrong? Do they know what's best for him, or are they just cramping his style? Who said Keep Off the Grass, and why? Who said he wasn't allowed to go There, wherever There happens to be?

It's his karma to be endlessly positive. And he may even find a career where everything depends on his relentless optimism. Men with Sagittarian planets and points are born hopeful. No matter how black a situation looks – no matter how much fear or pain is involved – this man has faith with a capital F. He is the living embodiment of the idea that where there is life, there is hope. Look for a smile that convinces and uplifts. Men with planets or points in this sign only have to beam your way and you instantly get the impression that everything's going to be okay. Even if he fails at his task, it's unlikely to stop him. He needs you to see that there are Reasons to be Cheerful. Even if there aren't.

Does he always succeed in sending people away smiling? Of course not. Sometimes his optimism or dedication to humanity's need for light relief is totally unjustified, and bleak reality will have a way of winning. This never stops him, however. And it doesn't stop people from placing their hope and trust in him, either. Most Sag types know that their job on this planet is to make things better. Always Look on the Bright Side of Life? Why not?

Does he have Sagittarius Rising? A reassuring, remarkably convincing smile will be a big part of his package. So will a fixation with the next place he wants to explore – locally or globally – or a massive emotional attachment to a place he's just come back from.

HIS CAPRICORN SIDE

If his Sun, Moon, Mercury, Venus, Mars and/or Rising Sign is in Capricorn, then this sign will be a big part of his personality. Is the Midheaven there too? Check at www.astro.com.

He needs to climb, socially or professionally, and doesn't mind waiting for success. It means more if he started life in a biscuit factory and ends up signing a business deal worth millions. If he has a number of planets in Capricorn, then his upward trajectory (along with his knack of hanging around with useful talents or connections) may be quite striking.

He knows that Rome wasn't built in a day, and Arnold Schwarzenegger didn't get a body like that in ten minutes, either. You too can start life as a bricklayer and end up as the prime minister, if you have this as your Moon sign.

If it's his Mercury sign, then he knows that life is all about being on the make and on the move, and if he hasn't started his upward trajectory by the age of twenty-nine, he worries that he's too late. If he has Mars in Capricorn, he's socially and professionally ambitious and always knows how to scale the next rung of the ladder. He climbs and he waits, and he climbs and he waits – until he makes it. This is the man who always has an exit strategy and a long-term plan. He never signs a contract without calculating how it's going to affect his life ten years from now.

With Mercury in Capricorn, he speaks with impressive authority and when required can make almost anything sound terribly, terribly serious. Nobody has more gravitas when he sings in the shower. A lot of men with this Mercury sign find their lives change during puberty as their voices break and they start to sound like real men for the first time. Watch them during an argument – you can bet money on the fact that they'll start booming in a baritone if they need a little respect. He can be a negative thinker – too cautious about life, and too motivated by fear. Depression can be the result, unless he trains himself to develop different mental patterns and lose his inner Eeyore.

If he has any planet or point in Capricorn, he will play the part of mentor, and mentored, throughout his life. Capricorn types need someone to look up to as they climb up the social or professional ladder, but they are also authority figures for others – guides, elders or teachers – along the path.

Capricorn is ruled by Saturn, the planet of responsibility. Sometimes it's his age, sometimes it's his experience, sometimes it's just his position at any given time, but the Capricorn type will always find himself taking responsibility for people who are either on the first rung of a ladder or taking their first baby steps into a new phase of life.

Relationships with people who are younger or greener are typical. So is a job or a weekend interest where the Capricorn type is required to carry other people on their shoulders. There is usually a burden involved. It may be practical (time or money) or psychological (the feeling of always having to look after others). Even if he has just one point or planet in Capricorn, though, it's part of his karma and it usually feels quite natural to him.

The Capricorn type is fated to be there when people leave the nest or learn the ropes in some way. They are often a magnet for anyone with their L-plates on, which often explains the slightly hunched look some of them get in their middle years – that's what happens when you carry other people too far for too long!

It's in his interest to set boundaries and make rules. And once he does this, life becomes far more manageable. This is particularly true in any professional or personal relationship where it's clear he's playing Big Daddy. If he doesn't set limits, then nobody else will. And unless the Capricorn type does this properly, he may well find that he is shouldering too much (or just putting up with too much!)

He can be a rock and make a lasting difference to the lives of his partners, kids, colleagues, students or other dependents. For his own sanity, though, the Capricorn type has to be a realist and set firm boundaries. For many people in his life, he is the reality check. He is often the gateway to maturity for others, because he lets them know what's what in a way that other signs cannot.

He knows life is hard and that the real world can be an

unforgiving place. All the more reason, then, to try and be firm with people so they can do all their learning in a safe place before they have to be released into life Out There. The Capricorn type feels a particularly strong sense of this with his own children, but also with anyone (or anything) who is dependent on him. The process can be painful but also deeply satisfying for him, because once the life lessons are over, he can walk away knowing he has played his part.

Feeling older and wiser makes him feel at home in his own skin, which is why so many men with a Capricorn chart signature end up with private lives, family relationships or professional set-ups where they have to help others climb to where they need to be. Are any of these relationships co-dependent? Frequently. But only for a time, because even Capricorn types have to let go eventually – and those they have mentored have to move on.

The irony for Capricorn is that those he takes on board also have to teach him something about the real world too. Tempting though it may be for both parties to stay locked in a parent–child connection, life has a funny way of breaking the pattern and waking everyone up. Capricorn types who get lost in the co-dependency of a friendship, relationship, working connection or parent–child relationship are missing the point. Hard though it is, they have to accept that the special chemistry they have with someone is not the whole story. Rather, it's a necessary part of a learning process that has to take place.

Is it good for younger, less experienced or more dependent people to lean on the Capricorn type? For a time – until they learn what they need to know. Sometimes, ironically, what they need to know most is independence. All of which takes a certain amount of burden from the Capricorn type's shoulders, but it also confronts him with reality in quite a different way. He's drawn to people who want to move onwards and upwards. But he also needs to understand that everyone grows up and moves on, be they child, lover or employee.

In his personal life, as well as his professional life, he needs to reconcile his need to be boss with his need to be wise. Sometimes what he does in the name of his own authority is unwise, and sometimes his more enlightened moves can actually undermine his place at the top. Sorting out this inner conflict can teach him a lot about himself.

The conflict can also be played out between himself and other people. The Capricorn type may well find himself laying down the law in the face of opposition from other people who claim to know more than he does – or at least to know what's true.

Alternatively, it may be the Capricorn type who is arguing on the side of wisdom while he is confronted with someone else who is an ultimate authority figure – a boss, perhaps, or his father, or even sections of the establishment. Who knows best? Who knows more? Who's in charge? Do they deserve to be in charge? Why are they in charge? Questions like this follow the Capricorn type around for a lifetime.

Life has a funny way of forcing wisdom onto Capricorn, even if he thinks he is successfully running the show – or that he naturally has the upper hand. Frequently, the people who enlighten him are those who represent truth in some way, or a wake-up call. Much as the Capricorn type would like to keep on running the show according to prescribed ideas or the usual rules, others often have their own ideas about showing him the light.

His biggest life lesson is this: it's possible to manage a situation by relying on knowledge, wisdom and enlightenment rather than by heavying other people. This is the twin message of Saturn, the ruler of Capricorn. It offers this man a choice between two kinds of authority, and at various points in his life he will find himself at a crossroads where he must decide to be genuinely right . . . or just in charge.

It's in his nature to look up to people, from childhood through to old age. Capricorn is associated with the Tenth House in astrology, which describes the process of climbing higher by hitching a ride on the shoulders of giants. For this reason, the Capricorn type needs to choose his mentors carefully. Fathers and father figures are associated with Saturn, the ruler of this sign – but men with planets or points in Capricorn can also find female guides and mentors too. In all cases, it's important that the person (or philosophy, or company) who is being elevated in his eyes is worthy of that position. Will he genuinely be taught by his mentors, or has he just found Donald Duck as a role model? The smart ones take their time before deciding if someone really is a suitable rock to lean on.

Does he have Capricorn Rising? He always seems grounded, down to earth and sensible – even when he's trying to be really weird and interesting. Whatever his Sun, Moon, Mercury, Venus and/or Mars sign, Capricorn Rising always appears to have his feet solidly planted on the ground. He seems ambitious too. He either wants to make it to the top or he's already on his way. This one seems awfully serious. When his face is relaxed, it tends to look slightly grim. On the plus side, he often uses this deadpan expression to make his jokes funnier. As they age, they can become craggy – but in a sexy Easter-Island-statue way!

HIS AQUARIUS SIDE

If his Sun, Moon, Mercury, Venus, Mars and/or Rising Sign is in Aquarius then this sign will be a big part of his personality. Is the Midheaven there too? Check at www.astro.com.

He's slightly Mork from Ork, this man, and he may sleep upside down in a wardrobe, drink with his finger or be seen in public wearing rainbow-striped suspenders. Prepare yourself. He's an absolute original. He poses the questions that everybody else is secretly thinking but nobody is brave enough to ask, and can occasionally leave everyone at the dinner table with their jaws on the floor. No matter what his age and generation, he is the quintessential sixties thinker, and in his mind it's always 1969 and the revolution is just around the corner.

He doesn't mind if the truth is shocking – he'd rather have honesty à la Jerry Springer than be stuck with a lot of fake opinions and polite dinner-party chat. If he has lots of points or planets in Aquarius, he may become well known for his eccentric streak, which usually reveals itself in the way he dresses or the way he speaks – or just his lifestyle.

Heavily Aquarian males are uniformly goony, loony or potty, so prepare yourself before you decide to take your clothes off. If he turns up with an identical twin and they're both naked *and* wearing glasses, you have some fast thinking to do. What if the rest of his chart is very different? Then his inner weirdness will only leak out periodically, but it never really goes away.

He has a head like a computer – but it's the kind of computer that's ahead of its time. He may even speak Venusian. If you give him a shed, a kettle and enough time to himself, he may emerge later with soot all over his face and the kind of home-made invention that makes Steve Jobs, Benjamin Franklin and Thomas Edison look like slow learners.

He does well in a group and understands why miracles happen through teamwork – no matter whether it's the Boy Scouts, a Buddhist monastery or the St Kilda Football Club.

Is his Venus sign Aquarius? His fantasy lover is probably one of Doctor Who's assistants – or he may even be genuinely aroused by the idea of a wild night with K9, the doctor's robotic dog. Whatever his Venus sign, as you read this the Aquarian type is already moving on from his love affair with the iPod to the next big thing. He is easily seduced by new technology and the cutting edge of computers, the New Age, astronomy or science.

When faced with a 'normal' relationship or a walk on the wild side, he'll take the walk on the wild side every time. He's drawn to eccentric, independent women with strong feminist views – either as friends or as lovers – and there are plenty of

Mad Hatters in his address book. Are you odd enough to be in Robert Ripley's Odditorium? Believe it or not, you're exactly the kind of woman the Aquarian man feels compelled by – the noticeably spaced out, odd, free-spirited or genuinely loopy.

He has radical views and alternative ideas about the world, and not everybody understands. He doesn't care. He needs the freedom to be as far-out as he likes, even if he sometimes gets drunk at dinner parties and shocks people with his *real* opinions on things. Part of him understands why Tony Blair had to build that Millennium Dome. He needs the weird and the wonderful. It comforts him. It's part of his induction into society, also, to be rejected by other people for being too radical. This is always a turning point for him, and helps define his personality for the rest of his life.

In his book *A Brief History of Time: A Reader's Companion*, Stephen Hawking wrote, 'I was born on January the 8th 1942, exactly three hundred years after the death of Galileo. However, I estimate that about two hundred thousand other babies were also born on that day. I don't know whether any of them were later interested in astronomy.' Well, maybe not. But, nevertheless, on January 8 1942 all babies being born (including tiny Stephen) had Venus in unusual, independent Aquarius. He's a Capricorn, but he's an Aquarian type. Professor Hawking has aspects (patterns) in his horoscope that involve Uranus too. Uranus is the ruler of Aquarius. It doubles the dose of brilliance and eccentricity. If your man has planets and/or points in Aquarius, calculate his chart at www.astro.com and see if there are lots of lines stretching across the horoscope wheel from the Uranus symbol, which looks like this: ♅.

Here are some famous Aquarian/Uranian types: **Lord Byron** – Venus in Aquarius, Uranus opposite Moon and Sun; **Alice Cooper** – Sun in Aquarius, Uranus opposite Moon and trine Sun; **Tom Baker** (*Doctor Who*) – Venus and Mars in Aquarius, Uranus sextile both; **Doctor Who** (the TV show) – Moon in Aquarius, Uranus square Sun and Mercury; **Billy Bragg** –

Venus in Aquarius, Uranus opposite Venus and trine Moon; **Gyles Brandreth** – Moon and Mercury in Aquarius, Uranus trine both; **Quentin Crisp** – Moon in Aquarius, Uranus sextile Mars; **Graeme Garden** – Venus in Aquarius, Uranus trine Venus; **Russell Grant** – Sun and Moon in Aquarius, Uranus trine Venus and Mars; **Eddie Izzard** – Sun, Venus, Mercury, Mars in Aquarius, Uranus opposite Venus; **Derek Jarman** – Sun, Venus, Mercury in Aquarius, Uranus square Mercury; **Elton John** – Venus in Aquarius, Uranus trine Venus and square Mercury; **Will Young** – Sun and Mars in Aquarius, Uranus sextile Mercury; **Bob Downe** – Sun and Mercury in Aquarius, Uranus opposite Sun; **Holly Johnson** – Sun in Aquarius, Uranus opposite Sun; **Gary Numan** – Venus in Aquarius, Uranus opposite Venus, Uranus square Moon; **Arthur Conan Doyle** – Moon and Midheaven in Aquarius, Uranus opposite Sun; **Douglas Adams** – Venus in Aquarius, Uranus square Mercury and trine Mars; **Jules Verne** – Midheaven, Sun and Mercury in Aquarius, Uranus sextile Mars; **Jean Paul Sartre** – Moon in Aquarius, Uranus square Midheaven; **Terry Jones** – Sun, Mercury, Venus in Aquarius, Uranus square Mercury; **Rik Mayall** – Venus in Aquarius, Uranus opposite Venus and sextile Moon; **Barry Humphries** – Sun and Venus in Aquarius, Uranus sextile Sun; **Peter Gabriel** – Sun and Venus in Aquarius, Uranus sextile Midheaven; **Jack Kerouac** – Mercury in Aquarius, Uranus square Midheaven and Mars; **Steve Jobs** – Mercury in Aquarius, Uranus opposite Venus; **Leonardo da Vinci** – Mars in Aquarius, Uranus sextile Venus; **H.G. Wells** – Moon in Aquarius, Ascendant in Aquarius, Uranus conjunct Mars.

Quite a lot of the men on this list surprise or even shock other people with their sexuality. They have private lives that, once they are in the public domain, *progress* things. They introduce new ideas about how to date, mate and relate – and with whom. Eddie Izzard describes himself as a male lesbian. Quentin Crisp, Derek Jarman, Elton John, Will Young, Leonardo da Vinci and Holly Johnson were, or are, famously gay. Billy Bragg – a strong Aquarian/Uranian type – once wrote a song called 'Sexuality' (also known at the time as 'Having a Shag with Billy Bragg'!) that became the safe-sex anthem.

I have known Aquarian/Uranians who are celibate, which shocks many of their friends. I have also known some of them to develop relationships with hookers who let them do the cleaning (in their underpants). Others are like camels: they have one-night stands and then stagger back into the desert for another six months. Then there are those who live in a separate home to their wife and they commute when they need the company.

In 1989, Q magazine interviewed super-Aquarian muso Peter Gabriel about the end of his marriage. According to the report, Gabriel managed this transition by (among other things) yoga, hanging upside down from 'gravity boots' and immersing himself in a samadhi flotation tank (a form of sensory deprivation he found restful). Men with Aquarian/Uranian influence in their charts do it in their own sweet, weird way, whether it's breaking up or falling in love.

Notice something else? An awful lot of them are into science or science fiction, or new technology or cutting-edge ideas. Russell Grant is an astrologer. Professor Hawking is an astronomer. Edwin 'Buzz' Aldrin, another Aquarian type, was an astronaut. 'Gus' Grissom, Jules Verne, Kurt Vonnegut and Philip K. Dick are Aquarian types too. It's the Doctor Who sign. Prepare yourself for sex with a timelord.

Behind all this stargazing and galaxy-inspecting, though, there is simply a need to know the truth. Space, if you think about it, is still the last great mystery. If we are to know the whole truth and nothing but the truth about this life then we need to understand life up there and out there too. The ocean is spoken for. For Aquarian/Uranians, only the cosmos will do.

Does he have Aquarius Rising? He'll present himself as a free spirit and, if you're really lucky, he'll reveal how one of his school reports or employer assessments described him as socially maladjusted. He seems mad, exciting, unpredictable and unusual. He has no interest in copying what everyone else is doing or fitting in for a quiet life. At least, that's the way it seems on the surface.

HIS PISCES SIDE

If his Sun, Moon, Mercury, Venus, Mars and/or Rising Sign is in Pisces then this sign will be a big part of his personality. Is the Midheaven there too? Check at www.astro.com.

His personal or professional life has to leave space for his sensitivity and imagination, or he feels astonishingly empty and unfulfilled. Remember, you are in the company of the original Lord of the Rings here – or the little boy who always wanted to dress up as the cat in KISS and get behind a drum kit with a set of furry ears.

If he has other planets in Pisces too, this man should be aware of the effect that alcohol and drugs have on his relationship with the real world, as it's not always a useful choice for him, and the contents of his head can end up looking like a ride on Disneyland.

He needs a lot of fantasy in his reality and likes escaping through theatre, poetry, film or computer games. His imagination is enormous, which explains why he may be the only person in the audience who ever understands what a mime artist is actually trying to say – or the only man in the world who can claim to comprehend James Joyce. He is intuitive, and may be psychic. Take his predictions seriously – they often come true.

He visualises things which the rest of us can't see and can't understand. He thinks in images, and they are as real to him as the book you are now reading. Poetry appeals to him for this reason. Anything too literal is just . . . dull.

If he is strongly Piscean then the line between make-believe and reality will be blurred, and he needs to find an outlet for that, otherwise the rest of the world may remain permanently dazed and confused by his thinking.

Neptune is 'the will-o-the-wisp and the mountain mist', wrote the legendary astrologer Charles Carter. Men with the Sun, Moon, Mercury, Venus, Mars, Ascendant and/or Midheaven in Pisces, and Neptune aspecting those planets and points, might as well change their name to Will Wisp by deed poll.

To check for aspects go to www.astro.com and look for this symbol in the horoscope ♆ with a lot of lines stretching out from it. The aspects are simply patterns – the conjunction, sextile, square, trine and opposition.

A wonderful selection of poets, Christians, Hare Krishnas, boozers, drug addicts, artists, photographers, meditators and dodgy devils are born with significant Neptune aspects and Pisces planets and/or points. The problems begin when their tendency to fantasise turns into awful self-deception. If they can avoid this trap, however, they end up floating ten feet higher above the ground than the rest of us.

Men who run with the fish include: **Damon Albarn** – Mercury and Venus in Pisces, Neptune trine Sun; **William Wordsworth** – Mercury in Pisces, Neptune conjunct Midheaven; **Prince** – Moon in Pisces, Neptune trine Moon and opposite Venus; **Rene Lalique** – Midheaven in Pisces, Neptune sextile Venus; **Elvis Presley** – Moon in Pisces, Neptune square Ascendant, trine Mercury and Sun; **Bob Dylan** – Mars in Pisces, Neptune square Mercury, Neptune trine Moon; **Paul Cézanne** – Moon in Pisces, Neptune conjunct Venus; **Ron L. Hubbard** – Sun and Mercury in Pisces, Neptune trine Mercury; **Hans Christian Andersen** – Venus in Pisces, Neptune trine Venus and Mars; **Ram Dass** – Midheaven and Venus in Pisces, Neptune opposite Venus, trine Mercury; **Jeffrey Archer** – Mercury in Pisces, Neptune opposite Mercury; **George Harrison** – Sun and Venus in Pisces, Neptune trine Mercury, opposite Venus; **Spike Milligan** – Venus in Pisces, Neptune square Mercury; **Ansel Adams** – Sun and Mars in Pisces, Neptune trine Mercury; **Kenneth Grahame** – Sun and Mercury in Pisces, both opposite Neptune; **Anthony Armstrong Jones** – Sun and Venus in Pisces, Neptune opposite Mercury; **Pierre Renoir** – Sun and Mercury in Pisces, Neptune conjunct Ascendant; **Percy Bysshe Shelley** – Moon in Pisces, Neptune opposite Ascendant; **Sri Meher Baba** – Sun and Mercury in Pisces, Neptune trine Ascendant; **Rudolph Steiner** – Sun and Mercury in Pisces, Neptune conjunct both; **W. H. Auden** – Sun and Mercury in Pisces, Neptune opposite Venus.

When you want a Pisces/Neptune type to be sensible and take things seriously, he will commonly wriggle around like a fish (which is the perfect image for Pisces) and swim away into fantasy land.

When once asked who his favourite poets were, Bob Dylan mentioned a flying-trapeze family from the circus, Smokey Robinson and W. C. Fields. When *Playboy* tried again on another occasion and asked Dylan what his songs were about, he said, 'Oh, some are about four minutes; some are about five; and some, believe it or not, are about eleven or twelve.' Dylan is slippery, like all Pisces/Neptune types. And he is also a poet, of course.

Some of them write this poetry down, some of them seek it out in the lyric sheets in CDs and in their favourite books or websites. Others make it up in an exercise book or conduct everyday conversations with you that sound like poetry instead. Some people do use the Internet for things other than cheap Viagra advertisements and penis enlargement; these are Piscean/Neptune types and, God bless them, they send poems or whimsical pieces about walruses. Neptune rules the imagination – Pisces is linked to fantasy. Why say you're going to the shop for a carton of milk when you could tell people you're sailing the wide ocean in search of fertile cows? A Pisces/Neptune type who is fluffing around like this can either restore your sense of perspective on life or irritate the hell out of you. It depends, often, how much Pisces/Neptune there is in your own natal chart.

These men know there's more out there than you do because they: took acid and understood the universe; got drunk once and met God; had a psychic experience with a deck of tarot cards; or went to heaven in their dreams and met Jesus. The unseen world speaks strongly to Pisces/Neptune types, and some of them know it from childhood and are consequently devout Christians by the time they turn twenty-one.

The fish symbol of Christianity also belongs to Pisces, and destiny dictates that these men have to confront this religion at some point in their lives. Aunty Maureen may have been a dedicated Anglican; a friend may go through a conversion; a priest may suddenly or unexpectedly enter their world; or they may find themselves surrounded by Buddhists, Hindus, Jews or Moslems and be forced to examine Christ that way. And just in case you think it's a heresy to discuss Jesus Christ in an astrology book, ask yourself what the three wise men did for a living if they were following a star.

Take this example from Spike Milligan, super-Neptunian, quoted in *Spike Milligan: The Biography* by Humphrey Carpenter. In 1995 he told a journalist that he still attends mass most Sundays, and goes to regular confession. 'So why do you believe in God?' Spike was asked. Back came the reply, 'I don't. I just like Jesus.' Towards the end of his life, Spike said, 'I'm a lapsed Catholic and a practising Catholic. I practise all the time. Then I lapse. Then I practise a bit more. It never stops.'

Meditative space is crucial to Pisces/Neptune types. Some find it in the bottom of a beer glass, others find it in a haze of smoke and some of them find it in yoga classes, churches or temples. It's hard to share and occasionally it's hard to understand, but it's part of what makes them tick.

The boundaries of Pisces/Neptune types are fuzzy, so they find it impossible not to feel the same emotions as other people – or even animals. This can lead to a kind of super-compassion and an acute sensitivity. On occasion, this is actually the motivation behind the spiritual beliefs or the need for drugs or alcohol: Pisces/Neptune either needs to find an answer for others' suffering or he needs to find a way to blot it all out. The army is not a very good place for them. Neither is the real world!

Some of them see life through the side of a bong, others through the bottom of a wine glass. Some can be blinded by their religious beliefs, which they use to justify the most peculiar moral choices. Others, sadly, lose the connection with reality altogether. All forms of Pisces/Neptune influences can lend themselves to temporary blindness – or even a life of self-evasion and moral confusion. Innocent confusion can cause as much trouble in the lives of Neptune/Pisces types as deliberate deceit, but it all comes from the same place: vision problems.

Pisces/Neptune is great for . . . creating characters for children's cartoons, establishing telepathic connections with cats or changing all the light bulbs in the house to purple. It's bad for self-deluding criminals, self-deceiving root rats or blokes with a victim complex (no, he is not Christ on the cross, and by the way, this is not Easter).

Does he have Pisces Rising? Look for a sensitive face with eyes that appear as if they could be moved to tears by poetry or at least by a steady stream of Nag Champa incense. Some of them even have eyes like pools, and when you are holding hands across a crowded speed-dating table, it may be easy to imagine you can hold your nose and just dive in. All this is no reflection of the person behind the mask, of course. Keep looking!

4 MORE ABOUT HER

If you haven't already looked up your partner's planet signs, turn to page 272 now. You probably already know her Sun Sign – it's her regular sign, the one you've read about in magazines or newspapers. To find out the inner workings of her soul, though, you also need her Moon Sign, Mercury Sign, Venus Sign, Mars Sign and Rising Sign.

HER ARIES SIDE

If her Sun, Moon, Mercury, Venus, Mars and/or Rising Sign is in Aries then this sign will be a big part of her personality. Want to know if the Midheaven is there too? Check www.astro.com.

Are you ready, boots? Then take a tip from Nancy Sinatra and *start walking*. She's an arm wrestler, a tease and, yes, she does look as if she was born to wear boots, and walk all over you too.

If her Aries side is well developed, then she deals extremely well with heated, urgent or high-friction environments that would make weaker women run away. Politics, competitive sport and the armed forces are all great places for the Aries type to do her stuff. So is the cutting edge of business or corporate life.

Nobody slams back a tennis ball as furiously as an Aries-influenced woman. Nobody bounces back faster on the end of a bungee rope either. As a child, she reads books about brave little helicopters and Amazonian tomboys, and gets all fired up. Cinderella doesn't really do it for her. She needs strong role models. Her aesthetic is more *Sports Illustrated* than *Victoria's Secret*. She is the anti frou-frou.

She makes an excellent karate student or a power forward in basketball. She's also extremely good at speeding in her car too – not to mention aiming the rifles at fluffy toys at fun fairs. Who makes 'Boom! Boom!' noises when she's shooting at a giant Bugs Bunny? A woman with planets or points in Aries.

When she's bad, she's very bad indeed – and is either caught for provoking traffic police or in possession of an unlicensed handgun. And when she's good? Nobody else is more fun to ride motorbikes with – even the straight ones secretly want to join Dykes on Bikes. Remember, even if she only has one point or planet in Aries, a large chunk of her personality is projected through this feisty, fiery sign.

One of my Venus in Aries website visitors says, 'I love it when people air their grievances openly.' An Aries type knows that anger is healthy – she doesn't mind teasing the cat to the point of open warfare, and enjoys a bit of quality hissing and paw-swiping.

As little girls they play with boys, and don't understand why they can't just shave their heads and change their name to Jimmy. As grown women they discover that not all is fair in love and war. This woman never slinks away and cries in the corner, though. She fights back. And when she fights back, baby, you'll *really* know about it.

In lesbian relationships, she is a reliably fast mover. Has someone had her paws on you, within nanoseconds of meeting you? Check her chart for Aries planets or points!

All of them adore hunting in the jungle of love, whatever their sexuality. The Aries type is a ruthless, reckless and fiercely competitive speed-dater. Dump her and you'll know about it too. She'll be seen around town with your best friend, probably semi-naked, and probably within six months (though she'd prefer six minutes).

There's not too much that's fluttery, helpless or fluffy about women with points or planets in Aries – although she can fake it if she has to. She prefers pants and jeans – or strong colours and statement frocks. She doesn't do girlie-tizzy, unless she's being ironic.

Does she have Mars in Aries? This horoscope placement needs special consideration. The unlucky Mars in Aries woman can end up in police mug shots. The lucky ones get by without legal interference, but their collection of martial arts DVDs does tend to raise eyebrows. Who really enjoys adding to her kitchen knife collection? A Mars in Aries woman.

Even the most restrained and apparently low-key of Mars in Aries women have an inner Lara Croft on standby, or a little bit of Karen Blixen in their soul . . . striding around the plains with her rifle sights trained on the big game is part of what she's all about.

Even if she has just one planet or point in Aries, she tends to come alive when she is competing against other women. Sport is an excellent outlet for this; affairs with married men are not, as she discovers when the wife she is cuckolding suddenly decides to stuff prawns in her curtain rods.

If she has more than one planet in Aries, it may be hard for her to walk past a tattoo parlour without fantasising about what might happen if she suddenly dropped in. There is a toughness about her femininity if she's a double, treble or quadruple Aries type. There is also a propensity to try and make it in an all-male domain, if she is heavily Aries influenced. She's a tough cookie, and once she's past the age of sixty, makes a street-smart old bird.

Even if she has just 20 per cent of her chart in Aries, smashing the glass ceiling appeals strongly to her, and she doesn't mind giving her career the occasional shot of Jackie Chan and Chuck Norris, even if she is wearing a skirt at the time. Sometimes she'll treat her career like Evel Knievel too – jumping over a water tank full of man-eating sharks, as she effortlessly clears fourteen Greyhound buses. She does well in professions where you have to be fast, tough and fearless.

As a child, she understands *completely* why Lucy in *Peanuts* felt compelled to pull the football away from Charlie Brown before he could get a chance to kick it. That impulse is in her astrological DNA as well.

Does she have Mercury in Aries? She's good on conversational attack and defence – to the point where she could probably run for congress one day, or compete in Aggressive Flirting at the next Olympics. She is not a waffler, nor is she a faffer. She doesn't do padding, and she always gets straight to the point. Sometimes she is in so much of a rush that she'll abbreviate everything or use acronyms. She does a very good impression of Laverne De Fazio in *Laverne and Shirley*, and can sound like one hell of a mean mother if she tries.

She needs a job or a weekend interest where she's allowed to pit herself against other people. Any profession or hobby where you're allowed to hurl insults or yell a lot is *fine*. She's an action woman, and if the cause is right, can turn herself into an instant activist just by snapping her fingers. She's the queen of tough grrrl quotes: 'Don't get mad, get even', 'Revenge is a dish best served cold', 'When the going gets tough, the tough get going' and 'All's fair in love and war'.

Does she have Aries as her Rising Sign? If it's the only thing she has in Aries, then it can be awfully misleading. The toughness will be an act! Destiny will often put her in situations where she has to compete against someone too. It may be a sibling, another woman, a professional rival or an ex-partner. This is the jutting-jaw Rising Sign, even if she has fluffy, blond hair and a frilly frock on. The vibe is daring, challenging. 'Don't even think about it!' is the Aries Rising message.

If she has planets and points in Aries and aspects involving Mars, the ruler of Aries, she may be assertive to the point of being aggressive. She can carry a lot of anger around. And she can make other people angry too. Check her chart at www.astro.com. If there are lots of lines stretching from the Mars symbol ♂ then she may need a job or weekend passion that is a safe container for her inner mud wrestler. Without it, steam often ends up coming out of her ears at inopportune moments.

Sometimes women with a strong Aries/Mars side don't admit they've got it – so they project it onto other people. Suddenly, everyone else becomes the aggressor, instead of them. So they feign innocence when you start hurling lampshades at them, and wonder why on earth you're shouting. Unconscious provocation can be the irritating speciality of many an unevolved Aries type!

Her energy is quite remarkable, by the way. She can turn almost any situation around through sheer force of personality. She has a load of yang in her character. Mars and Aries are masculine energies in astrology, and there is a side to her that can take charge like a cross between Winston Churchill, His Holiness the Dalai Lama and Abraham Lincoln . . . even when she's wearing heels.

Nobody is more firm in the face of chaos or madness in others. The Aries type sets boundaries and draws the line. If she has the Sun in Aries you'll already know about her ability to put out spot fires. If she has the Moon, Mercury or other points or planets in this sign, that ability is also there. Having her around is like having a human fire extinguisher on the premises. And here's another analogy for you: a cowgirl with a lassoo. Who ropes and ties the cattle when they've all gone crazy? The Aries type.

Motivation will not be an issue with her, by the way. Even if only one planet or point is in this sign, she'll have no problems moving on her priorities – *now*. This one doesn't need to learn assertiveness skills. She has them in the cot. And when those tiny fists start whirling, all around know – instantly – where the buck has to stop, and with whom.

HER TAURUS SIDE

If her Sun, Moon, Mercury, Venus, Mars and/or Rising Sign is in Taurus then this sign will be a big part of her personality. Want to know if the Midheaven is there too? Check www.astro.com.

Are 628 pieces of jewellery too many for one woman? Not if you have planets or points in Taurus. What about owning property in three countries? Once again, not a problem. The only exception to this rule is the Taurus type who subscribes to a left-wing view of the planet, and drops out of shopaholic, capitalist society altogether. She still accumulates and collects, though – even if it's only flowers from her garden. Alternatively, she'll make a fortune, just so she can give it away.

Her views on the taxation system are emotional. Don't ever talk about it at a dinner party unless you want to be there for several hours.

Her values are the key to her personality. They may be Christian (donate it to the needy), capitalist (take me to Fifth Avenue), communist (let's visit Karl Marx in Highgate Cemetery), feminist (why should women get paid less?) or pure eco-warrior (you can't put a price on wilderness). Unless you can fathom what she will and won't sell out for, however, you'll never really understand her. It influences everything – from the way she wheels a trolley around the supermarket to the way she sees you.

Lots of them are funny about their money and possessions. It pushes their buttons and triggers their insecurity. Always pay them back on time. Always return their stuff, too, if you've borrowed it.

Is she one of the shopaholic Taurus types? Then heaven is a mall to her, and she can do it all, from Foot Locker to Benetton to Hallmark Cards and Victoria's Secret. Some of them use Betty Rubble in *The Flintstones* as their personal role model: 'Charge it!'

The exception to this is the Taurus type who becomes so emotional about financial and economic issues that she bucks the system and boycotts consumer madness altogether. She still needs her gorgeous things – but they will be second-hand, homemade or very few in number. The Taurean types who downsize and live simply (e.g. cheaply) are still sensualists. But instead of being turned on by Prada bags, they salivate over the colour of their knitting wool, the texture of their pumpkins and the scent of their lavender plants. They all like a family heirloom. And a priceless family heirloom is, well, priceless . . .

If she is one of the cash-conscious Taurean types, then by her forties she has typically learnt to think like a businesswoman and talk like Wall Street – result? An enviable lifestyle, or a substantial investment in charity. This is the woman who chases the *Antique Roadshow* film crew down the street until they identify her Picassos. It's also the woman who runs a stall at a local market and turns it into a dot com. If she has other planets in Taurus as well, she could be a natural entrepreneur and take a family business and turn it into a goldmine.

If she has Taurus Rising, and other planets in Taurus too, then what you see is what you get – someone who is intensely practical and packed with common sense: in a word, grounded. No planets in Taurus, Virgo or Capricorn (the other earth signs)? Then she'll be utterly convincing in the practical role, and even roll her sleeves up for you – but at the end of the day it will be just that, a role. Be careful with Rising Signs. They're just packaging, you know.

Does she have Mars in Taurus? She could end up being one of the richest women on the planet, if that's her bag, and Harvard Business School may have something to learn from her. Lots of Taurean types do well in retail or sales without even trying – ker-ching!

Whatever her Taurean planets, she is amazingly resourceful. If times are tough, she goes without silk stockings and dyes her legs with diluted cocoa. She knows how to hoard, and she knows how to ration herself when necessary. Make do and mend! Yes, yes, yes!

Not surprisingly, though, most Taurus types would honestly prefer to be so rich that they can snap up Frida Kahlos at auction and wear Cartier. The only exception to this rule is the politically or socially conscious Taurus type, as discussed, who may reject consumerism altogether, and deliberately drop out of 'Spend, spend, spend' society.

Either way, money, property and business are big issues with the Taurus type. Whatever the rest of her horoscope looks like, 20 per cent of her is Taurean, and she takes her games of Monopoly more seriously than most. She's a canny player, in all senses of the word.

When the Mars in Taurus woman becomes angry with people, she proceeds on the basis that she is Richie Rich or Scrooge McDuck. She grits her teeth, fumes and sends psychic signals to other people that say 'That cost me a lot of money, you know' or 'After everything I've done for you!' or 'My Christmas present cost more than yours' or 'What about that fifty bucks you still owe me?' The really fortunate ones are able to yell, 'I could buy or sell you a million times over!' In Hollywood, it's known as f— you money.

It doesn't matter if she has Mars, the Sun, Moon, Mercury, Venus or the Rising Sign (or the Midheaven) here, though – being broke changes her more dramatically than anything else. You can double that message, too, if the Taurus type faces redundancy, theft, bankruptcy or stock-exchange losses – almost any kind of wipe-out, in fact.

It's all about the same thing: a sense of personal worth. On the surface, these wipe-outs (and even Her Majesty the Queen has faced tax bills!) seem to be about cash. Or *stuff*. Or security. But what actually takes place during these fated crises is a chance for the Taurus type to add up what really counts in her life.

This is when the famous resourcefulness of the Taurean type usually comes into play. She is gifted at scooping up talent, time, contacts – and whatever she has left, materially or financially –

to shore herself up. Even in the middle of insecurity, she can secure her life.

Some of them have to learn lessons about credit cards. Others have to deal with the reality of investments or gambling. Hopefully these are all lessons that the Taurus type only has to take on board once.

Cash and property are emotional issues for her, and trigger much soul-searching. The world around her puts its own value on life, but she is fated to sort out her own personal stock exchange. In the process she discovers how much love costs, or pride, freedom or self-worth. All the clichés (not to mention all the old Beatles songs) about money make genuine sense to a woman born with planets or points in Taurus, because it's part of her karma to fix her own price on what matters.

Because of this, she has a value system that is unique to her, and remarkably powerful. It can withstand almost anything, from a tax bill to an expensive divorce. The Taurus type counts her own costs and creates her own mental balance sheet of what (and who) is truly worth it in life, and what can be written off. She has the most complex and interesting view of money and what constitutes real spiritual 'wealth' of any sign, and perhaps it isn't surprising that so many women with points and planets here come to hold strong political or religious views.

What rewards her? That's a central question for any woman with a developed Taurus side in her horoscope. Fate often hands her relationships, jobs, projects or plans that come without guarantees or backing. This can make the Taurus type feel decidedly nervous. At heart, she prefers to know what's in her garden and when it's going to appear; or, to put it another way, she'd rather have solid capital behind her concepts than mere enthusiasm and encouraging pats on the back. Destiny tells the Taurus type to trust the process, though, and in time she comes to discover that some things have their own reward, and it has nothing whatsoever to do with a financial pay-off.

What does she believe and hold dear? What does she refuse

to sell out for? What does she *know* money can't buy? If you are going to move in with someone who has Taurus in her chart, you had better get to the bottom of her value system before you discover that you both believe in different things. She has principles and standards the way other women have poodles and pedicures. Understanding where her allegiance lies is the key to unlocking her character, and you need to know exactly where her beliefs, ethics, morals, loyalties and allegiances really lie.

Her values aren't just ideals floating around in her head. She has a way of translating them in practical ways – everything from her voting habits to her choice of lifestyle. Taurus is an earth sign that manifests in concrete ways. This woman walks her talk in a way that might surprise you if you haven't encountered a Taurus type before. Other women might have strong feelings, but this woman is capable of applying her values to her personal or professional life with total commitment. She's the environmentalist who recycles, the patriot who flies the flag, the pacifist who pulls her investment out of pro-arms trade banks, the Labour voter who donates to the party, the arch-Conservative who builds a statue of Margaret Thatcher in the garden, or the Christian who won't sell out the Bible.

HER GEMINI SIDE

If her Sun, Moon, Mercury, Venus, Mars and/or Rising Sign is in Gemini, then this sign will be a big part of her personality. Want to know if the Midheaven is there too? Check www.astro.com.

She has a way with words and accents. When she reads aloud from the newspaper over the breakfast toast and marmalade, she sounds like a CBS anchorwoman. At school, she was always the girl who could do languages. Their vocabularies are full of old family words, TV catchphrases and in-jokes. The Americans tend to do an extremely good version of posh British; the English can do very good Scots, and the Australians do a remarkably good Texan or fake Parisian. Ooh la la!

If the rest of her chart agrees, she may end up with a job in media, education, publishing or the entertainment industry. At the very least, whatever career or life path she chooses, she's always endlessly (and reliably) amusing about shopping, weight, dating and family. When she's on the end of a phone, it's better than listening to 'Woman's Hour'. She does well in jobs where a bit of chat is required . . . or preferably a *lot* of chat.

She articulates what other people are feeling, and has a way of *putting* things. Other people struggle to say it, but the Gemini type can get it all out in three minutes flat. As a child, she can recite entire songs off by heart, or learn lines from TV and radio shows and shoot them back at her baffled parents. Gemini types are bright – interested, and interesting too.

Does she have Venus in Gemini? Then she flirts like Murphy Brown – she's funny, cool, breezy and intelligent, all at the same time. She has trouble sleeping with idiots too, unless she can turn it into a funny story for her friends afterwards.

If there are several planets in Gemini in her horoscope, she may as well quit work right now and go to work for *Time* magazine. Whatever her chosen profession, though, women with the Moon and Venus in Gemini (in particular) are the Lois Lanes of love. They report on their feelings to girlfriends, or turn them into long essays in diaries or letters. This one is capable of finding a date online, conducting the relationship by email, breaking it up by email and then emailing the sad news to her girlfriends.

Does she have more than one planet or point in Gemini? She has a book in her, if she's typical – or at least she's prepared to pay someone else to ghostwrite it for her one day. In the meantime, modern technology is harnessed in the interests of her private life.

Venus in Gemini is the consummate faxer and sex-texter of the zodiac. No other woman depends on the written or spoken word in love quite so much. As a teenager, she has to cross her legs tightly when the boys in class go through the dictionary for rude words. Erotica by Anaïs Nin, *Belle de Jour*, the short stories in *Scarlet* magazine or a $1.99 phone call to a pre-recorded sex line can all get her hot and bothered.

Here's something to remember about the woman who has the Sun, Moon, Mercury, Venus, Mars and/or Rising Sign in Gemini . . . she doesn't do bimbo. And if she does squeeze her bottom into a pair of hotpants, it's because she's being post-feminist, post-modern and ironic. She gets annoyed when people miss the humour in the way she dresses. That fur hat – does nobody get the joke? She does (frequently) do glasses, however, or books in bed, or five newspapers rolled up in her hand luggage. Her preferred artwork – like Frida Kahlo – has a message, too. Her preferred T-shirts *always* have a message.

She loves regular, short bursts of travel, and if she had the time and money, would live on one-hour flights and weekend car trips. Unless she has planets in Sagittarius, though, long-haul overseas treks are not for her. She bores easily and prefers moving on. If the cash is there, she likes doing San Francisco–Hawaii, Sydney–Melbourne, Auckland–Sydney, Montreal–New York and London–Paris.

She renames herself by her thirties, or is known by two or more different names (nicknames, for example) to the people in her closest circle. She also likes making up names for her lovers, and the naming game can also extend to animals, cars and plants.

She attracts friends and lovers who are as funny and clever as she is and speed-dials them. If she has more than one planet in Gemini then her connection to a sibling holds a big key to her personality too. For better or worse, siblings play an important role.

Is her Rising Sign Gemini? She's a clever dresser. A lot of thought goes into the wardrobe, the hair and the accessories because she knows how clothes *communicate*. The image is bright, witty, interested – and interesting. Do you get the joke? You better, if you're sitting on an aeroplane next to a Gemini Rising female.

If she has planets in Gemini too then she will find a natural career in any profession where people have plugged into ideas or connected to places. The well-known Gemini Rising sense of humour will also be a huge part of who she really is.

Does she have Mercury in Gemini? Then she's the original go-between. Audrey Hepburn had this Mercury sign – as a child, during World War II, she carried messages for the Resistance in her ballet shoes. Women with Mercury in Gemini are networkers, connectors, talkers, thinkers, writers, students and teachers. The propaganda queen Tokyo Rose had this Mercury sign too. Nobody is cleverer or trickier in front of a microphone. The more her Mercury sign dominates her personality, the bigger the gossip (or diary-keeper) she is likely to be. She needs to talk about it and write about it. Discretion is not really her thing, as her therapist is the first to discover.

Does she have Mars in Gemini? Don't be mean to her, or she'll do you the same way Kitty Kelley does the rich and famous. Words are her weapon, and anyone attacking a Mars in Gemini woman should be aware that her emails, letters and gossip can be lethal. Other people's pens are filled with black ink. Hers is permanently filled with arsenic, just in case. She's a world-class flamer too.

With this Mars sign, her energy is sharp, fast, witty and light, and when life is going her way she can be funnier than Barbra Streisand in *Funny Girl*. At school, she joins the debating team at the last minute and wipes the floor with her opponents. When she makes a point, it can feel like she's jabbing you with knitting needles. She has Opinions with a capital O, so be ready. No film remains undiscussed with her.

If she has any point or planet in Gemini, then her conversations are often conducted like ping-pong games, but only when her opponent is worthy of her. In order to feel complete, she desperately needs a partner who can be relied upon to bat the ball back in discussions. Without that dynamic in her relationship, she may find that part of her withers and dies.

A mute husband hiding behind the *New York Times* at breakfast will cause her huge problems. And a dumb-dumb girlfriend who can only say 'yes', 'no' or 'maybe' will drive her insane. She needs funny people around her too – because she is funny – and postcards that make her laugh and yellowing cartoons stuck on the loo wall or the office noticeboard. At least 20 per cent of her astrological DNA is pure comedy.

She needs to be careful with everything from answering-machine messages to Post-it notes and emails, because when she speaks or writes in haste (and in anger) what remains behind can screw up her love life, her social life or her career forever. In some cases, it may even cause her legal problems. Her words are usually her karma.

When she gets one of her periodical energy surges, she will remind you of a multi-armed Indian love god. At her most active and motivated, she is capable of dialling with one hand, typing with another and talking two languages – while running to catch a plane and listening to the news on her iPod. Not surprisingly, focus tends to go out of the window.

The best lesson she can learn is that a worthwhile cause – just one person, perhaps, or even something vast and global – always needs her. A Gemini type who is fighting the good fight has a unique ability to articulate the rights and wrongs, and – better still – raise a smile or a big laugh along the way. She is even capable of amusing her enemies. Her hardest lesson? She needs to learn that people never forget what she says or writes, and that even when she thinks she's merely being assertive, her words can leave scorch marks.

She is here to transmit, to connect and to inform. People really listen when Gemini types talk. Some of them are highly educated, others never make it beyond high school, but they all know how to communicate effectively and have an intuitive sense of how to get through to people.

She's clever and funny, if she's typical of her Gemini birthright, and it's common for women with this sign in their charts to use their way with words in order to achieve the goals set by the other signs in their horoscopes. If she has Taurus planets too, for example, this woman might use her 'human radio' skills to make money, or to make a point.

HER CANCER SIDE

If her Sun, Moon, Mercury, Venus, Mars and/or Rising Sign is in Cancer then this sign will be a big part of her personality. Want to know if the Midheaven is there too? Check www.astro.com.

If she has more than one planet in Cancer, she'll never just own property – she'll have a profound emotional relationship with it, and nothing will ever hurt like the sale of her first home.

Remember, whatever the rest of her chart looks like, 20 per cent of her is pure Martha Stewart. She thinks in terms of domestic detail, and is secretly pleased that fairy cakes are hip again. Does she have planets in Virgo too? Then the contents of her fridge and pantry will really, *really* matter. Don't go messing around in there or feed her stuff that's not up to her own special standards.

She thinks in terms of the family. She looks around her world and understands how the Windsors or the Kennedys got that way. No other sign understands all those family trees at the start of Jilly Cooper novels except the Cancer type! Professional relationships can be dissected in the same way. Who's like a sister to her? Who's playing mother? Who's the father figure in the business?

She thinks in terms of feelings – as in the Morris Albert song – whoa, whoa, whoa, feelings. Logic and commonsense don't have much to do with it. It's all emotion, memory and mood, and it increases with the amount of Cancer she has in her chart.

Even with one planet or point in this sign, she has a strong sense of belonging and place. Cancerian types watch the Olympics on television and can't help but reach for the tissues when the national anthem is played. Patriotism is an emotional business for her. And it comforts her enormously to know where she comes from and where she fits. When she feels vulnerable, this woman will always retreat to her class, her upbringing and everything she was taught as a child. Crisis takes her back to her roots, every time. The rare exception to this is the crab-influenced woman who has such traumatic experiences in her own country that she has to emigrate. If so, her new country becomes her first adopted love – and she will feel just as passionate about it.

Does she have Venus in Cancer? She really, really loves Monopoly – and if she ever gets the time and money, she'll play it in real life too, with large chunks of Manhattan real estate.

She has strong feelings about children – either her own or other people's. She makes a tireless worker or fundraiser for children's aid organisations or a wonderfully dedicated godmother or aunt; the kids don't necessarily have to be hers. A cat or dog can sometimes become a child substitute. Venus in Cancer wanders into an animal shelter and weeps.

Whatever planets or points she has in Cancer, she genuinely cares. Nobody is better at looking after you when you're ill – life for her often means being Florence Nightingale. She is fiercely protective and *genuinely* cares about you, even when you're being boring about your symptoms.

Food is important to her comfort zone, and it's got to be familiar or old-school. When they travel, American Cancer-influenced women crave Aunt Jemima's pancake mix and Goober Grape jelly. The English want to know where the Cooper's Oxford is. The Australians long for their Vegemite on principle, even if they don't really like the stuff. Lots of them believe in nice cups of tea – or strong cups of coffee. It goes back to childhood, and it's the Cancerian type's version of medicine.

She understands her mother's or grandmother's heritage, and

it shows in her home, on her bookcase or in her wardrobe. She has an instinct for vintage clothing, but prefers it if she can haul out a family heirloom frock and wear it to a party. Other women forget where they come from, but the Cancer type feels a huge affinity with even the oldest and crumbliest branches on her family tree.

Her mother is the key to her soul. If she has more than one planet in Cancer, then it's the key to almost 50 per cent of her entire personality. Good, bad or indifferent, the mother–daughter relationship speaks volumes about the emotional state of this woman. She is seldom ambivalent about the mother–daughter relationship, and if she talks about it for long enough, it will produce moist eyes either way. This is one woman who doesn't make a good latchkey kid, by the way. And don't get her started on bottle-feeding either.

If she loves you, then she'll mother you. She has no trouble attracting lovers who need the top sliced off their boiled eggs or their toast cut into soldiers. Whether she actually needs them long term, however, depends on the rest of her horoscope.

Don't ever underestimate the influence her entire family has on her. A mother, father, aunt, uncle, grandfather, grandmother, sister or brother can shape her life to an astonishing degree – much more than any school or university ever could. If she's typical of her Cancer side, she'll have extreme clan consciousness and either blame stuff on that or happily attribute it. There's no middle ground.

Her maternal instinct is an important part of her psychological make-up, and it may be expressed towards her own children in an obvious way – but also to any living creature who is in pain or vulnerable. This may incline her towards the caring professions, if the rest of her chart agrees. Lots of them still have their Cabbage Patch doll adoption certificates (purchased, embarrassingly enough, at the age of 39). She can mother vulnerable friends, other people's children or stray cats. It's in her nature to want to protect and comfort.

Does she have Cancer Rising? Now, this is someone you can feel at home with. She may have different qualities on the inside, but the image is Mobile Comfort Zone. There is a cosy familiarity about Cancer Rising women – they could be your sister, aunt or mother. Often, they bring their childhood accents with them. They speak their class or local background, because it's part of their outer packaging.

History strikes a chord. If she's British, then Mary Queen of Scots and Oliver Cromwell will really matter. If she's American or Australian, she wanders around English National Trust buildings in the English countryside, secretly wondering if one of her distant ancestors ever used the loo. The past has a tremendously emotional pull on this woman. African–American Cancer types look backwards to their roots in order to move forwards. It sustains them.

It's hard for the Cancer type to make out a will and leave her property to anyone – because she has such a strong attachment to her home. Gardens also have the same effect on her (and home towns, childhood villages and favourite streets).

She has a tremendous sense of place, and understands how certain buildings or towns can carry their own karma or weave their own magic. She prefers to live in a house with a name. A number never really conveys enough personality for her, and all her residences have character. A Cancerian type wrote in to my website, explaining how she had connected with London Bridge during her time in that city! If she has planets or points in Cancer, then she genuinely feels the spirit in her favourite places.

She sees herself in terms of her town, her suburb, her village, her country or her state/county. Cancer Rising women tell you 'I'm an Eastender' or 'I'm an Aussie' or 'I'm from Austin, Texas'. Their sense of home is part of who they are, and they dress that way and behave that way. No matter how many time zones the Cancer Rising woman crosses, to the people at home she always looks as if she never left.

Does she have Mars in Cancer? If she has children, fierce maternal pride will be much in evidence, and you criticise her sons or daughters at your cost. A lot of her energy will be channelled into kids – or nannying pets/friends/lovers – if she's typical of her Mars sign.

A small business based on baking, cleaning or any other housewifely art could make her a fortune, so don't laugh at her sponge cakes or mock her Mrs Mop side. Real estate, renovation, gardening and interior design bring out a fierce, almost manic, energy in her – she channels a huge amount of her lust for life into her home, and could probably make a difference to yours as well.

Is she a lunar type too? Look for Moon aspects at www.astro.com (lots of lines stretching across the chart from the Moon symbol: ☽). She'll have a thing about food – and probably a thing about bras as well, believe it or not. Cancer types with Moon aspects sometimes have a round, open face – just like *la Luna*. The Moon describes her mother as well as her own issues around being a parent. If she has planets or points in Cancer and a strong set of Moon aspects, this is going to be an *enormous* deal in her life.

HER LEO SIDE

If her Sun, Moon, Mercury, Venus, Mars and/or Rising Sign is in Leo then this sign will be a big part of her personality. Want to know if the Midheaven is there too? Check www.astro.com.

A Leo type carries herself with amazing dignity, even when her life resembles a paddock full of horse manure. She oozes royal breeding and *noblesse oblige*, even if she was raised by thugs and crooks. Typically, though, the Leo type has impressive lineage, and if you trawl through her family tree long enough, you are bound to find someone who's danced with a man who's danced with a girl who's danced with the Prince of Wales (or J.F.K.)

Alternatively, a surprisingly high number of Leo types have their own anecdotes about the rich, the royal or the famous. It may be a tiny detail in history (her great-great-uncle once made the King a bacon sandwich) but it will matter to her – and it should matter to you, too, if you want to be with her for longer than five minutes. Lots of them have vaguely famous friends, exes or old classmates.

Friends who court her or colleagues who respect the fact that she needs to hold court make her feel wonderfully reassured, and she is never more at home than when she is being appreciated. Respect!

Does she have the Moon in Leo? Queen Elizabeth has this Moon position, and so does that other well-known royal, Queen Latifah. This woman needs a classy hairstyle, a hair salon with chandeliers overhead or the *right* hat. It doesn't take too much imagination to picture her in 10 Downing Street; waving regally from the balcony of Buckingham Palace or the White House. If she has lots of planets or points in Leo, then a connection to top people and top places is in her DNA.

Is her Rising Sign Leo? She is always given the aristocratic roles in school drama groups, even if she opens her mouth and the suburbs comes out. She has a little class, and a little style. Lots of them look as if they should permanently be clad in tweed suits. Leo Rising women switch on the BBC World Service and accidentally find themselves talking with beautifully rounded vowels. This applies even if they live in the Bronx. Class rubs off on them.

Dignity and presence are the Leo Rising woman's armour against the world, and she'll use them in job interviews, on first dates, at parties, in court cases and at meetings. Short Leo Rising women seem taller than they really are. And tall Leo Rising women put on heels deliberately, just so they can rule the room. They know how to stand up straight and strut their stuff. And destiny has a strange way of putting them in jobs or relationship roles where this becomes necessary.

All Leo Rising women have eyes that freeze or glaze over. You'll experience the freeze effect if you do or say anything vulgar or insulting. And if you've really gone beyond the pale? You'll get *the glaze*. Leo Rising eyes say, 'I don't wish to draw attention to your ghastliness, but your insolence has been noted.'

Whatever her Leo chart signature, the business card is key. The little girls with Mercury in Leo long to have them printed at F.A.O. Schwarz or Smythson, with a gold teddy bear on the top. As a child or teen, there is also an awful lot of signature-doodling, as she tries to find the most impressive way of signing her name. And if her name is too ordinary? She'll change it by the time she's thirty. The only way she can bear being called Madge is if she knows it's short for Your Majesty.

Does she have Mercury in Leo? If she writes, talks, records, teaches or studies for a living, then her Leo side will be the most obvious thing about her. There will be a little of the star, actress, princess, dame or queen about her. She may even be the queen of her own personal Algonquin round table.

All of them are incredibly good at dramatising. If she runs into her ex in the street on a wet Thursday afternoon, it may become the basis for an entire country 'n' western epic, complete with three-part harmonies. And when her high-school teacher asks her to take a turn at reading from Shakespeare, her fellow students will be treated to the bloodiest and most melodramatic version of Lady Macbeth they have ever heard – with frenzied hand-rubbing thrown in. She has a gift for staging and display, even if she's just having friends around for pasta. And if there is a capital O Occasion coming up? The Leo type goes mad.

She does not have a bog-standard email address, if she's typical of this sign. She hates knowing that her name has already been taken, and refuses to end up as janetjones1974@hotmail.com. Marital name-changes bring on a frenzy of fantasising. Should she or shouldn't she? Is his name better than hers? Or what about a double-barrelled surname? Embarrassingly enough for the Leo type, this ritual can take place during every first date she has.

Speeches (at births, deaths, marriages and bar mitzvahs) bring out the Hollywood in her, so be prepared. She doesn't stammer, um and ah or cough. She'll play it like a professional. She's a natural storyteller too, so all the bits and pieces of her life – or someone else's – will be effortlessly gathered into a kind of grand narrative. Nobody else can make her kid's first day at school sound like Harry Potter's first day at Hogwarts.

She can try to fool around and be funny, but she always comes out sounding like Angelica Houston. There is nothing cute, wacky, squeaky or silly about the voice of the typical Leo. And if she's born with Minnie Mouse vowels, she forces herself to learn how to sound cool.

Her worst sin is ego expressed at loud volume. Name-dropping, big-noting herself, referring to herself in the third person or leading every conversation back to herself are all common faults. Once this woman realises how deeply, deeply tacky this is, though, she brings it under control, and you will seldom hear the 'Me' word ever again.

Does she have Mars in Leo? When she gets angry, she behaves like Scarlett O'Hara: tossing her head, beating her fists on the ground and making dramatic declarations. She is also remarkably good at the Miss Piggy karate chop, complete with black-velvet gloves. *Hi-yaaa*! Best of all, though, is her stately Dame Edith Sitwell impersonation – it keeps the peasants at bay. How does she attack you? By being classier than you, that's how. And when she's on form, her enemies can come away feeling remarkably grubby. She is never classier than when she's really, *really* angry – and anyone who makes the mistake of challenging her will feel as if Lady Penelope has just ordered Parker to run over them several times with her pink Rolls-Royce. Roaring does her good. It's not socially acceptable, of course, but an imperious, outraged howl can be a wonderful release for her.

Does she have more than one point or planet in Leo? Her energy may be noticeably feline – like a Siamese cat prowling her territory, or Serena Williams slinking around a tennis court – or distinctly regal, like Princess Anne on duty.

She gives good pout. She can be fierce when she's angry, and even her enemies find it deeply impressive – intimidating too. All of them need to be big shots, boss ladies or queens of their domain. A career that allows her to send memos is probably a safe bet – or a personal life where she gets to strut.

Leo types love a bit of luxe. She was born to lie on a chaise longue with a box of Prestat chocolates and a tiara in the safe. She loves anyone special, famous and important too – but please note, she often ends up that way herself. She reads *Vanity Fair* in the doctor's waiting room and fantasises about buying all the luxury luggage. She'd rather spend extra on getting the best (single malt Scotch, French champagne, German cars) than save money. It's usually quality, not quantity, with her. She doesn't understand why any woman would pay the same amount of money for five pairs of Gap jeans when she could get a pair of vintage Yves St Laurents or Diane von Fursternbergs for just a *leetle* bit more.

One of my Venus in Leo website visitors writes, 'I secretly like going to places where I'm known, or where I know I'll be noticed'. That's quite an admission. But a surprising number of Venus in Leo women prefer to return to restaurants where the staff know who they are, and they don't mind overdoing it (just slightly) for a neighbour's party either.

It's all about the hair for Venus in Leo. It's usually long and thick – true Hollywood hair. In her dreams, she gets a blow-dry before every single public outing. Lots of them unwittingly have hair like the Leo symbol too – luxuriously flipped up at the ends.

All Leo types can read film-star autobiographies and relate. She likes tales of classy dames who sink knee-deep into serious amounts of *merde*, and yet handle themselves like aristocrats.

She admires people who go through hell and still hold their heads high.

She's creative. She can design handbags and start novels, write, shoot, edit (and star) in her own DVD epics and do extremely self-expressive, self-choreographed dance routines, particularly when sloshed. She prefers sport where she can wave her arms around and be photographed with a trophy – and jobs or interests where she is guaranteed VIP treatment if she makes it. The giveaway for this sign? Total dignity. Even if she has to work for twenty years to discover and develop it, she'll make sure you know exactly *why* respect is due.

HER VIRGO SIDE

If her Sun, Moon, Mercury, Venus, Mars and/or Rising Sign is Virgo, then this sign will be a big part of her personality. Want to know if the Midheaven is there too? Check www.astro.com.

Virgo types only feel truly secure and comfortable once all their routines are in place. For some that means a glass of hot water with lemon upon rising and a Salute to the Sun after breakfast; or a bowl of porridge shortly before mucking out the stables and polishing six pairs of riding boots. For other Virgo types, method and routine just mean a Toblerone before, during and after work. She's funny about her health, and her body. This applies no matter whether it's operating perfectly or like Mama Cass on a bad day.

Her habits, routines and personal peccadillos commonly revolve around food, drink and cigarettes. Those who smoke have a particular ritual surrounding their cigarettes. Those who don't can become extremely passionate on the subject of people who blow Benson & Hedges at them in public.

Sheets and pillowcases matter to Virgo types too – she has *opinions* about domestic routine. She dots the i's and crosses the t's (she knows why Lynne Truss matters), and the Virgo type also has an endearing habit of tutting to herself when she watches *The Weakest Link* and notices other people being hopelessly sloppy with facts and dates.

Whatever the rest of her horoscope looks like, if she has a planet or point in Virgo then she needs her food and drink (and any other substance) exactly the way it runs on the list inside her head. She's fussy about GM food, animal testing, vitamin and mineral counts, the gooeyness of the jam inside her doughnuts, wheat allergies, dairy allergies – and the purity of her hash.

She is strangely drawn by any situation, relationship or person that resembles a Rubik's cube. Over three billion combinations and just one solution? Perfect! This is one of the very few women in the world who can Scrabble you to death. She's a Googler too. In fact, she *loves* to Google. She Googles herself (ego-Googling) and then she Googles you too. Oooh!

A lot of vegetarians have Virgo planets and points, it must be said, but so do women who only eat ham sandwiches on alternate Thursdays – and then only with French mustard and no butter. Either way, fridge contents really count; so do the mealtimes, occasionally the Vitamin A count and the metric conversion weight of the food.

She loves a list, and whenever she listens to Desert Island Discs, mentally starts composing her own. In her fantasies, life is just one great big chapter of Harry Potter, complete with a Sorting Hat. She longs for people to be classified and tidied away, and wishes reality could be more like Hogwarts, where everyone knows where they *really* stand.

Does she have Venus in Virgo? Then she understands relationships that are based on service, both in bed and out of it. She can remind you of Barbara Eden in *I Dream Of Jeannie*: 'Thou may ask anything of thy slave, Master!' or alternatively get illicit thrills from having her lover service her. Either way, she is aroused by the idea of naked servitude.

Virgo rules small animals. Dogs, cats and birds matter to her, too, with this Venus sign. A pet is never just a pet – it's a trusted friend. She loves the fact that pets can have passports now, and be described as companions.

It doesn't matter which planet or point she has in Virgo – the physical dictates the mental, the emotional and the spiritual for her. So let's hope she is living in a body that feels like a temple. If it feels like the Betty Ford Centre, it can affect everything about her being. How she feels *physically* dictates everything else.

If she has more than one planet in Virgo then she will be a hard worker and a perfectionist who finds God in the details. It's the tiny stitches in the big tapestry that make her successful, and she knows it. She likes intricate plots in books and she likes epic trilogies that show the author's really, *really* worked at it. Words are her thing – Mercury is Virgo's ruling planet.

Does she have Virgo Rising? She can present two images – the first is the body-conscious, water-guzzling, yoga-adoring, lycra-loving fitness fan. The second is the ailing maiden whose cholesterol problems, bacterial infections or battles with illness make her the local source for anyone who can't get to their doctor or acupuncturist. Either way, when you look at Virgo Rising, you get the body. It's not surprising that so many spend a lifetime working on it, and when they do work, they can look like forty going on twenty.

When all is well in the Virgo Rising bodily temple, she has a chance to work on her style as well as her substance – and that style is neat. It's a look that frequently seems to depend on hair product, and it works. Clean colours, new-looking shoes, carefully blow-dried hair. It's all about the details, and when she goes all-out for a special occasion, you can sometimes feel as if you are looking at a piece of outstanding work by a Hollywood props department – the earrings will be the right kind of earrings, the rings will be on all the right fingers . . . Virgo Rising can do polished extremely well.

Whatever her Virgo placements, no matter how successful this one becomes, there is always a sense that she is doing her duty or serving people. She gives the impression that she genuinely cares about what she is delivering – and it has to be as perfect as she can make it.

Is her Mars sign Virgo? She defends herself by letting you know that she's working harder than you, and she's being more methodical. She gets what she wants by putting in the hours and by being word-perfect (or numerically correct). Part of her is a natural critic and editor too – born to plan, to classify, to categorise, to file away and to get the job absolutely right. It's her way of setting boundaries.

Whatever points or planets are in Virgo, this woman needs a lifestyle and daily schedule that allows her to manage her famous capacity for work along with her equally famous need for a healthy life. It's usually a continuing process for her because of the ever-changing nature of her career, and the fluctuations in her lifestyle. All women with Virgo in their charts need to sort it out, but part of the fun of being a Virgo type is that the ongoing obsession with work, rest and play never ends.

Is she a workaholic, as so many astrology features and books claim? She can fall into it. But the smart Virgo types understand that holidays, long lunches and even the occasional siesta all have their benefits. Wellbeing and workload are two prime areas of concern for her, and she can spend a lot of time and energy trying to make them fit together – with good reason. If she forgets that she has a body as well as a mind, a desk, a phone and a computer, then health problems flare up.

The true Virgo type is hip to meditation, relaxation and stress – because she has to be. She is also the first employee to examine contracts for the fine print on overtime and holidays. Virgo-influenced women who are self-employed need to be particularly careful, however, as they can end up being their own hellish bosses, unless they develop a realistic-looking diary. This sign is all about the balance between productivity and self-care, and balancing this out will take up a lot more of her energy and attention than you might expect.

There is a direct connection between her job satisfaction and her health, which she needs to fully understand in order to function happily in life. Sometimes she falls in love with her job and lets the eight-hour rule slide (eight hours for sleeping, eight hours for working and eight hours for fun). If you know a Virgo type who is stealing time from her sleeping and fun schedules, then it's very likely that her health and wellbeing will become an issue sooner or later. It's almost a rule with women who have planets in this sign.

And if she hates her job? Once again, the body–mind connection has a funny way of making itself felt. With this sign in her horoscope, she needs to develop a work style as well as a lifestyle that accommodates her need to do the job, *enjoy* the job and look after her energy levels as well. Signs of immense overproductivity or striking underproductivity should not be ignored. They are more important with Virgo types than other signs, and point to bigger issues than she (or you) might suspect.

People born in the 1960s – today's influential adults – were born with Pluto, the planet of obsession, in the sign of Virgo. It's hard to believe, but before the Pluto in Virgo women came along, running shoes were not worn by anyone but athletes and yoga was hardly practised outside India. Water came out of a tap instead of a plastic bottle, and health-food shops were but a twinkle in an entrepreneur's eye. That should give you another angle on this sign. Women who have planets or points in Virgo are more concerned with purity and perfection than other people, and it can be a lifetime mission for them to sort out their yoga mats and Evian supplies along with their commitment to a job done well. Their little life (and work) experiments often set the agenda around the world, as what the Virgo type tunes into is typically what the influential sixties Pluto in Virgo generation also tune into.

HER LIBRA SIDE

If her Sun, Moon, Mercury, Venus, Mars and/or Rising Sign is in Libra then this sign will be a big part of her personality. Want to know if the Midheaven is there too? Check www.astro.com.

Her partnership is her safety net, and it gives her the protection and emotional security she craves. Take her to a tennis court and she'll ask, 'Shall we play mixed doubles?'

Does she have the Moon in Libra? Lots of Libran types like dancing – tap, ballet, jazz or strictly ballroom. You too can be Josephine Baker or Twyla Tharp with this Moon sign. It's the combination of coupledom and pulling graceful shapes that appeals to her. That, and the shoes.

Does she have Venus in Libra? When required, she can be a woman's woman and a man's woman simultaneously. Whatever the rest of her horoscope looks like, if she has Venus in Libra, then she does heels, hairdos and girlie charm with great aplomb – it's all Barbie dress-ups to her, and she has fun with it. Clothes really count too. Libra is the design sign. Her miniskirts are statements. Her floor-length gypsy skirts are statements too.

If she also has planets in Scorpio she can become fixated by love, and obsessed by a crush. Unrequited longing can take over her life, and a break-up can decimate her. When this happens, the Venus in Libra woman needs to lean hard on the non-Libra, non-Scorpio aspects of her personality to restore some perspective.

All Libran types need to inhabit a fair planet. Equality really matters – between races, sexes, classes, rich and poor, and between animals and humans. Exploitation of any kind deeply troubles her. Peace for all living things is her motto. Any system where people, animals or the environment are unfairly trashed seriously upsets her. One of my Libran-influenced website-visitors says, 'I love hearing success stories of people who've battled for animal welfare and won.' If Libra chooses to have children or adopt them, they will all be treated equally, no matter whether they are Japanese, Finnish, Jewish or African.

She loves the idea of love conquering class barriers too. It appeals to the side of her that is romantic, as well as the side of her that believes we're all equal under the sun. Her heart beats faster when she gets out *Saturday Night Fever* from the video shop, and watches rough-as-guts Brooklyn boy Tony Manero seducing his precious Manhattan yuppie princess. *Dirty Dancing*, *West Side Story* and *Titanic* have exactly the same effect on her. Can a posh girl on the upper decks really find love and happiness with a below-decks yobbo with a flat cap? *Oh God*, Venus in Libra swoons, *if only*.

She's a romantic. She loves it when people pair off properly. She likes happy endings in love stories where everyone ends up at the altar and the baddies end up with nobody. A separation or divorce can seriously rock her world – much more than it affects other women. She cries at the double-wedding scene at the end of the BBC's *Pride and Prejudice*.

Is her Mars sign Libra? She thrives in a marriage or partnership and likes to get things done as one half of a couple. If she's not careful, she can end up joined at the hip to her significant other, and her friends will worry that she's lost her identity. If her partner truly lets her shine, though, the double-act can end up showcasing her in a way that single life would never do. Could you be Tommy Lee to her Pamela Anderson? If so, you could make a fortune with your DVD.

Whatever the rest of her horoscope looks like, with this Mars placement she is 20 per cent Libran, so you are dealing with a charmer and a diplomat who likes professional and personal relationships to be utterly fair and balanced. Injustice really, *really* gets to her. But it's hard for her to fight it, unless she can kill the opposition with charm. She'll get awfully reasonable with you when she's really fired up. 'Is this fair?' asks the Mars in Libra woman. 'Aren't we all equal, deep down?' she coaxes. Justice and equality push all kinds of buttons with her, and she knows she is on solid ground when she uses them as her guiding lights.

Is her Rising Sign Libra? She just looks nice. There is no other word for it – nice. And she wouldn't be offended by that, because she *is* nice. Absolutely charming, and always easy to get on with. What's on the inside, of course, depends on her other planets, as Libra Rising is simply the outer packaging. She is her own best public relations person, because she instinctively knows how to apply the rules of PR to life. Her smile is her make-up (though, it has to be said, lots of them are mad about make-up as well).

Whatever points or planets are in Libra, this is the Noah's Ark sign. Once they find a soulmate or a business partner, they tend to arrive everywhere in a unit of two, or bring their other half into the conversation with them. Being single for too long is a problem for them, and that can also be worn like a badge.

Is her Mercury sign Libra? *Romeo and Juliet* really resonates with this woman, and she doesn't think 'Romeo, Romeo, wherefore art thou Romeo?' is funny at all. She understands the pure romance of it. She thinks in terms of partnerships – me and you, as opposed to me, me, me, and throughout her working life she'll be given plenty of chances to become involved in professional duets or business double-acts. Who can she get on her side? She'll use more diplomacy than Elizabeth I if she has to, to win over her potential allies. She's a natural feminist, but may also be concerned with animal rights or the environment. A lop-sided world is no world at all, in her opinion.

The Libran-influenced woman tends to think like a lawyer, no matter what profession she's in. Her immediate question about any situation, personal or professional, is simple: is it fair?

She thinks in pictures and images too. This is the little girl who grows up playing endlessly with her Etch-A-Sketch, and then turns into the kind of woman who actually pays to walk around an art gallery with headphones on. They all have a sixth sense about haircuts, hair colour, curtains, shoe heights and cushions. In fact, say it loud and say it proud – Libra is probably *the* cushion sign. They have a feeling for texture, colour and form that makes the Tate Gallery the perfect place to leave them on a rainy day . . . or even a sunny one.

All of them want equilibrium. You can rock the boat when a Libran type is around, but she will soon steer it somewhere safe. Sometimes she can rock the boat herself – but she will typically rescue the situation. Perhaps this is why so many Libran types are famous for their calming effect. The ancients decided to interpret the constellation of Libra as a set of scales because of one word: *balance*.

Her capacity to adapt to anything and anybody is astonishing. She has a gift for adjusting, bending and, if necessary, twisting and turning. Surfing is a Libran sport. Even if she's never been on a board in her life, the Libran type can usually identify with the art of wave management. She intuitively understands how to lean to the right, lean to the left, lean to the right again . . . and survive the ride.

Because the constellation of Libra is associated with a set of scales the Libran type classically finds herself in careers, families or relationships where she must keep the scales even. Here's another classically Libran image – the circus tightrope.

It is her spectacular people skills, given to her by Venus, that enable her to charm, pacify, calm and correct. The Libran scales themselves encourage her to find equilibrium and harmony. Even if she only has one planet or point in this sign, her Libran side will still be in evidence through her life – particularly in crisis situations, which is when her grace and graciousness is usually most obvious.

This sign is associated with fence-sitting and indecision in quite a few astrology books. But women with Libran qualities are much more focused than that. It is their mission to seek the calm centre in any situation. To get there, the Libran type needs to be skilful at negotiating life's extremes. She knows how easily a set of scales can tip, or how quickly a situation can overturn. Even if this sometimes means she's leaning to the left while simultaneously preparing to lean to the right, it doesn't make her lily-livered or weak. Rough experiences in her personal or professional life make her highly conscious of the need for balance, that's all.

Does she create her own storms? Some of them do. But all Libran types have an instinctive wariness about any person, plan, project or set-up that is swinging between wild extremes, and will typically do whatever it takes to restore balance and harmony.

HER SCORPIO SIDE

If her Sun, Moon, Mercury, Venus, Mars and/or Rising Sign is in Scorpio then this sign will be a big part of her personality. Want to know if the Midheaven is there too? Check www.astro.com.

There is a lot in opera, Oprah, or soap opera that calls her. The murders, suicides, incest, secret adoptions, brushes with death, voices from beyond the grave and hidden abortions (yes, you *can* talk about taboo subjects when a Scorpio type is reading) all resonate. Does she have a lot of planets in Scorpio? Then her private life needs to be kept extremely private, lest the local archbishop publicly labels her a wayward hussy, or she be invited to appear in a new series of the *Carry On* films.

Is her Mercury sign Scorpio? She says what you're not supposed to say – and thinks about ideas that other people prefer to bury or hide. Some of them concern death. Others concern sex or the occult. Still more concern the particular balance of power in her personal or professional world. Other people say, 'Let's not talk about it' but Mercury in Scorpio women close the door, hang up a Do Not Disturb sign and say, 'Okay, let's talk about it.'

She carries secrets too. Lots and lots of secrets – in fact, nobody else needs a paper shredder more. Scorpio types need secrets. Her diary should probably have a skull and crossbones on the front and a combination lock on the back. It doesn't matter if she's writing about family, friends or lovers – it all tends to sound like a bleeped-out episode of *The Osbournes*.

Is she intense? Oh, not really. Just enough to burn holes in your cushions, that's all. Nobody is capable of staring longer and deeper than a Scorpio type – or saying so much with her eyes.

If she has several planets in Scorpio she may work in a field where discretion is everything and great depth is required. She'll choose a professional niche where she can be powerful and change people's lives. Don't trust any of them who do fluffy bunny impersonations. Underneath the big white ears and pink high heels lurks the next prime minister.

Does she have the Moon in Scorpio? She'll look at you and see your underwear. Lots of them are familiar with bondage, too – or at the very least, bondage-style black leather bras – and some of them make seriously spectacular cross-dressers. The religious Moon in Scorpio types just immerse themselves in intense rituals, with enough candles to light the Vatican, and try to deal with their awful sinfulness that way.

Sometimes it's the occult that is a comfort, rather than the world of sex or intense religion. She may be comforted by the mysteries of tarot or astrology, or cushioned by a belief in something more powerful and hidden than the rest of us see. Many prominent wiccans and stargazers have the Moon in Scorpio, by the way.

Whatever planets or points are in Scorpio, she needs makeovers, and if she can't practise them on herself, she will commandeer her friends, do their hair and make-up and change them forever. She makes over houses and flats too, and if she's in a job where she's allowed to take other people (or just other people's work) and overhaul them, she's in heaven. She's here to create new beginnings from whatever she hurls in the garbage, or she can save a situation or person that is breaking down and resurrect it.

If she has planets or points in Scorpio, then whatever society buries, ignores, represses, forgets, edits or censors is her life's blood. She has a need for taboo, and is drawn towards film, music, art and books that reflect this. Lesbian crime fiction? No problem. Concentration camp diaries? Essential! Public debates about racism? Great! She's the schoolgirl who reads *Cosmopolitan* under the desk. Her first orgasm changes her life, by the way. Never underestimate its effect on her.

With planets or points in this sign, she reconstructs herself at regular intervals, usually after a psychological or emotional crash. It's quite true that her mood ring can get stuck on black. When that happens, she needs to go down, down, down into her personal abyss with plenty of good deep music and a slow-burning candle. She needs to plunge, in order to come up again renewed. This is why Scorpio types are so brilliant if you are suffering from depression, anxiety or Total Life Screw Up. She genuinely understands and will get down and dirty with you, to help you survive the journey.

Does she have Venus in Scorpio? Welcome to the world of Batgirl. Even the blond Venus in Scorpio women have their dark side. She can imagine making love to a vampire – or even becoming one. And she can also imagine herself being effortlessly transplanted into a chapter of Jackie Collins. This woman transforms herself at regular intervals. If her relationship fails, she'll go to ground for a year, then re-emerge with new hair, a new attitude and a new life. If she battles breast cancer, she'll survive it and come back as a charity fundraiser. If she dies on the operating table, she'll be reborn as a psychic. If she is sexually assaulted, she'll rise again to become a powerful feminist activist – it's in her nature to regenerate.

Ah, Scorpio types. Nobody else could enjoy a job in a morgue more – or relish the chance to visit a medium. Nobody else could sing along to 'Je T'Aime, Moi Non Plus' with quite so much feeling, or quite so much unnecessarily heavy breathing. And it's hard to think of any woman who could grab a ticket to *The Vagina Monologues* with quite so much enthusiasm too. In fact, some might say her entire *life* is a vagina monologue.

Her music is passionate and mysterious. One of my website correspondents is addicted to flamenco guitar. Another goes gooey over Nick Cave. They don't do airhead pop.

If you fast-forward your *Pride and Prejudice* DVD to the bit where Mr Darcy emerges from a lake, dripping wet in tight, white jodhpurs, you probably have planets or points in Scorpio, and no doubt you can imagine the missing sex scenes in Jane Austen too.

The Scorpio type can see the point of cricket, or any of the more psychological sports. She psychs out the players from the comfort of her sofa. She enjoys control. If she has more than one planet in Scorpio you may be surprised at how much an entire evening can be secretly dictated by her. Is she aware that she's pulling the strings? Not always. She has an intuitive understanding of people politics and the way power actually works. This is the *I, Claudius* sign.

If she's typical of her Scorpio side, then she will love the mystery and power of astrology and the deeper places that it can take you; and the world of mediumship and psychic ability compels her too.

She really loves a powerful career, and her passion for work is doubled if she gets to keep a lot of secrets as part of the job. It depends on the rest of her chart, but if she's channelling her Scorpio side in a major way, she will find a role where she is obviously (or secretly) in charge, and also in a position to create genuine, lasting and powerful change.

Expect strong views on pornography. Is it really just erotica with bad lighting, or is it something more sinister? A Scorpio type's sexuality is deeply important to her, and her feelings about sex in the public domain are usually complex and intense.

They all understand survival and are drawn to jobs (and people) where life and death are on the line. It's the intensity. This woman also likes wrecked gardens – she rebuilds them – and other people's disaster zones: magazines that need remoulding, manuscripts that need reworking, entire neighbourhoods that have been flooded and need reconstructing. Put the 're' in front of almost any word, and that's the Scorpio type's domain. She's the resurrectionist!

Does she have Mars in Scorpio? Her sexuality is her power, and her power can move and shake anything. When she finally discovers this and embraces it, she is capable of having the same effect on men that Sandra Dee had on John Travolta in *Grease* – but only after she changed into skintight black lycra and high heels. Remember that image of k.d. lang shaving Cindy Crawford on the cover of *Vanity Fair*? Ooof! Mars in Scorpio, baby! Menstruation, menopause, magic – all are fair game for the Mars in Scorpio woman, even if she keeps it private.

Scorpio types attract intense, secretive friends and lovers: people with a past, or people with secrets to keep. Part of her will always duck and dive in the shadows of life, because she isn't afraid of people (or issues) that other people find confronting. And when she gets going at a dinner party? You'll feel as if you're watching a confessional with Oprah Winfrey, or the best bits from *Eastenders*.

Is her Rising Sign Scorpio? She has a way of looking at you, halfway through a conversation, that banishes any idea you had about uncovering her life story. She can be wonderfully tight-lipped about almost anything you care to think of – though love and money are her special subjects, and these are two lines you may not cross unless she gives you permission. This intense privacy is a major part of her image. She's powerful too, or genuinely influential. She's attached to her sunglasses, by the way. Don't ever walk off with them.

HER SAGITTARIUS SIDE

If her Sun, Moon, Mercury, Venus, Mars and/or Rising Sign is in Sagittarius this sign will be a big part of her personality. Want to know if the Midheaven is there too? Check www.astro.com.

Is her Venus sign Sagittarius? Anywhere from Hanoi to Poland is on her list of places to love, so if you get into a serious relationship with her, make sure your passport is updated. She can understand why some people want to inhabit a real-life version of *Endless Summer* – Africa, Australia, New Zealand, Tahiti, Hawaii, South America – what's wrong with that?

She loves comedy and funny people, and may be a natural comedienne herself. One of my Venus in Sagittarius website visitors writes, 'I love anyone who has a ridiculous Pythonesque sense of humour – but real life is also funnier than any script.' The same woman teaches children with learning and mental disabilities, and loves her job because of all the 'wise, funny, talented and supportive clowns' in her class. Humour makes the world go around for Venus in Sagittarius, because it puts everything in perspective.

If she has more than one planet in Sagittarius, her world will be a multicultural melting pot, with more accents than you'll find on a Monday morning at the UN. Her computer will be her passport to London, New York, Montreal, Auckland, Sydney, Botswana and Minsk.

All of them need to believe in a meaningful universe, and after a life crisis or three, will go on The Big Search. It can take her in any direction, from Buddhism to astrology to born-again Christianity. The idea of living in a random, meaningless, chaotic jungle of DNA and stray atoms destroys her lust for life.

The Sagittarian type reads *The Motorcycle Diaries* and *completely relates*. This is the woman who goes mad if she is forced to stay stuck in the suburbs – and jumps on a bus in the middle of the night, just to get away. She craves exotic holidays, foreign visitors and round-the-world tickets.

She needs meaning in her life and typically finds it in cultures and belief systems outside her own. Comparing and contrasting them to the beliefs she was taught at school or at home gives her the perspective she needs. Narrow minds make her feel uncomfortable. She needs the freedom to explore ideas of all kinds, and great minds from all eras.

Is this the woman most likely to emigrate? Perhaps. It certainly crosses her mind on a regular basis – although her usual recurring fantasy is the overseas sabbatical, also known as My Year Off. Some Sagittarian types are just effortlessly international and don't seem to have any fixed nationality, even though their birth certificates say they are from downtown Woy Woy. She cringes when she hears about the number of Americans who don't hold valid passports. In fact, it makes her itchy all over.

She's good at funny faces. She can do a blank deadpan, or mad monkey eyes. She knows when to exaggerate and when to underplay. Anything, as long as it keeps you amused.

Does she have Mercury in Sagittarius? She thinks in jokes. Even a perfectly serious conversation about politics, death or religion will probably end up reminding you of a Bette Midler monologue – or Tracey Ullman doing Woody Allen. Vast exaggeration is her speciality, but she also knows how to dramatically underplay big subjects – all in the name of free entertainment for you. She knows why Jane Austen is funny. She knows why *The Office* is funny too.

This is the no worries, hakuna matata Mercury sign. She doesn't find it hard to think positively. If she has planets in Scorpio as well, then this side of her personality can stop her from becoming too dark.

All of them know that you grow by learning, and she may be a student of life, *all* her life. Her brain needs a lot of room to explore every angle, and all the options. Narrow-minded people shut her down. So does a career that won't allow her to explore intellectually.

She's a natural philosopher too, and likes wading through the non-fiction sections of bookshops in search of an answer (or three) to life's big questions. The more planets she has in Sagittarius, the more obvious this philosophical, questing side of her personality will be.

Is her Rising Sign Sagittarius? If she has planets in Sagittarius as well as this Sagittarian 'mask', then she'll be effortlessly funny

– a natural impressionist, or a walking sitcom. And some of them have no planets in Sagittarius at all, but quickly realise how useful a sense of humour can be, personally or professionally, so use their Sagittarius Rising Sign packaging to put this across.

Is her Mars Sign Sagittarius? She uses humour as a weapon. When it's important to defend what is dear to her – or attack her enemies – she'll come on like a stand-up comic with an unruly audience. Her idea of a real man is Carl Jung or Joseph Campbell, His Holiness the Dalai Lama or Ben 'Obi-Wan' Kenobe. She identifies with philosophers and sages, and the occasional guru too.

Whatever planets or points she has in Sagittarius, she lives in the future for a lot of the time, and has a forward-thinking, positive attitude towards her personal and her professional life. Her personal traffic lights are occasionally on amber, but usually stuck on green – she has no interest in stagnating in the past, or even being particularly satisfied with the present.

The joy of life for the Sagittarian type is its close resemblance to a travel agency full of brochures. She likes the thrill of not knowing where she's going; it makes the journey more enjoyable. For this reason, women born with planets or points in this sign tend to do well in careers where they are constantly being asked to engage in forward planning. Jupiter is the ruler of Sagittarius and it is associated with optimism and expansion. Sagittarian types can be astonishingly fearless about the future, and have an incredible faith in what's possible, which only other women with Sagittarian planets can properly understand. The rest of us just have to look on and admire her sense of conviction, which is always strong. This applies even if Sagittarian types fail at their projects, or find their plans go belly-up. The Jupiter influence in her horoscope helps her to move on and look forward.

Some signs are about living in the past and looking backwards. Some signs are about living in the present – the power of now. Sagittarius is about tomorrow, next Wednesday, next

August and the year 2020 too. She is influenced by the element of fire, if she has planets or points in this sign. To get a stronger sense of who she is, visualise the way that flames move upwards and race ahead. That's her energy, and that's her way of negotiating life.

Sagittarius is associated with the Ninth House in astrology, which rules new horizons. As a child, the Sagittarian type is typically fascinated by the idea that a horizon is never-ending. Swim far enough and you won't fall off the edge of the Earth. Fly far enough and you'll never stop seeing that thin line in front of you, receding into the distance. The concept of limitless horizons is a big part of her psyche. It's in her nature to keep moving across them, whenever and wherever she can.

The big farewell, or the 'au revoir' wave, is part of this journey. All women leave jobs, lovers, friends, family or places. For Sagittarian types, it's a necessary part of her own growth and evolution. Even if she has just one point or planet in this sign, she'll have a pattern of moving on and moving forward – and there is something organic, natural and positive about the pattern that feeds her need to keep growing, and keep going too.

How can she travel to Egypt if she's not prepared to hand in her key? How can she explore new horizons in her personal life if she's not ready to let someone go? How can she race towards the next professional horizon unless she's ready to turn her back on what went before? Sagittarian types can be wonderfully philosophical about these end points in their lives. Her motto is 'Don't Look Back', and she means it.

Jupiter, which has such an influence on her horoscope, helps her to give other people room to move too. She is the person least likely to cramp your style, and the last woman in the world who would try to limit, confine or restrict you in any way. Jupiter is about giving. The Sagittarian type typically gives you all the space you need, and more, if you want to explore bigger possibilities, or, just like her, new horizons.

She's an opportunist. She's hip to life's open doors. She has the soul of a gambler in many ways, because she places so much trust in what the future might bring her. She does not ask for guarantees from the universe, or even a note from her mother. All she requires is the space to pursue the next unravelling horizon.

She is not someone who hangs onto relationships or marriages out of fear, or the need for familiarity and security. She has much more faith in tomorrow than that. Nor does she need anyone to hold her hand as she steps towards the next big possibility. That can make for an interesting relationship, if you both truly understand each other; but it can also lead to a parting of the ways, particularly if she reaches a point in her life when the next unfolding horizon is in a part of the world where you have no intention of going!

HER CAPRICORN SIDE

If her Sun, Moon, Mercury, Venus, Mars and/or Rising Sign is in Capricorn, then this sign will be a big part of her personality. Is the Midheaven there too? Check www.astro.com.

The motto 'onwards and upwards' is her mantra, and her friends and lovers need to remember how much she needs to make it – and keep climbing too. Hold her back and she'll just be miserable. If the rest of her horoscope agrees, then this woman is destined for amazing success, no matter how hard she has to push herself to get there, or how far she has to slog up the social or professional ladder.

If she chooses parenthood, she will need to seriously confront her own ambition and weigh up nappies against the challenge of abseiling through the glass ceiling.

Does she have more than one planet in Capricorn? Then she will have natural gravitas, and a steady, serious side to her personality which is deeply impressive to a certain kind of corporate male.

If she has the choice between marrying the President and marrying the bellboy, you won't even have to ask – no matter how well-endowed the bellboy is. She has an instinctive understanding of class systems, caste systems and corporate systems – and how to make them work for her. She has what it takes to get to the top of them too.

Is her Rising Sign Capricorn? She projects seriousness, even if she's forced to put on a fluffy duck costume for a fancy-dress party. She appears to be a contender or a player from a young age – and the serious gaze can even be evident in baby photos.

She appears to be one of life's realists. Talk to her long enough and you'll pick up the distinct impression that life wasn't meant to be easy – and she knows, because she's lived it. Whatever role, career or vocation life hands her, the Capricorn Rising woman handles it with complete professionalism. It doesn't matter if she's a full-time wife and mother, a sales rep or a magician – she projects experience and competence.

Is her Venus Sign Capricorn?A surprisingly significant number of them end up with trophy husbands or partners who help them vault effortlessly up the social ladder. She is far too cool to admit it, but *Pretty Woman* struck a chord. She can relate to rags-to-riches stories or even hooker-to-wife stories, come to that. Who is photocopying in the office one day and racing off to marry a member of the royal family the next? The Venus in Capricorn woman.

She doesn't do low-cut tops, T-shirts with messages on the front or loud trousers. The only exception to this is the Venus in Capricorn woman whose profession requires that she dresses like Britney crossed with Jordan. In that case, expect yards of naked breast and vulgar heels, because it will be a work uniform. This one does work uniforms like no other woman. The clothes have to be practical, you see. She doesn't like anything that shows the dirt or looks as if it's going to shrink, even if *Vogue* does tell her that it's this season's must-have. Common sense defeats *haute couture* for her, every time. The Venus in Capricorn woman is practical in other ways too. Drop her on a desert island and she'll reach for her Swiss Army Knife.

Whatever planets or points she has in Capricorn, she always does what she says she's going to do, and turns up on time. The only exception to this rule is the Capricorn type who also has planets in Aquarius and Pisces, who is slightly Cadbury's Flake. Most of them are as dependable as the NASA clock, though, and as solid as a rock.

She thinks in terms of building solid structures, based on firm foundations. Some people go to Manhattan and wonder how the skyscrapers can possibly stay up. Capricorn types have no such doubts, because her entire life is like a skyscraper, constructed bit by bit, and she understands that if you put enough hard work and time into something, it tends to stay up – forever.

If it all goes horribly wrong in her life, she rebuilds everything from scratch using the lessons she has learnt to make sure she's on a firmer footing next time. She learns from experience, which is why she always seems so wise – or just so streetwise.

Manhattan speaks to her in other ways too. The very existence of New York City proves to her that it's possible to arrive on Ellis Island with nothing and end up owning half of the Upper West Side. The Capricorn type also understands the longing that bridge-and-tunnel types have for Fifth Avenue life. *Working Girl* is a Capricorn film and 'Uptown Girl' is a Capricorn song. All women with this sign in their charts are aware of class and social status – it's part of their astrological DNA.

Her brain is wired for upward mobility, and she instinctively understands how hierarchies work, in any sphere of society – from corporate life to political parties to the established order in her workplace. She understands the public service very, very well (and how to work it, natch). She finds it deeply satisfying that there are still some rules you can follow in life that will guarantee success. Patience and hard work are her tools. That, and a strong understanding of how you get there from here.

Is her Mars sign Capricorn? All her energy is focused on making it, which is why she may start out in a family of vacuum-cleaner salesmen and end up marrying the President.

If she has more than one planet in Capricorn then she has what it takes to build an empire. She knows how to lay firm foundations and structure her life according to real world laws. Capricorn types are typically wonderfully practical and have a gritty grasp of reality that can be extremely useful if you ever need sane advice on love, work or money. She knows what's what, who's who and what fits where. All of them are quietly canny about the way *life actually is* – which can be a blessing, if you're one of her less practical friends.

They're all into self-development. This doesn't necessarily mean a New Age course either (though if she also has planets in Aquarius, it may). Capricorn is associated with the Tenth House in astrology, which is all about climbing to the next rung of the evolutionary ladder. If she is properly supervised or mentored, the Capricorn type can haul herself up to any level she likes – professionally, emotionally, intellectually, spiritually or just physically.

Her family dictates where she enters the world. Her parents' financial position, social status or class describes where she starts out. From there, it's the Capricorn type's mission to move onwards and upwards, on her own terms. This is why so many of them start off in the suburbs and end up in the corridors of power. She's big on learning and training herself to go to the next level . . . wherever she believes that to be.

Like the male Capricorn type, she acts as a mentor for people throughout her life, often at the same time that she is mentored. Age, wisdom or experience gaps are common in her partnerships or in her professional relationships. Even if she only has one point or planet in this sign, it is her karma to understand what it means to take responsibility for others who are relying on her to take them to the next level.

Is she aware of status, class and social position, as so many astrology books claim? With Saturn's rulership of this sign, it is hard for her to ever properly relax and see people as people. She is, after all, a realist – and even the real world has first and third status! The Capricorn type works out her own pecking order, though, and draws conclusions about where she fits in, along with everybody else. Does she lead, follow or serve? What about you? Women with points or planets in Capricorn need to know the score.

Her famous realism means that she has an intensely practical approach to her professional and personal life. She knows all about prescribed roles and labels, for example, but she's much more interested in what actually goes on between people and how the system works. Is the top dog really the top dog, or does the cat in the alley run the show?

It's not hard for her to see herself in her children, employers, employees, clients, staff, lovers or partners. She's a mentor and guide – at the same time that she's a work in progress. She's down the bottom of the pecking order – at the same time that she's a few rungs above. The Capricorn type understands hierarchies, at home or at work, because she often finds herself in jobs or relationships where she's simultaneously balancing her heels on different rungs of the ladder of life. She's higher/lower/older/younger – all at once.

It's her karma to be put in a position where she constantly has to be responsible for others at the same time that she is guided or mentored. It's also her destiny to be thrown into relationships or careers where age, class or financial gaps teach her to develop her own wisdom about how life actually works. Of course, she knows that we're all the same under the skin, and we're all dependent on each other. Nevertheless, it is a curious fact of life that Capricorn types are repeatedly drawn into situations where they have to work within a system where everyone has their place in the scheme of things and where she is required to examine it, understand it – and see where there's room to move on up too.

HER AQUARIUS SIDE

If her Sun, Moon, Mercury, Venus, Mars and/or Rising Sign is in Aquarius, then this sign will be a big part of her personality. Want to know if the Midheaven is there too? Check www.astro.com.

As a child, she reads *Little Women* and identifies with Jo, or devours *The Famous Five* and identifies with George. She doesn't do Barbie, unless she's organising the caravan as a commune and has permission to put Ken upside-down in the pool with his shorts over his head.

She needs space. A flat next door to yours – or, as Virginia Woolf described it, 'A room of one's own'. Too much gooey togetherness and icky intimacy messes with her mind.

Does she have Mercury in Aquarius? She's a radical. Her views may be dramatically out of step with other people's and dinner parties can sometimes end in tears or handbag-throwing. She's 'anti' a lot of things: anti-sexism, anti-racism and anti-war, for a start. Don't make the mistake of thinking you can predict exactly what she's against, however. Some of them are even against the United Nations – and Germaine Greer.

If she has more than one planet in Aquarius she may be considered radical, strange or a little odd. Don't dismiss her as Miss Looney Tunes, though. A lot of her current life choices will become yours, about twenty years from now.

She needs a lot of New Age in her life, although she doesn't think of it as New Age – she prefers to think in terms of ordinary reality and non-ordinary reality. Quantum physics does something to her insides, and she can't stop herself from thinking about the *planet*.

Aquarian types have their own logic, and she needs to be true to herself, even when her decisions leave other people in a state of shock – or just scratching their heads. To compromise or conform for the sake of it feels like a sell-out to her. And, more than that, it just seems plain dumb.

She thinks in terms of her friendships or the groups that she is a part of. What do her friends think about her new lover? What would her friends do if the boss threw them out of the office tomorrow? She's brilliant at removing herself from a situation and thinking collectively. With this sign in her horoscope, at least 20 per cent of her is pure team player – even though she hangs onto her uniqueness and independence inside the group.

She has unique, original taste, and may carry a gold-tipped walking cane or tote around a green handbag with a secret compartment. Alternatively, she may remind you of Carole King on the cover of *Tapestry*, complete with bare feet, jeans, cushions and a cat – or Sporty Spice, complete with nose-piercing, tracksuit and gold-capped tooth.

She's the Lisa Simpson in her family and doesn't ever want to turn into Marge. She's also the Lieutenant Uhura on the Starship Enterprise, and lots of these brilliant, offbeat women also happen to know that Uhura is Swahili for freedom. Aha!

Does she have Venus in Aquarius? She is frequently Girl Alone, because she loves her independence and space just as much as she loves being in a relationship. Or she attracts people who can't or won't give her stability. Either way, she gets time out from intimacy.

Free at last! She is more open to relationship alternatives than other women. She may even believe that marriage is an obscene bourgeois institution designed to keep women in chains – or that woman is the nigger of the world (to quote John Lennon). She's good at platonic love, unpredictable on–off relationships and 'Let's have separate homes' relationships.

For the Venus in Aquarius type, the sex is often zipless. It can happen in the lavatory on a 747 or in a supermarket storeroom (just as long as nobody feels obliged to call back the next day). It can happen with a 16-year-old unemployed teenager, with some guy she picked up in a Texan pickup truck or in the back row at a Sex Pistols' reunion concert.

With planets or points in Venus, her taste in music, art,

fashion or interiors is extremely unconventional and occasionally downright bizarre. She's first with the latest, no matter whether she's streaming underground music from a website or starting a one-woman Gary Numan revival.

Does she have more than one point or planet in Aquarius? Sometimes she comes to the front door and forgets how mad she looks: when left to her own devices on a Sunday, the strongly Aquarian type is capable of throwing almost anything (and everything) on.

Nobody enjoys breaking up more – or leaving home more – than the Aquarius-influenced woman. She may even be seen hurling her hat in the air at the traffic lights, *à la* Mary Tyler Moore, a few moments after her grand exit. The emotions kick in later when she realises that maybe freedom isn't all it's cracked up to be. She secretly thinks that an awful lot of the girls she went to school with have turned into Stepford Wives – but she's too cool to mention it.

She likes experimenting with clothes, careers, relationships, her social life and her home life, and sets trends that other women follow. She has the soul of a suffragette, a flapper, a dolly bird and a punk – and she will not be told what to wear: by you, or by Stella McCartney. She longs for anything (or anybody) that is exciting, new, real, unexpected, different and out there. Her heart breaks when something (or someone) that she's held dear to her non-conformist heart suddenly becomes mainstream.

Does she have the Moon in Aquarius? Other girls say, 'When I grow up I want to be an air hostess,' while the Moon in Aquarius woman says, 'When I grow up I want to be an anthropologist/activist/astrologer/lesbian supermodel.' They don't do normal. They do *unusual*, baby.

All of them dig *Big Chill*-style friendships. Lots of men and women, all together, making space for each other's quirks – *brilliant*! She also loves it when her friends allow her to skip the big group barbecue and curl up in an armchair alone, reading

Colette. She needs space and the freedom to be herself. Friends who can give her this will be friends for life.

Domestically, the truly Aquarian type is a law unto herself. She is not like the women in the ads or the magazine lifestyle features. She skips the pyjamas and sleeps in Chanel No. 5, or she may dress up her dog in outfits to match her own. Eating roast beef out of the fridge at 4 a.m. with her bare hands? No problem. Throwing burned saucepans out of the window? Absolutely. If you live with her long enough, you'll see all the madness.

She likes alternative anything. Alternative music, alternative religions or alternative medicine can quickly put her back in her comfort zone. She needs a bit of boho, hippie or New Age to get by. Even at her most conservative and conventional (and she can play that game, if she has to) she'll never be able to hide her originality completely. The wedding dress may be white, but the train will be so long it will require six people to carry it into the church. The real-estate investments will be respectable, but decided by the *I Ching*.

She is a humanitarian, and feels strongly about children in the developing world – to the point where she'll consider adopting. Or she signs petitions, buys *The Big Issue*, believes in Bob Geldof and wears a wristband for AIDS fundraising. She feels uncomfortable unless she is changing the world, even in a small way. Sometimes just going vegetarian will do it.

When she can combine those *Big Chill*-styled groups of friends with a common cause, she finds that she has the kind of emotional security she has been looking for all of her life. Even then, she'll never blend seamlessly into the group. She'll always be a little outside it, and apart from it. The Aquarian type is never really one of the gang.

This woman's mantra is 'Space, independence and freedom' and without those things in her life, she can feel awful. Lovers who hold her tightly, gaze into her eyes and tell her that they'll be together forever just make her long to open all the windows and let the oxygen in. Part of her just doesn't have that level of passion or intensity.

Share households, families or marriages where there are lots of rules about mowing the lawn, fetching the newspaper on Sundays or having pasta on Wednesday nights are a disaster for her. She can't do it – *won't* do it – and is physically incapable of doing it. Her family tree contains at least one eccentric; their DNA has been passed down to her too.

Is her Mars sign Aquarius? One of these things is not like the other – and it's usually her. Her energy is wired and wild. She functions best when she's barefoot. If she's over forty, she was probably a punk – or all her friends were punks, so she decided to wear cashmere twinsets and sensible shoes. Freedom matters to the Mars in Aquarius woman. She knows why the caged bird sings, and she also understands why some women want to run with the wolves.

All of them do things in groups or through their friends. She is here to change the world, and does this most effectively when she is part of a posse. Aquarian types are gifted at no-strings, unconditional, *real* friendship, and have a cool, light touch that makes it work.

HER PISCES SIDE

If her Sun, Moon, Mercury, Venus, Mars and/or Rising Sign is in Pisces then this sign will be a big part of her personality. Want to know if the Midheaven is there too? Check www.astro.com.

Some of them hear voices – Piscean type Joan of Arc did. Others have eerily accurate dreams, or think of a friend and find her on the phone five minutes later.

What's her poison? It may be brandy and opium – or herbal tea, incense and a book on dream interpretation. Christmas carols in church can do it for her too – this is the sign that rules big faith as well as big escapes.

Give her anything, but give her emotion. Her bottom lip quivers when she sings ballads at karaoke nights, and she specialises in Big Shiny Eyes when you have deep and meaningful conversations over a bottle of wine.

One of my website correspondents who has Venus in Pisces says she loves rare perfumes from the thirties and forties, with essential oils rather than synthetics. This sign cares about chemicals, and also has a sensitive nose for wine – and (my informants tell me) a connoisseur's appreciation of hydroponic dope. Pisces is about substances, be they sold over the counter at Harrod's or round the back of a pub on a Saturday night.

Some Pisces types know that drugs and alcohol don't work for them, and abstain for life. Others enjoy weaving them into their week on a regular basis. In all cases, though, this woman can understand the homeless drunk on the corner, and will throw him fifty bucks anyway.

Compassion is her thing. She is part-psychic if she has planets or points in Pisces, and she knows what it feels like to be you. Or him. Or her.

She loves experiences that are hard to put into words and impossible to run through a computer or check out with science. Spiritual healing and reiki fascinate her. So does poetry, which speaks to her soul. She is drawn to people who ask her to take on trust what cannot be measured, seen or proven. They have faith, and faith speaks to her – even if she's being asked to believe that she was Sir Walter Raleigh in a previous existence or that consciousness survives death.

Love can be blind with her, particularly if Venus aspects Neptune (check this at www.astro.com). Relationships with attached people or dodgy, two-timing lovers may be a risk if this is the case. She can be blind to her own role in proceedings too. Careful!

Does she have Venus or the Moon in Pisces? She may be

inclined to wear beer goggles when choosing one-night stands, and should be careful, lest she wakes up with someone who resembles a deep-sea monster.

Give her a camera if you really want to know how extraordinary her imagination is, or hand her a paintbox and a book on the surrealists. She loves playing around with visual images or wandering around art galleries and losing herself in other people's realities.

The Pisces type needs to escape, and if things go badly wrong, may do so via a whisky bottle in the wardrobe, a morphine prescription or a line of cocaine. Her favourite music is pure prose and emotion – the kind that nobody else really understands. Sad songs and films make her misty-eyed, and she can be quiveringly emotional about almost anything, from other people's tragedies to the kitten she just found on the highway.

She needs to know there is more to the universe than Mars Bars. Some of them are attracted to Buddhism, some to Scientology. They all believe in a higher power.

She needs fantasy and alternative realities, even if they're for kids. Take her to Brisbane (also known as Brisneyland) and she will buy tickets to Sea World, Movie World, Dream World and Underwater World and emerge feeling perfectly normal. It's the ghastliness of mundane existence that does her head in.

She goes to see her accountant about her tax return, but daydreams about being the social director on *The Love Boat* instead, sailing the *Pacific Princess* en route to Puerto Vallarta. Children's books can make her feel safe and cosy also, when life becomes too crashingly difficult. *Mary Poppins* can do it for her, and so can the loopier parts of *Harry Potter*. She likes to eat breakfast cereal that has a spokes-elf, like Lucky Charms. Heaven is a bowl full of green clovers, orange stars, pink hearts, yellow moons and blue diamonds.

Does she have Mars in Pisces? If she loses her way in life, the frustration and anger may be channelled via a vodka bottle or through the bottom of a bong. Waving her arms around to trance music is probably safer – though one of my website correspondents defends drugs too. 'I love acid,' she wrote to me, 'because it made me question my whole brain's function and showed me how flimsy our perceptions can be.'

Lots of them become more spiritual or religious as they deal with life's storms. Having a doctrine, dogma or faith becomes their first line of defence. Buddhism helps many Mars in Pisces women face the day. When she's angry with the world, she can make a poetic sacrifice of herself and do the tragic heroine thing ad infinitum. Sensible friends can help, as can an awareness of the other more fiery or practical aspects of her horoscope. Some Mars in Pisces women are Cadbury's Flakes, and desperately need grounding. Wobbling around in high heels waving a champagne glass around is not good for them.

Is her Mercury sign Pisces? She has the soul of Emily Dickinson and Patti Smith, and knows how a rabbit feels – or a daisy, come to that. It is almost impossible for this woman to buy battery-hen eggs because she has the ability to stare deeply into a chicken's eyes and read its mind. Part of her wishes it was still the Sixties, so she could grab a seat on Ken Kesey's Magic Bus with the destination FURTHER on the front. She is one of the very few people on the planet who can actually see the pictures in *Magic Eye* books, and she typically sees a few extra images that other people miss.

All of them love the intriguing idea that the human family is probably descended from three cavewomen, all hanging around in the same tree and sharing the same banana. *Vive* the Daughters of Eve! A woman with Pisces in her chart is fascinated by the mysterious idea that all of us are swimming around in the same pool somehow.

Neptune rules Pisces. It describes a oneness – a lack of boundaries. Even if she isn't remotely religious or spiritual, the Piscean type knows that we are all mixed up together in the game of life. The connections she feels to you, to your great-great-grandmother and to everyone else might be mysterious, but they are still there.

She instinctively understands Jung's idea of the collective unconscious, and Joseph Campbell's take on shared human myths. Across class, culture, time, gender and nationality, Piscean types understand that we are linked by the same invisible threads. Your bits are her bits. And her bits are someone else's bits, 1000 years ago, and 500 kilometres away. She feels the unity of all life, and senses the threads that bind us together.

She knows that what separates people from each other is illusory, and she is much more interested in the fascinating idea that humanity is deeply, profoundly and irrevocably linked. It appeals to her Neptunian side – the part of her that is at a loss to understand why people pretend there are so many barriers separating them.

Piscean types can be forgiven for occasionally seeming lost, dazed and confused. They feel at home in the world of the imagination, but logic is often lost to her. She can grasp the bigger picture and get the overall essence – but fall down flat if she is required to point out exactly how A is connected to B, and how C ended up where D was supposed to be.

Her sense of identity is always related to her connection to others, which is also where the confusion sets in. Is she your lover, her sister's sister, her father's daughter, her aunt's niece or just the great-great-great-great-granddaughter of an exotic dancer in Paris who ran off with a minor member of Spanish parliament, who was in turn related to a Hungarian weightlifter named Boris? She is fascinated by *Six Degrees of Separation*, and also Six Degrees of Kevin Bacon.

She cannot separate herself from other people, even though she can't always make out the precise nature of the link. Sometimes it is psychic. Sometimes it is spiritual. Sometimes it is just – unfathomable. When she looks in the mirror, who does she see? If she has planets or points in Pisces, she never finds herself alone in there. She carries all of us with her, to one degree or another, because she intuitively understands that our separateness from each other is a myth. More than that, she knows it's unscientific. Forgive the Pisces type her occasional cross-eyed expression, her umming and aahing or her crossed wires. It's a reflection of her connection to the rest of us. When she is part of your cocktail and you are part of hers, how can you expect her not to get cross-eyed and mixed up?

5 YOUR CHEMISTRY

What follows are the fifty-four most common chemistry experiments you'll find in any relationship. They describe most of the games that people play according to their Sun, Moon, Mercury, Venus and Mars signs.

Which of the following games are you playing? Some couples stick with one pattern all the time, because it works so well. Others rotate several over the course of their partnership. Sometimes, getting locked in one particular chemistry experiment can cause an explosion, though. Switching the formulas around can help!

Think of relationships as a dialogue between all the different sides of you and your partner. It's the way the individual signs in your character – your Sun, Moon, Mercury, Venus, and Mars Sign – communicate with the different 'people' locked inside your partner's personality too. It's like having ten people in bed.

To begin with, the most common chemistry connection of all is this one – a planet in the same sign. That means you'll have matching twin sides, and an instant bond. It doesn't guarantee the longevity of the partnership, but it does guarantee an incredible sense of recognition and familiarity, right from the first date.

If you have planets in Aries and so does your partner, there will be a feeling of togetherness from the start. If you have planets in Sagittarius and your partner also has them, your basic similarities will make it easier to relate, to identify and *to shag*.

As you read on, you'll notice that some of the chemistry experiments you conduct with your partner are volatile. Others are more enjoyable.

Some partnerships fail because one partner feels incomplete. This is often because you are both trading too heavily on a connection that is easy while ignoring the other connections that are more troublesome. Some people edit or censor a side of their personality because it doesn't fit the relationship – but if so, expect to feel unfulfilled.

As you read on, you'll also see how limited traditional compatibility ratings are. There is so much more to both of you than just your Sun Sign! To get the whole picture of a relationship, it's essential that you find out what the Moon, Mercury, Venus and Mars are doing as well. These are the emotional and sexual keys in any relationship.

At the end of this section, you'll find the charts of some famous chemistry experiments – many of these people have planets in the same sign. These examples also show why your bonk-in-law often has a horoscope with uncanny similarities to your own. Look up the horoscopes of all your ex-lovers and see if you're guilty!

FIFTY-FOUR COMMON RELATIONSHIP PATTERNS

Now that you know which signs your planets are in – and your lover's – you can sort out which chemistry experiments are taking place in your personal love lab. You might be used to thinking of chemistry in terms of 'I'm an Aries' or 'He's a Gemini' or 'She's a Virgo and I'm a Pisces', but for a proper picture of all the games you play with each other, look up all your planet signs. Not just the Sun – but the Moon, Mercury, Venus and Mars also. Compare your planets with your partner's planets and see if you share any of the fifty-four most common relationship patterns, listed below.

For example, Yoko Ono and John Lennon had Aquarius–Libra, Aquarius–Scorpio, Sagittarius–Libra, Sagittarius–Aquarius, Sagittarius–Virgo, Pisces–Scorpio, Pisces–Virgo, Virgo–Scorpio and Virgo–Virgo planet chemistry experiments taking place in their partnership. As a rule, the more links between planet signs you share, the more complicated, extraordinary and life-changing your relationship will be.

If you need to double-check your planet signs and your partner's again, turn to page 272.

Aries Planets + Aries Planets

Imagine if Xena got into bed with the cast of *Gladiator*. Imagine if Lucy from *Peanuts* got into bed with herself. Imagine if Rocky had fallen for another boxer in *Rocky II*. This is a little of what you can expect from the Aries–Aries connection in your horoscopes. Of course, the way through is to find a common enemy. Alternatively, find a common goal – preferably one that requires you to push other people out of the way. Together, you are *terrifying*. There's an impulse to compete against each other too – especially in bed. Biting is optional.

Aries Planets + Gemini Planets

One of you prefers to act without thinking – *carpe diem* is where it's at – and the other partner finds this deeply unintelligent. The other partner would never do anything without a couple of calls, a question-and-answer session over the breakfast table and a quick check on the Internet. You are both fast on your feet, but one of you behaves as if they have just been jet-propelled from the mouth of a cannon. There has to be time to talk. And talk. *And talk*. Otherwise, the arguments will run for several months.

Aries Planets + Cancer Planets

One of you is hung up on family. It's either a hate–hate relationship, a love–hate relationship or a love–love *Brady Bunch* extravaganza. And in the middle of all this, Mum is the star of the show – for better or worse. To avoid arguments, it's essential that both partners have exactly the same view of the clan. Goodies or baddies? Manson family or Partridge family? Only then will the other partner know whether they should be whirling a chainsaw over their head during Christmas dinner, or distributing Moët.

Aries Planets + Leo Planets

One of you wastes no time when it comes to flowers, restaurant bookings, arm-wrestling and other seduction tactics. The other person finds this deeply gratifying, and within days the relationship is on. A mutual admiration society helps this relationship. One of you has bags of energy, initiative and *chutzpah*. The other partner has class, style and a teaspoon of star quality. As long as you keep on flattering and thanking each other (and *kicking against the same pricks*), this connection works well.

Aries Planets + Libra Planets

One of you thinks in terms of Me, and the other one thinks in terms of Us. Fortunately, the one who thinks in terms of Us has a natural gift for relationships and expresses a large part of their personality through a partnership. What brings you together? Any person or situation that you find deeply unfair, unbalanced or unjust. That's when you both swing into action and realise you do have common ground after all. Apart from that, you are astonishingly different human beings; it's Margot Fonteyn meets The Hulk.

Aries Planets + Sagittarius Planets

Thank goodness you've finally found someone who can provide the rocket fuel for your personal NASA expedition. One partner in this relationship wants to explore, travel, study, teach, get a book published, stay on an ashram, learn French, cook Spanish . . . and more. The other one will join in immediately, enthusiastically and unequivocally – or at least cheer you on while they go off on their own mad mission. What will you fight about? Any religious, political or philosophical differences. Non-believers will be shot.

Aries Planets + Capricorn Planets

A mad impulse can destroy careers and reputations, you know. Or do you? One partner in this relationship clearly has no idea, no matter how many quietly disapproving looks are thrown their way. This is a clash of opposites, between the tortoise and the adrenaline-pumped hare. One of you knows that slow and steady wins the race, and that Rome wasn't built in a day – and neither was a Lego car park. The other one wants action *right now*, or else. One of you crawls, the other one pushes. It happens in bed too.

Aries Planets + Aquarius Planets

One of you has radical ideas about making the world a better place by banning GM food from the local school or selling fund-raising ribbons for AIDS. If the other partner is moved strongly enough to get actively involved, the relationship will get a huge energy boost, and so will the campaign. It's essential that you both agree to disagree if some issues divide you – otherwise one of you will attack and the other will rebel. Together you can do anything, but only if one of you is fine about the other's loopier qualities.

Taurus Planets + Taurus Planets

Are you socialists, communists, capitalists or economic rationalists? Strangely enough, all four kinds of Taurus/Taurus couples still share exactly the same addiction to mashed potato. The mash won't help when you're making your wills, though. Do make sure you are coming from the same place economically, philosophically, politically and spiritually, before it gets ugly. If you are both committed to saving and investing money, though, you could end up richer than you think. It's the Taurus 'Kerching!' factor.

Taurus Planets + Cancer Planets

Once you've agreed on your household budget, anything is possible. Joy Division sang 'Love Will Tear Us Apart', but with you two, it's likely to be cash. Once the salaries have been combined, however, and common values agreed on, you can create the sort of home life that other couples fantasise about. One of you knows exactly what is required in terms of real estate, lifestyle, gardening and the kitchen cupboards. The other has strong ideas too. If they match, you'll find your shared home is a relationship bedrock.

Taurus Planets + Leo Planets

One of you recoils at undignified money discussions, but the other one is deeply practical and knows that cash matters. One of you has a strong set of core values that come straight from family, church, class, politics or – the school of life. The other could secretly not care less, but must still cultivate respect or there will be trouble ahead. Should one of you be a Material Girl or Boy in this relationship, be careful. If it all ends up in tears, a battle royal is possible, and the money issues could become a little ugly.

Taurus Planets + Virgo Planets

One of you believes in working hard. The other believes in being productive. There will be times when you look like two of the seven dwarves, singing 'Hi Ho, Hi Ho' as you shuffle off to the salt mines. You both have an incredibly practical, grounded, common-sense side to your personalities that finds a safe home in this relationship. For one of you, the body is a temple. Temples can be expensive to run, though. So let's hope both partners agree that the cost is worth it. Let's hope you agree on what to eat as well.

Taurus Planets + Scorpio Planets

Your mutual assets, loans, possessions and property will be a big issue, right from the start. Scorpio rules joint finances. Taurus rules individual finances. Put that together, and it is unlikely you can just let your tax returns go – never mind a divorce settlement, if it ever comes to that. One of you wants passion, intensity, emotion, depth. The other one just wants to know what the sensible thing to do is. These two signs are opposite each other on the zodiac wheel – so this part of your relationship is a tug of war.

Taurus Planets + Capricorn Planets

What price stability? You both really, really need it – and in this relationship you could have it. If you both want to be rich and successful, you might just do it. At the very least, the bills will be paid on time, and one of you will steadily add notches to your CV the way other people add notches to their bedpost. If you focus on this dynamic in the relationship (and forget the rest) you could get by on success alone. Leave other couples to their mood lamps and drug-addled credit-card binges. You want a car space!

Taurus Planets + Aquarius Planets

This set-up in a relationship commonly results in clashes over money or personal values and beliefs, with both partners counting the cost in terms of cash – or integrity. Both of you have a stubborn streak, which doesn't help. The rare exception to this pattern is the Taurus–Aquarius couple who find a shared cause. Even so, there will be several occasions when expletives have to be deleted, thanks to one person's wildly unpredictable moments of loopy behaviour, and the other person's lack of tolerance.

Taurus Planets + Pisces Planets

One of you is convinced that if only the money was there, it could be put into the vegetable garden/spent at Tiffany's/signed away to Oxfam. How to acquire the *moolah*, though? That's where the other partner's imagination comes in. And what seemed to be an unlikely vision or an unfocused flight of fancy can become a lucrative reality, once the more grounded, cash-conscious partner becomes involved. Sexually, this is a fascinating match. It should be possible to get the erotic highs that money can't buy.

Gemini Planets + Gemini Planets

Once you know you're both speaking the same language, you will go one step further and invent a new language of your own. Nicknames, buzz words, private jokes and acronyms are the currency of your love. You will need to play another relationship game apart from this one if you're ever going to get down to serious sex. Otherwise, it will be all head and no heart – and certainly no condoms. Talking without really saying anything is a risk with this connection. You're both funny, though, and you know it.

Gemini Planets + Leo Planets

One of you is endlessly entertained, informed and amused by the other – but the gossip and anecdotes must never, *ever* take cheap shots at the sexual or emotional side of your relationship or heads will roll. Impressively clever compliments and thesaurus-crafted funny cards will help things along, as it's clear that one of you needs to be the unofficial scribe and court jester in the relationship. And it's flattering to be in the service of someone so special, isn't it? Ahem. Let's hope that's a 'yes' from one of you.

Gemini Planets + Virgo Planets

One of you likes weekend breaks and little overseas jaunts. The other will come along for the ride, but the familiar rituals and routines of home will have to come along too, as well as various work anxieties. You both live in your heads a lot of the time, and too much thinking will definitely get in the way of this relationship. You'll need a stronger emotional or sexual connection from other planets in your charts to really make this work. You share books, magazines and radio stations, but what about the grunt factor?

Gemini Planets + Libra Planets

Oh, the joy of this connection. It's so civilised, for a start. It's a chatty, charming, light, bright, easy part of your relationship that you can return to any time you like. One of you likes to talk. The other one is happy to listen – and nod a lot. One of you articulates sexual or romantic feelings with wit, intelligence and quotable quotes. The other's romantic soul is massaged by the message. You may play other games in your relationships at various times, but neither of you will ever be bored by this one.

Gemini Planets + Sagittarius Planets

One partner finds Jung fascinating. The other partner finds it fascinating that you can make so many bad puns out of Carl Jung's name. One partner sees the big global picture. The other partner sees the gossip at popbitch.com and immediately forgets there is supposed to be a big global picture at all. You do have some similarities – travel turns you both on, and you'll share a few dog-eared paperbacks too. At heart, though, one of you is a believer with a capital B – and the other is totally unconvinced.

Gemini Planets + Aquarius Planets

Other people eavesdrop when you two start talking, and with good reason. Your dinner conversations sound like Oprah Winfrey interviewing E. T. One of you is drawn towards everything (and everybody) that is alternative, fringe, out there, new, sexy-techy or ahead of its time. The other is perennially curious and longs to find out more so that it can be parcelled up and passed on. One of you is used to being misunderstood; the other has a talent for understanding and translating. It's an orgasmic meeting of minds.

Gemini Planets + Pisces Planets

One of you is sensitive and emotional and finds that only music, film, poetry and art can really contain and express the feelings involved in any relationship. The other one is listening to the radio while channel surfing, texting and reading *The National Enquirer*. One of you is all about information and communication – the other one finds words hard. One of you is intuitive and doesn't need anything spelled out. The other believes email keeps love alive. Sexually, it's like Lois Lane in bed with Flipper.

Cancer Planets + Cancer Planets

It's all about the breasts – and the kitchen. It's also about the parents (yours, or your partner's) and the incredible allure of the real estate agent's front window. Something happens to Cancerian-influenced lovers when they buy their first home together – it's a kind of morgasm: a mortgage crossed with an orgasm. Even if one of you has Problem Parents with a capital P, the endless angst about them will bring you together. You need children, or animals that are child substitutes, to bring out your best qualities.

Cancer Planets + Virgo Planets

This connection works extremely well once you move in together, as the details of your shared domestic life come together in a way that would have Martha Stewart salivating. It's the list on the fridge that makes it all work, as one of you knows. That and the fact that one partner is genuinely caring, particularly when the flu hits – or even more pressing health problems, come to that. Once you work out the food issues (and there will always be food issues), you can cook your way into each other's hearts.

Cancer Planets + Libra Planets

One of you operates in terms of the family (or the clan). The other operates in terms of your partnership, and has a Noah's

Ark approach to life. If you both agree that your family and your partnership are equally important, you will find common ground. If not, clashes are likely. One partner is much more emotional than the other and is dominated by feelings and memories. The other person is more detached. One of you believes a house is not a home without a lot of photos. The other prefers original art.

Cancer Planets + Scorpio Planets

Common-sense has nothing to do with this connection. It's about sex, irrational need and illogical emotion – who cares about love being sensible? This link between you can work brilliantly, and link you on a profoundly deep level. One of you will have a nipple fixation, too, which always helps. One partner is extremely intense – a survivor of various life crises. The other genuinely cares about that and wants to tend to the damaged goods. This is about close, complicated and *very* private love.

Cancer Planets + Capricorn Planets

This works right up to the point when hard decisions have to be made about career versus family or success versus home life. If one of you has relatives who are down the scale socially, don't be surprised if they are locked in a wardrobe during the wedding reception. This cosmic blend in your relationship is famously difficult. One of you is ambitious, practical and patient. The other is emotional, dominated by feelings and needs (oh, those needs). These are opposite signs and you can expect a tug of war.

Cancer Planets + Pisces Planets

Caring and compassionate. Nurturing and sensitive. Emotional and . . . emotional. You two are the couple most likely to cry at *Bambi*, and should not be allowed in unsupervised to any film starring orphaned animals. This is an incredibly sexy, ooshy, gooshy relationship connection. You're both big on dream homes – those fantasy palaces you see in *Vogue Living*, with indoor lap pools. One of you has to be careful using drugs or alcohol. The other has strong feelings about the family. You look after each other. Aaah!

Leo Planets + Leo Planets

You are secretly united in the knowledge that you are both far more talented, special or important than other people. And it helps you overcome the main obstacle to your love, which is accepting the hideous truth that you've both had (shudder) *other lovers* before. Oral sex needs to be organised on a scrupulously fair 50–50 sex roster system, with stopwatches to ensure nobody gets a superior deal. The same applies to housework. You both loathe menial domestic tasks. Split the cost of a cleaner, or else.

Leo Planets + Libra Planets

One of you could charm for your country at the next Olympics. The other is relieved to finally be with a partner who can be shunted around nightclub openings, New Year parties and family Christmas dinners and make them look good. One partner has a great eye, a good wardrobe and a sound grasp of Hair Theory. The other just likes being seen with somebody who *Vanity Fair* might photograph. It's a partnership full of little ego massages and favours. It has *style* – like a classic old Hollywood romance.

Leo Planets + Scorpio Planets

If one of you wants to try sexual games or positions that the other one finds demeaning or undignified, then there will be serious problems – so forget the dog biscuits and the whip. The combination of Leo and Scorpio planets in this relationship makes the balance of power a huge issue. Both of you have a controlling streak, and both of you will be stubborn about backing down. One of you plays the king or queen, while the other plays Richard III – the secretive arch-plotter in the corner.

Leo Planets + Sagittarius Planets

As long as the funny stories in this relationship are never at the expense of the Leo-influenced partner – or tacky, cheap and vulgar *in any way* – this connection will work well. There is a lot to admire and respect about the Sagittarius-influenced partner, after all – the noble quest for knowledge, the global mindset, the sexy foreign stamps in the passport . . . no wonder the Leo-influenced partner is so happy to be courted. Infidelity could crack this one wide open, though – so forget about playing away, baby.

Leo Planets + Aquarius Planets

You are both stubborn about what matters most. For one partner, this is undoubtedly the Absolutely Fabulous World of Me. This results in mad acts of rebellion by the other person, who feels like one of the Sex Pistols during the Royal Jubilee. Over the long term, this game of monarch and punk could create a rift. One of you is undoubtedly much more radical and offbeat than the other. In order for this connection to work, the more conservative partner will need to appreciate any reflected cool this brings them!

Virgo Planets + Virgo Planets

It's all about the domestic routine. Cats and dogs are usually vital to this shared daily bonding, though birds on the window ledge will do too. Visitors who look after the home of a Virgo–Virgo type couple arrive to find eight pages of notes telling them how far to twiddle the tap in the laundry, and why the bathroom mirror fogs up. *Great* book collection, though. Health issues bring you together if you both have Virgo planets. Just don't get sick at the same time. You are both aroused by doing crosswords naked.

Virgo Planets + Scorpio Planets

This is a great astrological link – and when you finally hit on the master–slave connection in bed, it will really take off. When you play this game together (in bed or out) you will both realise that one of you is pushing total control and world domination while the other is scurrying around like one of the maids from *Upstairs Downstairs*. If you both respect each other's role, though, so what? However, there may be personal hygiene issues, particularly if one of you is all maid and the other one is all (messy) master.

Virgo Planets + Sagittarius Planets

One of you gets the map and starts calculating distances. The other one gets the map, throws it out of the car window and drives off. This is a hard connection to work with in your charts. The big picture is far more important to one partner – but the lack of respect for crucial details will drive the other one loco. It's also important that both of you agree on the same beliefs and ideologies (no matter whether this means Catholicism or the Labour party or astrology). If you don't, the debates could be picky, critical and hard.

Virgo Planets + Capricorn Planets

Practical and Patient. Methodical and Wise. Are either of you bored yet? It doesn't seem likely with this combination, which is excellent in bed too. One of you knows that orgasms just don't happen and is prepared to do the work. The other one appreciates subtle, fine details – the precise trajectory of the tongue from nipple to navel, the weave on the sheets . . . It all adds up to quite a promising partnership connection for you, and although one of you is enslaved to work, those alternate Sundays off will be special.

Virgo Planets + Pisces Planets

These two signs are opposite each other on the zodiac wheel, and significant chunks of your two personalities are also remarkably opposite. One of you surfs the waves of life and likes to get lost in the chaos. The other one prefers to sit on the sand, where life feels more solid and manageable. Together, you work best if you find a person or cause you both believe is worth serving and sacrificing for. Your ailing dog will do, if all else fails. At heart, though, one of you is into order, and the other one prefers to escape it.

Libra Planets + Libra Planets

Your initial emails to each other consist of the same subject header, over and over again – 'Me Too!' – although sometimes this is varied to 'I Agree!' This is a fantastic connection to have in your charts, and it works sexually and emotionally. There will be moments when your relationship runs like Jane Austen on powerful drugs. Despite all the agreeing and nodding, which can seem a little exhausting after a while, this particular relationship game is enough to sustain your partnership for an entire lifetime.

Libra Planets + Sagittarius Planets

This is an excellent game to play in your relationship, and is something you can return to if other games aren't working so well. One of you will do anything for a harmonious partnership, including listening to bizarre theories about aliens or accompanying the loved one on arduous potholing trips to rural Wales. This is fantastic for the more adventurous partner whose head is full of interesting ideas and whose DNA is all about exploration. Fidelity is vital, though. No solo voyages with naked local entertainment!

Libra Planets + Capricorn Planets

One of you needs a partner to take to work functions and to wheel out at important parties. The other one is fine about all that – what is life without a few handshakes and some deeply meaningless talk about the weather? One of you knows all this social lubricating keeps the universe smooth and well-oiled, while the other one knows just how important networking is for success. Problems will arise if one of you allows professional or social ambition to get in the way of what is just or fair, however!

Libra Planets + Aquarius Planets

One of you is perfectly charming about the other person's mad streak. This is a revelation to the mad person, who is amazed at how tolerant some people can actually be. One of you is a born romantic who loves the delicate art of fine-tuning relationships until balance is achieved. This is why the prospect of making it work with El Loopy is so seductive. What you may not have realised, however, is quite how much *space* your other half requires. Just give it to them. Like magic, the scales will suddenly balance.

Scorpio Planets + Scorpio Planets

It's the silences that speak in this relationship. Your first date is like a Pinter play. You stare, you sweat and you steam up the windows. You lick your lips, narrow your eyes, cross your legs and you uncross them. Then you go home and one of you notices . . . black underwear in the wardrobe. Whoa, mama! You are both demented control freaks, and at some point one of you will use a triangular relationship situation to increase the pain, the passion and the power. It's hellish, *non*? But the sex is grrreat.

Scorpio Planets + Capricorn Planets

Lord help us if you two ever get into the White House. Did you meet at work? If so, your colleagues have every right to demand that you be separated during working hours. You're far too lethal as a team, like the raptors in *Jurassic Park* but with briefcases. One of you is powerful; the other one is ambitious. One of you understands that sexual rewards are often the secret appeal of success. The other one just wants you to hurry up and oblige. Your ability to help each other climb socially and professionally is *key*.

Scorpio Planets + Aquarius Planets

One of you thinks human beings should have progressed beyond pornography by now. The other one has a fine collection. One of you can't believe it when people live their lives as if they were rehashed plots from *Dynasty*. One of you secretly wishes *Dynasty* was still on. One partner expresses their personality by trying to control; the other one expresses their personality by rebelling madly. This part of your relationship will be hard work. Sexually, it's like Elvira, Mistress of the Dark getting into bed with Dr Spock. One of you needs a lot of space.

Scorpio Planets + Pisces Planets

Psychic sex! You don't need to bark orders at each other in bed, and even groaning isn't strictly necessary. It's all accomplished through naked ESP, and it's amazing how one partner knows exactly *when* to go in – and how long to go on. You are both connected by your emotions, which are deep (in one partner) and extremely sensitive (in the other). One of you will have more power and control in the relationship than the other – but it may be a bargain you are both satisfied with. Your fantasies are totally taboo.

Sagittarius Planets + Sagittarius Planets

You encourage each other to go over the top – with anecdotes, with idiotic outfits for fancy-dress parties and with funny stories. Life is a cartoon, and you both know it. One of you has emigrated, is on a working holiday, or has just come back from one overseas trek and is planning the next one. One of you has studied before, but wants to go to the next level on another course. You are both natural explorers and perennial students of life, and appreciate this in one another. Shagging on top of the pyramids? Why not.

Sagittarius Planets + Aquarius Planets

A fascination with the same country, the same culture – or the same unusual belief system – is typical. Anything from Madagascar to Scientology can bring you together. There is a mutual need for space and freedom too. One of you wants to travel, the other one wants to go out with friends. One of you wants to take an evening class, the other one wants to log onto an Internet forum. Together you can be intellectually enlightened beings, but sexually and emotionally you need other, deeper connections.

Sagittarius Planets + Pisces Planets

This connection between you is all about yearning, longing, daydreaming and exploring life's more fantastic possibilities. You are both escape artists in different ways, and it's always about The Summer Holiday with you two. Even though a dislike of too much reality, normality and familiarity binds you together, remember that you also have major differences. One of you is much more enthusiastic and fired-up than the other, and one of you is far more raw, emotional and sensitive than the other.

Capricorn Planets + Capricorn Planets

If you hold hands for the next twenty years, you can climb any mountain together. There will be a tremendously practical, sensible streak in your relationship if you have this combination. Once you click into the Capricorn–Capricorn game, there will be no time for silliness or fluffery in the relationship. You can be two wise old birds together, learning your life lessons sagely and responsibly, and steadily building the kind of foundations in your life that will bring you the position and success you both need.

Capricorn Planets + Pisces Planets

One of you needs a break from all that hard work (success always comes at a price, and it is usually your *joie de vivre*) so the other partner can be a useful escape route. One of you is awfully responsible, wise, patient, realistic and sensible. The other one is not. Or at least, when you play this game together, that's the way it's going to appear. This can work well, if one partner is always there with the bubble bath and the weird music when the other one gets home and puts the briefcase down. Fantasy plus reality works.

Aquarius Planets + Aquarius Planets

You are both weird, but in completely different ways. You give each other a huge amount of space and freedom, because you appreciate how unbearable it is to feel suffocated or trapped in a relationship. No rules or timetables for you! All the space can sometimes make you feel as if you are on opposite ends of an airport runway, though. You will need to lean on other connections between you to feel the heat. The shared weirdness extends to your sex life, which may be a) fully clothed or b) involve parrots.

Pisces Planets + Pisces Planets

You both manage to take out-of-focus photographs of each other – much to the amazement of the woman at Kodak. One of you has appalling eyesight and for some reason, the glasses or contact lenses are never where they're supposed to be. One of you is also constitutionally unable to either understand tax or pay it on time. Sexually, you both spend so much time fantasising that cold bedroom realities can be a let-down. Bring on the mood lighting and video camera! More Vaseline! More J. R. R. Tolkien!

FAMOUS CHEMISTRY EXPERIMENTS

Princess Diana	Prince Charles	Camilla Parker-Bowles
Sun in Cancer	Sun in Scorpio	Sun in Cancer
Moon in Aquarius	Moon in Taurus	Moon in Cancer
Mercury in Cancer	Mercury in Scorpio	Mercury in Cancer
Venus in Taurus	Venus in Libra	Venus in Cancer
Mars in Virgo	Mars in Sagittarius	Mars in Gemini

Bob Geldof	Paula Yates	Michael Hutchence
Sun in Libra	Sun in Taurus	Sun in Aquarius
Moon in Sagittarius	Moon in Scorpio	Moon in Scorpio
Mercury in Libra	Mercury in Aries	Mercury in Capricorn
Venus in Virgo	Venus in Gemini	Venus in Sagittarius
Mars in Virgo	Mars in Cancer	Mars in Capricorn

Mia Farrow	Woody Allen	Diane Keaton
Sun in Aquarius	Sun in Sagittarius	Sun in Capricorn
Moon in Capricorn	Moon in Aquarius	Moon in Aquarius
Mercury in Aquarius	Mercury in Sagittarius	Mercury in Sagittarius
Venus in Aries	Venus in Libra	Venus in Capricorn
Mars in Capricorn	Mars in Capricorn	Mars in Cancer

Anne Heche	Ellen de Generes
Sun in Gemini	Sun in Aquarius
Moon in Virgo	Moon in Aries
Mercury in Gemini	Mercury in Capricorn
Venus in Aries	Venus in Aquarius
Mars in Sagittarius	Mars in Sagittarius

Angelina Jolie

Sun in Gemini
Moon in Aries
Mercury in Gemini
Venus in Cancer
Mars in Aries

Brad Pitt

Sun in Sagittarius
Moon in Capricorn
Mercury in Capricorn
Venus in Capricorn
Mars in Capricorn

Jennifer Aniston

Sun in Aquarius
Moon in Sagittarius
Mercury in Aquarius
Venus in Aries
Mars in Scorpio

Hillary Clinton

Sun in Scorpio
Moon in Pisces
Mercury in Scorpio
Venus in Scorpio
Mars in Leo

Bill Clinton

Sun in Leo
Moon in Taurus
Mercury in Leo
Venus in Libra
Mars in Libra

Monica Lewinsky

Sun in Leo
Moon in Taurus
Mercury in Cancer
Venus in Leo
Mars in Aries

Arthur Miller

Sun in Libra
Moon in Aquarius
Mercury in Scorpio
Venus in Scorpio
Mars in Leo

Marilyn Monroe

Sun in Gemini
Moon in Aquarius
Mercury in Gemini
Venus in Aries
Mars in Pisces

John F. Kennedy

Sun in Gemini
Moon in Virgo
Mercury in Taurus
Venus in Gemini
Mars in Taurus

Spencer Tracey

Sun in Aries
Moon in Gemini
Mercury in Pisces
Venus in Taurus
Mars in Pisces

Katherine Hepburn

Sun in Taurus
Moon in Taurus
Mercury in Taurus
Venus in Aries
Mars in Capricorn

Ted Hughes	Sylvia Plath
Sun in Leo	Sun in Scorpio
Moon in Gemini	Moon in Libra
Mercury in Virgo	Mercury in Scorpio
Venus in Libra	Venus in Virgo
Mars in Gemini	Mars in Leo

Paul McCartney	Linda McCartney
Sun in Gemini	Sun in Libra
Moon in Leo	Moon in Scorpio
Mercury in Gemini	Mercury in Libra
Venus in Taurus	Venus in Scorpio
Mars in Leo	Mars in Aries

Sandra Bernhard	Madonna	Guy Ritchie
Sun in Gemini	Sun in Leo	Sun in Virgo
Moon in Sagittarius	Moon in Virgo	Moon in Aries
Mercury in Gemini	Mercury in Virgo	Mercury in Libra
Venus in Taurus	Venus in Leo	Venus in Libra
Mars in Cancer	Mars in Taurus	Mars in Leo

Yoko Ono	John Lennon
Sun in Aquarius	Sun in Libra
Moon in Sagittarius	Moon in Aquarius
Mercury in Pisces	Mercury in Scorpio
Venus in Aquarius	Venus in Virgo
Mars in Virgo	Mars in Libra

Peter Sellers	Brigitte Bardot
Sun in Virgo	Sun in Libra
Moon in Taurus	Moon in Gemini
Mercury in Leo	Mercury in Libra
Venus in Libra	Venus in Virgo
Mars in Virgo	Mars in Leo

Courtney Love	Kurt Cobain
Sun in Cancer	Sun in Pisces
Moon in Cancer	Moon in Cancer
Mercury in Leo	Mercury in Pisces
Venus in Gemini	Venus in Pisces
Mars in Gemini	Mars in Scorpio

Ray Davies	Chrissie Hynde
Sun in Cancer	Sun in Virgo
Moon in Cancer	Moon in Scorpio
Mercury in Gemini	Mercury in Virgo
Venus in Cancer	Venus in Virgo
Mars in Leo	Mars in Leo

Sid Vicious	Nancy Spungen
Sun in Taurus	Sun in Pisces
Moon in Libra	Moon in Gemini
Mercury in Taurus	Mercury in Pisces
Venus in Taurus	Venus in Aquarius
Mars in Cancer	Mars in Capricorn

Oscar Wilde	Lord Alfred (Bosie) Douglas
Sun in Libra	Sun in Libra
Moon in Leo	Moon in Libra
Mercury in Scorpio	Mercury in Libra
Venus in Libra	Venus in Libra
Mars in Sagittarius	Mars in Leo

Tony Blair	Cherie Blair
Sun in Taurus	Sun in Virgo
Moon in Aquarius	Moon in Leo
Mercury in Aries	Mercury in Libra
Venus in Aries	Venus in Scorpio
Mars in Gemini	Mars in Capricorn

MORE CHEMISTRY LESSONS

When all your planets are clustered together, the bits of yourself you can't live with can easily be projected onto your partner – which is rather like having a fight with a mirror when you're in a bad mood. Equally, the stuff you love about yourself and your life can be neatly captured in your partner (another projection) especially when you are madly in love. Here are some examples of people who share signs projecting happily – and not so happily.

Meg has the Sun in Cancer, and her boyfriend David has Mercury and Venus in Cancer. Meg says, 'We're both into the house, and for that matter, real estate in general. And we're both close to his family.'

Paul has the Moon in Virgo, and Mark also has the Moon in Virgo. Paul says, 'Mark's such a perfectionist about details that he never finishes anything because he's so worried it won't be good enough. Sometimes he doesn't start anything either, for the same reason, and it's incredibly frustrating!'

Mark says, 'Paul's really self-critical and I worry that he'll never get what he deserves at work because he's so down on himself. Sometimes he's too frightened to put his ideas out there, because he doesn't think they're polished enough. It drives me nuts!'

Mark and Paul both contain an inner Virgo, thanks to their Virgo planets – and both are seeing the more difficult traits associated with that sign in each other. Astrology can wake them up to what they are doing, though.

Meg and David are happy to share and recognise their Cancerian traits. But with both couples, the people involved are simply mirroring each other, negatively or positively, depending on how they feel about themselves and the relationship.

Writing in *Relationship Signs* about this very phenomenon, the legendary Linda Goodman said, 'When you stress the positive side of the doubled energies, you find couples who can accomplish the near impossible.' So, despite the possibility for unfair projections ('He's a neurotic Virgo type and – oh dear – so am I!') there is also maximum potential for an amazingly powerful double-act if you share planets in signs. As with everything astrological, it all depends on your attitude.

THE SKINNY ON YOUR SHARED SIGNS

Here's the lowdown on the connection you share if you both have a personal planet in the same sign.

Aries

You are fighters. You both had childhood enemies or rivals, and perhaps you both have them in adulthood too. You share the need to get sporty or physical, or at least cheer on someone else and wave a big flag. One of you probably has scars from rushing around/crashing/falling out of things. Both of you are fast off the mark. It won't be a slow-paced romance. When you compete with each other you feel a little buzz.

The emotional connection

Fast and energetic. You don't muck around. Sinus-clearing arguments are very common as well.

Why have you found each other?

As a couple, you can be braver, stronger and faster than the rest of us. So let's hope your cause is a good one. Together, you get things done. You can also back each other up when the world outside wants a fight. At the highest level, you will encourage each other to take on an enemy, come first, or win a glittering prize.

Excuuuse me!

Watch out for accusations of pushiness, selfishness or aggression. You're just mirroring each other.

Taurus

You have both gone through some heavy money, business, career or property questions that have dramatically decided which kind of Taurean you'll be: rich and getting richer, or morally above money. Compare stories about selling out/not selling out. Compare big financial gain or loss stories in your lives to bond faster. What's worth more: honey from your own garden or Fortnum and Mason's jam? Discuss!

The emotional connection

Shared values are the key. Did you both take pay cuts to get fulfilling jobs? Or do you both invest in art?

Why have you found each other?

Together you are a walking lesson for the rest of us in what's valuable. Your shared shares can set the tone for entire stock-market shifts. You could make each other rich, or you could inspire each other to pursue a philosophical, political or spiritual direction that lifts you above filthy lucre. You define each other's values.

Excuuuse me!

Isn't it funny how one of you seems to be so materialistic, money-mad or hung up on being poor?

Gemini

Siblings are a big deal, for better or worse. You both like making up words for things and nicknames for each other. You're both witty, clever and often hilarious to eavesdrop on. You share a mobile phone and email dependency. Galloping curiosity about each other is likely. Dinner will be a series of hovering question marks. Switch the phones off, for the love of Mike. A lot of your conversation starts with, 'Did you read/hear . . . ?'

The emotional connection

It's brain to brain. You admire each other's heads. You connect through a shared sense of humour too.

Why have you found each other?

Together you will connect people, places and ideas. You two plug into the world, link people up, pass on information, gossip, joke and talk a lot. You are here to be an information HQ for your street or the Internet. One of you has a book/play/script/poem inside you. The other partner could easily bring it out.

Excuuuse me!

Oh dear. He's so superficial, flighty, irritatingly shallow, gossipy and lightweight. Or is he just your evil twin?

Cancer

You click on food, children or small animals; also (and this is very important), your mothers, families and home. How strongly you bond depends on how negative or positive these things are for you. Will you moan together or share the joys? You will provide excellent free therapy for each other if family relationships were damaged in any way. Two people sharing Cancerian bits together can cluck over each other like hens, especially when one of you is doing the cooking.

The emotional connection

Protective, nurturing, caring. You are his mum; he is your mum. When you get sick, he genuinely worries.

Why have you found each other?

Together you will look after kids, sick people or animals. Together you will accumulate the best his 'n' hers recipe book in your street. You have found each other to share the importance of family, home and country. At its highest level, this relationship will produce a solid home and family, and a strong sense of kinship.

Excuuuse me!

'All you ever think about is your mother/your damn family'; 'Why do we always have to stay home?', etc.

Leo

You're both well known, or you both know famous people. You feel it's noble to give to people too. When you're together, you secretly know you're better than the poor old proletariat. It's awful, but isn't it true? One of you has back problems. You're both in the PLU club – People Like Us. It may be a cult of two, but never mind. You don't have hobbies or interests; you have outlets for your talents. There is a difference, you know.

The emotional connection

Enthusiastic and warm. When you two get together other signs stand back because of the energy blast.

Why have you found each other?

You will collaborate on a creative project or get deeply involved with children (your own or other people's). You also use each other as a yardstick for proper, noble behaviour. Together you work out 'what is correct'. It's not necessarily what the royal family does, either. (Well, one would hope not, given their recent behaviour.) Together you set standards for the rest of us.

Excuuuse me!

One of you is a snob, hung up on class or glamorous people, pompous and obsessed with *moi*. Oh dear . . . it is *moi*!

Virgo

Your health, diet and lifestyle dominate your lives. If you're the king and queen of macrobiotics, fantastic. If you're sick all the time, or addicted to something, that will take over too. You both take work ultra-seriously. You're both fussy about details. You care about each other's bodily functions as much as you care about life. When one of you has a computer malfunction, the other one despairs on your behalf. It's the worry, you know.

The emotional connection

It's through the head, not the heart. You analyse each other – and the relationship – a lot.

Why have you found each other?

Together you can be a well-run machine, quite literally the most productive couple on the block. You both care more about your physical state than other signs, so you'll support each other there as well. At its highest level, this partnership will make work demons out of both of you and get you seriously healthy.

Excuuuse me!

'Shut up about spinach losing its nutrients in the microwave!' Is he mirroring your own nutrition neuroses?

Libra

You know how to get on with people and you both have excellent party skills. You two can work a room like no other couple. You share an eye for form, colour, design or texture. You need a partner – in work or in love – to function properly. Popularity matters to you. You share a belief that conflict is to be avoided, unless it's the price you have to pay for peace or justice. You have antennae that detect unpleasantness a mile off. Run! Run!

The emotional connection

So sweet and nice, it makes other people turn pale green. But you truly believe in love and it works for you.

Why have you found each other?

Together you can mend arguments among friends, family or work colleagues. You should both be in the diplomatic corps. Together you can pursue your taste in homes and clothes. You'll find Cupid too. At its highest level, this could be an authentically romantic relationship – the kind Parisians invented for us.

Excuuuse me!

Nice can be bland. And bland can be boring. Do principles count less than being liked? Oh, is he your mirror?

Scorpio

You are both obsessive, passionate people. You don't spill your secrets easily because that means giving away your control or power, and you hate that. You know about taboo stuff – hush-hush sexuality issues, the drama of dealing with death and very possibly the occult. You share laser-beam eyes (you can scorch at ten paces) and a deep well of emotion gurgling under your ribs.

One of you will show the other how power actually works. Your dark sides are blacker than black.

The emotional connection

Intense. Sometimes manipulative – think power-tripping, game-playing or even outright battles for control. You two are passionately committed and involved.

Why have you found each other?

You can talk about the stuff that other people shrink from. You are both survivors and can find comparing survival stories very healing. Together, you're powerful. You can transform lives, projects, people and even the world. At its highest level, this partnership will transform both of you – and heal and change others.

Excuuuse me!

Hung up on sex, secretive, control-freak, string-puller . . . is this you dissing him, or is this him dissing you?

Sagittarius

Travel is the big one, or an addiction to learning. More knowledge! Gimme more! You both like the big global picture, either on cable TV or on your bookshelf. You may also have read books by the same thinkers/gurus/experts. You both need freedom and a huge amount of space to experiment and explore. You share a yok-yok-yok sense of humour too. One of you will influence the other to 'think big' – to do more and be more. Your combined library is enormous.

The emotional connection

Generous, expansive, broad. This isn't petty, domestic or jealous. You let each other explore and discover.

Why have you found each other?

You'll do a lot of globetrotting together. Or you'll encourage each other to go back to school and sign up for some unlikely, yet fascinating, evening class. You're here to explore ideas or new places and share it with us. At its highest level, this partnership will produce PhD degrees and incredible discoveries/explorations.

Excuuuse me!

The meaning of life isn't in a book, you know. And it's not in frickin' Tibet either. (But is this him . . . or you?)

Capricorn

You are both goal-driven. You've moved several leagues ahead of where you were, socially or professionally, at the age of twenty-one. You're cautious people. You're both grounded, down-to-earth and ambitious to make it. You share a seriousness about life that isn't terribly fashionable, so it's a relief when you find each other. You are two little Bob the Builders. You plod away forever, creating secure structures in your life. It takes years.

The emotional connection

Practical. You help each other to achieve your goals in life. Together you can build houses or businesses.

Why have you found each other?

Without people like you, there would be no solid foundations in our society. You are the builders and developers, and you get things done. Life hasn't been easy for either of you – that's another common factor. At its highest level this partnership will produce solid, enduring structures, professionally and personally.

Excuuuse me!

'You only fell in love with me because I was useful'; 'You only married me to get my second name.'

Aquarius

Friends are vital to both of you. There's membership of a group, band, club, team or committee. You both have gangs of buddies. You both have unusual, alternative or frankly weird interests as well. Time or money goes into good causes or humanitarian goals. You both know what it's like to feel like a fruit-bat outsider and love the freedom of being yourselves with each other. You're into making the world a better place, even if it's just sitting in front of the news a lot and moaning.

The emotional connection

Breezy and matey but often buzzy and exciting too. Intellectual, not overly physical or emotional. You give each other lots of space.

Why have you found each other?

You'll encourage each other to be less conventional and conformist, more free and more honest. You'll electrify each other and come up with new ways to date, mate or relate that challenge other people's social rules. At its highest level, this partnership will progress or advance the human race in some way. So why wait?

Excuuuse me!

He's so stubborn, deliberately 'different' and impossible to fathom . . . it almost makes you want to ask for a mirror.

Pisces

You share the need to escape into other realities. That can mean drugs, drink, computer games or art. You both rely on your sixth sense. There's a deep compassion and empathy for animals or people who are suffering. You are both extremely sensitive, to the point of being raw like sushi. You both go underwater in the pool for the thrill of seeing 'another world'. One of you will never be on time, or never be where they're supposed to be. You're into poems, meditation and surreal whimsy. One of you has vision problems or wears tinted sunglasses.

The emotional connection

Inspiring. Spiritual. Vague . . . and totally impractical. It's never grounded in other people's reality, but who needs that anyway?

Why have you found each other?

You have found each other to understand why psychic connections can be louder than emails. Together you can pursue the most imaginative, fantastic projects. You can help or heal pets/people who need it. At its highest level, this partnership can produce great art or great healing. Which one appeals to you?

Excuuuse me!

You like Cadbury's Flake, but not to live with. Is he ever on time? (More to the point, are you guilty as well?)

KARMIC CRUNCHES – AND NOW . . . THE PROBLEM AREAS

Matching signs can actually take you to the heights, as Linda Goodman observed, but you'll both need to be pretty sussed about yourselves in order to get there. In the meantime, be cautious about playing the projection game. If you think all your Taurean faults (materialism, greed, selling out for a buck) belong to your vile Taurus girlfriend, then chances are you're more unconsciously hung up on *moolah* than you think.

Really difficult issues between partners – the kind that lead to sudden dumpings or long, painful divorces – are often the result of two people having planets in incompatible signs. Planets in signs that naturally oppose each other or square off to each other can cause the real tension or 'You just don't get it!' elements of a relationship. There are so many pressures on couples over the long term (kids, money, mortgages, redundancies, stress, illness, people who become addicted to reality TV, etc.) that it's often these weaker links in the chain between you that can create the snapping sounds. Here's the score.

EXPECT SOME TENSION AND DIFFERENCES IF YOUR COMBINED PLANETS ARE IN . . .

If your Sun, Moon, Mercury, Venus, and/or Mars are in signs that clash with his Sun, Moon, Mercury, Venus and/or Mars, then you can expect relationship challenges. If you have Mercury in Aries, for example, and he has Venus in Capricorn, there will be tension. If you have Venus and Mars in Taurus and he has the Sun and Moon in Scorpio, there will also be tension! Follow this checklist to see where the snags are. If there are a lot of different clashes going on, then you'll have a stormy partnership.

Aries–Libra
Aries–Cancer
Aries–Capricorn
Aries–Libra–Cancer
Aries–Libra–Capricorn
Aries–Cancer–Capricorn
Aries–Cancer–Libra–Capricorn
Taurus–Scorpio
Taurus–Leo
Taurus–Aquarius
Taurus–Leo–Scorpio
Taurus–Aquarius–Scorpio
Taurus–Leo–Aquarius
Taurus–Leo–Scorpio–Aquarius
Gemini–Sagittarius
Gemini–Pisces
Gemini–Virgo
Gemini–Virgo–Sagittarius
Gemini–Pisces–Sagittarius
Gemini–Virgo–Pisces
Gemini–Virgo–Sagittarius–Pisces
Cancer–Capricorn
Cancer–Libra
Cancer–Aries
Leo–Aquarius
Leo–Scorpio
Leo–Taurus
Virgo–Pisces

Virgo–Sagittarius
Virgo–Gemini
Libra–Aries
Libra–Capricorn
Libra–Cancer
Scorpio–Taurus
Scorpio–Aquarius
Scorpio–Leo
Sagittarius–Gemini
Sagittarius–Pisces
Sagittarius–Virgo
Capricorn–Cancer
Capricorn–Aries
Capricorn–Libra
Aquarius–Leo
Aquarius–Taurus
Aquarius–Scorpio
Pisces–Virgo
Pisces–Gemini
Pisces–Sagittarius

DECODING THE SIGNS WHEN THERE'S A PROBLEM

Aries

The person with the Aries planet in their chart may seem too tough, too fast, too quick to snap or just too short-fused to the person with Cancer, Libra or Capricorn planets. They may be confronted by the Aries' speed or aggression, either in the workplace or in love-life tactics.

Taurus

The person with the Taurus planet may seem too money-conscious (even if they are an avowed anti-materialist) or too hung up on business or property to the person with Leo, Scorpio or Aquarius planets. They may seem stubborn too.

Gemini

The person with the Gemini planet may seem to inhabit their head (rather than their heart) and this can make the person with

Virgo, Sagittarius or Pisces planets uncomfortable. It may feel as if there is too much talking (or too many books) and not enough other stuff.

Cancer

The person with the Cancer planet may seem too hung up on Mum (or the family) to the person with Libra, Capricorn or Aries planets. Alternatively, they could appear too irrationally emotional – or too fond of safety and comfort at the expense of living.

Leo

The person with the Leo planet could seem like an egomaniac to the person with planets in Scorpio, Aquarius or Taurus. How proud (or how pompous!) can a person be, after all? They may seem over-confident or far too grand, somehow, for the other party.

Virgo

The person with the Virgo planet could classically present all the 'wrong' traits of this sign to their lover, friend or family member with planets in Sagittarius, Pisces or Gemini. Fussy, hung up on health, pedantic, neurotic about work, neurotic full stop . . . the list goes on!

Libra

The person with the Libra planet may seem rather too interested in popularity votes as opposed to decision-making for the person with Capricorn, Aries or Cancer planets. How on earth do they ever get anything done? When will they ever actually make a stand?

Scorpio

The person with the Scorpio planet could seem way too private (to the point of annoying secrecy) to the person with Aquarius,

Taurus or Leo planets. Then there's the complexity, the intensity and the emotion to deal with, not to mention the secret lust for control.

Sagittarius

The person with the Sagittarius planet could seem carelessly optimistic about important career or financial situations to the person with Pisces, Gemini or Virgo planets. Then there is the belief system of the Sagittarian to contend with. His/her faith, politics or religion may not compute.

Capricorn

The person with the Capricorn planet may appear to be far too professionally or socially ambitious to the person with Aries, Cancer or Libra planets. They may seem hung up on crawling to the top or staying at the top, and far too cautious about life and people generally.

Aquarius

The person with the Aquarius planet may seem barking mad to the person with planets in Taurus, Leo or Scorpio! They could seem so fixed about a particular way of life or belief system that the other party may recoil. The Aquarian type will be stubbornly independent too.

Pisces

The person with the Pisces planet will seem vague, unreliable, unrealistic or frankly out to lunch to the person with planets in Gemini, Virgo or Sagittarius. They may appear to have way too many fantasies or illusions, either about themselves or their lives, for the other person.

YES, BUT WILL MY FRIENDS LIKE HIM? THE ASTROLOGY OF GROUP PSYCHOLOGY

Shared households, step-families and big collections of friends are just three areas where group chemistry can either work with – or against – your lover. It's a surprisingly important part of life for lots of couples, and it's funny how often friends or families can make your relationship work or . . . hard work.

Really successful shared households, gangs of friends and families – even rock bands and sports teams, come to that – need to be composed of individuals who have both common bonds and a few creative clashes in their charts. Do you and your partner fit in with your flatmates, or his extended family?

Common bonds

You (as a couple) and the group will have lots of common bonds if you have planets in the same element – Fire, Earth, Air or Water. See below for the best blends.

Planets in Fire blend – Aries, Leo, Sagittarius
Planets in Earth blend – Taurus, Virgo, Capricorn
Planets in Air blend – Gemini, Libra, Aquarius
Planets in Water blend – Cancer, Scorpio, Pisces

Creative clashes

You (as a couple) and the group will have problems if there are lots of planets in clashing signs – Fire and Water don't mix! See below.

Planets in Aries and Cancer, Aries and Libra, Aries and Capricorn clash.

Planets in Taurus and Leo, Taurus and Scorpio, Taurus and Aquarius clash.

Planets in Gemini and Virgo, Gemini and Sagittarius, Gemini and Pisces clash.

Planets in Cancer and Libra, Cancer and Capricorn, Cancer and Aries clash.

Planets in Leo and Scorpio, Leo and Aquarius, Leo and Taurus clash.

Planets in Virgo and Sagittarius, Virgo and Pisces, Virgo and Gemini clash.

Planets in Libra and Capricorn, Libra and Aries, Libra and Cancer clash.

Planets in Scorpio and Aquarius, Scorpio and Taurus, Scorpio and Leo clash.

Planets in Sagittarius and Pisces, Sagittarius and Gemini, Sagittarius and Virgo clash.

Planets in Capricorn and Aries, Capricorn and Cancer, Capricorn and Libra clash.

Planets in Aquarius and Taurus, Aquarius and Leo, Aquarius and Scorpio clash.

Planets in Pisces and Gemini, Pisces and Virgo, Pisces and Sagittarius clash.

The Beatles had common bonds in Pisces, Scorpio and Cancer. George Harrison had the Sun in Pisces, John Lennon had Mercury in Scorpio and Ringo Starr had the Sun in Cancer. It generated that famously emotional, passionate energy current in their music that made people want to fall in love – or weep all over their kaftans.

The band was also the centrepiece of a huge astrological clash involving Paul McCartney and Yoko Ono. All four Beatle charts show this clash in the signs Leo, Scorpio and Aquarius, as George, John, Paul and Ringo each have important planets or points in these incompatible signs. And guess what? Yoko has her Sun in Aquarius too.

Life is never boring if you have lots of common bonds along with a few clash points – but remember, any outsiders (like your new lover) who walk into the lives of couples and groups with particular planetary combinations (and who hook into them with their own planets and points) can have a make-or-break effect. This often happens with families when a new baby is born too. Amazingly, the baby plugs into the pattern and suddenly unresolved tensions of many years' standing need to be faced and hopefully resolved!

Look at shared households, bands, work teams, families or any other small cluster of people you intuitively know has big, powerful, connections with you – for better or worse. Then look at how your partner affects the chemistry as a whole.

FAMILY FLOW

If you have the Sun in Aries, your partner has Mercury in Leo and your daughter has Venus in Sagittarius, for example, no matter what else is sticking or stalling in the family unit, there will always be a strong, noisy, loud, show-off bond between you!

You can stretch the group of three rule to a group of four, by the way. If the majority of you form one of these patterns in the family, some extraordinary projects, plans, dreams and wishes will come out of your house. In this particular instance, three out of four really won't be too bad.

The Aries–Leo–Sagittarius dominated family

If you share most or all of your personal planets in these signs, you will be an energetic, extroverted, optimistic combination. One person will take on the Tarzan role; another will play the show-off. Nobody will take no for an answer and any wet blankets who go dripping around the place will be thrown on the bonfire in front of a live TV audience. This combination of people is very oomphy, loud and lots of fun. When you go to a party, you tend to arrive together and then attract other people to your corner through sheer force of personality. Who wants to jump on a cheap flight tomorrow? You do! Who wants to organise a fancy-dress football match right now? You all do!

The Taurus–Virgo–Capricorn dominated family

Money, success and take your vitamins! If you share most or all of your personal planets in these signs, you will form an extremely practical, down-to-earth, grounded combination. It lacks the sheer enthusiasm and attention-grabbing factors you get with Aries–Leo–Sagittarius, but there is something utterly determined, wonderfully focused and stubbornly sensible about this combo. In a few cases, this type of family will end up rejecting the modern world and turn to alternative lifestyles, compost heaps and secondhand markets, but it's more common for all involved to end up with costly, luscious 'good life' lifestyles. There is a low tolerance for silliness, laziness and weirdness in this combo. Don't muck around and for God's sake, don't talk about UFOs at seven o'clock in the morning.

The Gemini–Libra–Aquarius dominated family

Huge phone and Internet bills are just a risk you're going to have to take if you share most or all of your personal planets in these signs. One of you is eccentric, offbeat, alternative, or – let's put this tactfully – certifiably insane. This is a light, stimulating, clever, breezy combination. It lacks true emotion but who needs that when you can all talk about your fave websites? A lot of book-lending and book-giving goes on in this sort of family, and anything remotely messy in the feelings department gets analysed so it can become more civilised. Some people will find it all a bit cold and clever-clever, but you all thrive on the brain massage and the wonderful space and freedom you extend to one another. The Aquarian streak often involves your family in causes or mad ideas.

The Cancer–Scorpio–Pisces dominated family

The Beatles had this combination. One of you has stared death in the face, or survived the deaths of other people. It lends the whole family a depth and intensity that other sign combinations lack. There are machinations and complications in this family too. Lots of secrets. Lots of private feelings. And sometimes, a lot of dark emotions. At some point, power will become the ugly issue that bites everyone in the bottom. However, no combination of people will push other people's buttons more powerfully! This combination is extremely deep and has layers upon layers. Importantly, the mother or grandmother in this collection of people is the key to just about everything. It tends to be a matriarchal clan and you can trace most of the highs and lows back to her influence.

6 FIND YOUR SIGNS

To find your or your partner's Moon Sign, Mercury Sign, Venus Sign, Mars Sign and Rising Sign, look up the following 1960–1985 birthday tables. Space doesn't allow for all twentieth-century dates to be shown in this book, but birthday tables for 1920–1960 and 1985–2000 can be found at www.jessicaadams.com.

The birthday tables show the time a planet entered a sign as well as the date. The time shown is Greenwich Mean Time (London time) which all astrologers use.

Because of this, if you were born outside England, you will need to work out what time it was in London at the moment you were born and then look yourself up. For example:

Drew Barrymore
Born February 22 1975
11.51 a.m. California, USA

(Details taken from her birth certificate, featured in *Profiles of Women* by Lois M. Rodden.) Drew is a Piscean. After we subtract the right number of hours from her California birth time to get it back to London time (GMT), it turns out she has this astrological profile:

Moon in Cancer
Mercury in Aquarius
Venus in Pisces
Mars in Capricorn

Another example:

Winona Ryder
Born October 29 1971
11.00 a.m. Cajarc, France

(Details taken from her birth certificate, recorded by Frank Clifford in *Profiles of Women* by Lois M. Rodden.) Winona is a Scorpio. After adjusting her birth time for France to get it to London time, we find:

Moon in Pisces
Mercury in Scorpio
Venus in Scorpio
Mars in Aquarius

If you don't know how many hours ahead or behind GMT (London time) you were on the day of your birth, visit www.astro.com and work out your chart online – it will do the maths for you in seconds – free! Don't know what time you were born? Use 6 a.m.

For most people reading this section, finding out the Mercury, Venus and Mars sign will be a snap – no hour-counting (or even birth time) required. So . . . what are you waiting for?

MOON 1960

1960
Jan 02 09:19 Pisces
Jan 04 15:21 Aries
Jan 07 01:22 Taurus
Jan 09 13:45 Gemini
Jan 12 02:23 Cancer
Jan 14 13:59 Leo
Jan 17 00:03 Virgo

. . . MOON 1960

Jan 19 08:14 Libra
Jan 21 13:59 Scorpio
Jan 23 17:03 Sagittarius
Jan 25 18:00 Capricorn
Jan 27 18:19 Aquarius
Jan 29 19:56 Pisces
Feb 01 00:39 Aries
Feb 03 09:16 Taurus
Feb 05 20:58 Gemini
Feb 08 09:37 Cancer
Feb 10 21:08 Leo
Feb 13 06:35 Virgo
Feb 15 13:55 Libra
Feb 17 19:24 Scorpio
Feb 19 23:12 Sagittarius
Feb 22 01:39 Capricorn
Feb 24 03:32 Aquarius
Feb 26 06:04 Pisces
Feb 28 10:37 Aries
Mar 01 18:18 Taurus
Mar 04 05:08 Gemini
Mar 06 17:37 Cancer
Mar 09 05:25 Leo
Mar 11 14:47 Virgo
Mar 13 21:19 Libra
Mar 16 01:37 Scorpio
Mar 18 04:37 Sagittarius
Mar 20 07:14 Capricorn
Mar 22 10:10 Aquarius
Mar 24 14:02 Pisces
Mar 26 19:29 Aries
Mar 29 03:13 Taurus
Mar 31 13:32 Gemini
Apr 03 01:46 Cancer
Apr 05 14:01 Leo
Apr 08 00:02 Virgo
Apr 10 06:35 Libra
Apr 12 10:01 Scorpio
Apr 14 11:37 Sagittarius
Apr 16 13:01 Capricorn
Apr 18 15:32 Aquarius
Apr 20 19:55 Pisces
Apr 23 02:23 Aries
Apr 25 10:50 Taurus
Apr 27 21:16 Gemini
Apr 30 09:22 Cancer
May 02 21:58 Leo
May 05 08:59 Virgo
May 07 16:30 Libra
May 09 20:07 Scorpio
May 11 20:55 Sagittarius
May 13 20:50 Capricorn
May 15 21:51 Aquarius
May 18 01:23 Pisces
May 20 07:55 Aries
May 22 17:00 Taurus
May 25 03:55 Gemini
May 27 16:06 Cancer
May 30 04:50 Leo
Jun 01 16:38 Virgo

. . . MOON 1960

Jun 04 01:31 Libra
Jun 06 06:20 Scorpio
Jun 08 07:31 Sagittarius
Jun 10 06:48 Capricorn
Jun 12 06:23 Aquarius
Jun 14 08:17 Pisces
Jun 16 13:42 Aries
Jun 18 22:33 Taurus
Jun 21 09:46 Gemini
Jun 23 22:10 Cancer
Jun 26 10:51 Leo
Jun 28 22:53 Virgo
Jul 01 08:46 Libra
Jul 03 15:08 Scorpio
Jul 05 17:42 Sagittarius
Jul 07 17:34 Capricorn
Jul 09 16:43 Aquarius
Jul 11 17:19 Pisces
Jul 13 21:07 Aries
Jul 16 04:48 Taurus
Jul 18 15:40 Gemini
Jul 21 04:09 Cancer
Jul 23 16:46 Leo
Jul 26 04:31 Virgo
Jul 28 14:33 Libra
Jul 30 21:55 Scorpio
Aug 02 02:04 Sagittarius
Aug 04 03:25 Capricorn
Aug 06 03:21 Aquarius
Aug 08 03:42 Pisces
Aug 10 06:21 Aries
Aug 12 12:35 Taurus
Aug 14 22:29 Gemini
Aug 17 10:43 Cancer
Aug 19 23:17 Leo
Aug 22 10:41 Virgo
Aug 24 20:09 Libra
Aug 27 03:23 Scorpio
Aug 29 08:19 Sagittarius
Aug 31 11:09 Capricorn
Sep 02 12:35 Aquarius
Sep 04 13:51 Pisces
Sep 06 16:26 Aries
Sep 08 21:44 Taurus
Sep 11 06:31 Gemini
Sep 13 18:10 Cancer
Sep 16 06:46 Leo
Sep 18 18:07 Virgo
Sep 21 02:58 Libra
Sep 23 09:18 Scorpio
Sep 25 13:42 Sagittarius
Sep 27 16:54 Capricorn
Sep 29 19:32 Aquarius
Oct 01 22:14 Pisces
Oct 04 01:46 Aries
Oct 06 07:09 Taurus
Oct 08 15:16 Gemini
Oct 11 02:18 Cancer
Oct 13 14:55 Leo
Oct 16 02:40 Virgo

. . . MOON 1960–1

Oct 18 11:32 Libra
Oct 20 17:06 Scorpio
Oct 22 20:15 Sagittarius
Oct 24 22:28 Capricorn
Oct 27 00:57 Aquarius
Oct 29 04:26 Pisces
Oct 31 09:11 Aries
Nov 02 15:27 Taurus
Nov 04 23:44 Gemini
Nov 07 10:26 Cancer
Nov 09 22:59 Leo
Nov 12 11:24 Virgo
Nov 14 21:07 Libra
Nov 17 02:53 Scorpio
Nov 19 05:16 Sagittarius
Nov 21 06:02 Capricorn
Nov 23 07:04 Aquarius
Nov 25 09:49 Pisces
Nov 27 14:50 Aries
Nov 29 21:59 Taurus
Dec 02 07:00 Gemini
Dec 04 17:52 Cancer
Dec 07 06:21 Leo
Dec 09 19:13 Virgo
Dec 12 06:10 Libra
Dec 14 13:13 Scorpio
Dec 16 16:07 Sagittarius
Dec 18 16:16 Capricorn
Dec 20 15:48 Aquarius
Dec 22 16:47 Pisces
Dec 24 20:34 Aries
Dec 27 03:30 Taurus
Dec 29 13:01 Gemini

1961

Jan 01 00:21 Cancer
Jan 03 12:54 Leo
Jan 06 01:48 Virgo
Jan 08 13:31 Libra
Jan 10 22:08 Scorpio
Jan 13 02:40 Sagittarius
Jan 15 03:41 Capricorn
Jan 17 02:55 Aquarius
Jan 19 02:32 Pisces
Jan 21 04:26 Aries
Jan 23 09:51 Taurus
Jan 25 18:50 Gemini
Jan 28 06:22 Cancer
Jan 30 19:05 Leo
Feb 02 07:48 Virgo
Feb 04 19:27 Libra
Feb 07 04:50 Scorpio
Feb 09 11:01 Sagittarius
Feb 11 13:50 Capricorn
Feb 13 14:14 Aquarius
Feb 15 13:53 Pisces
Feb 17 14:40 Aries
Feb 19 18:21 Taurus
Feb 22 01:51 Gemini
Feb 24 12:48 Cancer
Feb 27 01:34 Leo

. . . MOON 1961

Mar 01 14:12 Virgo
Mar 04 01:21 Libra
Mar 06 10:23 Scorpio
Mar 08 17:03 Sagittarius
Mar 10 21:19 Capricorn
Mar 12 23:29 Aquarius
Mar 15 00:26 Pisces
Mar 17 01:32 Aries
Mar 19 04:25 Taurus
Mar 21 10:32 Gemini
Mar 23 20:22 Cancer
Mar 26 08:48 Leo
Mar 28 21:29 Virgo
Mar 31 08:21 Libra
Apr 02 16:36 Scorpio
Apr 04 22:34 Sagittarius
Apr 07 02:52 Capricorn
Apr 09 06:02 Aquarius
Apr 11 08:31 Pisces
Apr 13 10:55 Aries
Apr 15 14:16 Taurus
Apr 17 19:55 Gemini
Apr 20 04:49 Cancer
Apr 22 16:43 Leo
Apr 25 05:31 Virgo
Apr 27 16:34 Libra
Apr 30 00:27 Scorpio
May 02 05:25 Sagittarius
May 04 08:39 Capricorn
May 06 11:24 Aquarius
May 08 14:22 Pisces
May 10 17:55 Aries
May 12 22:25 Taurus
May 15 04:34 Gemini
May 17 13:16 Cancer
May 20 00:45 Leo
May 22 13:38 Virgo
May 25 01:17 Libra
May 27 09:34 Scorpio
May 29 14:11 Sagittarius
May 31 16:20 Capricorn
Jun 02 17:44 Aquarius
Jun 04 19:50 Pisces
Jun 06 23:23 Aries
Jun 09 04:37 Taurus
Jun 11 11:40 Gemini
Jun 13 20:49 Cancer
Jun 16 08:15 Leo
Jun 18 21:12 Virgo
Jun 21 09:32 Libra
Jun 23 18:50 Scorpio
Jun 26 00:05 Sagittarius
Jun 28 01:59 Capricorn
Jun 30 02:18 Aquarius
Jul 02 02:52 Pisces
Jul 04 05:12 Aries
Jul 06 10:01 Taurus
Jul 08 17:27 Gemini
Jul 11 03:13 Cancer
Jul 13 14:56 Leo

. . . MOON 1961

Jul 16 03:54 Virgo
Jul 18 16:38 Libra
Jul 21 03:04 Scorpio
Jul 23 09:42 Sagittarius
Jul 25 12:28 Capricorn
Jul 27 12:41 Aquarius
Jul 29 12:12 Pisces
Jul 31 12:55 Aries
Aug 02 16:18 Taurus
Aug 04 23:04 Gemini
Aug 07 08:56 Cancer
Aug 09 20:59 Leo
Aug 12 10:00 Virgo
Aug 14 22:43 Libra
Aug 17 09:44 Scorpio
Aug 19 17:43 Sagittarius
Aug 21 22:07 Capricorn
Aug 23 23:25 Aquarius
Aug 25 23:02 Pisces
Aug 27 22:48 Aries
Aug 30 00:36 Taurus
Sep 01 05:52 Gemini
Sep 03 15:00 Cancer
Sep 06 03:00 Leo
Sep 08 16:05 Virgo
Sep 11 04:33 Libra
Sep 13 15:22 Scorpio
Sep 15 23:54 Sagittarius
Sep 18 05:42 Capricorn
Sep 20 08:43 Aquarius
Sep 22 09:36 Pisces
Sep 24 09:40 Aries
Sep 26 10:41 Taurus
Sep 28 14:31 Gemini
Sep 30 22:19 Cancer
Oct 03 09:43 Leo
Oct 05 22:45 Virgo
Oct 08 11:03 Libra
Oct 10 21:19 Scorpio
Oct 13 05:20 Sagittarius
Oct 15 11:23 Capricorn
Oct 17 15:37 Aquarius
Oct 19 18:10 Pisces
Oct 21 19:35 Aries
Oct 23 21:06 Taurus
Oct 26 00:24 Gemini
Oct 28 07:02 Cancer
Oct 30 17:29 Leo
Nov 02 06:17 Virgo
Nov 04 18:42 Libra
Nov 07 04:40 Scorpio
Nov 09 11:50 Sagittarius
Nov 11 16:59 Capricorn
Nov 13 20:59 Aquarius
Nov 16 00:18 Pisces
Nov 18 03:10 Aries
Nov 20 06:02 Taurus
Nov 22 09:59 Gemini
Nov 24 16:20 Cancer
Nov 27 02:01 Leo

. . . MOON 1961–2

Nov 29 14:25 Virgo
Dec 02 03:08 Libra
Dec 04 13:30 Scorpio
Dec 06 20:24 Sagittarius
Dec 09 00:30 Capricorn
Dec 11 03:11 Aquarius
Dec 13 05:41 Pisces
Dec 15 08:44 Aries
Dec 17 12:38 Taurus
Dec 19 17:47 Gemini
Dec 22 00:49 Cancer
Dec 24 10:25 Leo
Dec 26 22:29 Virgo
Dec 29 11:26 Libra
Dec 31 22:41 Scorpio
1962
Jan 03 06:23 Sagittarius
Jan 05 10:24 Capricorn
Jan 07 12:00 Aquarius
Jan 09 12:53 Pisces
Jan 11 14:33 Aries
Jan 13 18:01 Taurus
Jan 15 23:42 Gemini
Jan 18 07:39 Cancer
Jan 20 17:49 Leo
Jan 23 05:53 Virgo
Jan 25 18:52 Libra
Jan 28 06:54 Scorpio
Jan 30 15:59 Sagittarius
Feb 01 21:09 Capricorn
Feb 03 22:56 Aquarius
Feb 05 22:52 Pisces
Feb 07 22:50 Aries
Feb 10 00:34 Taurus
Feb 12 05:18 Gemini
Feb 14 13:19 Cancer
Feb 17 00:03 Leo
Feb 19 12:26 Virgo
Feb 22 01:21 Libra
Feb 24 13:36 Scorpio
Feb 26 23:46 Sagittarius
Mar 01 06:38 Capricorn
Mar 03 09:51 Aquarius
Mar 05 10:16 Pisces
Mar 07 09:32 Aries
Mar 09 09:40 Taurus
Mar 11 12:35 Gemini
Mar 13 19:25 Cancer
Mar 16 05:55 Leo
Mar 18 18:32 Virgo
Mar 21 07:28 Libra
Mar 23 19:28 Scorpio
Mar 26 05:48 Sagittarius
Mar 28 13:45 Capricorn
Mar 30 18:43 Aquarius
Apr 01 20:42 Pisces
Apr 03 20:41 Aries
Apr 05 20:25 Taurus
Apr 07 21:59 Gemini
Apr 10 03:12 Cancer

. . . MOON 1962

Apr 12 12:36 Leo
Apr 15 00:56 Virgo
Apr 17 13:53 Libra
Apr 20 01:36 Scorpio
Apr 22 11:26 Sagittarius
Apr 24 19:19 Capricorn
Apr 27 01:07 Aquarius
Apr 29 04:40 Pisces
May 01 06:12 Aries
May 03 06:49 Taurus
May 05 08:16 Gemini
May 07 12:27 Cancer
May 09 20:35 Leo
May 12 08:11 Virgo
May 14 21:02 Libra
May 17 08:42 Scorpio
May 19 18:02 Sagittarius
May 22 01:08 Capricorn
May 24 06:30 Aquarius
May 26 10:29 Pisces
May 28 13:14 Aries
May 30 15:16 Taurus
Jun 01 17:40 Gemini
Jun 03 21:56 Cancer
Jun 06 05:23 Leo
Jun 08 16:12 Virgo
Jun 11 04:50 Libra
Jun 13 16:44 Scorpio
Jun 16 02:03 Sagittarius
Jun 18 08:29 Capricorn
Jun 20 12:48 Aquarius
Jun 22 15:58 Pisces
Jun 24 18:43 Aries
Jun 26 21:34 Taurus
Jun 29 01:09 Gemini
Jul 01 06:18 Cancer
Jul 03 13:55 Leo
Jul 06 00:22 Virgo
Jul 08 12:47 Libra
Jul 11 01:05 Scorpio
Jul 13 11:00 Sagittarius
Jul 15 17:32 Capricorn
Jul 17 21:07 Aquarius
Jul 19 23:00 Pisces
Jul 22 00:33 Aries
Jul 24 02:56 Taurus
Jul 26 06:56 Gemini
Jul 28 13:00 Cancer
Jul 30 21:20 Leo
Aug 02 07:57 Virgo
Aug 04 20:17 Libra
Aug 07 08:55 Scorpio
Aug 09 19:48 Sagittarius
Aug 12 03:17 Capricorn
Aug 14 07:07 Aquarius
Aug 16 08:16 Pisces
Aug 18 08:25 Aries
Aug 20 09:19 Taurus
Aug 22 12:27 Gemini
Aug 24 18:33 Cancer

. . . MOON 1962–3

Aug 27 03:29 Leo
Aug 29 14:35 Virgo
Sep 01 03:00 Libra
Sep 03 15:46 Scorpio
Sep 06 03:26 Sagittarius
Sep 08 12:19 Capricorn
Sep 10 17:26 Aquarius
Sep 12 19:01 Pisces
Sep 14 18:32 Aries
Sep 16 18:00 Taurus
Sep 18 19:28 Gemini
Sep 21 00:25 Cancer
Sep 23 09:06 Leo
Sep 25 20:30 Virgo
Sep 28 09:07 Libra
Sep 30 21:48 Scorpio
Oct 03 09:39 Sagittarius
Oct 05 19:34 Capricorn
Oct 08 02:21 Aquarius
Oct 10 05:28 Pisces
Oct 12 05:40 Aries
Oct 14 04:43 Taurus
Oct 16 04:50 Gemini
Oct 18 08:04 Cancer
Oct 20 15:30 Leo
Oct 23 02:31 Virgo
Oct 25 15:13 Libra
Oct 28 03:48 Scorpio
Oct 30 15:19 Sagittarius
Nov 02 01:17 Capricorn
Nov 04 09:02 Aquarius
Nov 06 13:52 Pisces
Nov 08 15:45 Aries
Nov 10 15:44 Taurus
Nov 12 15:43 Gemini
Nov 14 17:48 Cancer
Nov 16 23:39 Leo
Nov 19 09:33 Virgo
Nov 21 21:57 Libra
Nov 24 10:33 Scorpio
Nov 26 21:43 Sagittarius
Nov 29 07:00 Capricorn
Dec 01 14:25 Aquarius
Dec 03 19:53 Pisces
Dec 05 23:17 Aries
Dec 08 00:59 Taurus
Dec 10 02:07 Gemini
Dec 12 04:21 Cancer
Dec 14 09:20 Leo
Dec 16 17:59 Virgo
Dec 19 05:41 Libra
Dec 21 18:17 Scorpio
Dec 24 05:32 Sagittarius
Dec 26 14:18 Capricorn
Dec 28 20:42 Aquarius
Dec 31 01:20 Pisces

1963

Jan 02 04:47 Aries
Jan 04 07:33 Taurus
Jan 06 10:14 Gemini

. . . MOON 1963

Jan 08 13:41 Cancer
Jan 10 19:00 Leo
Jan 13 03:07 Virgo
Jan 15 14:04 Libra
Jan 18 02:35 Scorpio
Jan 20 14:20 Sagittarius
Jan 22 23:23 Capricorn
Jan 25 05:13 Aquarius
Jan 27 08:35 Pisces
Jan 29 10:43 Aries
Jan 31 12:54 Taurus
Feb 02 16:03 Gemini
Feb 04 20:40 Cancer
Feb 07 03:05 Leo
Feb 09 11:36 Virgo
Feb 11 22:18 Libra
Feb 14 10:38 Scorpio
Feb 16 22:57 Sagittarius
Feb 19 09:00 Capricorn
Feb 21 15:23 Aquarius
Feb 23 18:17 Pisces
Feb 25 19:05 Aries
Feb 27 19:38 Taurus
Mar 01 21:38 Gemini
Mar 04 02:07 Cancer
Mar 06 09:14 Leo
Mar 08 18:33 Virgo
Mar 11 05:34 Libra
Mar 13 17:51 Scorpio
Mar 16 06:26 Sagittarius
Mar 18 17:34 Capricorn
Mar 21 01:21 Aquarius
Mar 23 05:04 Pisces
Mar 25 05:37 Aries
Mar 27 04:56 Taurus
Mar 29 05:12 Gemini
Mar 31 08:13 Cancer
Apr 02 14:45 Leo
Apr 05 00:20 Virgo
Apr 07 11:49 Libra
Apr 10 00:13 Scorpio
Apr 12 12:47 Sagittarius
Apr 15 00:26 Capricorn
Apr 17 09:33 Aquarius
Apr 19 14:53 Pisces
Apr 21 16:29 Aries
Apr 23 15:50 Taurus
Apr 25 15:06 Gemini
Apr 27 16:26 Cancer
Apr 29 21:24 Leo
May 02 06:12 Virgo
May 04 17:42 Libra
May 07 06:15 Scorpio
May 09 18:42 Sagittarius
May 12 06:13 Capricorn
May 14 15:51 Aquarius
May 16 22:31 Pisces
May 19 01:47 Aries
May 21 02:21 Taurus
May 23 01:53 Gemini

. . . MOON 1963

May 25 02:28 Cancer
May 27 05:58 Leo
May 29 13:21 Virgo
Jun 01 00:08 Libra
Jun 03 12:38 Scorpio
Jun 06 01:00 Sagittarius
Jun 08 12:06 Capricorn
Jun 10 21:21 Aquarius
Jun 13 04:20 Pisces
Jun 15 08:46 Aries
Jun 17 10:54 Taurus
Jun 19 11:43 Gemini
Jun 21 12:46 Cancer
Jun 23 15:43 Leo
Jun 25 21:56 Virgo
Jun 28 07:40 Libra
Jun 30 19:47 Scorpio
Jul 03 08:11 Sagittarius
Jul 05 19:02 Capricorn
Jul 08 03:36 Aquarius
Jul 10 09:52 Pisces
Jul 12 14:16 Aries
Jul 14 17:14 Taurus
Jul 16 19:27 Gemini
Jul 18 21:44 Cancer
Jul 21 01:15 Leo
Jul 23 07:06 Virgo
Jul 25 16:02 Libra
Jul 28 03:38 Scorpio
Jul 30 16:07 Sagittarius
Aug 02 03:12 Capricorn
Aug 04 11:25 Aquarius
Aug 06 16:45 Pisces
Aug 08 20:06 Aries
Aug 10 22:37 Taurus
Aug 13 01:15 Gemini
Aug 15 04:39 Cancer
Aug 17 09:16 Leo
Aug 19 15:40 Virgo
Aug 22 00:25 Libra
Aug 24 11:38 Scorpio
Aug 27 00:15 Sagittarius
Aug 29 11:57 Capricorn
Aug 31 20:37 Aquarius
Sep 03 01:37 Pisces
Sep 05 03:52 Aries
Sep 07 05:02 Taurus
Sep 09 06:45 Gemini
Sep 11 10:07 Cancer
Sep 13 15:29 Leo
Sep 15 22:47 Virgo
Sep 18 07:59 Libra
Sep 20 19:10 Scorpio
Sep 23 07:49 Sagittarius
Sep 25 20:15 Capricorn
Sep 28 06:03 Aquarius
Sep 30 11:46 Pisces
Oct 02 13:47 Aries
Oct 04 13:49 Taurus
Oct 06 13:58 Gemini

. . . MOON 1963–4

Oct 08 16:00 Cancer
Oct 10 20:53 Leo
Oct 13 04:34 Virgo
Oct 15 14:24 Libra
Oct 18 01:52 Scorpio
Oct 20 14:32 Sagittarius
Oct 23 03:20 Capricorn
Oct 25 14:19 Aquarius
Oct 27 21:36 Pisces
Oct 30 00:39 Aries
Nov 01 00:42 Taurus
Nov 02 23:48 Gemini
Nov 05 00:08 Cancer
Nov 07 03:23 Leo
Nov 09 10:13 Virgo
Nov 11 20:07 Libra
Nov 14 07:56 Scorpio
Nov 16 20:39 Sagittarius
Nov 19 09:22 Capricorn
Nov 21 20:51 Aquarius
Nov 24 05:32 Pisces
Nov 26 10:25 Aries
Nov 28 11:49 Taurus
Nov 30 11:14 Gemini
Dec 02 10:44 Cancer
Dec 04 12:19 Leo
Dec 06 17:26 Virgo
Dec 09 02:21 Libra
Dec 11 14:04 Scorpio
Dec 14 02:53 Sagittarius
Dec 16 15:21 Capricorn
Dec 19 02:28 Aquarius
Dec 21 11:28 Pisces
Dec 23 17:40 Aries
Dec 25 20:57 Taurus
Dec 27 21:58 Gemini
Dec 29 22:06 Cancer
Dec 31 23:08 Leo

1964

Jan 03 02:47 Virgo
Jan 05 10:09 Libra
Jan 07 21:03 Scorpio
Jan 10 09:49 Sagittarius
Jan 12 22:13 Capricorn
Jan 15 08:47 Aquarius
Jan 17 17:03 Pisces
Jan 19 23:10 Aries
Jan 22 03:23 Taurus
Jan 24 06:04 Gemini
Jan 26 07:51 Cancer
Jan 28 09:45 Leo
Jan 30 13:08 Virgo
Feb 01 19:25 Libra
Feb 04 05:12 Scorpio
Feb 06 17:35 Sagittarius
Feb 09 06:10 Capricorn
Feb 11 16:39 Aquarius
Feb 14 00:08 Pisces
Feb 16 05:09 Aries
Feb 18 08:44 Taurus

. . . MOON 1964

Feb 20 11:47 Gemini
Feb 22 14:49 Cancer
Feb 24 18:10 Leo
Feb 26 22:30 Virgo
Feb 29 04:46 Libra
Mar 02 13:53 Scorpio
Mar 05 01:46 Sagittarius
Mar 07 14:35 Capricorn
Mar 10 01:35 Aquarius
Mar 12 09:05 Pisces
Mar 14 13:15 Aries
Mar 16 15:30 Taurus
Mar 18 17:25 Gemini
Mar 20 20:11 Cancer
Mar 23 00:14 Leo
Mar 25 05:41 Virgo
Mar 27 12:47 Libra
Mar 29 22:03 Scorpio
Apr 01 09:40 Sagittarius
Apr 03 22:35 Capricorn
Apr 06 10:24 Aquarius
Apr 08 18:46 Pisces
Apr 10 23:08 Aries
Apr 13 00:36 Taurus
Apr 15 01:05 Gemini
Apr 17 02:23 Cancer
Apr 19 05:39 Leo
Apr 21 11:17 Virgo
Apr 23 19:07 Libra
Apr 26 05:00 Scorpio
Apr 28 16:45 Sagittarius
May 01 05:42 Capricorn
May 03 18:06 Aquarius
May 06 03:43 Pisces
May 08 09:15 Aries
May 10 11:09 Taurus
May 12 11:01 Gemini
May 14 10:53 Cancer
May 16 12:31 Leo
May 18 17:02 Virgo
May 21 00:41 Libra
May 23 10:57 Scorpio
May 25 23:02 Sagittarius
May 28 11:59 Capricorn
May 31 00:32 Aquarius
Jun 02 11:01 Pisces
Jun 04 18:02 Aries
Jun 06 21:19 Taurus
Jun 08 21:50 Gemini
Jun 10 21:16 Cancer
Jun 12 21:34 Leo
Jun 15 00:27 Virgo
Jun 17 06:53 Libra
Jun 19 16:48 Scorpio
Jun 22 05:03 Sagittarius
Jun 24 18:01 Capricorn
Jun 27 06:21 Aquarius
Jun 29 16:56 Pisces
Jul 02 00:52 Aries
Jul 04 05:42 Taurus

. . . MOON 1964

Jul 06 07:42 Gemini
Jul 08 07:56 Cancer
Jul 10 08:00 Leo
Jul 12 09:44 Virgo
Jul 14 14:41 Libra
Jul 16 23:32 Scorpio
Jul 19 11:27 Sagittarius
Jul 22 00:26 Capricorn
Jul 24 12:30 Aquarius
Jul 26 22:35 Pisces
Jul 29 06:25 Aries
Jul 31 12:00 Taurus
Aug 02 15:28 Gemini
Aug 04 17:13 Cancer
Aug 06 18:11 Leo
Aug 08 19:50 Virgo
Aug 10 23:51 Libra
Aug 13 07:31 Scorpio
Aug 15 18:44 Sagittarius
Aug 18 07:38 Capricorn
Aug 20 19:38 Aquarius
Aug 23 05:13 Pisces
Aug 25 12:15 Aries
Aug 27 17:23 Taurus
Aug 29 21:15 Gemini
Sep 01 00:13 Cancer
Sep 03 02:36 Leo
Sep 05 05:12 Virgo
Sep 07 09:19 Libra
Sep 09 16:19 Scorpio
Sep 12 02:47 Sagittarius
Sep 14 15:30 Capricorn
Sep 17 03:47 Aquarius
Sep 19 13:22 Pisces
Sep 21 19:43 Aries
Sep 23 23:46 Taurus
Sep 26 02:46 Gemini
Sep 28 05:39 Cancer
Sep 30 08:52 Leo
Oct 02 12:42 Virgo
Oct 04 17:44 Libra
Oct 07 00:56 Scorpio
Oct 09 11:02 Sagittarius
Oct 11 23:31 Capricorn
Oct 14 12:15 Aquarius
Oct 16 22:32 Pisces
Oct 19 05:04 Aries
Oct 21 08:24 Taurus
Oct 23 10:03 Gemini
Oct 25 11:37 Cancer
Oct 27 14:13 Leo
Oct 29 18:25 Virgo
Nov 01 00:24 Libra
Nov 03 08:24 Scorpio
Nov 05 18:43 Sagittarius
Nov 08 07:05 Capricorn
Nov 10 20:08 Aquarius
Nov 13 07:28 Pisces
Nov 15 15:10 Aries
Nov 17 18:56 Taurus

. . . MOON 1964–5

Nov 19 19:58 Gemini
Nov 21 20:03 Cancer
Nov 23 20:58 Leo
Nov 26 00:02 Virgo
Nov 28 05:54 Libra
Nov 30 14:30 Scorpio
Dec 03 01:23 Sagittarius
Dec 05 13:53 Capricorn
Dec 08 02:57 Aquarius
Dec 10 14:59 Pisces
Dec 13 00:12 Aries
Dec 15 05:32 Taurus
Dec 17 07:21 Gemini
Dec 19 07:02 Cancer
Dec 21 06:30 Leo
Dec 23 07:41 Virgo
Dec 25 12:04 Libra
Dec 27 20:11 Scorpio
Dec 30 07:20 Sagittarius

1965

Jan 01 20:06 Capricorn
Jan 04 09:04 Aquarius
Jan 06 21:06 Pisces
Jan 09 07:07 Aries
Jan 11 14:10 Taurus
Jan 13 17:48 Gemini
Jan 15 18:34 Cancer
Jan 17 17:57 Leo
Jan 19 17:54 Virgo
Jan 21 20:27 Libra
Jan 24 03:00 Scorpio
Jan 26 13:32 Sagittarius
Jan 29 02:21 Capricorn
Jan 31 15:17 Aquarius
Feb 03 02:55 Pisces
Feb 05 12:43 Aries
Feb 07 20:23 Taurus
Feb 10 01:36 Gemini
Feb 12 04:13 Cancer
Feb 14 04:54 Leo
Feb 16 05:05 Virgo
Feb 18 06:44 Libra
Feb 20 11:45 Scorpio
Feb 22 20:56 Sagittarius
Feb 25 09:16 Capricorn
Feb 27 22:14 Aquarius
Mar 02 09:38 Pisces
Mar 04 18:44 Aries
Mar 07 01:49 Taurus
Mar 09 07:14 Gemini
Mar 11 11:02 Cancer
Mar 13 13:22 Leo
Mar 15 14:55 Virgo
Mar 17 17:03 Libra
Mar 19 21:31 Scorpio
Mar 22 05:36 Sagittarius
Mar 24 17:06 Capricorn
Mar 27 05:58 Aquarius
Mar 29 17:31 Pisces
Apr 01 02:18 Aries

. . . MOON 1965

Apr 03 08:28 Taurus
Apr 05 12:54 Gemini
Apr 07 16:24 Cancer
Apr 09 19:23 Leo
Apr 11 22:14 Virgo
Apr 14 01:38 Libra
Apr 16 06:41 Scorpio
Apr 18 14:31 Sagittarius
Apr 21 01:23 Capricorn
Apr 23 14:03 Aquarius
Apr 26 02:02 Pisces
Apr 28 11:12 Aries
Apr 30 17:03 Taurus
May 02 20:26 Gemini
May 04 22:38 Cancer
May 07 00:49 Leo
May 09 03:47 Virgo
May 11 08:04 Libra
May 13 14:09 Scorpio
May 15 22:31 Sagittarius
May 18 09:19 Capricorn
May 20 21:50 Aquarius
May 23 10:14 Pisces
May 25 20:18 Aries
May 28 02:48 Taurus
May 30 05:58 Gemini
Jun 01 07:05 Cancer
Jun 03 07:46 Leo
Jun 05 09:33 Virgo
Jun 07 13:29 Libra
Jun 09 20:03 Scorpio
Jun 12 05:09 Sagittarius
Jun 14 16:20 Capricorn
Jun 17 04:51 Aquarius
Jun 19 17:28 Pisces
Jun 22 04:29 Aries
Jun 24 12:16 Taurus
Jun 26 16:18 Gemini
Jun 28 17:20 Cancer
Jun 30 16:58 Leo
Jul 02 17:11 Virgo
Jul 04 19:42 Libra
Jul 07 01:37 Scorpio
Jul 09 10:53 Sagittarius
Jul 11 22:28 Capricorn
Jul 14 11:07 Aquarius
Jul 16 23:44 Pisces
Jul 19 11:12 Aries
Jul 21 20:14 Taurus
Jul 24 01:48 Gemini
Jul 26 03:53 Cancer
Jul 28 03:37 Leo
Jul 30 02:54 Virgo
Aug 01 03:54 Libra
Aug 03 08:20 Scorpio
Aug 05 16:49 Sagittarius
Aug 08 04:22 Capricorn
Aug 10 17:09 Aquarius
Aug 13 05:37 Pisces
Aug 15 16:56 Aries

. . . MOON 1965

Aug 18 02:27 Taurus
Aug 20 09:20 Gemini
Aug 22 13:04 Cancer
Aug 24 14:01 Leo
Aug 26 13:36 Virgo
Aug 28 13:52 Libra
Aug 30 16:53 Scorpio
Sep 01 23:59 Sagittarius
Sep 04 10:51 Capricorn
Sep 06 23:33 Aquarius
Sep 09 11:56 Pisces
Sep 11 22:49 Aries
Sep 14 07:56 Taurus
Sep 16 15:06 Gemini
Sep 18 20:00 Cancer
Sep 20 22:35 Leo
Sep 22 23:29 Virgo
Sep 25 00:15 Libra
Sep 27 02:46 Scorpio
Sep 29 08:41 Sagittarius
Oct 01 18:28 Capricorn
Oct 04 06:48 Aquarius
Oct 06 19:13 Pisces
Oct 09 05:53 Aries
Oct 11 14:16 Taurus
Oct 13 20:39 Gemini
Oct 16 01:26 Cancer
Oct 18 04:51 Leo
Oct 20 07:13 Virgo
Oct 22 09:20 Libra
Oct 24 12:31 Scorpio
Oct 26 18:08 Sagittarius
Oct 29 03:04 Capricorn
Oct 31 14:49 Aquarius
Nov 03 03:22 Pisces
Nov 05 14:21 Aries
Nov 07 22:29 Taurus
Nov 10 03:54 Gemini
Nov 12 07:29 Cancer
Nov 14 10:13 Leo
Nov 16 12:54 Virgo
Nov 18 16:10 Libra
Nov 20 20:36 Scorpio
Nov 23 02:56 Sagittarius
Nov 25 11:45 Capricorn
Nov 27 23:03 Aquarius
Nov 30 11:39 Pisces
Dec 02 23:22 Aries
Dec 05 08:11 Taurus
Dec 07 13:27 Gemini
Dec 09 15:56 Cancer
Dec 11 17:08 Leo
Dec 13 18:35 Virgo
Dec 15 21:33 Libra
Dec 18 02:40 Scorpio
Dec 20 10:01 Sagittarius
Dec 22 19:26 Capricorn
Dec 25 06:44 Aquarius
Dec 27 19:17 Pisces
Dec 30 07:39 Aries

. . . MOON 1966

1966
Jan 01 17:46 Taurus
Jan 04 00:06 Gemini
Jan 06 02:40 Cancer
Jan 08 02:49 Leo
Jan 10 02:34 Virgo
Jan 12 03:53 Libra
Jan 14 08:08 Scorpio
Jan 16 15:39 Sagittarius
Jan 19 01:44 Capricorn
Jan 21 13:26 Aquarius
Jan 24 01:58 Pisces
Jan 26 14:32 Aries
Jan 29 01:42 Taurus
Jan 31 09:43 Gemini
Feb 02 13:41 Cancer
Feb 04 14:13 Leo
Feb 06 13:11 Virgo
Feb 08 12:50 Libra
Feb 10 15:14 Scorpio
Feb 12 21:33 Sagittarius
Feb 15 07:25 Capricorn
Feb 17 19:25 Aquarius
Feb 20 08:05 Pisces
Feb 22 20:30 Aries
Feb 25 07:53 Taurus
Feb 27 17:02 Gemini
Mar 01 22:48 Cancer
Mar 04 00:56 Leo
Mar 06 00:36 Virgo
Mar 07 23:48 Libra
Mar 10 00:46 Scorpio
Mar 12 05:18 Sagittarius
Mar 14 13:55 Capricorn
Mar 17 01:34 Aquarius
Mar 19 14:18 Pisces
Mar 22 02:33 Aries
Mar 24 13:31 Taurus
Mar 26 22:41 Gemini
Mar 29 05:23 Cancer
Mar 31 09:12 Leo
Apr 02 10:31 Virgo
Apr 04 10:39 Libra
Apr 06 11:29 Scorpio
Apr 08 14:53 Sagittarius
Apr 10 22:01 Capricorn
Apr 13 08:42 Aquarius
Apr 15 21:13 Pisces
Apr 18 09:27 Aries
Apr 20 20:00 Taurus
Apr 23 04:26 Gemini
Apr 25 10:47 Cancer
Apr 27 15:09 Leo
Apr 29 17:49 Virgo
May 01 19:31 Libra
May 03 21:23 Scorpio
May 06 00:52 Sagittarius
May 08 07:12 Capricorn
May 10 16:51 Aquarius
May 13 04:54 Pisces

. . . MOON 1966

May 15 17:15 Aries
May 18 03:49 Taurus
May 20 11:39 Gemini
May 22 17:00 Cancer
May 24 20:37 Leo
May 26 23:22 Virgo
May 29 02:00 Libra
May 31 05:11 Scorpio
Jun 02 09:38 Sagittarius
Jun 04 16:10 Capricorn
Jun 07 01:20 Aquarius
Jun 09 12:56 Pisces
Jun 12 01:26 Aries
Jun 14 12:29 Taurus
Jun 16 20:26 Gemini
Jun 19 01:05 Cancer
Jun 21 03:29 Leo
Jun 23 05:07 Virgo
Jun 25 07:22 Libra
Jun 27 11:03 Scorpio
Jun 29 16:31 Sagittarius
Jul 01 23:51 Capricorn
Jul 04 09:14 Aquarius
Jul 06 20:39 Pisces
Jul 09 09:15 Aries
Jul 11 21:03 Taurus
Jul 14 05:51 Gemini
Jul 16 10:44 Cancer
Jul 18 12:27 Leo
Jul 20 12:46 Virgo
Jul 22 13:38 Libra
Jul 24 16:31 Scorpio
Jul 26 22:04 Sagittarius
Jul 29 06:04 Capricorn
Jul 31 16:01 Aquarius
Aug 03 03:35 Pisces
Aug 05 16:14 Aries
Aug 08 04:37 Taurus
Aug 10 14:38 Gemini
Aug 12 20:41 Cancer
Aug 14 22:50 Leo
Aug 16 22:35 Virgo
Aug 18 22:05 Libra
Aug 20 23:24 Scorpio
Aug 23 03:50 Sagittarius
Aug 25 11:37 Capricorn
Aug 27 21:55 Aquarius
Aug 30 09:48 Pisces
Sep 01 22:27 Aries
Sep 04 10:59 Taurus
Sep 06 21:52 Gemini
Sep 09 05:26 Cancer
Sep 11 09:01 Leo
Sep 13 09:25 Virgo
Sep 15 08:33 Libra
Sep 17 08:34 Scorpio
Sep 19 11:21 Sagittarius
Sep 21 17:52 Capricorn
Sep 24 03:48 Aquarius
Sep 26 15:48 Pisces

. . . MOON 1966–7

Sep 29 04:29 Aries
Oct 01 16:47 Taurus
Oct 04 03:43 Gemini
Oct 06 12:12 Cancer
Oct 08 17:24 Leo
Oct 10 19:27 Virgo
Oct 12 19:29 Libra
Oct 14 19:21 Scorpio
Oct 16 20:59 Sagittarius
Oct 19 01:55 Capricorn
Oct 21 10:40 Aquarius
Oct 23 22:20 Pisces
Oct 26 11:03 Aries
Oct 28 23:05 Taurus
Oct 31 09:27 Gemini
Nov 02 17:42 Cancer
Nov 04 23:36 Leo
Nov 07 03:09 Virgo
Nov 09 04:54 Libra
Nov 11 05:53 Scorpio
Nov 13 07:36 Sagittarius
Nov 15 11:36 Capricorn
Nov 17 19:03 Aquarius
Nov 20 05:52 Pisces
Nov 22 18:31 Aries
Nov 25 06:36 Taurus
Nov 27 16:30 Gemini
Nov 29 23:49 Cancer
Dec 02 05:01 Leo
Dec 04 08:48 Virgo
Dec 06 11:43 Libra
Dec 08 14:17 Scorpio
Dec 10 17:13 Sagittarius
Dec 12 21:30 Capricorn
Dec 15 04:19 Aquarius
Dec 17 14:17 Pisces
Dec 20 02:39 Aries
Dec 22 15:07 Taurus
Dec 25 01:13 Gemini
Dec 27 07:58 Cancer
Dec 29 11:57 Leo
Dec 31 14:33 Virgo

1967

Jan 02 17:03 Libra
Jan 04 20:16 Scorpio
Jan 07 00:28 Sagittarius
Jan 09 05:53 Capricorn
Jan 11 13:05 Aquarius
Jan 13 22:44 Pisces
Jan 16 10:48 Aries
Jan 18 23:39 Taurus
Jan 21 10:38 Gemini
Jan 23 17:51 Cancer
Jan 25 21:20 Leo
Jan 27 22:36 Virgo
Jan 29 23:32 Libra
Feb 01 01:43 Scorpio
Feb 03 05:55 Sagittarius
Feb 05 12:10 Capricorn
Feb 07 20:17 Aquarius

. . . MOON 1967

Feb 10 06:19 Pisces
Feb 12 18:17 Aries
Feb 15 07:18 Taurus
Feb 17 19:15 Gemini
Feb 20 03:47 Cancer
Feb 22 08:04 Leo
Feb 24 09:04 Virgo
Feb 26 08:44 Libra
Feb 28 09:09 Scorpio
Mar 02 11:53 Sagittarius
Mar 04 17:35 Capricorn
Mar 07 02:03 Aquarius
Mar 09 12:41 Pisces
Mar 12 00:53 Aries
Mar 14 13:54 Taurus
Mar 17 02:19 Gemini
Mar 19 12:10 Cancer
Mar 21 18:03 Leo
Mar 23 20:08 Virgo
Mar 25 19:50 Libra
Mar 27 19:10 Scorpio
Mar 29 20:08 Sagittarius
Apr 01 00:10 Capricorn
Apr 03 07:48 Aquarius
Apr 05 18:28 Pisces
Apr 08 06:56 Aries
Apr 10 19:56 Taurus
Apr 13 08:14 Gemini
Apr 15 18:36 Cancer
Apr 18 01:54 Leo
Apr 20 05:42 Virgo
Apr 22 06:41 Libra
Apr 24 06:19 Scorpio
Apr 26 06:26 Sagittarius
Apr 28 08:53 Capricorn
Apr 30 14:57 Aquarius
May 03 00:47 Pisces
May 05 13:09 Aries
May 08 02:09 Taurus
May 10 14:08 Gemini
May 13 00:10 Cancer
May 15 07:49 Leo
May 17 12:52 Virgo
May 19 15:31 Libra
May 21 16:29 Scorpio
May 23 17:06 Sagittarius
May 25 18:58 Capricorn
May 27 23:43 Aquarius
May 30 08:18 Pisces
Jun 01 20:06 Aries
Jun 04 09:04 Taurus
Jun 06 20:52 Gemini
Jun 09 06:17 Cancer
Jun 11 13:19 Leo
Jun 13 18:23 Virgo
Jun 15 21:58 Libra
Jun 18 00:25 Scorpio
Jun 20 02:20 Sagittarius
Jun 22 04:46 Capricorn
Jun 24 09:11 Aquarius

. . . MOON 1967

Jun 26 16:49 Pisces
Jun 29 03:52 Aries
Jul 01 16:42 Taurus
Jul 04 04:38 Gemini
Jul 06 13:47 Cancer
Jul 08 19:58 Leo
Jul 11 00:07 Virgo
Jul 13 03:19 Libra
Jul 15 06:17 Scorpio
Jul 17 09:22 Sagittarius
Jul 19 12:59 Capricorn
Jul 21 17:59 Aquarius
Jul 24 01:28 Pisces
Jul 26 12:00 Aries
Jul 29 00:40 Taurus
Jul 31 13:00 Gemini
Aug 02 22:32 Cancer
Aug 05 04:26 Leo
Aug 07 07:36 Virgo
Aug 09 09:34 Libra
Aug 11 11:44 Scorpio
Aug 13 14:52 Sagittarius
Aug 15 19:18 Capricorn
Aug 18 01:17 Aquarius
Aug 20 09:18 Pisces
Aug 22 19:47 Aries
Aug 25 08:21 Taurus
Aug 27 21:08 Gemini
Aug 30 07:34 Cancer
Sep 01 14:08 Leo
Sep 03 17:07 Virgo
Sep 05 18:03 Libra
Sep 07 18:44 Scorpio
Sep 09 20:40 Sagittarius
Sep 12 00:42 Capricorn
Sep 14 07:08 Aquarius
Sep 16 15:53 Pisces
Sep 19 02:46 Aries
Sep 21 15:20 Taurus
Sep 24 04:21 Gemini
Sep 26 15:45 Cancer
Sep 28 23:41 Leo
Oct 01 03:38 Virgo
Oct 03 04:34 Libra
Oct 05 04:14 Scorpio
Oct 07 04:32 Sagittarius
Oct 09 07:03 Capricorn
Oct 11 12:45 Aquarius
Oct 13 21:37 Pisces
Oct 16 08:57 Aries
Oct 18 21:41 Taurus
Oct 21 10:38 Gemini
Oct 23 22:27 Cancer
Oct 26 07:40 Leo
Oct 28 13:19 Virgo
Oct 30 15:31 Libra
Nov 01 15:26 Scorpio
Nov 03 14:51 Sagittarius
Nov 05 15:44 Capricorn
Nov 07 19:45 Aquarius

. . . MOON 1967–8

Nov 10 03:42 Pisces
Nov 12 14:58 Aries
Nov 15 03:52 Taurus
Nov 17 16:40 Gemini
Nov 20 04:13 Cancer
Nov 22 13:47 Leo
Nov 24 20:45 Virgo
Nov 27 00:48 Libra
Nov 29 02:13 Scorpio
Dec 01 02:10 Sagittarius
Dec 03 02:25 Capricorn
Dec 05 04:57 Aquarius
Dec 07 11:19 Pisces
Dec 09 21:43 Aries
Dec 12 10:32 Taurus
Dec 14 23:18 Gemini
Dec 17 10:23 Cancer
Dec 19 19:21 Leo
Dec 22 02:21 Virgo
Dec 24 07:27 Libra
Dec 26 10:36 Scorpio
Dec 28 12:09 Sagittarius
Dec 30 13:11 Capricorn

1968

Jan 01 15:23 Aquarius
Jan 03 20:35 Pisces
Jan 06 05:45 Aries
Jan 08 18:02 Taurus
Jan 11 06:54 Gemini
Jan 13 17:54 Cancer
Jan 16 02:09 Leo
Jan 18 08:11 Virgo
Jan 20 12:47 Libra
Jan 22 16:28 Scorpio
Jan 24 19:23 Sagittarius
Jan 26 21:57 Capricorn
Jan 29 01:06 Aquarius
Jan 31 06:16 Pisces
Feb 02 14:39 Aries
Feb 05 02:15 Taurus
Feb 07 15:09 Gemini
Feb 10 02:34 Cancer
Feb 12 10:50 Leo
Feb 14 16:03 Virgo
Feb 16 19:21 Libra
Feb 18 22:00 Scorpio
Feb 21 00:48 Sagittarius
Feb 23 04:12 Capricorn
Feb 25 08:37 Aquarius
Feb 27 14:42 Pisces
Feb 29 23:14 Aries
Mar 03 10:27 Taurus
Mar 05 23:17 Gemini
Mar 08 11:21 Cancer
Mar 10 20:27 Leo
Mar 13 01:51 Virgo
Mar 15 04:23 Libra
Mar 17 05:33 Scorpio
Mar 19 06:53 Sagittarius
Mar 21 09:34 Capricorn

. . . MOON 1968

Mar 23 14:16 Aquarius
Mar 25 21:15 Pisces
Mar 28 06:32 Aries
Mar 30 17:55 Taurus
Apr 02 06:40 Gemini
Apr 04 19:12 Cancer
Apr 07 05:28 Leo
Apr 09 12:04 Virgo
Apr 11 15:01 Libra
Apr 13 15:32 Scorpio
Apr 15 15:23 Sagittarius
Apr 17 16:23 Capricorn
Apr 19 19:57 Aquarius
Apr 22 02:45 Pisces
Apr 24 12:32 Aries
Apr 27 00:22 Taurus
Apr 29 13:11 Gemini
May 02 01:50 Cancer
May 04 12:54 Leo
May 06 20:58 Virgo
May 09 01:21 Libra
May 11 02:30 Scorpio
May 13 01:53 Sagittarius
May 15 01:30 Capricorn
May 17 03:22 Aquarius
May 19 08:52 Pisces
May 21 18:14 Aries
May 24 06:15 Taurus
May 26 19:12 Gemini
May 29 07:43 Cancer
May 31 18:53 Leo
Jun 03 03:52 Virgo
Jun 05 09:49 Libra
Jun 07 12:30 Scorpio
Jun 09 12:42 Sagittarius
Jun 11 12:05 Capricorn
Jun 13 12:46 Aquarius
Jun 15 16:42 Pisces
Jun 18 00:50 Aries
Jun 20 12:25 Taurus
Jun 23 01:22 Gemini
Jun 25 13:43 Cancer
Jun 28 00:30 Leo
Jun 30 09:26 Virgo
Jul 02 16:10 Libra
Jul 04 20:20 Scorpio
Jul 06 22:05 Sagittarius
Jul 08 22:24 Capricorn
Jul 10 23:03 Aquarius
Jul 13 02:03 Pisces
Jul 15 08:51 Aries
Jul 17 19:30 Taurus
Jul 20 08:13 Gemini
Jul 22 20:31 Cancer
Jul 25 06:55 Leo
Jul 27 15:10 Virgo
Jul 29 21:32 Libra
Aug 01 02:11 Scorpio
Aug 03 05:11 Sagittarius
Aug 05 06:57 Capricorn

. . . MOON 1968

Aug 07 08:37 Aquarius
Aug 09 11:45 Pisces
Aug 11 17:53 Aries
Aug 14 03:36 Taurus
Aug 16 15:51 Gemini
Aug 19 04:15 Cancer
Aug 21 14:40 Leo
Aug 23 22:21 Virgo
Aug 26 03:45 Libra
Aug 28 07:38 Scorpio
Aug 30 10:40 Sagittarius
Sep 01 13:22 Capricorn
Sep 03 16:19 Aquarius
Sep 05 20:27 Pisces
Sep 08 02:49 Aries
Sep 10 12:06 Taurus
Sep 12 23:54 Gemini
Sep 15 12:28 Cancer
Sep 17 23:25 Leo
Sep 20 07:16 Virgo
Sep 22 12:00 Libra
Sep 24 14:39 Scorpio
Sep 26 16:30 Sagittarius
Sep 28 18:44 Capricorn
Sep 30 22:11 Aquarius
Oct 03 03:21 Pisces
Oct 05 10:35 Aries
Oct 07 20:07 Taurus
Oct 10 07:43 Gemini
Oct 12 20:23 Cancer
Oct 15 08:08 Leo
Oct 17 16:59 Virgo
Oct 19 22:05 Libra
Oct 22 00:06 Scorpio
Oct 24 00:32 Sagittarius
Oct 26 01:13 Capricorn
Oct 28 03:43 Aquarius
Oct 30 08:54 Pisces
Nov 01 16:51 Aries
Nov 04 03:01 Taurus
Nov 06 14:48 Gemini
Nov 09 03:26 Cancer
Nov 11 15:45 Leo
Nov 14 01:55 Virgo
Nov 16 08:26 Libra
Nov 18 11:06 Scorpio
Nov 20 11:04 Sagittarius
Nov 22 10:20 Capricorn
Nov 24 11:02 Aquarius
Nov 26 14:52 Pisces
Nov 28 22:26 Aries
Dec 01 08:58 Taurus
Dec 03 21:06 Gemini
Dec 06 09:43 Cancer
Dec 08 22:02 Leo
Dec 11 09:00 Virgo
Dec 13 17:09 Libra
Dec 15 21:31 Scorpio
Dec 17 22:28 Sagittarius
Dec 19 21:32 Capricorn

. . . MOON 1968–9

Dec 21 20:59 Aquarius
Dec 23 23:01 Pisces
Dec 26 05:02 Aries
Dec 28 14:57 Taurus
Dec 31 03:11 Gemini
1969
Jan 02 15:53 Cancer
Jan 05 03:55 Leo
Jan 07 14:42 Virgo
Jan 09 23:33 Libra
Jan 12 05:32 Scorpio
Jan 14 08:19 Sagittarius
Jan 16 08:39 Capricorn
Jan 18 08:17 Aquarius
Jan 20 09:21 Pisces
Jan 22 13:43 Aries
Jan 24 22:13 Taurus
Jan 27 09:53 Gemini
Jan 29 22:36 Cancer
Feb 01 10:29 Leo
Feb 03 20:41 Virgo
Feb 06 05:00 Libra
Feb 08 11:18 Scorpio
Feb 10 15:23 Sagittarius
Feb 12 17:28 Capricorn
Feb 14 18:31 Aquarius
Feb 16 20:03 Pisces
Feb 18 23:49 Aries
Feb 21 07:02 Taurus
Feb 23 17:41 Gemini
Feb 26 06:11 Cancer
Feb 28 18:12 Leo
Mar 03 04:07 Virgo
Mar 05 11:34 Libra
Mar 07 16:56 Scorpio
Mar 09 20:48 Sagittarius
Mar 11 23:40 Capricorn
Mar 14 02:09 Aquarius
Mar 16 05:04 Pisces
Mar 18 09:27 Aries
Mar 20 16:20 Taurus
Mar 23 02:12 Gemini
Mar 25 14:19 Cancer
Mar 28 02:37 Leo
Mar 30 12:54 Virgo
Apr 01 20:03 Libra
Apr 04 00:22 Scorpio
Apr 06 02:57 Sagittarius
Apr 08 05:05 Capricorn
Apr 10 07:46 Aquarius
Apr 12 11:41 Pisces
Apr 14 17:13 Aries
Apr 17 00:43 Taurus
Apr 19 10:28 Gemini
Apr 21 22:17 Cancer
Apr 24 10:51 Leo
Apr 26 21:57 Virgo
Apr 29 05:44 Libra
May 01 09:50 Scorpio
May 03 11:19 Sagittarius

. . . MOON 1969

May 05 11:57 Capricorn
May 07 13:28 Aquarius
May 09 17:04 Pisces
May 11 23:09 Aries
May 14 07:28 Taurus
May 16 17:41 Gemini
May 19 05:31 Cancer
May 21 18:12 Leo
May 24 06:07 Virgo
May 26 15:08 Libra
May 28 20:05 Scorpio
May 30 21:30 Sagittarius
Jun 01 21:07 Capricorn
Jun 03 21:04 Aquarius
Jun 05 23:13 Pisces
Jun 08 04:37 Aries
Jun 10 13:06 Taurus
Jun 12 23:49 Gemini
Jun 15 11:52 Cancer
Jun 18 00:35 Leo
Jun 20 12:54 Virgo
Jun 22 23:04 Libra
Jun 25 05:31 Scorpio
Jun 27 08:00 Sagittarius
Jun 29 07:44 Capricorn
Jul 01 06:49 Aquarius
Jul 03 07:26 Pisces
Jul 05 11:16 Aries
Jul 07 18:53 Taurus
Jul 10 05:31 Gemini
Jul 12 17:47 Cancer
Jul 15 06:29 Leo
Jul 17 18:42 Virgo
Jul 20 05:20 Libra
Jul 22 13:04 Scorpio
Jul 24 17:11 Sagittarius
Jul 26 18:09 Capricorn
Jul 28 17:35 Aquarius
Jul 30 17:31 Pisces
Aug 01 19:55 Aries
Aug 04 02:02 Taurus
Aug 06 11:50 Gemini
Aug 08 23:57 Cancer
Aug 11 12:39 Leo
Aug 14 00:33 Virgo
Aug 16 10:51 Libra
Aug 18 18:54 Scorpio
Aug 21 00:12 Sagittarius
Aug 23 02:49 Capricorn
Aug 25 03:36 Aquarius
Aug 27 04:04 Pisces
Aug 29 05:57 Aries
Aug 31 10:50 Taurus
Sep 02 19:24 Gemini
Sep 05 06:57 Cancer
Sep 07 19:36 Leo
Sep 10 07:21 Virgo
Sep 12 17:02 Libra
Sep 15 00:25 Scorpio
Sep 17 05:42 Sagittarius

. . . MOON 1969–70

Sep 19 09:14 Capricorn
Sep 21 11:31 Aquarius
Sep 23 13:22 Pisces
Sep 25 15:56 Aries
Sep 27 20:29 Taurus
Sep 30 04:06 Gemini
Oct 02 14:52 Cancer
Oct 05 03:25 Leo
Oct 07 15:22 Virgo
Oct 10 00:49 Libra
Oct 12 07:19 Scorpio
Oct 14 11:33 Sagittarius
Oct 16 14:35 Capricorn
Oct 18 17:21 Aquarius
Oct 20 20:26 Pisces
Oct 23 00:17 Aries
Oct 25 05:33 Taurus
Oct 27 13:00 Gemini
Oct 29 23:13 Cancer
Nov 01 11:35 Leo
Nov 04 00:00 Virgo
Nov 06 09:59 Libra
Nov 08 16:18 Scorpio
Nov 10 19:30 Sagittarius
Nov 12 21:09 Capricorn
Nov 14 22:53 Aquarius
Nov 17 01:52 Pisces
Nov 19 06:32 Aries
Nov 21 12:52 Taurus
Nov 23 20:59 Gemini
Nov 26 07:10 Cancer
Nov 28 19:22 Leo
Dec 01 08:14 Virgo
Dec 03 19:17 Libra
Dec 06 02:30 Scorpio
Dec 08 05:43 Sagittarius
Dec 10 06:20 Capricorn
Dec 12 06:27 Aquarius
Dec 14 07:56 Pisces
Dec 16 11:56 Aries
Dec 18 18:35 Taurus
Dec 21 03:28 Gemini
Dec 23 14:09 Cancer
Dec 26 02:21 Leo
Dec 28 15:20 Virgo
Dec 31 03:18 Libra

1970

Jan 02 12:04 Scorpio
Jan 04 16:33 Sagittarius
Jan 06 17:30 Capricorn
Jan 08 16:48 Aquarius
Jan 10 16:37 Pisces
Jan 12 18:48 Aries
Jan 15 00:21 Taurus
Jan 17 09:07 Gemini
Jan 19 20:14 Cancer
Jan 22 08:40 Leo
Jan 24 21:33 Virgo
Jan 27 09:43 Libra
Jan 29 19:34 Scorpio

. . . MOON 1970

Feb 01 01:50 Sagittarius
Feb 03 04:22 Capricorn
Feb 05 04:20 Aquarius
Feb 07 03:37 Pisces
Feb 09 04:17 Aries
Feb 11 07:59 Taurus
Feb 13 15:29 Gemini
Feb 16 02:17 Cancer
Feb 18 14:54 Leo
Feb 21 03:42 Virgo
Feb 23 15:30 Libra
Feb 26 01:24 Scorpio
Feb 28 08:38 Sagittarius
Mar 02 12:54 Capricorn
Mar 04 14:35 Aquarius
Mar 06 14:49 Pisces
Mar 08 15:16 Aries
Mar 10 17:44 Taurus
Mar 12 23:37 Gemini
Mar 15 09:19 Cancer
Mar 17 21:40 Leo
Mar 20 10:30 Virgo
Mar 22 21:57 Libra
Mar 25 07:10 Scorpio
Mar 27 14:07 Sagittarius
Mar 29 19:00 Capricorn
Mar 31 22:08 Aquarius
Apr 03 00:01 Pisces
Apr 05 01:32 Aries
Apr 07 04:02 Taurus
Apr 09 09:02 Gemini
Apr 11 17:33 Cancer
Apr 14 05:16 Leo
Apr 16 18:07 Virgo
Apr 19 05:35 Libra
Apr 21 14:16 Scorpio
Apr 23 20:15 Sagittarius
Apr 26 00:27 Capricorn
Apr 28 03:43 Aquarius
Apr 30 06:38 Pisces
May 02 09:33 Aries
May 04 13:05 Taurus
May 06 18:18 Gemini
May 09 02:17 Cancer
May 11 13:22 Leo
May 14 02:11 Virgo
May 16 14:03 Libra
May 18 22:50 Scorpio
May 21 04:11 Sagittarius
May 23 07:13 Capricorn
May 25 09:26 Aquarius
May 27 11:59 Pisces
May 29 15:27 Aries
May 31 20:03 Taurus
Jun 03 02:10 Gemini
Jun 05 10:26 Cancer
Jun 07 21:17 Leo
Jun 10 10:02 Virgo
Jun 12 22:28 Libra
Jun 15 08:02 Scorpio

. . . MOON 1970

Jun 17 13:39 Sagittarius
Jun 19 16:05 Capricorn
Jun 21 17:01 Aquarius
Jun 23 18:12 Pisces
Jun 25 20:52 Aries
Jun 28 01:35 Taurus
Jun 30 08:24 Gemini
Jul 02 17:21 Cancer
Jul 05 04:26 Leo
Jul 07 17:11 Virgo
Jul 10 06:03 Libra
Jul 12 16:41 Scorpio
Jul 14 23:26 Sagittarius
Jul 17 02:19 Capricorn
Jul 19 02:45 Aquarius
Jul 21 02:37 Pisces
Jul 23 03:43 Aries
Jul 25 07:18 Taurus
Jul 27 13:53 Gemini
Jul 29 23:14 Cancer
Aug 01 10:44 Leo
Aug 03 23:35 Virgo
Aug 06 12:33 Libra
Aug 08 23:57 Scorpio
Aug 11 08:07 Sagittarius
Aug 13 12:25 Capricorn
Aug 15 13:31 Aquarius
Aug 17 13:01 Pisces
Aug 19 12:50 Aries
Aug 21 14:46 Taurus
Aug 23 20:04 Gemini
Aug 26 04:58 Cancer
Aug 28 16:38 Leo
Aug 31 05:36 Virgo
Sep 02 18:26 Libra
Sep 05 05:55 Scorpio
Sep 07 14:58 Sagittarius
Sep 09 20:52 Capricorn
Sep 11 23:34 Aquarius
Sep 13 23:57 Pisces
Sep 15 23:35 Aries
Sep 18 00:21 Taurus
Sep 20 04:02 Gemini
Sep 22 11:41 Cancer
Sep 24 22:55 Leo
Sep 27 11:54 Virgo
Sep 30 00:33 Libra
Oct 02 11:36 Scorpio
Oct 04 20:32 Sagittarius
Oct 07 03:10 Capricorn
Oct 09 07:26 Aquarius
Oct 11 09:30 Pisces
Oct 13 10:12 Aries
Oct 15 11:00 Taurus
Oct 17 13:43 Gemini
Oct 19 19:59 Cancer
Oct 22 06:13 Leo
Oct 24 18:57 Virgo
Oct 27 07:37 Libra
Oct 29 18:15 Scorpio

. . . MOON 1970–71

Nov 01 02:24 Sagittarius
Nov 03 08:33 Capricorn
Nov 05 13:11 Aquarius
Nov 07 16:33 Pisces
Nov 09 18:52 Aries
Nov 11 20:50 Taurus
Nov 13 23:49 Gemini
Nov 16 05:23 Cancer
Nov 18 14:36 Leo
Nov 21 02:50 Virgo
Nov 23 15:39 Libra
Nov 26 02:25 Scorpio
Nov 28 10:03 Sagittarius
Nov 30 15:06 Capricorn
Dec 02 18:45 Aquarius
Dec 04 21:56 Pisces
Dec 07 01:04 Aries
Dec 09 04:25 Taurus
Dec 11 08:33 Gemini
Dec 13 14:32 Cancer
Dec 15 23:22 Leo
Dec 18 11:05 Virgo
Dec 21 00:02 Libra
Dec 23 11:27 Scorpio
Dec 25 19:28 Sagittarius
Dec 28 00:02 Capricorn
Dec 30 02:24 Aquarius

1971

Jan 01 04:08 Pisces
Jan 03 06:27 Aries
Jan 05 10:01 Taurus
Jan 07 15:09 Gemini
Jan 09 22:09 Cancer
Jan 12 07:24 Leo
Jan 14 18:58 Virgo
Jan 17 07:54 Libra
Jan 19 20:04 Scorpio
Jan 22 05:16 Sagittarius
Jan 24 10:33 Capricorn
Jan 26 12:36 Aquarius
Jan 28 13:02 Pisces
Jan 30 13:36 Aries
Feb 01 15:49 Taurus
Feb 03 20:35 Gemini
Feb 06 04:07 Cancer
Feb 08 14:07 Leo
Feb 11 01:58 Virgo
Feb 13 14:51 Libra
Feb 16 03:22 Scorpio
Feb 18 13:46 Sagittarius
Feb 20 20:37 Capricorn
Feb 22 23:43 Aquarius
Feb 25 00:06 Pisces
Feb 26 23:30 Aries
Feb 28 23:54 Taurus
Mar 03 03:02 Gemini
Mar 05 09:48 Cancer
Mar 07 19:56 Leo
Mar 10 08:11 Virgo
Mar 12 21:06 Libra

. . . MOON 1971

Mar 15 09:32 Scorpio
Mar 17 20:24 Sagittarius
Mar 20 04:38 Capricorn
Mar 22 09:29 Aquarius
Mar 24 11:08 Pisces
Mar 26 10:46 Aries
Mar 28 10:16 Taurus
Mar 30 11:44 Gemini
Apr 01 16:51 Cancer
Apr 04 02:06 Leo
Apr 06 14:17 Virgo
Apr 09 03:17 Libra
Apr 11 15:28 Scorpio
Apr 14 02:03 Sagittarius
Apr 16 10:39 Capricorn
Apr 18 16:46 Aquarius
Apr 20 20:08 Pisces
Apr 22 21:09 Aries
Apr 24 21:07 Taurus
Apr 26 21:59 Gemini
Apr 29 01:44 Cancer
May 01 09:35 Leo
May 03 21:03 Virgo
May 06 10:00 Libra
May 08 22:04 Scorpio
May 11 08:08 Sagittarius
May 13 16:09 Capricorn
May 15 22:20 Aquarius
May 18 02:40 Pisces
May 20 05:11 Aries
May 22 06:32 Taurus
May 24 08:01 Gemini
May 26 11:26 Cancer
May 28 18:17 Leo
May 31 04:48 Virgo
Jun 02 17:27 Libra
Jun 05 05:37 Scorpio
Jun 07 15:29 Sagittarius
Jun 09 22:45 Capricorn
Jun 12 04:03 Aquarius
Jun 14 08:02 Pisces
Jun 16 11:06 Aries
Jun 18 13:39 Taurus
Jun 20 16:24 Gemini
Jun 22 20:30 Cancer
Jun 25 03:13 Leo
Jun 27 13:07 Virgo
Jun 30 01:23 Libra
Jul 02 13:46 Scorpio
Jul 04 23:59 Sagittarius
Jul 07 07:04 Capricorn
Jul 09 11:27 Aquarius
Jul 11 14:15 Pisces
Jul 13 16:33 Aries
Jul 15 19:11 Taurus
Jul 17 22:47 Gemini
Jul 20 03:57 Cancer
Jul 22 11:17 Leo
Jul 24 21:10 Virgo
Jul 27 09:12 Libra

. . . MOON 1971

Jul 29 21:51 Scorpio
Aug 01 08:50 Sagittarius
Aug 03 16:32 Capricorn
Aug 05 20:47 Aquarius
Aug 07 22:35 Pisces
Aug 09 23:27 Aries
Aug 12 00:56 Taurus
Aug 14 04:11 Gemini
Aug 16 09:50 Cancer
Aug 18 17:58 Leo
Aug 21 04:19 Virgo
Aug 23 16:23 Libra
Aug 26 05:09 Scorpio
Aug 28 16:57 Sagittarius
Aug 31 01:55 Capricorn
Sep 02 07:04 Aquarius
Sep 04 08:51 Pisces
Sep 06 08:44 Aries
Sep 08 08:38 Taurus
Sep 10 10:25 Gemini
Sep 12 15:21 Cancer
Sep 14 23:38 Leo
Sep 17 10:29 Virgo
Sep 19 22:48 Libra
Sep 22 11:33 Scorpio
Sep 24 23:44 Sagittarius
Sep 27 09:53 Capricorn
Sep 29 16:39 Aquarius
Oct 01 19:37 Pisces
Oct 03 19:41 Aries
Oct 05 18:42 Taurus
Oct 07 18:53 Gemini
Oct 09 22:11 Cancer
Oct 12 05:31 Leo
Oct 14 16:17 Virgo
Oct 17 04:48 Libra
Oct 19 17:31 Scorpio
Oct 22 05:32 Sagittarius
Oct 24 16:06 Capricorn
Oct 27 00:12 Aquarius
Oct 29 04:57 Pisces
Oct 31 06:26 Aries
Nov 02 05:56 Taurus
Nov 04 05:28 Gemini
Nov 06 07:15 Cancer
Nov 08 12:57 Leo
Nov 10 22:45 Virgo
Nov 13 11:06 Libra
Nov 15 23:50 Scorpio
Nov 18 11:30 Sagittarius
Nov 20 21:37 Capricorn
Nov 23 05:53 Aquarius
Nov 25 11:48 Pisces
Nov 27 15:04 Aries
Nov 29 16:09 Taurus
Dec 01 16:26 Gemini
Dec 03 17:51 Cancer
Dec 05 22:17 Leo
Dec 08 06:41 Virgo
Dec 10 18:20 Libra

. . . MOON 1971–72

Dec 13 07:02 Scorpio
Dec 15 18:38 Sagittarius
Dec 18 04:08 Capricorn
Dec 20 11:33 Aquarius
Dec 22 17:10 Pisces
Dec 24 21:10 Aries
Dec 26 23:46 Taurus
Dec 29 01:39 Gemini
Dec 31 04:02 Cancer

1972

Jan 02 08:22 Leo
Jan 04 15:51 Virgo
Jan 07 02:34 Libra
Jan 09 15:04 Scorpio
Jan 12 02:58 Sagittarius
Jan 14 12:26 Capricorn
Jan 16 19:04 Aquarius
Jan 18 23:28 Pisces
Jan 21 02:36 Aries
Jan 23 05:18 Taurus
Jan 25 08:14 Gemini
Jan 27 12:02 Cancer
Jan 29 17:22 Leo
Feb 01 00:56 Virgo
Feb 03 11:07 Libra
Feb 05 23:18 Scorpio
Feb 08 11:38 Sagittarius
Feb 10 21:51 Capricorn
Feb 13 04:37 Aquarius
Feb 15 08:11 Pisces
Feb 17 09:51 Aries
Feb 19 11:12 Taurus
Feb 21 13:36 Gemini
Feb 23 17:53 Cancer
Feb 26 00:15 Leo
Feb 28 08:40 Virgo
Mar 01 19:01 Libra
Mar 04 07:01 Scorpio
Mar 06 19:37 Sagittarius
Mar 09 06:50 Capricorn
Mar 11 14:43 Aquarius
Mar 13 18:40 Pisces
Mar 15 19:37 Aries
Mar 17 19:28 Taurus
Mar 19 20:13 Gemini
Mar 21 23:27 Cancer
Mar 24 05:47 Leo
Mar 26 14:48 Virgo
Mar 29 01:42 Libra
Mar 31 13:49 Scorpio
Apr 03 02:28 Sagittarius
Apr 05 14:21 Capricorn
Apr 07 23:38 Aquarius
Apr 10 04:58 Pisces
Apr 12 06:33 Aries
Apr 14 05:55 Taurus
Apr 16 05:17 Gemini
Apr 18 06:46 Cancer
Apr 20 11:47 Leo
Apr 22 20:25 Virgo

. . . MOON 1972

Apr 25 07:35 Libra
Apr 27 19:56 Scorpio
Apr 30 08:31 Sagittarius
May 02 20:29 Capricorn
May 05 06:36 Aquarius
May 07 13:28 Pisces
May 09 16:35 Aries
May 11 16:48 Taurus
May 13 15:58 Gemini
May 15 16:16 Cancer
May 17 19:38 Leo
May 20 02:56 Virgo
May 22 13:37 Libra
May 25 02:01 Scorpio
May 27 14:34 Sagittarius
May 30 02:13 Capricorn
Jun 01 12:16 Aquarius
Jun 03 19:52 Pisces
Jun 06 00:28 Aries
Jun 08 02:15 Taurus
Jun 10 02:25 Gemini
Jun 12 02:45 Cancer
Jun 14 05:10 Leo
Jun 16 11:04 Virgo
Jun 18 20:39 Libra
Jun 21 08:43 Scorpio
Jun 23 21:15 Sagittarius
Jun 26 08:37 Capricorn
Jun 28 18:03 Aquarius
Jul 01 01:19 Pisces
Jul 03 06:23 Aries
Jul 05 09:25 Taurus
Jul 07 11:05 Gemini
Jul 09 12:30 Cancer
Jul 11 15:06 Leo
Jul 13 20:17 Virgo
Jul 16 04:49 Libra
Jul 18 16:16 Scorpio
Jul 21 04:47 Sagittarius
Jul 23 16:11 Capricorn
Jul 26 01:08 Aquarius
Jul 28 07:29 Pisces
Jul 30 11:51 Aries
Aug 01 14:58 Taurus
Aug 03 17:34 Gemini
Aug 05 20:18 Cancer
Aug 07 23:57 Leo
Aug 10 05:23 Virgo
Aug 12 13:28 Libra
Aug 15 00:20 Scorpio
Aug 17 12:50 Sagittarius
Aug 20 00:38 Capricorn
Aug 22 09:44 Aquarius
Aug 24 15:29 Pisces
Aug 26 18:41 Aries
Aug 28 20:43 Taurus
Aug 30 22:56 Gemini
Sep 02 02:12 Cancer
Sep 04 06:54 Leo
Sep 06 13:16 Virgo

. . . MOON 1972–73

Sep 08 21:37 Libra
Sep 11 08:16 Scorpio
Sep 13 20:43 Sagittarius
Sep 16 09:08 Capricorn
Sep 18 19:05 Aquarius
Sep 21 01:10 Pisces
Sep 23 03:45 Aries
Sep 25 04:28 Taurus
Sep 27 05:15 Gemini
Sep 29 07:39 Cancer
Oct 01 12:26 Leo
Oct 03 19:31 Virgo
Oct 06 04:35 Libra
Oct 08 15:28 Scorpio
Oct 11 03:53 Sagittarius
Oct 13 16:45 Capricorn
Oct 16 03:52 Aquarius
Oct 18 11:13 Pisces
Oct 20 14:23 Aries
Oct 22 14:38 Taurus
Oct 24 14:03 Gemini
Oct 26 14:45 Cancer
Oct 28 18:15 Leo
Oct 31 01:00 Virgo
Nov 02 10:28 Libra
Nov 04 21:47 Scorpio
Nov 07 10:17 Sagittarius
Nov 09 23:12 Capricorn
Nov 12 11:03 Aquarius
Nov 14 19:57 Pisces
Nov 17 00:45 Aries
Nov 19 01:53 Taurus
Nov 21 01:05 Gemini
Nov 23 00:31 Cancer
Nov 25 02:12 Leo
Nov 27 07:25 Virgo
Nov 29 16:16 Libra
Dec 02 03:43 Scorpio
Dec 04 16:23 Sagittarius
Dec 07 05:07 Capricorn
Dec 09 16:54 Aquarius
Dec 12 02:33 Pisces
Dec 14 09:00 Aries
Dec 16 12:00 Taurus
Dec 18 12:25 Gemini
Dec 20 11:57 Cancer
Dec 22 12:35 Leo
Dec 24 16:03 Virgo
Dec 26 23:22 Libra
Dec 29 10:11 Scorpio
Dec 31 22:52 Sagittarius

1973

Jan 03 11:31 Capricorn
Jan 05 22:48 Aquarius
Jan 08 08:03 Pisces
Jan 10 14:58 Aries
Jan 12 19:25 Taurus
Jan 14 21:41 Gemini
Jan 16 22:39 Cancer
Jan 18 23:41 Leo

. . . MOON 1973

Jan 21 02:24 Virgo
Jan 23 08:17 Libra
Jan 25 17:53 Scorpio
Jan 28 06:11 Sagittarius
Jan 30 18:55 Capricorn
Feb 02 05:56 Aquarius
Feb 04 14:23 Pisces
Feb 06 20:29 Aries
Feb 09 00:54 Taurus
Feb 11 04:11 Gemini
Feb 13 06:45 Cancer
Feb 15 09:13 Leo
Feb 17 12:32 Virgo
Feb 19 17:59 Libra
Feb 22 02:36 Scorpio
Feb 24 14:15 Sagittarius
Feb 27 03:05 Capricorn
Mar 01 14:23 Aquarius
Mar 03 22:32 Pisces
Mar 06 03:38 Aries
Mar 08 06:51 Taurus
Mar 10 09:31 Gemini
Mar 12 12:30 Cancer
Mar 14 16:08 Leo
Mar 16 20:43 Virgo
Mar 19 02:49 Libra
Mar 21 11:16 Scorpio
Mar 23 22:27 Sagittarius
Mar 26 11:16 Capricorn
Mar 28 23:13 Aquarius
Mar 31 07:56 Pisces
Apr 02 12:49 Aries
Apr 04 14:59 Taurus
Apr 06 16:12 Gemini
Apr 08 18:05 Cancer
Apr 10 21:32 Leo
Apr 13 02:47 Virgo
Apr 15 09:50 Libra
Apr 17 18:52 Scorpio
Apr 20 06:02 Sagittarius
Apr 22 18:50 Capricorn
Apr 25 07:22 Aquarius
Apr 27 17:10 Pisces
Apr 29 22:54 Aries
May 02 01:02 Taurus
May 04 01:16 Gemini
May 06 01:35 Cancer
May 08 03:37 Leo
May 10 08:13 Virgo
May 12 15:31 Libra
May 15 01:10 Scorpio
May 17 12:42 Sagittarius
May 20 01:31 Capricorn
May 22 14:18 Aquarius
May 25 01:06 Pisces
May 27 08:15 Aries
May 29 11:28 Taurus
May 31 11:53 Gemini
Jun 02 11:21 Cancer
Jun 04 11:50 Leo

. . . MOON 1973

Jun 06 14:52 Virgo
Jun 08 21:16 Libra
Jun 11 06:52 Scorpio
Jun 13 18:43 Sagittarius
Jun 16 07:37 Capricorn
Jun 18 20:20 Aquarius
Jun 21 07:29 Pisces
Jun 23 15:49 Aries
Jun 25 20:38 Taurus
Jun 27 22:18 Gemini
Jun 29 22:09 Cancer
Jul 01 21:56 Leo
Jul 03 23:31 Virgo
Jul 06 04:24 Libra
Jul 08 13:06 Scorpio
Jul 11 00:48 Sagittarius
Jul 13 13:46 Capricorn
Jul 16 02:16 Aquarius
Jul 18 13:08 Pisces
Jul 20 21:44 Aries
Jul 23 03:41 Taurus
Jul 25 06:59 Gemini
Jul 27 08:11 Cancer
Jul 29 08:30 Leo
Jul 31 09:35 Virgo
Aug 02 13:13 Libra
Aug 04 20:36 Scorpio
Aug 07 07:38 Sagittarius
Aug 09 20:30 Capricorn
Aug 12 08:53 Aquarius
Aug 14 19:15 Pisces
Aug 17 03:16 Aries
Aug 19 09:14 Taurus
Aug 21 13:27 Gemini
Aug 23 16:08 Cancer
Aug 25 17:50 Leo
Aug 27 19:34 Virgo
Aug 29 22:53 Libra
Sep 01 05:18 Scorpio
Sep 03 15:25 Sagittarius
Sep 06 04:02 Capricorn
Sep 08 16:31 Aquarius
Sep 11 02:41 Pisces
Sep 13 09:57 Aries
Sep 15 15:00 Taurus
Sep 17 18:48 Gemini
Sep 19 22:01 Cancer
Sep 22 00:57 Leo
Sep 24 03:59 Virgo
Sep 26 08:01 Libra
Sep 28 14:19 Scorpio
Sep 30 23:48 Sagittarius
Oct 03 12:03 Capricorn
Oct 06 00:49 Aquarius
Oct 08 11:24 Pisces
Oct 10 18:29 Aries
Oct 12 22:36 Taurus
Oct 15 01:09 Gemini
Oct 17 03:29 Cancer
Oct 19 06:25 Leo

. . . MOON 1973–4

Oct 21 10:19 Virgo
Oct 23 15:29 Libra
Oct 25 22:28 Scorpio
Oct 28 07:58 Sagittarius
Oct 30 19:58 Capricorn
Nov 02 08:59 Aquarius
Nov 04 20:27 Pisces
Nov 07 04:20 Aries
Nov 09 08:26 Taurus
Nov 11 10:00 Gemini
Nov 13 10:47 Cancer
Nov 15 12:20 Leo
Nov 17 15:42 Virgo
Nov 19 21:16 Libra
Nov 22 05:07 Scorpio
Nov 24 15:11 Sagittarius
Nov 27 03:13 Capricorn
Nov 29 16:18 Aquarius
Dec 02 04:33 Pisces
Dec 04 13:51 Aries
Dec 06 19:09 Taurus
Dec 08 20:58 Gemini
Dec 10 20:52 Cancer
Dec 12 20:45 Leo
Dec 14 22:21 Virgo
Dec 17 02:54 Libra
Dec 19 10:44 Scorpio
Dec 21 21:20 Sagittarius
Dec 24 09:42 Capricorn
Dec 26 22:43 Aquarius
Dec 29 11:11 Pisces
Dec 31 21:35 Aries

1974

Jan 03 04:38 Taurus
Jan 05 08:00 Gemini
Jan 07 08:29 Cancer
Jan 09 07:43 Leo
Jan 11 07:42 Virgo
Jan 13 10:22 Libra
Jan 15 16:55 Scorpio
Jan 18 03:13 Sagittarius
Jan 20 15:48 Capricorn
Jan 23 04:50 Aquarius
Jan 25 17:01 Pisces
Jan 28 03:32 Aries
Jan 30 11:42 Taurus
Feb 01 16:54 Gemini
Feb 03 19:06 Cancer
Feb 05 19:12 Leo
Feb 07 18:52 Virgo
Feb 09 20:11 Libra
Feb 12 00:59 Scorpio
Feb 14 10:02 Sagittarius
Feb 16 22:17 Capricorn
Feb 19 11:21 Aquarius
Feb 21 23:16 Pisces
Feb 24 09:13 Aries
Feb 26 17:12 Taurus
Feb 28 23:11 Gemini
Mar 03 03:00 Cancer

. . . MOON 1974

Mar 05 04:49 Leo
Mar 07 05:34 Virgo
Mar 09 06:52 Libra
Mar 11 10:40 Scorpio
Mar 13 18:21 Sagittarius
Mar 16 05:42 Capricorn
Mar 18 18:39 Aquarius
Mar 21 06:34 Pisces
Mar 23 16:03 Aries
Mar 25 23:10 Taurus
Mar 28 04:34 Gemini
Mar 30 08:40 Cancer
Apr 01 11:41 Leo
Apr 03 13:57 Virgo
Apr 05 16:23 Libra
Apr 07 20:25 Scorpio
Apr 10 03:28 Sagittarius
Apr 12 13:57 Capricorn
Apr 15 02:35 Aquarius
Apr 17 14:45 Pisces
Apr 20 00:21 Aries
Apr 22 06:54 Taurus
Apr 24 11:11 Gemini
Apr 26 14:18 Cancer
Apr 28 17:04 Leo
Apr 30 20:01 Virgo
May 02 23:39 Libra
May 05 04:44 Scorpio
May 07 12:06 Sagittarius
May 09 22:16 Capricorn
May 12 10:35 Aquarius
May 14 23:04 Pisces
May 17 09:20 Aries
May 19 16:11 Taurus
May 21 19:55 Gemini
May 23 21:46 Cancer
May 25 23:12 Leo
May 28 01:26 Virgo
May 30 05:16 Libra
Jun 01 11:11 Scorpio
Jun 03 19:22 Sagittarius
Jun 06 05:49 Capricorn
Jun 08 18:03 Aquarius
Jun 11 06:44 Pisces
Jun 13 17:53 Aries
Jun 16 01:47 Taurus
Jun 18 05:59 Gemini
Jun 20 07:22 Cancer
Jun 22 07:30 Leo
Jun 24 08:12 Virgo
Jun 26 10:58 Libra
Jun 28 16:41 Scorpio
Jul 01 01:21 Sagittarius
Jul 03 12:20 Capricorn
Jul 06 00:42 Aquarius
Jul 08 13:26 Pisces
Jul 11 01:11 Aries
Jul 13 10:22 Taurus
Jul 15 15:55 Gemini
Jul 17 17:57 Cancer

. . . MOON 1974

Jul 19 17:44 Leo
Jul 21 17:10 Virgo
Jul 23 18:19 Libra
Jul 25 22:46 Scorpio
Jul 28 07:00 Sagittarius
Jul 30 18:11 Capricorn
Aug 02 06:47 Aquarius
Aug 04 19:27 Pisces
Aug 07 07:16 Aries
Aug 09 17:13 Taurus
Aug 12 00:16 Gemini
Aug 14 03:49 Cancer
Aug 16 04:27 Leo
Aug 18 03:43 Virgo
Aug 20 03:45 Libra
Aug 22 06:38 Scorpio
Aug 24 13:35 Sagittarius
Aug 27 00:16 Capricorn
Aug 29 12:53 Aquarius
Sep 01 01:30 Pisces
Sep 03 12:59 Aries
Sep 05 22:51 Taurus
Sep 08 06:37 Gemini
Sep 10 11:40 Cancer
Sep 12 13:55 Leo
Sep 14 14:13 Virgo
Sep 16 14:17 Libra
Sep 18 16:14 Scorpio
Sep 20 21:47 Sagittarius
Sep 23 07:22 Capricorn
Sep 25 19:39 Aquarius
Sep 28 08:15 Pisces
Sep 30 19:26 Aries
Oct 03 04:40 Taurus
Oct 05 12:01 Gemini
Oct 07 17:31 Cancer
Oct 09 21:03 Leo
Oct 11 22:56 Virgo
Oct 14 00:11 Libra
Oct 16 02:24 Scorpio
Oct 18 07:15 Sagittarius
Oct 20 15:44 Capricorn
Oct 23 03:21 Aquarius
Oct 25 15:57 Pisces
Oct 28 03:14 Aries
Oct 30 12:00 Taurus
Nov 01 18:23 Gemini
Nov 03 23:02 Cancer
Nov 06 02:31 Leo
Nov 08 05:19 Virgo
Nov 10 07:59 Libra
Nov 12 11:24 Scorpio
Nov 14 16:39 Sagittarius
Nov 17 00:42 Capricorn
Nov 19 11:39 Aquarius
Nov 22 00:12 Pisces
Nov 24 12:00 Aries
Nov 26 21:05 Taurus
Nov 29 02:58 Gemini
Dec 01 06:22 Cancer

. . . MOON 1974–5

Dec 03 08:32 Leo
Dec 05 10:40 Virgo
Dec 07 13:43 Libra
Dec 09 18:14 Scorpio
Dec 12 00:35 Sagittarius
Dec 14 09:04 Capricorn
Dec 16 19:49 Aquarius
Dec 19 08:13 Pisces
Dec 21 20:36 Aries
Dec 24 06:45 Taurus
Dec 26 13:16 Gemini
Dec 28 16:16 Cancer
Dec 30 17:05 Leo

1975

Jan 01 17:33 Virgo
Jan 03 19:22 Libra
Jan 05 23:39 Scorpio
Jan 08 06:40 Sagittarius
Jan 10 15:59 Capricorn
Jan 13 03:04 Aquarius
Jan 15 15:24 Pisces
Jan 18 04:04 Aries
Jan 20 15:22 Taurus
Jan 22 23:23 Gemini
Jan 25 03:21 Cancer
Jan 27 04:01 Leo
Jan 29 03:14 Virgo
Jan 31 03:14 Libra
Feb 02 05:54 Scorpio
Feb 04 12:11 Sagittarius
Feb 06 21:43 Capricorn
Feb 09 09:17 Aquarius
Feb 11 21:46 Pisces
Feb 14 10:23 Aries
Feb 16 22:10 Taurus
Feb 19 07:35 Gemini
Feb 21 13:19 Cancer
Feb 23 15:14 Leo
Feb 25 14:38 Virgo
Feb 27 13:39 Libra
Mar 01 14:34 Scorpio
Mar 03 19:06 Sagittarius
Mar 06 03:40 Capricorn
Mar 08 15:10 Aquarius
Mar 11 03:50 Pisces
Mar 13 16:19 Aries
Mar 16 03:53 Taurus
Mar 18 13:44 Gemini
Mar 20 20:49 Cancer
Mar 23 00:32 Leo
Mar 25 01:22 Virgo
Mar 27 00:52 Libra
Mar 29 01:08 Scorpio
Mar 31 04:10 Sagittarius
Apr 02 11:09 Capricorn
Apr 04 21:46 Aquarius
Apr 07 10:18 Pisces
Apr 09 22:45 Aries
Apr 12 09:54 Taurus
Apr 14 19:15 Gemini

. . . MOON 1975

Apr 17 02:28 Cancer
Apr 19 07:15 Leo
Apr 21 09:43 Virgo
Apr 23 10:42 Libra
Apr 25 11:40 Scorpio
Apr 27 14:20 Sagittarius
Apr 29 20:09 Capricorn
May 02 05:34 Aquarius
May 04 17:35 Pisces
May 07 06:03 Aries
May 09 17:04 Taurus
May 12 01:45 Gemini
May 14 08:08 Cancer
May 16 12:39 Leo
May 18 15:46 Virgo
May 20 18:05 Libra
May 22 20:26 Scorpio
May 24 23:52 Sagittarius
May 27 05:31 Capricorn
May 29 14:10 Aquarius
Jun 01 01:33 Pisces
Jun 03 14:02 Aries
Jun 06 01:19 Taurus
Jun 08 09:50 Gemini
Jun 10 15:22 Cancer
Jun 12 18:46 Leo
Jun 14 21:11 Virgo
Jun 16 23:41 Libra
Jun 19 03:00 Scorpio
Jun 21 07:35 Sagittarius
Jun 23 13:56 Capricorn
Jun 25 22:33 Aquarius
Jun 28 09:34 Pisces
Jun 30 22:03 Aries
Jul 03 09:55 Taurus
Jul 05 18:59 Gemini
Jul 08 00:24 Cancer
Jul 10 02:51 Leo
Jul 12 03:56 Virgo
Jul 14 05:22 Libra
Jul 16 08:23 Scorpio
Jul 18 13:33 Sagittarius
Jul 20 20:46 Capricorn
Jul 23 05:56 Aquarius
Jul 25 16:59 Pisces
Jul 28 05:28 Aries
Jul 30 17:54 Taurus
Aug 02 04:03 Gemini
Aug 04 10:18 Cancer
Aug 06 12:44 Leo
Aug 08 12:54 Virgo
Aug 10 12:51 Libra
Aug 12 14:31 Scorpio
Aug 14 19:00 Sagittarius
Aug 17 02:26 Capricorn
Aug 19 12:10 Aquarius
Aug 21 23:33 Pisces
Aug 24 12:03 Aries
Aug 27 00:45 Taurus
Aug 29 11:54 Gemini

. . . MOON 1975–6

Aug 31 19:36 Cancer
Sep 02 23:09 Leo
Sep 04 23:30 Virgo
Sep 06 22:38 Libra
Sep 08 22:46 Scorpio
Sep 11 01:41 Sagittarius
Sep 13 08:12 Capricorn
Sep 15 17:52 Aquarius
Sep 18 05:32 Pisces
Sep 20 18:08 Aries
Sep 23 06:44 Taurus
Sep 25 18:14 Gemini
Sep 28 03:07 Cancer
Sep 30 08:21 Leo
Oct 02 10:04 Virgo
Oct 04 09:39 Libra
Oct 06 09:09 Scorpio
Oct 08 10:36 Sagittarius
Oct 10 15:29 Capricorn
Oct 13 00:10 Aquarius
Oct 15 11:41 Pisces
Oct 18 00:21 Aries
Oct 20 12:44 Taurus
Oct 22 23:52 Gemini
Oct 25 08:58 Cancer
Oct 27 15:20 Leo
Oct 29 18:47 Virgo
Oct 31 19:56 Libra
Nov 02 20:08 Scorpio
Nov 04 21:10 Sagittarius
Nov 07 00:46 Capricorn
Nov 09 08:00 Aquarius
Nov 11 18:42 Pisces
Nov 14 07:18 Aries
Nov 16 19:38 Taurus
Nov 19 06:15 Gemini
Nov 21 14:37 Cancer
Nov 23 20:49 Leo
Nov 26 01:05 Virgo
Nov 28 03:48 Libra
Nov 30 05:37 Scorpio
Dec 02 07:34 Sagittarius
Dec 04 10:59 Capricorn
Dec 06 17:13 Aquarius
Dec 09 02:52 Pisces
Dec 11 15:07 Aries
Dec 14 03:40 Taurus
Dec 16 14:13 Gemini
Dec 18 21:49 Cancer
Dec 21 02:54 Leo
Dec 23 06:28 Virgo
Dec 25 09:28 Libra
Dec 27 12:28 Scorpio
Dec 29 15:53 Sagittarius
Dec 31 20:17 Capricorn

1976

Jan 03 02:33 Aquarius
Jan 05 11:36 Pisces
Jan 07 23:22 Aries
Jan 10 12:10 Taurus

. . . MOON 1976

Jan 12 23:20 Gemini
Jan 15 07:01 Cancer
Jan 17 11:16 Leo
Jan 19 13:26 Virgo
Jan 21 15:11 Libra
Jan 23 17:49 Scorpio
Jan 25 21:52 Sagittarius
Jan 28 03:25 Capricorn
Jan 30 10:35 Aquarius
Feb 01 19:47 Pisces
Feb 04 07:18 Aries
Feb 06 20:14 Taurus
Feb 09 08:17 Gemini
Feb 11 16:59 Cancer
Feb 13 21:33 Leo
Feb 15 22:59 Virgo
Feb 17 23:14 Libra
Feb 20 00:14 Scorpio
Feb 22 03:19 Sagittarius
Feb 24 08:55 Capricorn
Feb 26 16:49 Aquarius
Feb 29 02:42 Pisces
Mar 02 14:23 Aries
Mar 05 03:19 Taurus
Mar 07 15:56 Gemini
Mar 10 01:59 Cancer
Mar 12 07:56 Leo
Mar 14 09:59 Virgo
Mar 16 09:45 Libra
Mar 18 09:18 Scorpio
Mar 20 10:34 Sagittarius
Mar 22 14:49 Capricorn
Mar 24 22:20 Aquarius
Mar 27 08:34 Pisces
Mar 29 20:38 Aries
Apr 01 09:34 Taurus
Apr 03 22:16 Gemini
Apr 06 09:07 Cancer
Apr 08 16:37 Leo
Apr 10 20:16 Virgo
Apr 12 20:55 Libra
Apr 14 20:15 Scorpio
Apr 16 20:15 Sagittarius
Apr 18 22:44 Capricorn
Apr 21 04:48 Aquarius
Apr 23 14:28 Pisces
Apr 26 02:37 Aries
Apr 28 15:38 Taurus
May 01 04:06 Gemini
May 03 14:54 Cancer
May 05 23:10 Leo
May 08 04:22 Virgo
May 10 06:40 Libra
May 12 07:03 Scorpio
May 14 07:05 Sagittarius
May 16 08:32 Capricorn
May 18 13:03 Aquarius
May 20 21:27 Pisces
May 23 09:07 Aries
May 25 22:08 Taurus

. . . MOON 1976

May 28 10:23 Gemini
May 30 20:39 Cancer
Jun 02 04:38 Leo
Jun 04 10:21 Virgo
Jun 06 14:00 Libra
Jun 08 15:59 Scorpio
Jun 10 17:07 Sagittarius
Jun 12 18:46 Capricorn
Jun 14 22:32 Aquarius
Jun 17 05:44 Pisces
Jun 19 16:33 Aries
Jun 22 05:22 Taurus
Jun 24 17:37 Gemini
Jun 27 03:30 Cancer
Jun 29 10:40 Leo
Jul 01 15:47 Virgo
Jul 03 19:35 Libra
Jul 05 22:34 Scorpio
Jul 08 01:06 Sagittarius
Jul 10 03:50 Capricorn
Jul 12 07:54 Aquarius
Jul 14 14:36 Pisces
Jul 17 00:40 Aries
Jul 19 13:12 Taurus
Jul 22 01:41 Gemini
Jul 24 11:40 Cancer
Jul 26 18:19 Leo
Jul 28 22:24 Virgo
Jul 31 01:14 Libra
Aug 02 03:56 Scorpio
Aug 04 07:04 Sagittarius
Aug 06 10:55 Capricorn
Aug 08 15:58 Aquarius
Aug 10 23:01 Pisces
Aug 13 08:49 Aries
Aug 15 21:06 Taurus
Aug 18 09:55 Gemini
Aug 20 20:34 Cancer
Aug 23 03:31 Leo
Aug 25 07:04 Virgo
Aug 27 08:42 Libra
Aug 29 10:05 Scorpio
Aug 31 12:29 Sagittarius
Sep 02 16:30 Capricorn
Sep 04 22:20 Aquarius
Sep 07 06:12 Pisces
Sep 09 16:19 Aries
Sep 12 04:31 Taurus
Sep 14 17:33 Gemini
Sep 17 05:07 Cancer
Sep 19 13:11 Leo
Sep 21 17:17 Virgo
Sep 23 18:28 Libra
Sep 25 18:34 Scorpio
Sep 27 19:22 Sagittarius
Sep 29 22:14 Capricorn
Oct 02 03:50 Aquarius
Oct 04 12:10 Pisces
Oct 06 22:50 Aries
Oct 09 11:12 Taurus

. . . MOON 1976–7

Oct 12 00:15 Gemini
Oct 14 12:24 Cancer
Oct 16 21:50 Leo
Oct 19 03:25 Virgo
Oct 21 05:27 Libra
Oct 23 05:17 Scorpio
Oct 25 04:49 Sagittarius
Oct 27 05:56 Capricorn
Oct 29 10:06 Aquarius
Oct 31 17:54 Pisces
Nov 03 04:46 Aries
Nov 05 17:23 Taurus
Nov 08 06:21 Gemini
Nov 10 18:28 Cancer
Nov 13 04:37 Leo
Nov 15 11:47 Virgo
Nov 17 15:34 Libra
Nov 19 16:32 Scorpio
Nov 21 16:04 Sagittarius
Nov 23 16:04 Capricorn
Nov 25 18:30 Aquarius
Nov 28 00:48 Pisces
Nov 30 11:02 Aries
Dec 02 23:42 Taurus
Dec 05 12:39 Gemini
Dec 08 00:21 Cancer
Dec 10 10:12 Leo
Dec 12 17:55 Virgo
Dec 14 23:14 Libra
Dec 17 02:02 Scorpio
Dec 19 02:54 Sagittarius
Dec 21 03:12 Capricorn
Dec 23 04:49 Aquarius
Dec 25 09:36 Pisces
Dec 27 18:32 Aries
Dec 30 06:44 Taurus

1977

Jan 01 19:43 Gemini
Jan 04 07:13 Cancer
Jan 06 16:21 Leo
Jan 08 23:24 Virgo
Jan 11 04:48 Libra
Jan 13 08:45 Scorpio
Jan 15 11:18 Sagittarius
Jan 17 13:02 Capricorn
Jan 19 15:12 Aquarius
Jan 21 19:31 Pisces
Jan 24 03:20 Aries
Jan 26 14:42 Taurus
Jan 29 03:38 Gemini
Jan 31 15:20 Cancer
Feb 03 00:12 Leo
Feb 05 06:18 Virgo
Feb 07 10:36 Libra
Feb 09 14:04 Scorpio
Feb 11 17:11 Sagittarius
Feb 13 20:14 Capricorn
Feb 15 23:45 Aquarius
Feb 18 04:45 Pisces
Feb 20 12:23 Aries

. . . MOON 1977

Feb 22 23:07 Taurus
Feb 25 11:50 Gemini
Feb 28 00:03 Cancer
Mar 02 09:25 Leo
Mar 04 15:19 Virgo
Mar 06 18:35 Libra
Mar 08 20:37 Scorpio
Mar 10 22:42 Sagittarius
Mar 13 01:40 Capricorn
Mar 15 06:00 Aquarius
Mar 17 12:06 Pisces
Mar 19 20:23 Aries
Mar 22 07:06 Taurus
Mar 24 19:39 Gemini
Mar 27 08:17 Cancer
Mar 29 18:41 Leo
Apr 01 01:25 Virgo
Apr 03 04:39 Libra
Apr 05 05:40 Scorpio
Apr 07 06:09 Sagittarius
Apr 09 07:41 Capricorn
Apr 11 11:24 Aquarius
Apr 13 17:50 Pisces
Apr 16 02:52 Aries
Apr 18 14:03 Taurus
Apr 21 02:38 Gemini
Apr 23 15:25 Cancer
Apr 26 02:43 Leo
Apr 28 10:52 Virgo
Apr 30 15:13 Libra
May 02 16:24 Scorpio
May 04 15:59 Sagittarius
May 06 15:54 Capricorn
May 08 18:00 Aquarius
May 10 23:29 Pisces
May 13 08:30 Aries
May 15 20:05 Taurus
May 18 08:51 Gemini
May 20 21:36 Cancer
May 23 09:14 Leo
May 25 18:31 Virgo
May 28 00:29 Libra
May 30 02:57 Scorpio
Jun 01 02:54 Sagittarius
Jun 03 02:08 Capricorn
Jun 05 02:44 Aquarius
Jun 07 06:36 Pisces
Jun 09 14:35 Aries
Jun 12 01:57 Taurus
Jun 14 14:50 Gemini
Jun 17 03:29 Cancer
Jun 19 14:54 Leo
Jun 22 00:29 Virgo
Jun 24 07:36 Libra
Jun 26 11:42 Scorpio
Jun 28 13:02 Sagittarius
Jun 30 12:48 Capricorn
Jul 02 12:56 Aquarius
Jul 04 15:31 Pisces
Jul 06 22:04 Aries

. . . MOON 1977

Jul 09 08:33 Taurus
Jul 11 21:15 Gemini
Jul 14 09:50 Cancer
Jul 16 20:52 Leo
Jul 19 05:59 Virgo
Jul 21 13:10 Libra
Jul 23 18:14 Scorpio
Jul 25 21:05 Sagittarius
Jul 27 22:15 Capricorn
Jul 29 23:05 Aquarius
Aug 01 01:24 Pisces
Aug 03 06:55 Aries
Aug 05 16:18 Taurus
Aug 08 04:30 Gemini
Aug 10 17:04 Cancer
Aug 13 03:57 Leo
Aug 15 12:26 Virgo
Aug 17 18:49 Libra
Aug 19 23:36 Scorpio
Aug 22 03:03 Sagittarius
Aug 24 05:31 Capricorn
Aug 26 07:41 Aquarius
Aug 28 10:47 Pisces
Aug 30 16:12 Aries
Sep 02 00:52 Taurus
Sep 04 12:27 Gemini
Sep 07 01:03 Cancer
Sep 09 12:14 Leo
Sep 11 20:35 Virgo
Sep 14 02:08 Libra
Sep 16 05:46 Scorpio
Sep 18 08:28 Sagittarius
Sep 20 11:05 Capricorn
Sep 22 14:12 Aquarius
Sep 24 18:30 Pisces
Sep 27 00:41 Aries
Sep 29 09:22 Taurus
Oct 01 20:34 Gemini
Oct 04 09:09 Cancer
Oct 06 20:58 Leo
Oct 09 05:59 Virgo
Oct 11 11:30 Libra
Oct 13 14:11 Scorpio
Oct 15 15:27 Sagittarius
Oct 17 16:51 Capricorn
Oct 19 19:36 Aquarius
Oct 22 00:27 Pisces
Oct 24 07:34 Aries
Oct 26 16:53 Taurus
Oct 29 04:08 Gemini
Oct 31 16:40 Cancer
Nov 03 05:03 Leo
Nov 05 15:17 Virgo
Nov 07 21:51 Libra
Nov 10 00:42 Scorpio
Nov 12 01:04 Sagittarius
Nov 14 00:51 Capricorn
Nov 16 02:00 Aquarius
Nov 18 05:59 Pisces
Nov 20 13:13 Aries

. . . MOON 1977–8

Nov 22 23:10 Taurus
Nov 25 10:49 Gemini
Nov 27 23:20 Cancer
Nov 30 11:53 Leo
Dec 02 23:06 Virgo
Dec 05 07:18 Libra
Dec 07 11:33 Scorpio
Dec 09 12:22 Sagittarius
Dec 11 11:26 Capricorn
Dec 13 11:00 Aquarius
Dec 15 13:09 Pisces
Dec 17 19:11 Aries
Dec 20 04:54 Taurus
Dec 22 16:52 Gemini
Dec 25 05:30 Cancer
Dec 27 17:52 Leo
Dec 30 05:14 Virgo

1978

Jan 01 14:32 Libra
Jan 03 20:35 Scorpio
Jan 05 23:04 Sagittarius
Jan 07 22:55 Capricorn
Jan 09 22:05 Aquarius
Jan 11 22:51 Pisces
Jan 14 03:05 Aries
Jan 16 11:31 Taurus
Jan 18 23:07 Gemini
Jan 21 11:51 Cancer
Jan 24 00:02 Leo
Jan 26 10:56 Virgo
Jan 28 20:08 Libra
Jan 31 03:04 Scorpio
Feb 02 07:14 Sagittarius
Feb 04 08:50 Capricorn
Feb 06 09:05 Aquarius
Feb 08 09:48 Pisces
Feb 10 12:57 Aries
Feb 12 19:51 Taurus
Feb 15 06:25 Gemini
Feb 17 18:56 Cancer
Feb 20 07:10 Leo
Feb 22 17:40 Virgo
Feb 25 02:04 Libra
Feb 27 08:28 Scorpio
Mar 01 13:02 Sagittarius
Mar 03 15:58 Capricorn
Mar 05 17:51 Aquarius
Mar 07 19:46 Pisces
Mar 09 23:08 Aries
Mar 12 05:18 Taurus
Mar 14 14:49 Gemini
Mar 17 02:49 Cancer
Mar 19 15:13 Leo
Mar 22 01:50 Virgo
Mar 24 09:42 Libra
Mar 26 15:01 Scorpio
Mar 28 18:38 Sagittarius
Mar 30 21:24 Capricorn
Apr 02 00:05 Aquarius
Apr 04 03:21 Pisces

. . . MOON 1978

Apr 06 07:51 Aries
Apr 08 14:22 Taurus
Apr 10 23:28 Gemini
Apr 13 10:59 Cancer
Apr 15 23:31 Leo
Apr 18 10:44 Virgo
Apr 20 18:53 Libra
Apr 22 23:39 Scorpio
Apr 25 02:00 Sagittarius
Apr 27 03:28 Capricorn
Apr 29 05:28 Aquarius
May 01 09:00 Pisces
May 03 14:27 Aries
May 05 21:52 Taurus
May 08 07:19 Gemini
May 10 18:42 Cancer
May 13 07:17 Leo
May 15 19:15 Virgo
May 18 04:25 Libra
May 20 09:39 Scorpio
May 22 11:31 Sagittarius
May 24 11:42 Capricorn
May 26 12:10 Aquarius
May 28 14:37 Pisces
May 30 19:52 Aries
Jun 02 03:50 Taurus
Jun 04 13:54 Gemini
Jun 07 01:30 Cancer
Jun 09 14:08 Leo
Jun 12 02:35 Virgo
Jun 14 12:56 Libra
Jun 16 19:29 Scorpio
Jun 18 22:01 Sagittarius
Jun 20 21:52 Capricorn
Jun 22 21:08 Aquarius
Jun 24 21:57 Pisces
Jun 27 01:53 Aries
Jun 29 09:21 Taurus
Jul 01 19:38 Gemini
Jul 04 07:34 Cancer
Jul 06 20:13 Leo
Jul 09 08:45 Virgo
Jul 11 19:48 Libra
Jul 14 03:47 Scorpio
Jul 16 07:50 Sagittarius
Jul 18 08:33 Capricorn
Jul 20 07:42 Aquarius
Jul 22 07:26 Pisces
Jul 24 09:46 Aries
Jul 26 15:51 Taurus
Jul 29 01:31 Gemini
Jul 31 13:28 Cancer
Aug 03 02:11 Leo
Aug 05 14:29 Virgo
Aug 08 01:30 Libra
Aug 10 10:12 Scorpio
Aug 12 15:43 Sagittarius
Aug 14 18:03 Capricorn
Aug 16 18:15 Aquarius
Aug 18 18:05 Pisces

. . . MOON 1978–9

Aug 20 19:30 Aries
Aug 23 00:06 Taurus
Aug 25 08:31 Gemini
Aug 27 19:59 Cancer
Aug 30 08:40 Leo
Sep 01 20:47 Virgo
Sep 04 07:16 Libra
Sep 06 15:38 Scorpio
Sep 08 21:39 Sagittarius
Sep 11 01:20 Capricorn
Sep 13 03:09 Aquarius
Sep 15 04:10 Pisces
Sep 17 05:50 Aries
Sep 19 09:43 Taurus
Sep 21 16:56 Gemini
Sep 24 03:31 Cancer
Sep 26 16:02 Leo
Sep 29 04:11 Virgo
Oct 01 14:17 Libra
Oct 03 21:48 Scorpio
Oct 06 03:07 Sagittarius
Oct 08 06:53 Capricorn
Oct 10 09:43 Aquarius
Oct 12 12:13 Pisces
Oct 14 15:06 Aries
Oct 16 19:22 Taurus
Oct 19 02:05 Gemini
Oct 21 11:53 Cancer
Oct 24 00:04 Leo
Oct 26 12:32 Virgo
Oct 28 22:51 Libra
Oct 31 05:53 Scorpio
Nov 02 10:04 Sagittarius
Nov 04 12:41 Capricorn
Nov 06 15:04 Aquarius
Nov 08 18:06 Pisces
Nov 10 22:12 Aries
Nov 13 03:35 Taurus
Nov 15 10:45 Gemini
Nov 17 20:16 Cancer
Nov 20 08:09 Leo
Nov 22 20:57 Virgo
Nov 25 08:07 Libra
Nov 27 15:39 Scorpio
Nov 29 19:24 Sagittarius
Dec 01 20:44 Capricorn
Dec 03 21:36 Aquarius
Dec 05 23:36 Pisces
Dec 08 03:40 Aries
Dec 10 09:51 Taurus
Dec 12 17:55 Gemini
Dec 15 03:50 Cancer
Dec 17 15:38 Leo
Dec 20 04:34 Virgo
Dec 22 16:40 Libra
Dec 25 01:32 Scorpio
Dec 27 06:08 Sagittarius
Dec 29 07:16 Capricorn
Dec 31 06:53 Aquarius

1979

. . . MOON 1979

Jan 02 07:08 Pisces
Jan 04 09:41 Aries
Jan 06 15:18 Taurus
Jan 08 23:43 Gemini
Jan 11 10:14 Cancer
Jan 13 22:16 Leo
Jan 16 11:10 Virgo
Jan 18 23:41 Libra
Jan 21 09:51 Scorpio
Jan 23 16:08 Sagittarius
Jan 25 18:28 Capricorn
Jan 27 18:12 Aquarius
Jan 29 17:25 Pisces
Jan 31 18:11 Aries
Feb 02 22:03 Taurus
Feb 05 05:33 Gemini
Feb 07 16:06 Cancer
Feb 10 04:26 Leo
Feb 12 17:18 Virgo
Feb 15 05:37 Libra
Feb 17 16:12 Scorpio
Feb 19 23:51 Sagittarius
Feb 22 04:01 Capricorn
Feb 24 05:12 Aquarius
Feb 26 04:52 Pisces
Feb 28 04:54 Aries
Mar 02 07:09 Taurus
Mar 04 12:58 Gemini
Mar 06 22:34 Cancer
Mar 09 10:48 Leo
Mar 11 23:43 Virgo
Mar 14 11:42 Libra
Mar 16 21:49 Scorpio
Mar 19 05:38 Sagittarius
Mar 21 10:56 Capricorn
Mar 23 13:52 Aquarius
Mar 25 15:05 Pisces
Mar 27 15:47 Aries
Mar 29 17:36 Taurus
Mar 31 22:08 Gemini
Apr 03 06:24 Cancer
Apr 05 17:58 Leo
Apr 08 06:52 Virgo
Apr 10 18:45 Libra
Apr 13 04:16 Scorpio
Apr 15 11:18 Sagittarius
Apr 17 16:23 Capricorn
Apr 19 20:02 Aquarius
Apr 21 22:41 Pisces
Apr 24 00:51 Aries
Apr 26 03:27 Taurus
Apr 28 07:49 Gemini
Apr 30 15:11 Cancer
May 03 01:56 Leo
May 05 14:41 Virgo
May 08 02:48 Libra
May 10 12:10 Scorpio
May 12 18:25 Sagittarius
May 14 22:26 Capricorn
May 17 01:26 Aquarius

. . . MOON 1979

May 19 04:18 Pisces
May 21 07:30 Aries
May 23 11:20 Taurus
May 25 16:28 Gemini
May 27 23:51 Cancer
May 30 10:08 Leo
Jun 01 22:41 Virgo
Jun 04 11:12 Libra
Jun 06 21:05 Scorpio
Jun 09 03:15 Sagittarius
Jun 11 06:23 Capricorn
Jun 13 08:06 Aquarius
Jun 15 09:56 Pisces
Jun 17 12:52 Aries
Jun 19 17:18 Taurus
Jun 21 23:23 Gemini
Jun 24 07:25 Cancer
Jun 26 17:47 Leo
Jun 29 06:14 Virgo
Jul 01 19:08 Libra
Jul 04 05:57 Scorpio
Jul 06 12:56 Sagittarius
Jul 08 16:07 Capricorn
Jul 10 16:59 Aquarius
Jul 12 17:23 Pisces
Jul 14 18:57 Aries
Jul 16 22:43 Taurus
Jul 19 05:00 Gemini
Jul 21 13:40 Cancer
Jul 24 00:30 Leo
Jul 26 13:01 Virgo
Jul 29 02:06 Libra
Jul 31 13:46 Scorpio
Aug 02 22:06 Sagittarius
Aug 05 02:23 Capricorn
Aug 07 03:28 Aquarius
Aug 09 03:06 Pisces
Aug 11 03:10 Aries
Aug 13 05:22 Taurus
Aug 15 10:41 Gemini
Aug 17 19:17 Cancer
Aug 20 06:29 Leo
Aug 22 19:11 Virgo
Aug 25 08:14 Libra
Aug 27 20:13 Scorpio
Aug 30 05:39 Sagittarius
Sep 01 11:34 Capricorn
Sep 03 13:59 Aquarius
Sep 05 14:03 Pisces
Sep 07 13:29 Aries
Sep 09 14:12 Taurus
Sep 11 17:54 Gemini
Sep 14 01:27 Cancer
Sep 16 12:25 Leo
Sep 19 01:15 Virgo
Sep 21 14:11 Libra
Sep 24 01:54 Scorpio
Sep 26 11:36 Sagittarius
Sep 28 18:40 Capricorn
Sep 30 22:49 Aquarius

. . . MOON 1979–80

Oct 03 00:23 Pisces
Oct 05 00:28 Aries
Oct 07 00:45 Taurus
Oct 09 03:07 Gemini
Oct 11 09:09 Cancer
Oct 13 19:12 Leo
Oct 16 07:51 Virgo
Oct 18 20:44 Libra
Oct 21 08:02 Scorpio
Oct 23 17:09 Sagittarius
Oct 26 00:11 Capricorn
Oct 28 05:17 Aquarius
Oct 30 08:29 Pisces
Nov 01 10:09 Aries
Nov 03 11:16 Taurus
Nov 05 13:26 Gemini
Nov 07 18:24 Cancer
Nov 10 03:14 Leo
Nov 12 15:20 Virgo
Nov 15 04:16 Libra
Nov 17 15:30 Scorpio
Nov 19 23:56 Sagittarius
Nov 22 06:01 Capricorn
Nov 24 10:37 Aquarius
Nov 26 14:17 Pisces
Nov 28 17:17 Aries
Nov 30 19:54 Taurus
Dec 02 23:02 Gemini
Dec 05 04:01 Cancer
Dec 07 12:09 Leo
Dec 09 23:33 Virgo
Dec 12 12:29 Libra
Dec 15 00:08 Scorpio
Dec 17 08:37 Sagittarius
Dec 19 13:55 Capricorn
Dec 21 17:13 Aquarius
Dec 23 19:50 Pisces
Dec 25 22:40 Aries
Dec 28 02:08 Taurus
Dec 30 06:32 Gemini

1980

Jan 01 12:29 Cancer
Jan 03 20:47 Leo
Jan 06 07:48 Virgo
Jan 08 20:38 Libra
Jan 11 08:55 Scorpio
Jan 13 18:17 Sagittarius
Jan 15 23:51 Capricorn
Jan 18 02:25 Aquarius
Jan 20 03:33 Pisces
Jan 22 04:52 Aries
Jan 24 07:32 Taurus
Jan 26 12:11 Gemini
Jan 28 19:03 Cancer
Jan 31 04:08 Leo
Feb 02 15:21 Virgo
Feb 05 04:04 Libra
Feb 07 16:46 Scorpio
Feb 10 03:19 Sagittarius
Feb 12 10:12 Capricorn

. . . MOON 1980

Feb 14 13:20 Aquarius
Feb 16 13:54 Pisces
Feb 18 13:43 Aries
Feb 20 14:35 Taurus
Feb 22 17:58 Gemini
Feb 25 00:34 Cancer
Feb 27 10:10 Leo
Feb 29 21:53 Virgo
Mar 03 10:40 Libra
Mar 05 23:23 Scorpio
Mar 08 10:38 Sagittarius
Mar 10 19:02 Capricorn
Mar 12 23:45 Aquarius
Mar 15 01:11 Pisces
Mar 17 00:41 Aries
Mar 19 00:13 Taurus
Mar 21 01:47 Gemini
Mar 23 06:55 Cancer
Mar 25 15:58 Leo
Mar 28 03:52 Virgo
Mar 30 16:49 Libra
Apr 02 05:21 Scorpio
Apr 04 16:35 Sagittarius
Apr 07 01:43 Capricorn
Apr 09 08:00 Aquarius
Apr 11 11:07 Pisces
Apr 13 11:40 Aries
Apr 15 11:11 Taurus
Apr 17 11:41 Gemini
Apr 19 15:11 Cancer
Apr 21 22:52 Leo
Apr 24 10:12 Virgo
Apr 26 23:09 Libra
Apr 29 11:35 Scorpio
May 01 22:22 Sagittarius
May 04 07:14 Capricorn
May 06 14:03 Aquarius
May 08 18:33 Pisces
May 10 20:44 Aries
May 12 21:24 Taurus
May 14 22:07 Gemini
May 17 00:52 Cancer
May 19 07:14 Leo
May 21 17:32 Virgo
May 24 06:11 Libra
May 26 18:37 Scorpio
May 29 05:05 Sagittarius
May 31 13:14 Capricorn
Jun 02 19:29 Aquarius
Jun 05 00:10 Pisces
Jun 07 03:23 Aries
Jun 09 05:30 Taurus
Jun 11 07:22 Gemini
Jun 13 10:29 Cancer
Jun 15 16:22 Leo
Jun 18 01:47 Virgo
Jun 20 13:55 Libra
Jun 23 02:26 Scorpio
Jun 25 13:02 Sagittarius
Jun 27 20:46 Capricorn

. . . MOON 1980

Jun 30 02:04 Aquarius
Jul 02 05:48 Pisces
Jul 04 08:46 Aries
Jul 06 11:30 Taurus
Jul 08 14:33 Gemini
Jul 10 18:44 Cancer
Jul 13 01:03 Leo
Jul 15 10:11 Virgo
Jul 17 21:55 Libra
Jul 20 10:33 Scorpio
Jul 22 21:42 Sagittarius
Jul 25 05:45 Capricorn
Jul 27 10:35 Aquarius
Jul 29 13:11 Pisces
Jul 31 14:53 Aries
Aug 02 16:55 Taurus
Aug 04 20:10 Gemini
Aug 07 01:12 Cancer
Aug 09 08:23 Leo
Aug 11 17:54 Virgo
Aug 14 05:32 Libra
Aug 16 18:15 Scorpio
Aug 19 06:08 Sagittarius
Aug 21 15:11 Capricorn
Aug 23 20:33 Aquarius
Aug 25 22:43 Pisces
Aug 27 23:11 Aries
Aug 29 23:41 Taurus
Sep 01 01:50 Gemini
Sep 03 06:39 Cancer
Sep 05 14:22 Leo
Sep 08 00:31 Virgo
Sep 10 12:22 Libra
Sep 13 01:06 Scorpio
Sep 15 13:28 Sagittarius
Sep 17 23:45 Capricorn
Sep 20 06:31 Aquarius
Sep 22 09:27 Pisces
Sep 24 09:37 Aries
Sep 26 08:53 Taurus
Sep 28 09:21 Gemini
Sep 30 12:46 Cancer
Oct 02 19:57 Leo
Oct 05 06:19 Virgo
Oct 07 18:30 Libra
Oct 10 07:15 Scorpio
Oct 12 19:37 Sagittarius
Oct 15 06:37 Capricorn
Oct 17 14:53 Aquarius
Oct 19 19:31 Pisces
Oct 21 20:43 Aries
Oct 23 19:55 Taurus
Oct 25 19:17 Gemini
Oct 27 21:00 Cancer
Oct 30 02:38 Leo
Nov 01 12:18 Virgo
Nov 04 00:31 Libra
Nov 06 13:19 Scorpio
Nov 09 01:25 Sagittarius
Nov 11 12:15 Capricorn

. . . MOON 1980–81

Nov 13 21:10 Aquarius
Nov 16 03:21 Pisces
Nov 18 06:22 Aries
Nov 20 06:51 Taurus
Nov 22 06:27 Gemini
Nov 24 07:18 Cancer
Nov 26 11:23 Leo
Nov 28 19:37 Virgo
Dec 01 07:13 Libra
Dec 03 20:00 Scorpio
Dec 06 07:57 Sagittarius
Dec 08 18:12 Capricorn
Dec 11 02:36 Aquarius
Dec 13 09:03 Pisces
Dec 15 13:21 Aries
Dec 17 15:36 Taurus
Dec 19 16:39 Gemini
Dec 21 18:03 Cancer
Dec 23 21:33 Leo
Dec 26 04:32 Virgo
Dec 28 15:05 Libra
Dec 31 03:36 Scorpio

1981

Jan 02 15:42 Sagittarius
Jan 05 01:41 Capricorn
Jan 07 09:12 Aquarius
Jan 09 14:42 Pisces
Jan 11 18:43 Aries
Jan 13 21:45 Taurus
Jan 16 00:17 Gemini
Jan 18 03:08 Cancer
Jan 20 07:21 Leo
Jan 22 14:02 Virgo
Jan 24 23:45 Libra
Jan 27 11:49 Scorpio
Jan 30 00:11 Sagittarius
Feb 01 10:37 Capricorn
Feb 03 17:55 Aquarius
Feb 05 22:21 Pisces
Feb 08 01:01 Aries
Feb 10 03:10 Taurus
Feb 12 05:51 Gemini
Feb 14 09:43 Cancer
Feb 16 15:10 Leo
Feb 18 22:34 Virgo
Feb 21 08:12 Libra
Feb 23 19:54 Scorpio
Feb 26 08:29 Sagittarius
Feb 28 19:46 Capricorn
Mar 03 03:51 Aquarius
Mar 05 08:12 Pisces
Mar 07 09:48 Aries
Mar 09 10:22 Taurus
Mar 11 11:42 Gemini
Mar 13 15:05 Cancer
Mar 15 21:02 Leo
Mar 18 05:20 Virgo
Mar 20 15:31 Libra
Mar 23 03:14 Scorpio
Mar 25 15:51 Sagittarius

. . . MOON 1981

Mar 28 03:52 Capricorn
Mar 30 13:15 Aquarius
Apr 01 18:41 Pisces
Apr 03 20:25 Aries
Apr 05 20:04 Taurus
Apr 07 19:47 Gemini
Apr 09 21:33 Cancer
Apr 12 02:36 Leo
Apr 14 10:56 Virgo
Apr 16 21:38 Libra
Apr 19 09:39 Scorpio
Apr 21 22:14 Sagittarius
Apr 24 10:31 Capricorn
Apr 26 20:57 Aquarius
Apr 29 03:56 Pisces
May 01 06:57 Aries
May 03 06:59 Taurus
May 05 06:01 Gemini
May 07 06:17 Cancer
May 09 09:40 Leo
May 11 16:55 Virgo
May 14 03:24 Libra
May 16 15:37 Scorpio
May 19 04:14 Sagittarius
May 21 16:20 Capricorn
May 24 03:00 Aquarius
May 26 11:05 Pisces
May 28 15:44 Aries
May 30 17:10 Taurus
Jun 01 16:48 Gemini
Jun 03 16:38 Cancer
Jun 05 18:43 Leo
Jun 08 00:25 Virgo
Jun 10 09:55 Libra
Jun 12 21:54 Scorpio
Jun 15 10:31 Sagittarius
Jun 17 22:21 Capricorn
Jun 20 08:36 Aquarius
Jun 22 16:44 Pisces
Jun 24 22:18 Aries
Jun 27 01:16 Taurus
Jun 29 02:21 Gemini
Jul 01 02:57 Cancer
Jul 03 04:47 Leo
Jul 05 09:26 Virgo
Jul 07 17:42 Libra
Jul 10 05:02 Scorpio
Jul 12 17:35 Sagittarius
Jul 15 05:19 Capricorn
Jul 17 15:02 Aquarius
Jul 19 22:26 Pisces
Jul 22 03:43 Aries
Jul 24 07:18 Taurus
Jul 26 09:42 Gemini
Jul 28 11:41 Cancer
Jul 30 14:20 Leo
Aug 01 18:54 Virgo
Aug 04 02:24 Libra
Aug 06 12:58 Scorpio
Aug 09 01:22 Sagittarius

. . . MOON 1981

Aug 11 13:20 Capricorn
Aug 13 22:56 Aquarius
Aug 16 05:34 Pisces
Aug 18 09:49 Aries
Aug 20 12:43 Taurus
Aug 22 15:18 Gemini
Aug 24 18:16 Cancer
Aug 26 22:10 Leo
Aug 29 03:31 Virgo
Aug 31 11:02 Libra
Sep 02 21:10 Scorpio
Sep 05 09:23 Sagittarius
Sep 07 21:48 Capricorn
Sep 10 07:58 Aquarius
Sep 12 14:34 Pisces
Sep 14 17:55 Aries
Sep 16 19:30 Taurus
Sep 18 20:59 Gemini
Sep 20 23:39 Cancer
Sep 23 04:08 Leo
Sep 25 10:29 Virgo
Sep 27 18:40 Libra
Sep 30 04:52 Scorpio
Oct 02 16:59 Sagittarius
Oct 05 05:49 Capricorn
Oct 07 17:01 Aquarius
Oct 10 00:32 Pisces
Oct 12 04:01 Aries
Oct 14 04:43 Taurus
Oct 16 04:41 Gemini
Oct 18 05:52 Cancer
Oct 20 09:34 Leo
Oct 22 16:04 Virgo
Oct 25 00:56 Libra
Oct 27 11:38 Scorpio
Oct 29 23:48 Sagittarius
Nov 01 12:46 Capricorn
Nov 04 00:50 Aquarius
Nov 06 09:52 Pisces
Nov 08 14:38 Aries
Nov 10 15:44 Taurus
Nov 12 14:59 Gemini
Nov 14 14:36 Cancer
Nov 16 16:32 Leo
Nov 18 21:53 Virgo
Nov 21 06:33 Libra
Nov 23 17:36 Scorpio
Nov 26 06:00 Sagittarius
Nov 28 18:52 Capricorn
Dec 01 07:09 Aquarius
Dec 03 17:16 Pisces
Dec 05 23:49 Aries
Dec 08 02:31 Taurus
Dec 10 02:30 Gemini
Dec 12 01:40 Cancer
Dec 14 02:08 Leo
Dec 16 05:38 Virgo
Dec 18 12:58 Libra
Dec 20 23:39 Scorpio
Dec 23 12:11 Sagittarius

. . . MOON 1981–2

Dec 26 00:59 Capricorn
Dec 28 12:53 Aquarius
Dec 30 23:01 Pisces
1982
Jan 02 06:33 Aries
Jan 04 11:02 Taurus
Jan 06 12:48 Gemini
Jan 08 13:01 Cancer
Jan 10 13:21 Leo
Jan 12 15:37 Virgo
Jan 14 21:17 Libra
Jan 17 06:46 Scorpio
Jan 19 19:00 Sagittarius
Jan 22 07:50 Capricorn
Jan 24 19:25 Aquarius
Jan 27 04:49 Pisces
Jan 29 11:58 Aries
Jan 31 17:03 Taurus
Feb 02 20:20 Gemini
Feb 04 22:18 Cancer
Feb 06 23:50 Leo
Feb 09 02:15 Virgo
Feb 11 07:02 Libra
Feb 13 15:16 Scorpio
Feb 16 02:45 Sagittarius
Feb 18 15:36 Capricorn
Feb 21 03:15 Aquarius
Feb 23 12:09 Pisces
Feb 25 18:17 Aries
Feb 27 22:32 Taurus
Mar 02 01:50 Gemini
Mar 04 04:48 Cancer
Mar 06 07:50 Leo
Mar 08 11:27 Virgo
Mar 10 16:34 Libra
Mar 13 00:16 Scorpio
Mar 15 11:03 Sagittarius
Mar 17 23:47 Capricorn
Mar 20 11:53 Aquarius
Mar 22 21:01 Pisces
Mar 25 02:37 Aries
Mar 27 05:39 Taurus
Mar 29 07:44 Gemini
Mar 31 10:09 Cancer
Apr 02 13:36 Leo
Apr 04 18:18 Virgo
Apr 07 00:26 Libra
Apr 09 08:33 Scorpio
Apr 11 19:06 Sagittarius
Apr 14 07:41 Capricorn
Apr 16 20:18 Aquarius
Apr 19 06:19 Pisces
Apr 21 12:23 Aries
Apr 23 14:59 Taurus
Apr 25 15:48 Gemini
Apr 27 16:43 Cancer
Apr 29 19:09 Leo
May 01 23:45 Virgo
May 04 06:32 Libra
May 06 15:24 Scorpio

. . . MOON 1982

May 09 02:16 Sagittarius
May 11 14:49 Capricorn
May 14 03:44 Aquarius
May 16 14:46 Pisces
May 18 22:04 Aries
May 21 01:22 Taurus
May 23 01:54 Gemini
May 25 01:38 Cancer
May 27 02:27 Leo
May 29 05:43 Virgo
May 31 12:02 Libra
Jun 02 21:11 Scorpio
Jun 05 08:31 Sagittarius
Jun 07 21:12 Capricorn
Jun 10 10:08 Aquarius
Jun 12 21:44 Pisces
Jun 15 06:20 Aries
Jun 17 11:07 Taurus
Jun 19 12:34 Gemini
Jun 21 12:12 Cancer
Jun 23 11:56 Leo
Jun 25 13:36 Virgo
Jun 27 18:30 Libra
Jun 30 03:01 Scorpio
Jul 02 14:25 Sagittarius
Jul 05 03:15 Capricorn
Jul 07 16:03 Aquarius
Jul 10 03:35 Pisces
Jul 12 12:49 Aries
Jul 14 19:00 Taurus
Jul 16 22:03 Gemini
Jul 18 22:46 Cancer
Jul 20 22:35 Leo
Jul 22 23:20 Virgo
Jul 25 02:45 Libra
Jul 27 09:58 Scorpio
Jul 29 20:47 Sagittarius
Aug 01 09:36 Capricorn
Aug 03 22:17 Aquarius
Aug 06 09:23 Pisces
Aug 08 18:20 Aries
Aug 11 01:00 Taurus
Aug 13 05:22 Gemini
Aug 15 07:40 Cancer
Aug 17 08:40 Leo
Aug 19 09:40 Virgo
Aug 21 12:22 Libra
Aug 23 18:21 Scorpio
Aug 26 04:11 Sagittarius
Aug 28 16:41 Capricorn
Aug 31 05:23 Aquarius
Sep 02 16:10 Pisces
Sep 05 00:24 Aries
Sep 07 06:27 Taurus
Sep 09 10:57 Gemini
Sep 11 14:18 Cancer
Sep 13 16:46 Leo
Sep 15 18:57 Virgo
Sep 17 22:03 Libra
Sep 20 03:32 Scorpio

. . . MOON 1982–3

Sep 22 12:30 Sagittarius
Sep 25 00:31 Capricorn
Sep 27 13:21 Aquarius
Sep 30 00:18 Pisces
Oct 02 08:05 Aries
Oct 04 13:09 Taurus
Oct 06 16:39 Gemini
Oct 08 19:39 Cancer
Oct 10 22:44 Leo
Oct 13 02:09 Virgo
Oct 15 06:22 Libra
Oct 17 12:20 Scorpio
Oct 19 21:02 Sagittarius
Oct 22 08:37 Capricorn
Oct 24 21:35 Aquarius
Oct 27 09:12 Pisces
Oct 29 17:25 Aries
Oct 31 22:03 Taurus
Nov 03 00:22 Gemini
Nov 05 01:59 Cancer
Nov 07 04:10 Leo
Nov 09 07:40 Virgo
Nov 11 12:45 Libra
Nov 13 19:42 Scorpio
Nov 16 04:51 Sagittarius
Nov 18 16:21 Capricorn
Nov 21 05:20 Aquarius
Nov 23 17:42 Pisces
Nov 26 03:07 Aries
Nov 28 08:31 Taurus
Nov 30 10:36 Gemini
Dec 02 10:57 Cancer
Dec 04 11:26 Leo
Dec 06 13:32 Virgo
Dec 08 18:10 Libra
Dec 11 01:34 Scorpio
Dec 13 11:26 Sagittarius
Dec 15 23:15 Capricorn
Dec 18 12:12 Aquarius
Dec 21 00:56 Pisces
Dec 23 11:34 Aries
Dec 25 18:36 Taurus
Dec 27 21:48 Gemini
Dec 29 22:12 Cancer
Dec 31 21:33 Leo

1983

Jan 02 21:49 Virgo
Jan 05 00:44 Libra
Jan 07 07:16 Scorpio
Jan 09 17:13 Sagittarius
Jan 12 05:26 Capricorn
Jan 14 18:26 Aquarius
Jan 17 07:02 Pisces
Jan 19 18:08 Aries
Jan 22 02:36 Taurus
Jan 24 07:40 Gemini
Jan 26 09:28 Cancer
Jan 28 09:10 Leo
Jan 30 08:34 Virgo
Feb 01 09:47 Libra

. . . MOON 1983

Feb 03 14:32 Scorpio
Feb 05 23:28 Sagittarius
Feb 08 11:33 Capricorn
Feb 11 00:40 Aquarius
Feb 13 13:01 Pisces
Feb 15 23:46 Aries
Feb 18 08:30 Taurus
Feb 20 14:52 Gemini
Feb 22 18:31 Cancer
Feb 24 19:47 Leo
Feb 26 19:49 Virgo
Feb 28 20:30 Libra
Mar 02 23:50 Scorpio
Mar 05 07:15 Sagittarius
Mar 07 18:29 Capricorn
Mar 10 07:30 Aquarius
Mar 12 19:47 Pisces
Mar 15 06:00 Aries
Mar 17 14:04 Taurus
Mar 19 20:20 Gemini
Mar 22 00:52 Cancer
Mar 24 03:43 Leo
Mar 26 05:18 Virgo
Mar 28 06:48 Libra
Mar 30 09:56 Scorpio
Apr 01 16:19 Sagittarius
Apr 04 02:29 Capricorn
Apr 06 15:06 Aquarius
Apr 09 03:30 Pisces
Apr 11 13:37 Aries
Apr 13 20:59 Taurus
Apr 16 02:14 Gemini
Apr 18 06:14 Cancer
Apr 20 09:26 Leo
Apr 22 12:11 Virgo
Apr 24 15:04 Libra
Apr 26 19:04 Scorpio
Apr 29 01:28 Sagittarius
May 01 11:01 Capricorn
May 03 23:09 Aquarius
May 06 11:43 Pisces
May 08 22:16 Aries
May 11 05:36 Taurus
May 13 10:03 Gemini
May 15 12:48 Cancer
May 17 15:01 Leo
May 19 17:36 Virgo
May 21 21:11 Libra
May 24 02:17 Scorpio
May 26 09:27 Sagittarius
May 28 19:06 Capricorn
May 31 06:59 Aquarius
Jun 02 19:41 Pisces
Jun 05 06:59 Aries
Jun 07 15:05 Taurus
Jun 09 19:37 Gemini
Jun 11 21:32 Cancer
Jun 13 22:21 Leo
Jun 15 23:38 Virgo
Jun 18 02:36 Libra

. . . MOON 1983

Jun 20 07:59 Scorpio
Jun 22 15:55 Sagittarius
Jun 25 02:08 Capricorn
Jun 27 14:06 Aquarius
Jun 30 02:51 Pisces
Jul 02 14:47 Aries
Jul 05 00:05 Taurus
Jul 07 05:41 Gemini
Jul 09 07:50 Cancer
Jul 11 07:54 Leo
Jul 13 07:43 Virgo
Jul 15 09:10 Libra
Jul 17 13:38 Scorpio
Jul 19 21:31 Sagittarius
Jul 22 08:11 Capricorn
Jul 24 20:26 Aquarius
Jul 27 09:11 Pisces
Jul 29 21:20 Aries
Aug 01 07:37 Taurus
Aug 03 14:43 Gemini
Aug 05 18:09 Cancer
Aug 07 18:37 Leo
Aug 09 17:49 Virgo
Aug 11 17:51 Libra
Aug 13 20:44 Scorpio
Aug 16 03:33 Sagittarius
Aug 18 13:59 Capricorn
Aug 21 02:25 Aquarius
Aug 23 15:10 Pisces
Aug 26 03:08 Aries
Aug 28 13:38 Taurus
Aug 30 21:48 Gemini
Sep 02 02:53 Cancer
Sep 04 04:47 Leo
Sep 06 04:36 Virgo
Sep 08 04:13 Libra
Sep 10 05:49 Scorpio
Sep 12 11:07 Sagittarius
Sep 14 20:33 Capricorn
Sep 17 08:45 Aquarius
Sep 19 21:30 Pisces
Sep 22 09:10 Aries
Sep 24 19:12 Taurus
Sep 27 03:24 Gemini
Sep 29 09:24 Cancer
Oct 01 12:54 Leo
Oct 03 14:15 Virgo
Oct 05 14:42 Libra
Oct 07 16:06 Scorpio
Oct 09 20:20 Sagittarius
Oct 12 04:30 Capricorn
Oct 14 16:00 Aquarius
Oct 17 04:41 Pisces
Oct 19 16:18 Aries
Oct 22 01:47 Taurus
Oct 24 09:10 Gemini
Oct 26 14:47 Cancer
Oct 28 18:50 Leo
Oct 30 21:33 Virgo
Nov 01 23:30 Libra

. . . MOON 1983–4

Nov 04 01:53 Scorpio
Nov 06 06:09 Sagittarius
Nov 08 13:31 Capricorn
Nov 11 00:10 Aquarius
Nov 13 12:40 Pisces
Nov 16 00:36 Aries
Nov 18 10:06 Taurus
Nov 20 16:45 Gemini
Nov 22 21:10 Cancer
Nov 25 00:19 Leo
Nov 27 03:02 Virgo
Nov 29 05:57 Libra
Dec 01 09:40 Scorpio
Dec 03 14:56 Sagittarius
Dec 05 22:28 Capricorn
Dec 08 08:39 Aquarius
Dec 10 20:53 Pisces
Dec 13 09:16 Aries
Dec 15 19:33 Taurus
Dec 18 02:23 Gemini
Dec 20 06:02 Cancer
Dec 22 07:44 Leo
Dec 24 09:01 Virgo
Dec 26 11:18 Libra
Dec 28 15:26 Scorpio
Dec 30 21:44 Sagittarius

1984

Jan 02 06:07 Capricorn
Jan 04 16:30 Aquarius
Jan 07 04:34 Pisces
Jan 09 17:15 Aries
Jan 12 04:36 Taurus
Jan 14 12:40 Gemini
Jan 16 16:47 Cancer
Jan 18 17:50 Leo
Jan 20 17:35 Virgo
Jan 22 18:07 Libra
Jan 24 21:04 Scorpio
Jan 27 03:12 Sagittarius
Jan 29 12:12 Capricorn
Jan 31 23:11 Aquarius
Feb 03 11:22 Pisces
Feb 06 00:04 Aries
Feb 08 12:05 Taurus
Feb 10 21:39 Gemini
Feb 13 03:20 Cancer
Feb 15 05:09 Leo
Feb 17 04:32 Virgo
Feb 19 03:39 Libra
Feb 21 04:44 Scorpio
Feb 23 09:22 Sagittarius
Feb 25 17:49 Capricorn
Feb 28 05:02 Aquarius
Mar 01 17:29 Pisces
Mar 04 06:07 Aries
Mar 06 18:09 Taurus
Mar 09 04:29 Gemini
Mar 11 11:48 Cancer
Mar 13 15:21 Leo
Mar 15 15:47 Virgo

. . . MOON 1984

Mar 17 14:51 Libra
Mar 19 14:48 Scorpio
Mar 21 17:41 Sagittarius
Mar 24 00:36 Capricorn
Mar 26 11:09 Aquarius
Mar 28 23:37 Pisces
Mar 31 12:14 Aries
Apr 02 23:55 Taurus
Apr 05 10:04 Gemini
Apr 07 17:59 Cancer
Apr 09 23:01 Leo
Apr 12 01:11 Virgo
Apr 14 01:29 Libra
Apr 16 01:41 Scorpio
Apr 18 03:43 Sagittarius
Apr 20 09:10 Capricorn
Apr 22 18:27 Aquarius
Apr 25 06:26 Pisces
Apr 27 19:02 Aries
Apr 30 06:30 Taurus
May 02 16:01 Gemini
May 04 23:26 Cancer
May 07 04:43 Leo
May 09 08:02 Virgo
May 11 09:54 Libra
May 13 11:22 Scorpio
May 15 13:50 Sagittarius
May 17 18:43 Capricorn
May 20 02:55 Aquarius
May 22 14:08 Pisces
May 25 02:39 Aries
May 27 14:13 Taurus
May 29 23:23 Gemini
Jun 01 05:53 Cancer
Jun 03 10:19 Leo
Jun 05 13:27 Virgo
Jun 07 16:03 Libra
Jun 09 18:48 Scorpio
Jun 11 22:26 Sagittarius
Jun 14 03:48 Capricorn
Jun 16 11:41 Aquarius
Jun 18 22:18 Pisces
Jun 21 10:40 Aries
Jun 23 22:38 Taurus
Jun 26 08:04 Gemini
Jun 28 14:09 Cancer
Jun 30 17:30 Leo
Jul 02 19:27 Virgo
Jul 04 21:27 Libra
Jul 07 00:28 Scorpio
Jul 09 05:03 Sagittarius
Jul 11 11:23 Capricorn
Jul 13 19:41 Aquarius
Jul 16 06:10 Pisces
Jul 18 18:26 Aries
Jul 21 06:52 Taurus
Jul 23 17:10 Gemini
Jul 25 23:44 Cancer
Jul 28 02:41 Leo
Jul 30 03:29 Virgo

. . . MOON 1984

Aug 01 04:03 Libra
Aug 03 06:04 Scorpio
Aug 05 10:30 Sagittarius
Aug 07 17:24 Capricorn
Aug 10 02:25 Aquarius
Aug 12 13:13 Pisces
Aug 15 01:28 Aries
Aug 17 14:13 Taurus
Aug 20 01:31 Gemini
Aug 22 09:20 Cancer
Aug 24 13:00 Leo
Aug 26 13:32 Virgo
Aug 28 12:57 Libra
Aug 30 13:23 Scorpio
Sep 01 16:30 Sagittarius
Sep 03 22:55 Capricorn
Sep 06 08:11 Aquarius
Sep 08 19:24 Pisces
Sep 11 07:46 Aries
Sep 13 20:33 Taurus
Sep 16 08:25 Gemini
Sep 18 17:36 Cancer
Sep 20 22:49 Leo
Sep 23 00:19 Virgo
Sep 24 23:41 Libra
Sep 26 23:04 Scorpio
Sep 29 00:32 Sagittarius
Oct 01 05:28 Capricorn
Oct 03 14:03 Aquarius
Oct 06 01:19 Pisces
Oct 08 13:51 Aries
Oct 11 02:28 Taurus
Oct 13 14:14 Gemini
Oct 16 00:00 Cancer
Oct 18 06:41 Leo
Oct 20 09:56 Virgo
Oct 22 10:32 Libra
Oct 24 10:08 Scorpio
Oct 26 10:43 Sagittarius
Oct 28 14:04 Capricorn
Oct 30 21:13 Aquarius
Nov 02 07:49 Pisces
Nov 04 20:20 Aries
Nov 07 08:53 Taurus
Nov 09 20:10 Gemini
Nov 12 05:31 Cancer
Nov 14 12:33 Leo
Nov 16 17:08 Virgo
Nov 18 19:29 Libra
Nov 20 20:30 Scorpio
Nov 22 21:34 Sagittarius
Nov 25 00:17 Capricorn
Nov 27 06:06 Aquarius
Nov 29 15:33 Pisces
Dec 02 03:42 Aries
Dec 04 16:20 Taurus
Dec 07 03:24 Gemini
Dec 09 11:56 Cancer
Dec 11 18:08 Leo
Dec 13 22:35 Virgo

. . . MOON 1984–5

Dec 16 01:52 Libra
Dec 18 04:27 Scorpio
Dec 20 06:58 Sagittarius
Dec 22 10:21 Capricorn
Dec 24 15:47 Aquarius
Dec 27 00:18 Pisces
Dec 29 11:49 Aries
1985
Jan 01 00:36 Taurus
Jan 03 12:00 Gemini
Jan 05 20:18 Cancer
Jan 08 01:28 Leo
Jan 10 04:40 Virgo
Jan 12 07:13 Libra
Jan 14 10:07 Scorpio
Jan 16 13:48 Sagittarius
Jan 18 18:29 Capricorn
Jan 21 00:38 Aquarius
Jan 23 09:02 Pisces
Jan 25 20:05 Aries
Jan 28 08:53 Taurus
Jan 30 21:00 Gemini
Feb 02 05:59 Cancer
Feb 04 11:02 Leo
Feb 06 13:09 Virgo
Feb 08 14:10 Libra
Feb 10 15:49 Scorpio
Feb 12 19:09 Sagittarius
Feb 15 00:27 Capricorn
Feb 17 07:36 Aquarius
Feb 19 16:38 Pisces
Feb 22 03:42 Aries
Feb 24 16:27 Taurus
Feb 27 05:11 Gemini
Mar 01 15:23 Cancer
Mar 03 21:28 Leo
Mar 05 23:43 Virgo
Mar 07 23:47 Libra
Mar 09 23:47 Scorpio
Mar 12 01:29 Sagittarius
Mar 14 05:54 Capricorn
Mar 16 13:11 Aquarius
Mar 18 22:50 Pisces
Mar 21 10:20 Aries
Mar 23 23:06 Taurus
Mar 26 12:02 Gemini
Mar 28 23:13 Cancer
Mar 31 06:51 Leo
Apr 02 10:25 Virgo
Apr 04 10:54 Libra
Apr 06 10:10 Scorpio
Apr 08 10:17 Sagittarius
Apr 10 12:57 Capricorn
Apr 12 19:04 Aquarius
Apr 15 04:30 Pisces
Apr 17 16:18 Aries
Apr 20 05:12 Taurus
Apr 22 18:00 Gemini
Apr 25 05:26 Cancer
Apr 27 14:10 Leo

. . . MOON 1985

Apr 29 19:24 Virgo
May 01 21:22 Libra
May 03 21:17 Scorpio
May 05 20:56 Sagittarius
May 07 22:11 Capricorn
May 10 02:38 Aquarius
May 12 10:56 Pisces
May 14 22:25 Aries
May 17 11:23 Taurus
May 20 00:01 Gemini
May 22 11:05 Cancer
May 24 19:54 Leo
May 27 02:06 Virgo
May 29 05:41 Libra
May 31 07:07 Scorpio
Jun 02 07:33 Sagittarius
Jun 04 08:34 Capricorn
Jun 06 11:52 Aquarius
Jun 08 18:46 Pisces
Jun 11 05:24 Aries
Jun 13 18:11 Taurus
Jun 16 06:45 Gemini
Jun 18 17:22 Cancer
Jun 21 01:32 Leo
Jun 23 07:32 Virgo
Jun 25 11:48 Libra
Jun 27 14:37 Scorpio
Jun 29 16:30 Sagittarius
Jul 01 18:22 Capricorn
Jul 03 21:36 Aquarius
Jul 06 03:40 Pisces
Jul 08 13:21 Aries
Jul 11 01:44 Taurus
Jul 13 14:23 Gemini
Jul 16 00:54 Cancer
Jul 18 08:25 Leo
Jul 20 13:29 Virgo
Jul 22 17:10 Libra
Jul 24 20:16 Scorpio
Jul 26 23:12 Sagittarius
Jul 29 02:21 Capricorn
Jul 31 06:25 Aquarius
Aug 02 12:33 Pisces
Aug 04 21:43 Aries
Aug 07 09:41 Taurus
Aug 09 22:31 Gemini
Aug 12 09:28 Cancer
Aug 14 16:57 Leo
Aug 16 21:15 Virgo
Aug 18 23:44 Libra
Aug 21 01:51 Scorpio
Aug 23 04:36 Sagittarius
Aug 25 08:24 Capricorn
Aug 27 13:31 Aquarius
Aug 29 20:25 Pisces
Sep 01 05:42 Aries
Sep 03 17:28 Taurus
Sep 06 06:27 Gemini
Sep 08 18:10 Cancer
Sep 11 02:27 Leo

. . . MOON 1985

Sep 13 06:53 Virgo
Sep 15 08:34 Libra
Sep 17 09:17 Scorpio
Sep 19 10:40 Sagittarius
Sep 21 13:49 Capricorn
Sep 23 19:11 Aquarius
Sep 26 02:50 Pisces
Sep 28 12:43 Aries
Oct 01 00:35 Taurus
Oct 03 13:36 Gemini
Oct 06 01:59 Cancer
Oct 08 11:34 Leo
Oct 10 17:10 Virgo
Oct 12 19:12 Libra
Oct 14 19:13 Scorpio
Oct 16 19:05 Sagittarius
Oct 18 20:35 Capricorn
Oct 21 00:54 Aquarius
Oct 23 08:27 Pisces
Oct 25 18:47 Aries
Oct 28 06:59 Taurus
Oct 30 19:59 Gemini
Nov 02 08:31 Cancer
Nov 04 19:04 Leo
Nov 07 02:18 Virgo
Nov 09 05:52 Libra
Nov 11 06:31 Scorpio
Nov 13 05:52 Sagittarius
Nov 15 05:53 Capricorn
Nov 17 08:25 Aquarius
Nov 19 14:42 Pisces
Nov 22 00:42 Aries
Nov 24 13:07 Taurus
Nov 27 02:08 Gemini
Nov 29 14:23 Cancer
Dec 02 00:59 Leo
Dec 04 09:14 Virgo
Dec 06 14:33 Libra
Dec 08 16:56 Scorpio
Dec 10 17:13 Sagittarius
Dec 12 17:00 Capricorn
Dec 14 18:15 Aquarius
Dec 16 22:50 Pisces
Dec 19 07:37 Aries
Dec 21 19:41 Taurus
Dec 24 08:45 Gemini
Dec 26 20:44 Cancer
Dec 29 06:44 Leo
Dec 31 14:44 Virgo

MERCURY 1960–1963

(R) indicates Mercury Retrograde

1960
Jan 04 08:24 Capricorn
Jan 23 06:16 Aquarius
Feb 09 10:13 Pisces
Apr 16 02:21 Aries
May 04 16:44 Taurus
May 19 03:26 Gemini
Jun 02 20:30 Cancer
Jul 01 01:07 Leo
Jul 06 01:29 Cancer (R)
Aug 10 17:48 Leo
Aug 27 03:11 Virgo
Sep 12 06:28 Libra
Oct 01 17:15 Scorpio
Dec 07 17:28 Sagittarius
Dec 27 07:19 Capricorn

1961
Jan 14 18:57 Aquarius
Feb 01 21:38 Pisces
Feb 24 20:24 Aquarius (R)
Mar 18 10:12 Pisces
Apr 10 09:20 Aries
Apr 26 14:32 Taurus
May 10 16:32 Gemini
May 28 17:20 Cancer
Aug 04 01:14 Leo
Aug 18 20:50 Virgo
Sep 04 22:30 Libra
Sep 27 12:12 Scorpio
Oct 22 02:33 Libra (R)
Nov 10 23:49 Scorpio
Nov 30 22:51 Sagittarius
Dec 20 01:01 Capricorn

1962
Jan 07 15:05 Aquarius
Mar 15 11:39 Pisces
Apr 03 02:29 Aries
Apr 18 04:07 Taurus
May 03 06:01 Gemini
Jul 11 07:33 Cancer
Jul 26 18:47 Leo
Aug 10 19:26 Virgo
Aug 29 15:44 Libra
Nov 05 02:16 Scorpio
Nov 23 17:27 Sagittarius
Dec 12 20:47 Capricorn

1963
Jan 02 01:05 Aquarius
Jan 20 05:04 Capricorn (R)
Feb 15 10:03 Aquarius
Mar 09 05:22 Pisces
Mar 26 03:49 Aries
Apr 09 22:00 Taurus
May 03 03:57 Gemini
May 10 21:02 Taurus (R)
Jun 14 23:14 Gemini
Jul 04 02:57 Cancer
Jul 18 06:16 Leo

. . . MERCURY 1963–1967

Aug 03 09:17 Virgo
Aug 26 20:25 Libra
Sep 16 20:36 Virgo (R)
Oct 10 16:39 Libra
Oct 28 19:50 Scorpio
Nov 16 11:02 Sagittarius
Dec 06 05:12 Capricorn
1964
Feb 10 21:26 Aquarius
Feb 29 22:46 Pisces
Mar 16 23:51 Aries
Apr 02 00:53 Taurus
Jun 09 15:41 Gemini
Jun 24 17:14 Cancer
Jul 09 00:35 Leo
Jul 27 11:31 Virgo
Oct 03 00:08 Libra
Oct 20 07:07 Scorpio
Nov 08 10:57 Sagittarius
Nov 30 19:23 Capricorn
Dec 16 14:37 Sagittarius (R)
1965
Jan 13 03:07 Capricorn
Feb 03 08:58 Aquarius
Feb 21 05:36 Pisces
Mar 09 02:15 Aries
May 15 13:14 Taurus
Jun 02 03:44 Gemini
Jun 16 02:01 Cancer
Jul 01 15:51 Leo
Jul 31 10:36 Virgo
Aug 03 08:57 Leo (R)
Sep 08 17:10 Virgo
Sep 25 05:46 Libra
Oct 12 21:11 Scorpio
Nov 02 05:59 Sagittarius
1966
Jan 07 18:22 Capricorn
Jan 27 04:06 Aquarius
Feb 13 10:15 Pisces
Mar 03 02:53 Aries
Mar 22 02:40 Pisces (R)
Apr 17 21:25 Aries
May 09 14:45 Taurus
May 24 17:57 Gemini
Jun 07 19:08 Cancer
Jun 26 19:01 Leo
Sep 01 10:33 Virgo
Sep 17 08:16 Libra
Oct 05 21:59 Scorpio
Oct 30 07:31 Sagittarius
Nov 13 03:31 Scorpio (R)
Dec 11 15:23 Sagittarius
1967
Jan 01 00:49 Capricorn
Jan 19 17:03 Aquarius
Feb 06 00:35 Pisces
Apr 14 14:35 Aries
May 01 23:24 Taurus
May 16 03:25 Gemini

. . . MERCURY 1967–1971

May 31 17:59 Cancer
Aug 08 22:08 Leo
Aug 24 06:16 Virgo
Sep 09 16:51 Libra
Sep 30 01:43 Scorpio
Dec 05 13:39 Sagittarius
Dec 24 20:31 Capricorn

1968

Jan 12 07:18 Aquarius
Feb 01 12:55 Pisces
Feb 11 18:56 Aquarius (R)
Mar 17 14:43 Pisces
Apr 07 01:00 Aries
Apr 22 16:17 Taurus
May 06 22:55 Gemini
May 29 22:40 Cancer
Jun 13 22:36 Gemini (R)
Jul 13 01:29 Cancer
Jul 31 06:10 Leo
Aug 15 00:53 Virgo
Sep 01 16:58 Libra
Sep 28 14:37 Scorpio
Oct 07 22:49 Libra (R)
Nov 08 10:59 Scorpio
Nov 27 12:46 Sagittarius
Dec 16 14:10 Capricorn

1969

Jan 04 12:18 Aquarius
Mar 12 15:19 Pisces
Mar 30 09:59 Aries
Apr 14 05:55 Taurus
Apr 30 15:18 Gemini
Jul 08 03:58 Cancer
Jul 22 19:12 Leo
Oct 08 04:22 Virgo
Oct 10 06:52 Libra
Nov 01 16:54 Scorpio
Nov 20 06:01 Sagittarius
Dec 09 13:22 Capricorn

1970

Feb 13 13:10 Aquarius
Mar 05 20:12 Pisces
Mar 22 08:00 Aries
Apr 06 07:41 Taurus
Jun 13 12:48 Gemini
Jun 30 06:24 Cancer
Jul 14 08:08 Leo
Jul 31 05:24 Virgo
Oct 07 18:06 Libra
Oct 25 06:18 Scorpio
Nov 13 01:19 Sagittarius
Dec 03 10:17 Capricorn

1971

Jan 02 23:31 Sagittarius (R)
Jan 14 02:23 Capricorn
Feb 07 20:54 Aquarius
Feb 26 08:00 Pisces
Mar 14 04:48 Aries
Apr 01 14:16 Taurus
Apr 18 21:46 Aries (R)

. . . MERCURY 1971–1975

May 17 03:37 Taurus
Jun 07 06:47 Gemini
Jun 21 16:27 Cancer
Jul 06 08:56 Leo
Jul 26 17:08 Virgo
Aug 29 20:35 Leo (R)
Sep 11 06:51 Virgo
Sep 30 09:21 Libra
Oct 17 17:52 Scorpio
Nov 06 07:02 Sagittarius

1972

Jan 11 18:22 Capricorn
Jan 31 23:50 Aquarius
Feb 18 12:57 Pisces
Mar 05 17:03 Aries
May 12 23:49 Taurus
May 29 06:49 Gemini
Jun 12 02:59 Cancer
Jun 28 16:56 Leo
Sep 05 11:40 Virgo
Sep 21 12:15 Libra
Oct 09 11:15 Scorpio
Oct 30 19:32 Sagittarius
Nov 29 07:03 Scorpio (R)
Dec 12 23:27 Sagittarius

1973

Jan 04 14:46 Capricorn
Jan 23 15:27 Aquarius
Feb 09 19:34 Pisces
Apr 16 21:22 Aries
May 06 02:58 Taurus
May 20 17:27 Gemini
Jun 04 04:46 Cancer
Jun 27 06:52 Leo
Jul 16 07:52 Cancer (R)
Aug 11 12:27 Leo
Aug 28 15:26 Virgo
Sep 13 16:20 Libra
Oct 02 20:17 Scorpio
Dec 08 21:34 Sagittarius
Dec 28 15:19 Capricorn

1974

Jan 16 04:01 Aquarius
Feb 02 22:47 Pisces
Mar 02 17:40 Aquarius (R)
Mar 17 20:21 Pisces
Apr 11 15:24 Aries
Apr 28 03:14 Taurus
May 12 04:58 Gemini
May 29 08:08 Cancer
Aug 05 11:46 Leo
Aug 20 09:07 Virgo
Sep 06 05:53 Libra
Sep 28 00:26 Scorpio
Oct 26 23:16 Libra (R)
Nov 11 16:11 Scorpio
Dec 02 06:22 Sagittarius
Dec 21 09:21 Capricorn

1975

Jan 08 22:02 Aquarius

. . . MERCURY 1975–1979

Mar 16 11:55 Pisces
Apr 04 12:31 Aries
Apr 19 17:23 Taurus
May 04 11:58 Gemini
Jul 12 09:00 Cancer
Jul 28 08:08 Leo
Aug 12 06:16 Virgo
Aug 30 17:25 Libra
Nov 06 09:01 Scorpio
Nov 25 01:48 Sagittarius
Dec 14 04:13 Capricorn

1976

Jan 02 20:26 Aquarius
Jan 25 01:26 Capricorn (R)
Feb 15 19:09 Aquarius
Mar 09 12:05 Pisces
Mar 26 15:39 Aries
Apr 10 09:32 Taurus
Apr 29 23:17 Gemini
May 19 19:14 Taurus (R)
Jun 13 19:25 Gemini
Jul 04 14:20 Cancer
Jul 18 19:38 Leo
Aug 03 16:44 Virgo
Aug 25 20:57 Libra
Sep 21 07:11 Virgo (R)
Oct 10 14:50 Libra
Oct 29 04:57 Scorpio
Nov 16 19:04 Sagittarius
Dec 06 09:27 Capricorn

1977

Feb 10 23:58 Aquarius
Mar 02 08:11 Pisces
Mar 18 11:58 Aries
Apr 03 02:48 Taurus
Jun 10 21:08 Gemini
Jun 26 07:09 Cancer
Jul 10 12:01 Leo
Jul 28 10:17 Virgo
Oct 04 09:18 Libra
Oct 21 16:25 Scorpio
Nov 09 17:21 Sagittarius
Dec 01 06:45 Capricorn
Dec 21 07:18 Sagittarius (R)

1978

Jan 13 20:09 Capricorn
Feb 04 15:55 Aquarius
Feb 22 16:12 Pisces
Mar 10 12:11 Aries
May 16 08:20 Taurus
Jun 03 15:26 Gemini
Jun 17 15:49 Cancer
Jul 02 22:28 Leo
Jul 27 06:11 Virgo
Aug 13 07:05 Leo (R)
Sep 09 19:24 Virgo
Sep 26 16:40 Libra
Oct 14 05:29 Scorpio
Nov 03 07:47 Sagittarius

1979

. . . MERCURY 1979–1982

Jan 08 22:33 Capricorn
Jan 28 12:49 Aquarius
Feb 14 20:38 Pisces
Mar 03 21:31 Aries
Mar 28 10:42 Pisces (R)
Apr 17 12:46 Aries
May 10 22:02 Taurus
May 26 07:43 Gemini
Jun 09 06:31 Cancer
Jun 27 09:50 Leo
Sep 02 21:38 Virgo
Sep 18 18:58 Libra
Oct 07 03:53 Scorpio
Oct 30 07:02 Sagittarius
Nov 18 03:12 Scorpio (R)
Dec 12 13:32 Sagittarius

1980

Jan 02 08:01 Capricorn
Jan 21 02:17 Aquarius
Feb 07 08:05 Pisces
Apr 14 15:55 Aries
May 02 10:54 Taurus
May 16 17:05 Gemini
May 31 22:03 Cancer
Aug 09 03:28 Leo
Aug 24 18:46 Virgo
Sep 10 01:58 Libra
Sep 30 01:13 Scorpio
Dec 05 19:42 Sagittarius
Dec 25 04:44 Capricorn

1981

Jan 12 15:45 Aquarius
Jan 31 17:31 Pisces
Feb 16 08:07 Aquarius (R)
Mar 18 04:28 Pisces
Apr 08 09:08 Aries
Apr 24 05:29 Taurus
May 08 09:40 Gemini
May 28 16:57 Cancer
Jun 22 23:02 Gemini (R)
Jul 12 21:01 Cancer
Aug 01 18:28 Leo
Aug 16 12:45 Virgo
Sep 02 22:36 Libra
Sep 27 10:54 Scorpio
Oct 14 02:16 Libra (R)
Nov 09 13:10 Scorpio
Nov 28 20:48 Sagittarius
Dec 17 22:17 Capricorn

1982

Jan 05 16:45 Aquarius
Mar 13 19:07 Pisces
Mar 31 20:56 Aries
Apr 15 18:51 Taurus
May 01 13:25 Gemini
Jul 09 11:23 Cancer
Jul 24 08:46 Leo
Aug 08 14:03 Virgo
Aug 28 03:17 Libra
Nov 03 01:06 Scorpio

. . . MERCURY 1982–1985

Nov 21 14:23 Sagittarius
Dec 10 20:00 Capricorn

1983

Jan 01 13:24 Aquarius
Jan 12 07:02 Capricorn (R)
Feb 14 09:31 Aquarius
Mar 07 04:20 Pisces
Mar 23 20:06 Aries
Apr 07 17:00 Taurus
Jun 14 08:01 Gemini
Jul 01 19:15 Cancer
Jul 15 20:54 Leo
Aug 01 10:19 Virgo
Aug 29 05:50 Libra
Sep 06 02:46 Virgo (R)
Oct 08 23:40 Libra
Oct 26 15:43 Scorpio
Nov 14 08:52 Sagittarius
Dec 04 11:18 Capricorn

1984

Feb 09 01:47 Aquarius
Feb 27 18:04 Pisces
Mar 14 16:24 Aries
Mar 31 20:20 Taurus
Apr 25 11:59 Aries (R)
May 15 12:24 Taurus
Jun 07 15:41 Gemini
Jun 22 06:37 Cancer
Jul 06 18:53 Leo
Jul 26 06:45 Virgo
Sep 30 19:41 Libra
Oct 18 02:58 Scorpio
Nov 06 12:05 Sagittarius
Dec 01 16:17 Capricorn
Dec 07 21:57 Sagittarius (R)

1985

Jan 11 18:21 Capricorn
Feb 01 07:41 Aquarius
Feb 18 23:39 Pisces
Mar 07 00:05 Aries
May 14 02:07 Taurus
May 30 19:42 Gemini
Jun 13 16:09 Cancer
Jun 29 19:31 Leo
Sep 06 19:37 Virgo
Sep 22 23:11 Libra
Oct 10 18:48 Scorpio
Oct 31 16:40 Sagittarius
Dec 04 19:29 Scorpio (R)
Dec 12 10:58 Sagittarius

VENUS 1960–1964

(R) indicates Venus Retrograde

1960
Jan 02 08:43 Sagittarius
Jan 27 04:46 Capricorn
Feb 20 16:47 Aquarius
Mar 16 01:53 Pisces
Apr 09 10:31 Aries
May 03 19:55 Taurus
May 28 06:10 Gemini
Jun 21 16:33 Cancer
Jul 16 02:10 Leo
Aug 09 10:53 Virgo
Sep 02 19:28 Libra
Sep 27 05:11 Scorpio
Oct 21 17:10 Sagittarius
Nov 15 08:55 Capricorn
Dec 10 08:32 Aquarius
1961
Jan 05 03:29 Pisces
Feb 02 04:44 Aries
Jun 05 19:20 Taurus
Jul 07 04:29 Gemini
Aug 03 15:25 Cancer
Aug 29 14:15 Leo
Sep 23 15:39 Virgo
Oct 18 02:54 Libra
Nov 11 05:29 Scorpio
Dec 05 03:36 Sagittarius
Dec 29 00:03 Capricorn
1962
Jan 21 20:27 Aquarius
Feb 14 18:05 Pisces
Mar 10 18:25 Aries
Apr 03 23:01 Taurus
Apr 28 09:18 Gemini
May 23 02:42 Cancer
Jun 17 05:26 Leo
Jul 12 22:27 Virgo
Aug 08 17:09 Libra
Sep 07 00:05 Scorpio
1963
Jan 06 17:29 Sagittarius
Feb 05 20:30 Capricorn
Mar 04 11:36 Aquarius
Mar 30 00:54 Pisces
Apr 24 03:34 Aries
May 19 01:15 Taurus
Jun 12 19:51 Gemini
Jul 07 11:13 Cancer
Jul 31 22:34 Leo
Aug 25 05:43 Virgo
Sep 18 09:37 Libra
Oct 12 11:44 Scorpio
Nov 05 13:19 Sagittarius
Nov 29 15:15 Capricorn
Dec 23 18:48 Aquarius
1964
Jan 17 02:48 Pisces
Feb 10 21:04 Aries

. . . VENUS 1964–1968

Mar 07 12:32 Taurus
Apr 04 02:56 Gemini
May 09 03:04 Cancer
Jun 17 18:28 Gemini (R)
Aug 05 08:43 Cancer
Sep 08 04:47 Leo
Oct 05 18:04 Virgo
Oct 31 08:48 Libra
Nov 25 01:19 Scorpio
Dec 19 06:57 Sagittarius

1965

Jan 12 07:55 Capricorn
Feb 05 07:37 Aquarius
Mar 01 07:50 Pisces
Mar 25 09:49 Aries
Apr 18 14:25 Taurus
May 12 22:02 Gemini
Jun 06 08:33 Cancer
Jun 30 21:54 Leo
Jul 25 14:46 Virgo
Aug 19 13:01 Libra
Sep 13 19:45 Scorpio
Oct 09 16:40 Sagittarius
Nov 05 19:30 Capricorn
Dec 07 04:28 Aquarius

1966

Feb 06 13:00 Capricorn (R)
Feb 25 10:39 Aquarius
Apr 06 15:47 Pisces
May 05 04:28 Aries
May 31 17:55 Taurus
Jun 26 11:36 Gemini
Jul 21 17:08 Cancer
Aug 15 12:43 Leo
Sep 08 23:36 Virgo
Oct 03 03:40 Libra
Oct 27 03:23 Scorpio
Nov 20 01:02 Sagittarius
Dec 13 22:05 Capricorn

1967

Jan 06 19:32 Aquarius
Jan 30 18:50 Pisces
Feb 23 22:27 Aries
Mar 20 09:53 Taurus
Apr 14 09:51 Gemini
May 10 06:01 Cancer
Jun 06 16:44 Leo
Jul 08 22:07 Virgo
Sep 09 12:05 Leo (R)
Oct 01 17:59 Virgo
Nov 09 16:29 Libra
Dec 07 08:45 Scorpio

1968

Jan 01 22:36 Sagittarius
Jan 26 17:33 Capricorn
Feb 20 04:54 Aquarius
Mar 15 13:30 Pisces
Apr 08 21:47 Aries
May 03 06:55 Taurus
May 27 17:00 Gemini

. . . VENUS 1968–1972

Jun 21 03:19 Cancer
Jul 15 12:58 Leo
Aug 08 21:48 Virgo
Sep 02 06:39 Libra
Sep 26 16:44 Scorpio
Oct 21 05:15 Sagittarius
Nov 14 21:47 Capricorn
Dec 09 22:39 Aquarius

1969

Jan 04 20:07 Pisces
Feb 02 04:45 Aries
Jun 06 01:49 Taurus
Jul 06 22:04 Gemini
Aug 03 05:31 Cancer
Aug 29 02:49 Leo
Sep 23 03:27 Virgo
Oct 17 14:18 Libra
Nov 10 16:40 Scorpio
Dec 04 14:42 Sagittarius
Dec 28 11:05 Capricorn

1970

Jan 21 07:28 Aquarius
Feb 14 05:06 Pisces
Mar 10 05:27 Aries
Apr 03 10:07 Taurus
Apr 27 20:35 Gemini
May 22 14:21 Cancer
Jun 16 17:51 Leo
Jul 12 12:19 Virgo
Aug 08 10:03 Libra
Sep 07 01:57 Scorpio

1971

Jan 07 01:05 Sagittarius
Feb 05 15:01 Capricorn
Mar 04 02:28 Aquarius
Mar 29 14:05 Pisces
Apr 23 15:47 Aries
May 18 12:51 Taurus
Jun 12 07:01 Gemini
Jul 06 22:06 Cancer
Jul 31 09:19 Leo
Aug 24 16:29 Virgo
Sep 17 20:30 Libra
Oct 11 22:47 Scorpio
Nov 05 00:34 Sagittarius
Nov 29 02:45 Capricorn
Dec 23 06:37 Aquarius

1972

Jan 16 15:06 Pisces
Feb 10 10:14 Aries
Mar 07 03:31 Taurus
Apr 03 22:54 Gemini
May 10 14:01 Cancer
Jun 11 19:58 Gemini (R)
Aug 06 01:36 Cancer
Sep 07 23:33 Leo
Oct 05 08:39 Virgo
Oct 30 21:45 Libra
Nov 24 13:28 Scorpio
Dec 18 18:39 Sagittarius

. . . VENUS 1973–1977

1973
Jan 11 19:20 Capricorn
Feb 04 18:49 Aquarius
Feb 28 18:51 Pisces
Mar 24 20:40 Aries
Apr 18 01:10 Taurus
May 12 08:48 Gemini
Jun 05 19:25 Cancer
Jun 30 09:01 Leo
Jul 25 02:19 Virgo
Aug 19 01:16 Libra
Sep 13 09:11 Scorpio
Oct 09 08:14 Sagittarius
Nov 05 15:45 Capricorn
Dec 07 21:46 Aquarius
1974
Jan 29 19:38 Capricorn (R)
Feb 28 14:39 Aquarius
Apr 06 14:24 Pisces
May 04 20:27 Aries
May 31 07:25 Taurus
Jun 25 23:50 Gemini
Jul 21 04:40 Cancer
Aug 14 23:53 Leo
Sep 08 10:33 Virgo
Oct 02 14:32 Libra
Oct 26 14:17 Scorpio
Nov 19 12:02 Sagittarius
Dec 13 09:11 Capricorn
1975
Jan 06 06:45 Aquarius
Jan 30 06:10 Pisces
Feb 23 09:59 Aries
Mar 19 21:47 Taurus
Apr 13 22:31 Gemini
May 09 20:16 Cancer
Jun 06 11:00 Leo
Jul 09 11:15 Virgo
Sep 02 15:23 Leo (R)
Oct 04 05:30 Virgo
Nov 09 13:57 Libra
Dec 07 00:33 Scorpio
1976
Jan 01 12:19 Sagittarius
Jan 26 06:13 Capricorn
Feb 19 16:55 Aquarius
Mar 15 01:04 Pisces
Apr 08 09:00 Aries
May 02 17:52 Taurus
May 27 03:47 Gemini
Jun 20 14:00 Cancer
Jul 14 23:40 Leo
Aug 08 08:40 Virgo
Sep 01 17:48 Libra
Sep 26 04:20 Scorpio
Oct 20 17:25 Sagittarius
Nov 14 10:45 Capricorn
Dec 09 12:56 Aquarius
1977
Jan 04 13:05 Pisces

. . . VENUS 1977–1981

Feb 02 05:59 Aries
Jun 06 06:13 Taurus
Jul 06 15:12 Gemini
Aug 02 19:21 Cancer
Aug 28 15:12 Leo
Sep 22 15:07 Virgo
Oct 17 01:38 Libra
Nov 10 03:53 Scorpio
Dec 04 01:50 Sagittarius
Dec 27 22:11 Capricorn

1978

Jan 20 18:31 Aquarius
Feb 13 16:08 Pisces
Mar 09 16:30 Aries
Apr 02 21:14 Taurus
Apr 27 07:54 Gemini
May 22 02:04 Cancer
Jun 16 06:19 Leo
Jul 12 02:15 Virgo
Aug 08 03:09 Libra
Sep 07 05:07 Scorpio

1979

Jan 07 06:37 Sagittarius
Feb 05 09:15 Capricorn
Mar 03 17:18 Aquarius
Mar 29 03:17 Pisces
Apr 23 04:01 Aries
May 18 00:27 Taurus
Jun 11 18:12 Gemini
Jul 06 09:01 Cancer
Jul 30 20:06 Leo
Aug 24 03:15 Virgo
Sep 17 07:19 Libra
Oct 11 09:46 Scorpio
Nov 04 11:47 Sagittarius
Nov 28 14:17 Capricorn
Dec 22 18:32 Aquarius

1980

Jan 16 03:34 Pisces
Feb 09 23:37 Aries
Mar 06 18:51 Taurus
Apr 03 19:42 Gemini
May 12 20:42 Cancer
Jun 05 05:54 Gemini (R)
Aug 06 14:20 Cancer
Sep 07 17:53 Leo
Oct 04 23:03 Virgo
Oct 30 10:34 Libra
Nov 24 01:31 Scorpio
Dec 18 06:17 Sagittarius

1981

Jan 11 06:45 Capricorn
Feb 04 06:04 Aquarius
Feb 28 05:58 Pisces
Mar 24 07:39 Aries
Apr 17 12:04 Taurus
May 11 19:40 Gemini
Jun 05 06:25 Cancer
Jun 29 20:15 Leo
Jul 24 14:00 Virgo

. . . VENUS 1981–1985

Aug 18 13:40 Libra
Sep 12 22:46 Scorpio
Oct 08 23:59 Sagittarius
Nov 05 12:33 Capricorn
Dec 08 20:43 Aquarius

1982

Jan 23 03:06 Capricorn (R)
Mar 02 11:15 Aquarius
Apr 06 12:14 Pisces
May 04 12:21 Aries
May 30 20:56 Taurus
Jun 25 12:08 Gemini
Jul 20 16:16 Cancer
Aug 14 11:04 Leo
Sep 07 21:32 Virgo
Oct 02 01:27 Libra
Oct 26 01:13 Scorpio
Nov 18 23:01 Sagittarius
Dec 12 20:14 Capricorn

1983

Jan 05 17:53 Aquarius
Jan 29 17:27 Pisces
Feb 22 21:30 Aries
Mar 19 09:46 Taurus
Apr 13 11:20 Gemini
May 09 10:50 Cancer
Jun 06 05:57 Leo
Jul 10 05:16 Virgo
Aug 27 11:54 Leo (R)
Oct 05 19:24 Virgo
Nov 09 10:46 Libra
Dec 06 16:09 Scorpio

1984

Jan 01 01:55 Sagittarius
Jan 25 18:46 Capricorn
Feb 19 04:48 Aquarius
Mar 14 12:30 Pisces
Apr 07 20:08 Aries
May 02 04:48 Taurus
May 26 14:35 Gemini
Jun 20 00:44 Cancer
Jul 14 10:26 Leo
Aug 07 19:36 Virgo
Sep 01 05:02 Libra
Sep 25 16:00 Scorpio
Oct 20 05:41 Sagittarius
Nov 13 23:49 Capricorn
Dec 09 03:22 Aquarius

1985

Jan 04 06:19 Pisces
Feb 02 08:24 Aries
Jun 06 08:48 Taurus
Jul 06 07:58 Gemini
Aug 02 09:07 Cancer
Aug 28 03:35 Leo
Sep 22 02:49 Virgo
Oct 16 13:00 Libra
Nov 09 15:04 Scorpio
Dec 03 12:57 Sagittarius
Dec 27 09:15 Capricorn

MARS 1960–1967

(R) indicates Mars Retrograde

1960
Jan 14 05:00 Capricorn
Feb 23 04:11 Aquarius
Apr 02 06:23 Pisces
May 11 07:17 Aries
Jun 20 09:03 Taurus
Aug 02 04:30 Gemini
Sep 21 04:02 Cancer

1961
May 06 01:06 Leo
Jun 28 23:42 Virgo
Aug 17 00:36 Libra
Oct 01 19:56 Scorpio
Nov 13 21:44 Sagittarius
Dec 24 17:44 Capricorn

1962
Feb 01 23:01 Aquarius
Mar 12 07:52 Pisces
Apr 19 16:51 Aries
May 28 23:40 Taurus
Jul 09 03:43 Gemini
Aug 22 11:29 Cancer
Oct 11 23:43 Leo

1963
Jun 03 06:17 Virgo
Jul 27 04:04 Libra
Sep 12 09:01 Scorpio
Oct 25 17:21 Sagittarius
Dec 05 08:54 Capricorn

1964
Jan 13 06:05 Aquarius
Feb 20 07:25 Pisces
Mar 29 11:15 Aries
May 07 14:31 Taurus
Jun 17 11:33 Gemini
Jul 30 18:13 Cancer
Sep 15 05:11 Leo
Nov 06 03:06 Virgo

1965
Jun 29 00:59 Libra
Aug 20 12:07 Scorpio
Oct 04 06:37 Sagittarius
Nov 14 07:10 Capricorn
Dec 23 05:29 Aquarius

1966
Jan 30 06:55 Pisces
Mar 09 12:48 Aries
Apr 17 20:27 Taurus
May 28 21:59 Gemini
Jul 11 03:07 Cancer
Aug 25 15:44 Leo
Oct 12 18:28 Virgo
Dec 04 00:46 Libra

1967
Feb 12 12:04 Scorpio
Mar 31 06:25 Libra (R)
Jul 19 22:49 Scorpio
Sep 10 01:39 Sagittarius

. . . MARS 1967–1975

Oct 23 02:09 Capricorn
Dec 01 20:08 Aquarius

1968

Jan 09 09:46 Pisces
Feb 17 03:15 Aries
Mar 27 23:40 Taurus
May 08 14:11 Gemini
Jun 21 05:01 Cancer
Aug 05 17:06 Leo
Sep 21 18:37 Virgo
Nov 09 06:07 Libra
Dec 29 22:07 Scorpio

1969

Feb 25 06:21 Sagittarius
Sep 21 06:37 Capricorn
Nov 04 18:52 Aquarius
Dec 15 14:24 Pisces

1970

Jan 24 21:33 Aries
Mar 07 01:32 Taurus
Apr 18 19:02 Gemini
Jun 02 06:54 Cancer
Jul 18 06:48 Leo
Sep 03 05:02 Virgo
Oct 20 11:02 Libra
Dec 06 16:40 Scorpio

1971

Jan 23 01:41 Sagittarius
Mar 12 10:19 Capricorn
May 03 21:05 Aquarius
Nov 06 12:40 Pisces
Dec 26 18:13 Aries

1972

Feb 10 14:13 Taurus
Mar 27 04:39 Gemini
May 12 13:23 Cancer
Jun 28 16:19 Leo
Aug 15 01:09 Virgo
Sep 30 23:33 Libra
Nov 15 22:26 Scorpio
Dec 30 16:22 Sagittarius

1973

Feb 12 06:01 Capricorn
Mar 26 21:08 Aquarius
May 08 04:18 Pisces
Jun 20 21:04 Aries
Aug 12 15:14 Taurus
Oct 29 22:36 Aries (R)
Dec 24 08:32 Taurus

1974

Feb 27 10:24 Gemini
Apr 20 08:29 Cancer
Jun 09 01:05 Leo
Jul 27 14:16 Virgo
Sep 12 19:19 Libra
Oct 28 07:14 Scorpio
Dec 10 22:15 Sagittarius

1975

Jan 21 18:59 Capricorn
Mar 03 05:41 Aquarius

. . . MARS 1975–1982

Apr 11 19:23 Pisces
May 21 08:21 Aries
Jul 01 04:02 Taurus
Aug 14 20:57 Gemini
Oct 17 09:04 Cancer
Nov 25 18:12 Gemini (R)

1976

Mar 18 13:26 Cancer
May 16 11:18 Leo
Jul 06 23:35 Virgo
Aug 24 06:02 Libra
Oct 08 20:29 Scorpio
Nov 20 23:58 Sagittarius

1977

Jan 01 00:47 Capricorn
Feb 09 12:02 Aquarius
Mar 20 02:24 Pisces
Apr 27 15:49 Aries
Jun 06 03:03 Taurus
Jul 17 15:17 Gemini
Sep 01 00:24 Cancer
Oct 26 18:59 Leo

1978

Jan 26 01:55 Cancer (R)
Apr 10 18:51 Leo
Jun 14 02:38 Virgo
Aug 04 09:08 Libra
Sep 19 20:56 Scorpio
Nov 02 01:19 Sagittarius
Dec 12 17:37 Capricorn

1979

Jan 20 17:07 Aquarius
Feb 27 20:24 Pisces
Apr 07 01:06 Aries
May 16 04:22 Taurus
Jun 26 01:52 Gemini
Aug 08 13:26 Cancer
Sep 24 21:16 Leo
Nov 19 21:28 Virgo

1980

Mar 11 20:58 Leo (R)
May 04 02:10 Virgo
Jul 10 17:52 Libra
Aug 29 05:44 Scorpio
Oct 12 06:19 Sagittarius
Nov 22 01:35 Capricorn
Dec 30 22:24 Aquarius

1981

Feb 06 22:43 Pisces
Mar 17 02:33 Aries
Apr 25 07:09 Taurus
Jun 05 05:18 Gemini
Jul 18 08:46 Cancer
Sep 02 01:43 Leo
Oct 21 01:45 Virgo
Dec 16 00:01 Libra

1982

Aug 03 11:35 Scorpio
Sep 20 01:10 Sagittarius
Oct 31 22:55 Capricorn

. . . MARS 1984–1985

Dec 10 06:08 Aquarius

1983

Jan 17 13:02 Pisces

Feb 25 00:11 Aries

Apr 05 13:54 Taurus

May 16 21:34 Gemini

Jun 29 06:44 Cancer

Aug 13 16:45 Leo

Sep 30 00:01 Virgo

Nov 18 10:14 Libra

1984

Jan 11 03:08 Scorpio

Aug 17 19:40 Sagittarius

Oct 05 05:54 Capricorn

Nov 15 18:01 Aquarius

Dec 25 06:31 Pisces

1985

Feb 02 17:13 Aries

Mar 15 05:00 Taurus

Apr 26 09:05 Gemini

Jun 09 10:33 Cancer

Jul 25 03:57 Leo

Sep 10 01:25 Virgo

Oct 27 15:08 Libra

Dec 14 18:53 Scorpio

RISING SIGN TABLES

For precision accuracy, please check your birth data at www.astro.com.

Aries born around dawn – Aries Rising
Aries born after dawn – Taurus Rising
Aries born mid-morning – Gemini Rising
Aries born around noon – Cancer Rising
Aries born early afternoon – Leo Rising
Aries born mid-afternoon – Virgo Rising
Aries born around sunset – Libra Rising
Aries born after dinner – Scorpio Rising
Aries born mid-evening – Sagittarius Rising
Aries born around midnight – Capricorn Rising
Aries born in the small hours – Aquarius Rising
Aries born before dawn – Pisces Rising

Taurus born around dawn – Taurus Rising
Taurus born after dawn – Gemini Rising
Taurus born mid-morning – Cancer Rising
Taurus born around noon – Leo Rising
Taurus born early afternoon – Virgo Rising
Taurus born mid-afternoon – Libra Rising
Taurus born around sunset – Scorpio Rising
Taurus born after dinner – Sagittarius Rising
Taurus born mid-evening – Capricorn Rising
Taurus born around midnight – Aquarius Rising
Taurus born in the small hours – Pisces Rising
Taurus born before dawn – Aries Rising

Gemini born around dawn – Gemini Rising
Gemini born after dawn – Cancer Rising
Gemini born mid-morning – Leo Rising
Gemini born around noon – Virgo Rising

Gemini born early afternoon – Libra Rising
Gemini born mid-afternoon – Scorpio Rising
Gemini born around sunset – Sagittarius Rising
Gemini born after dinner – Capricorn Rising
Gemini born mid-evening – Aquarius Rising
Gemini born around midnight – Pisces Rising
Gemini born in the small hours – Aries Rising
Gemini born before dawn – Taurus Rising

Cancer born around dawn – Cancer Rising
Cancer born after dawn – Leo Rising
Cancer born mid-morning – Virgo Rising
Cancer born around noon – Libra Rising
Cancer born early afternoon – Scorpio Rising
Cancer born mid-afternoon – Sagittarius Rising
Cancer born around sunset – Capricorn Rising
Cancer born after dinner – Aquarius Rising
Cancer born mid-evening – Pisces Rising
Cancer born around midnight – Aries Rising
Cancer born in the small hours – Taurus Rising
Cancer born before dawn – Gemini Rising

Leo born around dawn – Leo Rising
Leo born after dawn – Virgo Rising
Leo born mid-morning – Libra Rising
Leo born around noon – Scorpio Rising
Leo born early afternoon – Sagittarius Rising
Leo born mid-afternoon – Capricorn Rising
Leo born around sunset – Aquarius Rising
Leo born after dinner – Pisces Rising
Leo born mid-evening – Aries Rising
Leo born around midnight – Taurus Rising
Leo born in the small hours – Gemini Rising
Leo born before dawn – Cancer Rising

Virgo born around dawn – Virgo Rising
Virgo born after dawn – Libra Rising
Virgo born mid-morning – Scorpio Rising
Virgo born around noon – Sagittarius Rising
Virgo born early afternoon – Capricorn Rising
Virgo born mid-afternoon – Aquarius Rising
Virgo born around sunset – Pisces Rising
Virgo born after dinner – Aries Rising
Virgo born mid-evening – Taurus Rising
Virgo born around midnight – Gemini Rising
Virgo born in the small hours – Cancer Rising
Virgo born before dawn – Leo Rising

Libra born around dawn – Libra Rising
Libra born after dawn – Scorpio Rising
Libra born mid-morning – Sagittarius Rising
Libra born around noon – Capricorn Rising
Libra born early afternoon – Aquarius Rising
Libra born mid-afternoon – Pisces Rising
Libra born around sunset – Aries Rising
Libra born after dinner – Taurus Rising
Libra born mid-evening – Gemini Rising
Libra born around midnight – Cancer Rising
Libra born in the small hours – Leo Rising
Libra born before dawn – Virgo Rising

Scorpio born around dawn – Scorpio Rising
Scorpio born after dawn – Sagittarius Rising
Scorpio born mid-morning – Capricorn Rising
Scorpio born around noon – Aquarius Rising
Scorpio born early afternoon – Pisces Rising
Scorpio born mid-afternoon – Aries Rising
Scorpio born around sunset – Taurus Rising
Scorpio born after dinner – Gemini Rising

Scorpio born mid-evening – Cancer Rising
Scorpio born around midnight – Leo Rising
Scorpio born in the small hours – Virgo Rising
Scorpio born before dawn – Libra Rising

Sagittarius born around dawn – Sagittarius Rising
Sagittarius born after dawn – Capricorn Rising
Sagittarius born mid-morning – Aquarius Rising
Sagittarius born around noon – Pisces Rising
Sagittarius born early afternoon – Aries Rising
Sagittarius born mid-afternoon – Taurus Rising
Sagittarius born around sunset – Gemini Rising
Sagittarius born after dinner – Cancer Rising
Sagittarius born mid-evening – Leo Rising
Sagittarius born around midnight – Virgo Rising
Sagittarius born in the small hours – Libra Rising
Sagittarius born before dawn – Scorpio Rising

Capricorn born around dawn – Capricorn Rising
Capricorn born after dawn – Aquarius Rising
Capricorn born mid-morning – Pisces Rising
Capricorn born around noon – Aries Rising
Capricorn born early afternoon – Taurus Rising
Capricorn born mid-afternoon – Gemini Rising
Capricorn born around sunset – Cancer Rising
Capricorn born after dinner – Leo Rising
Capricorn born mid-evening – Virgo Rising
Capricorn born around midnight – Libra Rising
Capricorn born in the small hours – Scorpio Rising
Capricorn born before dawn – Sagittarius Rising

Aquarius born around dawn – Aquarius Rising
Aquarius born after dawn – Pisces Rising
Aquarius born mid-morning – Aries Rising

Aquarius born around noon – Taurus Rising
Aquarius born early afternoon – Gemini Rising
Aquarius born mid-afternoon – Cancer Rising
Aquarius born around sunset – Leo Rising
Aquarius born after dinner – Virgo Rising
Aquarius born mid-evening – Libra Rising
Aquarius born around midnight – Scorpio Rising
Aquarius born in the small hours – Sagittarius Rising
Aquarius born before dawn – Capricorn Rising

Pisces born around dawn – Pisces Rising
Pisces born after dawn – Aries Rising
Pisces born mid-morning – Taurus Rising
Pisces born around noon – Gemini Rising
Pisces born early afternoon – Cancer Rising
Pisces born mid-afternoon – Leo Rising
Pisces born around sunset – Virgo Rising
Pisces born after dinner – Libra Rising
Pisces born mid-evening – Scorpio Rising
Pisces born around midnight – Sagittarius Rising
Pisces born in the small hours – Capricorn Rising
Pisces born before dawn – Aquarius Rising

USEFUL BOOKS AND WEBSITES

These are the astrology books and websites I always go back to. I hope you like them too. I've included my own website, where you'll find some exclusive *Astrolove* extras.

Books

Aspects in Astrology, Sue Tompkins, Rider, London, 2001
Astrology in the Year Zero, Garry Phillipson, Flare, London, 2000
The Book of World Horoscopes, Nicholas Campion, Cinnabar, London, 1992
Key Words for Astrology, Hajo Banzhaf & Anna Haebler, Weiser, York Beach, 1996
Making the Gods Work for You, Caroline W. Casey, Three Rivers Press, New York, 1998
The Moment of Astrology, Geoffrey Cornelius, Arkana, London, 1994
Secrets from a Stargazer's Notebook, Debbi Kempton-Smith, Bantam, New York, 1982
360 Degrees of Wisdom, Lynda Hill, Plume, New York, 1995
True as the Stars Above, Neil Spencer, Victor Gollancz, London, 2000

Websites

Jessica Adams – www.jessicaadams.com
The Astrological Lodge of London – www.astrolodge.co.uk
Astrology New York City – www.astrologynyc.org
Nick Campion – www.nickcampion.com
The Company of Astrologers – www.coa.org.uk
Robert Currey – www.astrology.co.uk
Adrian Duncan – www.world-of-wisdom.com
Federation of Australian Astrologers – www.faainc.org.au
Patty Greenall – www.pattygreenall.com
Lynda Hill – www.sabiansymbols.com
Deborah Houlding – www.skyscript.co.uk
Debbi Kempton-Smith – www.topquarkia.com

London School of Astrology – www.londonschoolofastrology.co.uk
Mystic Medusa – www.mysticmedusa.com
Garry Phillipson – www.astrozero.co.uk
Adam Smith – www.astroboogie.com
Neil Spencer – www.observer.co.uk
Julian Venables – www.julestheastrologer.co.uk

NOTES FOR ASTROLOGERS

Astrolove has been written and researched using Solar and Natal charts. The majority of the data used in this book has a rocking Rodden rating of AA, A or B and comes from the Astrodatabank software and website (www.astrodatabank.com). The remainder comes from *British Entertainers*, by Frank C. Clifford, Flare Publications (visit www.flareuk.com) and finally from the Internet's leading gay and lesbian site, www.astroqueer.com.

The planetary tables in Astrolove are the work of the mighty Mick Soar (www.llun.net) and all biographical dates have been checked at the BBC along with other news sources.

Any errors or updates (particularly data!) should be directed to me at jessicaadams.com, as gremlins have inevitably been known to sneak in with a book of this kind. Finally, I would like to acknowledge the team at www.astro.com who have made astrology free and accessible to everyone. This book would not work at all without this wonderful website.

Sources for quoted material

Page 39, David Beckham, *David Beckham: My Side*, reprinted by permission of HarperCollins Publishers Ltd © D. Beckham, 2003; page 106, Virginia Nicholson, *Among the Bohemians: Experiments in Living 1900–1939*, Penguin Books; page 107, Graeme Thomson, *Complicated Shadows: The Life and Music of Elvis Costello*, Canongate Books Ltd; page 120, Edgar Rice Burroughs, *Tarzan the Magnificent*, Ballantine Books; page 124, Tom Hopkinson, *Picture Post 1938–1950*, Salem House Publishing; page 130, Paul Gallagher & Terry Christian, *Brothers: From Childhood to Oasis*, Virgin Books; page 131, Neville Marten & Jeffrey Hudson, *The Kinks*, Sanctuary Publishing House Limited; page 131, Hunter Davies, *The Beatles*, W.W. Norton & Company Inc.; page 131, Christy Brown, *My Left Foot*, Secker & Warburg, reprinted by permission of The Random House Group Ltd; page 134, Nelson Mandela, *Long Walk to Freedom: The Autobiography of Nelson Mandela*, Little Brown & Company; page 148, Christopher Reeve, *Still Me*, Random House; page 153, Linda Goodman, *Linda Goodman's Sun Signs*, Taplinger Publishing Co.; page 153, Debbi Kempton-Smith, *Secrets from a Stargazer's Notebook: Making Astrology Work for You*, Bantam; page 154, Lin Cook, *Something Like Fire: Peter Cook Remembered*, David Higham Associates Ltd; page 165, Stephen Hawking, *A Brief History of Time: A Reader's Companion*, Bantam Books; page 169, Charles E. O. Carter, *Essays on the Foundations of Astrology*, Theosophical Publishing House; page 171, Humphrey Carpenter, *Spike Milligan: The Biography*, Hodder Stoughton; page 253, Linda Goodman, *Linda Goodman's Relationship Signs*, PanMacmillan.

Acknowledgements

Cheers to Anouska Jones and Saskia Adams for their thoughtful editing, and to Adam Smith, the astrologer for *Sunday Life* at the *Sunday Age* in Melbourne and the *Sun-Herald* in Sydney for his help as editorial consultant. Huge thanks to Mark Ferguson, Julie 'Jewels' Gibbs, Lynda Hill, Fiona Inglis, Pippa Masson, Jonathan Lloyd, Julian Venables and James Williams. Special thanks to Mick Soar for generating the planetary tables.

21st CENTURY GODDESS
Jessica Adams, Jelena Glisic, Anthea Paul

TUNE IN TO THE ALTERNATIVE YOU . . .

You're a modern woman who's always on the go, busy with work, keeping up with friends and family, and trying to stay fit and healthy. You communicate by phone, email, text message and your life is on fast forward as there are never enough hours in the day. It's a challenge, but you juggle your many responsibilities and still stay smiling . . .

Would you like to make it all easier?

It's time for you to welcome the Goddess and find the stardust in your DNA – to learn about yourself and your true essence.

Investigate astrology to really understand how the planets affect you and why. Work out how the spelling of your name affects your personality and your destiny. Learn the true meanings of the Tarot cards, and how to use crystals, oils and remedies for protection, inspiration and relaxation. Tune into your psychic sense to see what the future holds in store, with the help of your spirit guide, and reveal what your subconscious is saying through your dreams. Delve into the rituals and magic of the Craft to revitalise and revive you, helping you to direct your energy and ultimately create everything that your heart desires.

The *21st Century Goddess* – understand the ancient roots to live more fully now.

www.21stcenturygoddess.net

0 552 15071 1

BLACK SWAN

THE SUMMER PSYCHIC
Jessica Adams

No-one can predict the future, can they?

When Katie Pickard is sent by her newspaper to interview Brighton psychic Jim Gabriel about his predictions for the year ahead she is shocked and sceptical, especially when he predicts that he's going to marry her.

Then Jim's other predictions start coming true and Katie is forced to take him seriously – despite the fact that she's just fallen in love with somebody else.

Will she and Jim really be married by the end of the summer? And can a famous psychic ever be wrong.

'HUGELY ENTERTAINING AND ADDICTIVE – THE KIND OF BOOK THAT YOU DON'T WANT TO END'
Cosmopolitan

0 552 77257 7
9780552772570

BLACK SWAN

COOL FOR CATS
Jessica Adams

'AN ELOQUENT LOOK AT THE BITTERSWEET NATURE OF SUCCESS'
Glamour

It's 1979 and Linda Tyler is an assistant cook, engaged to a bank clerk in a sleepy town called Withingdean, when she answers an ad in a music paper. Suddenly, she gets the job that everyone else in England wants.

Within weeks, her life changes beyond recognition. She finds herself in London, working as a journalist on *NWW*, a punk and new wave music magazine. Free records by Blondie, Squeeze and The Clash land on her desk, and her name is permanently on the guest list.

Before the year is out she will be propositioned by four members of staff (including the work experience boy) and meet some rising stars (and occasionally spill Knickerbocker Glory on them). Along the way, though, Linda Tyler will also discover who and what she loves most – and make the most important decision of her life.

'ADAMS' LATEST NOVEL IS HUGELY TOUCHING, WITH A STOICAL AND FUNNY HEROINE'
Marie Claire

0 552 77084 1

BLACK SWAN

SINGLE WHITE E-MAIL
Jessica Adams

'SEXY, FUNNY, SMART. FOR ANY WOMAN WHO HAS EVER BEEN SINGLE'
Cosmopolitan

Dumped on her 30th birthday by the man she thought she would marry, Victoria Shepworth – known as Victoria 'Total Bloody Relationships Disaster' Shepworth to her friends – is feeling desperate.

So desperate that she cuts her hair, contemplates becoming a born-again lesbian and even throws herself into internet dating. Armed with a new computer and an anonymous nickname, she soon starts to feel human again – especially when she starts receiving e-mails from a fantastic Frenchman in Paris who claims to be a single white male seeking single white e-mail.

Soon, everything else in Victoria's life begins to seem boring, from her job in advertising, to her old friends and neighbours. It's only when tragedy strikes that her potential Monsieur Right is finally unmasked, though, and Victoria realizes that her love life will never be the same again.

'SINGLE *WHITE* E-*MAIL* HAS AN INNATE HONESTY ABOUT IT THAT KEEPS YOU ENTERTAINED TO THE END. AT TIMES DISARMINGLY HARSH AND DECIDEDLY CANDID, ADAMS' DÉBUT INTO THE LITERARY WORLD IS FRESH, FRENETIC AND FUN'
Elle

0 552 77278 X

BLACK SWAN